WE FEW

WE FEW

NICK BROKHAUSEN

CASEMATE

Philadelphia & Oxford

Published in the United States of America and Great Britain in 2018 by
CASEMATE PUBLISHERS
1950 Lawrence Road, Havertown, PA 19083, USA
and
The Old Music Hall, 106–108 Cowley Road, Oxford OX4 1JE, UK

Hardcover Edition: ISBN 978-1-61200-580-5
Digital Edition: ISBN 978-1-61200-581-2 (epub)

A CIP record for this book is available from the Library of Congress and the British Library

Printed and bound in the United States of America

For a complete list of Casemate titles, please contact:

CASEMATE PUBLISHERS (US)
Telephone (610) 853-9131
Fax (610) 853-9146
Email: casemate@casematepublishers.com
www.casematepublishers.com

CASEMATE PUBLISHERS (UK)
Telephone (01865) 241249
Fax (01865) 794449
Email: casemate-uk@casematepublishers.co.uk
www.casematepublishers.co.uk

"But we in it shall be remember'd;

We few, we happy few, we band of brothers;

For he to-day that sheds his blood with me

Shall be my brother;"

Henry V

William Shakespeare

To my peers I told you I would get even I hope I did you proud.

Contents

Acknowledgements		xi
Author's Note		xiii
Prologue		xvii

1	The Road to Mandalay	1
2	Keys to the Kingdom	15
3	First Blood	25
4	Cold Storage	35
5	Buffaloes Can Dance	43
6	The Coolest Man Alive	51
7	Polite Society Meets Reality	60
8	We Few, We Happy Few	71
9	Luck is a Fickle Mistress	77
10	Blue Eyes	89
11	Operation Afrika Corps	104
12	Selection Process	110
13	Bright Light	119
14	The Anthill Mob	129
15	With Texans Expect Bumps	137
16	As Through a Glass Darkly	143
17	Saltwater Therapy	148
18	Monkeyshines	156
19	Isn't Science Wonderful	164
20	The Cuckoo's Nest	176
21	Little Island in the Sun	187
22	King of the Cannibals	213
23	Rubik's Cube	221
24	Gin and Heartbreak	235

Acknowledgements

This is to acknowledge the people that helped me through this catharsis and still remained sane.

The first and foremost would have to be my editor, Mary Lisa Allen, who had to change her name to Icepick Kelly to satisfy the need for protective camouflage on her part. Icepick worked long and laborious hours to pull my crazed ramblings and dementia into focus, whilst bearing invective-laced comments about being tainted by too much education. She accomplished the impossible by pulling it all together and for this should get all the accolades. Life being capricious, she will probably be part of the public flogging.

To Dennis Cummings, my publisher, goes the Gonads of the Decade Award.

And finally, to those of you not hung up on the flinty-eyed, strong-jawed poster image sold by the spin doctors, and who share that splash of reality only war gives, do something inane and embarrassing in front of your kids to go along with this acknowledgement. I salute you.

Author's Note

This book is the first of two detailing the actions and experiences of a small group of Americans and their indigenous allies who were the backbone of ground reconnaissance in the Republic of Vietnam during the war.

The unit that is described here was part of MACV-SOG (Military Assistance Command Vietnam Studies and Observations Group), or Studies and Observations Group as it was innocuously called. In the eight years that it existed, the small recon companies that were the center of its activities conducted some of the most dangerous and daring missions of the war. Originally conceived as a unit capable of infiltrating the heart of the areas controlled by the North Vietnamese in both Laos and Vietnam, it expanded its reach to North Vietnam, Cambodia and a few other places best left unmentioned.

During that time the companies never exceeded more than 30 Americans, yet they were the best source for the enemy's disposition and were key to the US Military being able to take the war to the enemy, through the air and on the ground. This was accomplished by utilizing new and innovative technology, but also heavily relied on the ability of the individual team members being able to use tactics as old as those from the French and Indian Wars.

In that process this small unit racked up one of the most impressive records of awards for valor of any unit in the history of the United States Army. It came at a terrible price, however; the number of wounded and killed in action resulted in the computation of a life expectancy that was measured in a matter of a few months. Those missions today seem suicidal. In 1970 they seemed equally so, yet these men went out day after day with their indigenous allies, consisting of Montagnard tribesmen, Vietnamese, and Chinese Nungs, and faced the challenges with courage and resolve.

After the fall of the Republic of Vietnam the indigenous survivors faced persecution, and in some cases, wholesale execution. Today the Montagnard minority is still being persecuted by the central government as their traditional life is being robbed along with the resources of their homelands in the mountains of Vietnam and Laos. In the end, the Communist regimes seem determined to wipe out these amazing people.

For their devotion to our cause and to the very standards that we hold as sacred, they were abandoned through political compromise, and except for a few staunch allies in this country consisting of Special Forces veterans, were left to become one more victim of tyranny. That terrible price for fidelity and devotion to duty is not yet fully paid.

Those veterans of CCN are a diverse lot. Some came home and did as our forefathers before have done war after war. They picked up where their lives had left off and became citizens and pursued a life outside the military. Others stayed in the harness and acquitted themselves with honor and distinction in the wars and conflicts since. Some have risen to positions of power and influence, and others have become examples of the bedrock of American society, average men with families, kids, mortgages and the loves and woes of just being.

Others were not so lucky. Some sought solace in the bottle and welded the cap on tight, sinking into dependency to numb the pain of surviving and the horrible scar that war puts on your soul. Some sought solace in isolation, away from the demands of society. These are still our casualties, and as brothers we continue to reach out to them for we are the only ones that really understand.

The majority of us, through hard living and age, have lost that lean hardness that combat gives you. But we share a set of common traits. We are joyous to be alive every single day because it is a gift not a burden. We love this country with a passion akin to religious fervor, though we are at times disappointed in how the system is abused by special interests using the freedoms that we paid for with our blood. We still have an aversion to bullies and self-righteous fools that are concerned more with power and authority than with what is right, fair, and just.

We are still a bad sort to back into a comer, and three hundred to one odds are something that we consider as unfair to the guy with two hundred and ninety nine of his buddies against us. There are anecdotes innumerable of people that have assumed wrongly that we are just a bunch of old people who can be buffaloed or intimidated. We survived the war on pure aggression and murderous efficiency and some things just don't mellow with time.

We are and will always be a band of brothers, bonded by war and bathed in the pure love for each other that only combat veterans can understand. These men are my peers and I am terribly proud to be one of their number.

In the recent past I have had the pleasure of working with the new generation of Special Forces soldier, both officers and enlisted. This country is just now beginning to see what these unique men are capable of doing in the face of adversity. To say that we are proud of them doesn't quite convey the idea. To us Special Forces is a way of life, not a job description, and that code of conduct is exemplified in today's force.

This book and its companion is my tribute to my peers; it was written neither as the "Great American Novel," nor with the intent to give the reader the impression that we were death-stalking giants of the battlefield. We had our weaknesses and we certainly had our fear. We all have our ghosts that haunt us in one way or another and at times, I am sure, regrets about not being a better person. I hope it gives the reader a window into the past. I hope it will convey the incredible strength and macabre sense of humor that one needs in order to survive. But most of all, I hope that the reader will come away with a sense of how fortunate we are as a people that we can produce these qualities in our youth. I am proud to be a member of that small brotherhood of unwashed, profane, ribald, joyously alive fraternity.

Prologue

I am dreaming again. I know I am dreaming because I can see the forested slopes and hills that ring the lake. I can see the sunlight dancing on the waves. I can smell the air so crisp and clean and feel a freshening breeze off the stem of the boat. But I know it is an illusion. Reality is a gray fog tugging at some part of my subconscious like a voice on the wind. I resist it because I do not want to go.

I want to stay here; it is a place that is so peaceful, so far away it belongs to another place or another person's memories. I want to stay here because there is no blood and no death, only the sun and the waters of the lake and the gentle rocking of the boat. It is so beautiful, so serene; this is home. It wraps around me like a warm embrace. But I cannot stay. I have the premonition that something terrible will wake me. I fight the awakening and the lake, the boat, and the feelings of home come back into focus. That I can do; I can will myself to stay and drift back into the dream.

I am not alone; my little brother is with me. This feels right. He is wearing that old yellow slicker my mom hates because he looks like a ragamuffin in it. It is two sizes too large for him, but he wears it all the time when there is a chill in the breeze. And if it's too hot he still brings it along. It's his lucky jacket. He always catches fish when he has it.

Atop his head is that faded green baseball hat with the black bill, a result of too many days in the sun and being left in the back window of my dad's car. He always has that with him as well. Even from a mile or more away, everyone can tell at a glance that it is Ron by these two items.

He is bent over in the stem and his back is to me. His shoulders are hunched and heaving as if he is sobbing. I reach out for him to shake his shoulder, to comfort him and to try and find the reason for his sorrow. As I reach forward I notice that my hand and the sleeve of my shirt are bloody. Why am I bleeding? Did I cut myself with the fillet knife cutting bait? My hand touches his shoulder and as I shake him it leaves a bloody smear. He is still sobbing and I can hear him moaning. I am frightened now. I don't want him to hurt; he is my little brother. His hat is pulled down tight to one side and there is a dark stain on it. He turns around.

This isn't my baby brother; it is a Vietnamese, and his visage is horrific. His head has been split open like a melon and his eyeball is hanging out of the socket on the left side. I reach over and jerk my brother's hat off his head and I can see the terrible wound more clearly. It has rent his head open and I can see his brain exposed. His one good eye looks at me and it is full of sorrow. I realize that I know this boy. He is the same age as my little brother, about sixteen. I know him because I killed him. I took an entrenching tool and cleaved his head almost in half. I want to kill him again because he terrifies me and I want to rip my brother's clothes off of him so he can't profane them, as if his wearing them was some harbinger of danger to my brother, to me. He is looking at me so reproachfully. I took his future and his parent's dreams. I took the sunlight and the smell of the breeze away forever.

I remember the grenade went off right next to me. It blew me off the hillside and down on top of him and two others. He was carrying a type 56 AK. All I had was the shovel that I had been frantically digging in with and I killed out of animal fear and primal anger. He whimpered like a child with the first blow; I hit him again and again to stop his whimpering because it was like a knife cutting into my sanity.

He turns to me and grasps my hand. His hand is so cold that it bums my flesh. I struggle to pull away, but I can't. He holds me in an iron grip so that I cannot free myself. He has stopped moaning and he looks at me, transfixing me with his one good eye. In contrast to the horror of his face, it is so, so, serene I am captivated by it. It's black and depthless like a shark's, but somehow almost warm. Eternal. He turns and steps off the back of the boat and together we drop into the dark waters of the lake. I don't want to escape now. Somehow I know he has a message for me; there is something in the depths I must know, I don't know why, but I must know. We go deeper and I can see the light fading and the shadow of the boat hull receding.

I can't breathe; I am struggling to fight the terrible inclination to fill my lungs. I know that if I do I will surely suck water and drown. My lungs are burning and still he holds me in a death grip as we plummet into the dark watery abyss. I am on fire inside; I am struggling. At last I cannot hold my breath any longer and I gasp in an effort to fill my lungs with air.

I come to drenched with sweat and trembling. I am halfway between relief that it was all a dream and terror from the dream itself. Why does he come back to this place in my dreams, the only place where I find some tranquility, some peace? This isn't the first time; he comes to me often and I am afraid to dream about being safe at home because he will be there waiting for me. Why doesn't he leave? I fan the poncho liner to get some air and lay there in my bunk. I am clammy and so is the bed. I have soaked the sheets and the mattress. I stumble up and stand there shaking. In the dark I fumble with my little stand next to the bed, find my pistol and some cigarettes. Grope around the floor until I find my trousers. I put them on, wrap the poncho liner around me and step outside. It is hot and the stars are so close that it seems that you can reach out and touch them. I can smell the sea; it is warm and saline like the ethereal nature's womb.

I light up a cigarette and pull the poncho liner closer because despite the heat, I am chilled. I sit there for a while. I do not want to go back to sleep lest I fall into the dream again. I am thinking and walking aimlessly around the company, until I realize that I am in front of the Yard huts. I look up and see the glow of a cigarette in the shadows. The figure steps forward and I can see that it is Bong, the old man. He is a shaman. He nods at me and we both sit down on the stoop of the porch. The pungent odor of gun oil, cooked fish, and all that I identify as Montagnard surrounds me. I get another cigarette out and offer him one, but he shakes his head and smiles a quiet smile. He smokes his Yard tobacco in the rough paper they use; sometimes they make them out of newspaper. The tobacco is harsh and pungent. It stings my nostrils with its acrid, sharp tang.

We sit there and watch the stars and a few shooting stars that blaze their way out to sea. I stand up and he opens the door to the darkened interior. I will sleep here tonight, where I always seek refuge after I have the bad dreams. Here they won't come back. They will make a hammock for me and will watch over me. It is funny, every time I have this dream I come here and the old man is outside as if he knows I am coming, that I am lost and desperately seeking help. I feel old, no, more than that I feel ancient, as if I must carry some terrible burden. I don't know how I can release this ghost from my life or why I must carry him with me. But the old man knows. He is my island I cling to in order not to drown in fear and sorrow.

This is real. I am here, the old man is here, and the war is here. I must think about this specter, my Jacob Marley, who haunts the fringes of my fears. I must go back and try and understand, back to the beginning, from where and how I started this journey. We go inside after smoking the cigarettes. I find a place in one of the hammocks. The sleeping figures are muted in the half-light of a single burning lantern. One stirs next to me as I settle into the hammock. It is Thua, but he doesn't wake. Bong motions me to sleep and settles in a chair near the door. He just sits there, as if to guard me from the spirits, so I can sleep. I settle in, and begin to drift. I must remember the beginning of my journey to this place. I need to find meaning in all this and lift this weight from my soul.

CHAPTER I

The Road to Mandalay

It's muggy. The heat blasts through me the minute they open the door of the 707 that has brought its cargo of melancholy souls to this vast quagmire cleverly disguised as a nation fighting for its existence. It has been a typical MAC (Military Airlift Command) charter with the usual goat rodeo beginning at the departure station in the Replacement Depot in Oakland, California.

I arrived three days late for my reporting date because I finished off a 30 day pre-deployment leave with all the earmarks of a major bender. I was on my second tour going to the esteemed Republic of South Vietnam and had every intention of spending my last dime sucking up every deranged fantasy I could while I was still breathing and able. By the time I got to Oakland I didn't have enough body fluids left to sweat properly. Actually going back to the war was looking pretty attractive. I had just enough of my uniform left (that I hadn't given away as tokens of affection) to get in the front gate without the "Manners Police" giving me a hard time.

Oakland was the same as it had been since Korea, a warehouse full of scared teenagers with orders shipping them off to what they had been watching on the nightly news. The place smelled of fear with a capital "F." You processed in and waited for your airlift, assigned to a holding company where you, as an NCO (noncommissioned officer), would be given charge of 40 or 50 junior enlisted to ensure they made it to the aircraft.

A couple of days babysitting the cannon fodder and you wanted to kill them yourself. Most of the poor bastards were infantry with a few other admin or techno-twinks thrown in for good measure. The kids going to line units tended to be of two personality types, the quietly resigned and the swaggering macho assholes. It didn't matter which because underneath both types were scared shitless. The worst ones to put up with were the whiners going to tech jobs. They always had an excuse for any infraction. After a few judicious suggestions that you could get their orders changed to the infantry, the whining ceased.

While waiting for my lift, I spent three days going to the NCO club with some of the other Special Forces and Airborne types that were on their second or third tours as well. We avoided the cherries like the plague unless we were broke and they were willing to buy the drinks and not get too eager for combat stories. We also watched each other's back so that some scum-sucking little Spec-6 from admin didn't change our orders to the Ninth Infantry Division. This was a time-honored method of procurement by the Infantry for acquiring seasoned NCOs. They'd get some little dickweed in personnel to look for SF types and divert them at the Replacement Depot, thus they could avoid being accused of shanghaiing us at the reception point in Vietnam.

Airlift day came and we boarded TWA or whatever airline the Military Airlift Command had contracted. Regular airline, regular airline fare, this was during those heady days when they served decent food on American carriers and the hostesses were all pretty, perky, and didn't look like your grandmother or have the attitude of a gut shot wolverine.

The 14 hour flight is a boring drudgery or drunken binge, depending on if you have money or not. NCOs can drink, but the lower enlisted swine are limited to two or three beers. The officer in charge of our lift is a major I knew from when he was a captain, so he and I are swapping lies with each other and watching the lieutenants trying desperately to get the stewardesses aroused, well, at least interested. Fat chance, Buckwheat. These girls make this trip twice a week, bringing FNGs (fucking new guys) in and taking survivors of their one-year tour out. They have heard enough lame lines to fill a set of encyclopedias. But the human libido is an amazing mechanism, and there is a constant stream of little pinheads taking shots at them. All part of the job; they take it well and still manage to be alluring little goddesses of the airways while serving up the food and drinks with good-natured grace.

The major is going up to some outfit called FANK, which is some sort of special project, working with the Cambodians. He offers to get me on the orders, but I'd worked with the Cambodes before and learned very quickly that the only thing faster at getting out of the line of fire than a Cambodian was a hero assigned to Saigon. Nope, that is not for me. I want to be surrounded by Iron Age warriors from the hill tribes, my kind of people. I politely decline and the hours drift between catnapping and quiet conversation. We start the descent into Saigon and the newbies all gawk out the windows as the ground comes into view. It's raining outside, the beads of rain streaking the windows as we bump a few times and then we are on the ground taxiing to the gate area.

The engines wind down and the intercom comes on with the captain jocularly welcoming us to our destination. After we stop and the engines shut down, a squat, overweight sergeant first class comes onboard barking instructions, the usual litany of dos and don'ts. After this stirring bit of introduction, we soon disembark to walk the few meters to the holding area just inside the terminal. After a 30 minute wait in the sweltering heat, the pus-gut from the "repo-depot" comes up and officiously instructs me to get the troops in line. I look him over for a moment and tell him to take his fat ass out of my face and get to it himself. He starts to say something when the major tells him basically the same thing, but adds an extra comment about how a reassignment to a line unit might do wonders for his waistline. He stomps off to "arf" at the privates and we wait until the buses pull up and they start loading everyone on for the trip over to the in-country reception area. The kids are all wide-eyed from the exotic smells and crowded streets packed with moped and cycle traffic. In the stalls that line the roads all manner of consumer products are marketed. Thin ascetic looking Vietnamese hawk everything from WD-40 to stereos. There is a kaleidoscope of garishly painted signs and a proliferation of girls in brightly colored *ao dais* with the slit down the side, the Suzy Wong skirt dress of Vietnam.

A few of the replacements are astute enough to notice that the buses all have an armed guard and the windows are screened with mesh to keep the odd Viet Cong or drunk cowboy from throwing a grenade through the window. We wind through Saigon to the barracks and the in-processing point where we are issued our jungle fatigues and another clothing packet, US Army, Tropical, one set each, and processed to our units. With me is another old troop, Bernie O. Bernie had been in the original Air Assault which eventually became the mighty First Cavalry Division. He's been around the military so long he's developed the easy grace of a seasoned pickpocket in a crowded subway car.

Bernie has a round Irish face that speaks of too much blarney and liberal amounts of fine Irish whiskey, which season his outlook on the way of the world. He is in his mid-forties, has a gimp leg, and the exalted rank of Buck Sergeant. One would suppose, because of his age, that here is a former master sergeant who has fallen from grace and is working his sins off in order to retire, but this is not the case with Bernie. His is a simple case of getting out of the Army in the late fifties and pursuing a career in the then high-tech field of refrigeration. Bad location and even worse accounting skills left him with the only safe alternative of returning to the "Great Green Womb." So here he is, back in the Army and absolutely thrilled with the prospect of soldiering again and, more importantly, away from the spit and polish of garrison duty. Add to that the certain prospect of picking up rank faster and the opportunity for a bit of larceny and what more could a man ask for?

After an afternoon of in-processing, we are assigned a barracks and the time is ours. I am lying on the bunk in the transient barracks as Bernie comes bustling through the door with a pleased look on his face and a net bag full of tepid Ba Mi Ba beers in the heavy gauge 14 oz. glass bottles. You get an extra two ounces of beer with the added bonus that the bottle, empty or full, is the perfect tool for adjusting the headspace on the odd marine or sailor who wants to get froggy.

He plops down in the bunk opposite from me and grins that lopsided, wiseass grin that the Irish have perfected over the centuries. He pulls out two bottles from the bag, hands me one, then pulls out a CO_2 fire extinguisher that is obviously missing from someone's wall bracket and sprays the beers liberally. Voila! Instant, chilled beer. I take a long slow pull, relishing the sharp tang of the beer and the ambience of brewing that uses formaldehyde in the aging process. It gives you a heady hangover, but it is still better than that swill, Black Label.

"I went over to see if we got orders yet," Bernie starts and then smiles. I smell the conspiracy coming. "The Infantry guys managed to poach a couple of the new kids and they had us on orders to go to the Big Red One."

I know tragedy hasn't overcome us because he is in a really good mood. The Big Red One is the 1st Infantry Division. With our ranks, had we been shanghaied, we would end up as platoon sergeants. The proud members of this division put the emphasis on the last word in their nickname; those of us who never want to set foot in it put the emphasis on the second word, "red." I'm waiting patiently for him to lay out the masterful stroke of wheedling and scheming that he has accomplished in order to save us from a fate worse than death.

He takes a long pull on his beer, belches, and then continues. "I ran into one of the E-8s that run the admin section. He was in Germany with me in '58. I was his platoon sergeant and he was a Davy Crockett crewman."

"Anyway, he owes me a few favors, so he tells me that the only way to get up to Nha Trang, to Group Headquarters is either know God and have him protect you from the press gangs from the infantry or take a voluntary to an outfit called CCN."

I am beginning to feel queasy about this. For sure the guy he is talking to is another Mick and there is only one group that can outdo them in fucking each other and that's attorneys. And if I remember rightly, the Davy Crockett System was a jeep-mounted device that fired a huge projectile, like a foot in diameter, which was a nuclear warhead. In fact, the manual said to put the jeep in gear, fire, and accelerate away keeping a ridgeline between you and the target. How quaint, Bernie's E-8 is not only some fellow traveler, but is obviously not too bright.

On top of that, wherever or whatever CCN is, it is obviously something someone wants to keep quiet or they would have spelled it out. A simple rule in the Army is that if it is called by its initials, it's a bad start. You should worry even more if the initials are real short, because it indicates the speed at which your ass gets blown away.

Now, I had specifically sent Bernie over to the S-1 to arrange that we get orders assigning us to the 5l SFGA (Special Forces Group, Airborne), which is what we had on our original orders and to use their phone to call Nha Trang and tell them we were at the depot. If he wasn't able to do that he was to call House 39 and get someone to come over and rescue us from the clutches of the legs. These were pretty simple instructions, for Christ's sake. Even a Mick could follow them. I knew we could get assigned to the Mike Force. They always needed bodies in the Mike Force because it wandered around out there where all the bad people were and picked fights with them. Besides, I knew a number of the guys and I wanted to go where there were people that I could trust.

I'm beginning to sweat because he says, "I got us both on orders to go up to Da Nang and," he pauses, "I was able to get all those cherries freed from their infantry assignment as well. They are going with us."

Suddenly I am fully alarmed. My warning bells are ringing and my memory banks are starting to wind up. This is starting to smell like bad, bad news. It's obvious that this is an SF assignment, because anything that will get you away from the Division press gangs has to have some heavy priority on it. Add to that the fact that the cherries were able to get on the list, and the little voice in the back of my head is screaming, "Uh-oh," in big red letters.

Bernie is obviously pleased with himself and doesn't want to hear that if the assignment can spring guys right out of the infantry press gangs, it's got to have some major priority. With priority comes bad operations, lots of people shooting at you, helicopters and jets falling out of the air, and lots of folks going home with missing parts or in body bags. This is not good. I reach over and liberate another beer from the bag and lower its body temperature with the fire extinguisher. Bernie is still rattling on about how lucky we are. This will be a real combat assignment, nothing but SF brothers, blah, blah, blah. I'm beginning to suspect that the O'Reilly in S-1 had some sort of grudge against Bernie. Maybe Bernie was slapping leather to the guy's wife in the distant past and now it was payback time. I can see him grinning like a shark as he types up our orders. Hail Caesar, we who are about to die….

I come back from nightmare land with Bernie saying, "Geez, you look a little pale, brother. Maybe you need to take a cold shower, get acclimated…" I'm spinning in a vortex of bad vibes and suddenly realizing why the Irish end up in every front line outfit since King Henry beat the snot out of the French nobility at Agincourt. It's obviously a genetic thing that attracts them toward loud noises and screaming. They probably think it's a wake in progress, ergo plenty of free booze, so let's get involved.

It's so hot that I am starting to melt, but the beer is giving me a mellow feeling. Well, mellow enough that I don't throttle Bernie. I look at him and make sure I enunciate the words carefully.

"ARE YOU FUCKING CRAZY?" He looks at me with the hurt expression that only your family and ex-girlfriends who show up at your wedding seem to be able to pull off.

"What are you pissed about? We ain't going to some leg infantry outfit; I tried to call the number you gave me but no one answered. Then Kevin suggested that we could guarantee not going if we wanted to volunteer for this MACV-SOG thing."

I am trying to comprehend why my spine feels like I just pissed on an electric fence. Then it hits me, CCN, Chuckle Chuckle North, Command and Control North. Shiva, Destroyer of Worlds! Chaos! Oh yeah, now, I remember.

You see, with an operation where you are using company-sized maneuver forces, it's go out, scrap it up, and the bad guys have 200 plus targets to shoot at. They move out of your way if they aren't big enough or can't get the drop on you. From what I remember, SOG is Recon with a capital "R." It is deep penetration and no artillery support because you are in his back yard. There is nothing but air support, provided, of course, that it can get to you in time. You would have better luck getting help in the Bermuda Triangle. I have a couple of friends that are there. They are good men, lots of combat time; I remember something about it being voluntary. Ah, that's better, that little caveat might be a possible loophole. By now I'm on my third beer, so I decide to let Bernie off the hook.

"Oh yeah, Kevin. I knew it, another O'Fitzfuckyerbuddy." He is miffed that I yelled at him when he thinks he has done us both a great favor. Bernie can't know what he is in for, so I smile my brightest scamming smile, finish my beer, pull another one out and frost it down. Then I lean back against the wall and fix him with my most sincere look.

"Jesus, I'm sorry Bernie, I must still be affected by the drop in pressure from the long flight. Great! You got us a SF assignment. What the hell, I didn't want to go to the Mike Force. I would just as soon play this tour out in some cushy job. It's probably one of those show camps. You know, where all the bunkers are covered with cement and whitewashed, complete with a stencil of the unit crest on each one. Yes, that's it, probably right outside, where'd you say it was? Da Nang? Yeah, great place. All you do is let visiting Congressmen and reporters and Donut Dollies fly in and you give them the grand tour of a real SF A Camp. Probably has its own laundry with starched tiger stripes for the uniform of the day. Shit, we'll probably be able to drive into Da Nang and go to the whorehouses, every night we aren't being interviewed by Huntley and Brinkley, that is."

He is trying to get that Gaelic mush that he calls a brain around the fact that apparently I am no longer mad, but I can see that he is nervous about the flash of panic and terror that had been me a mere thirty seconds before. He gets into the swing of it, though, and spills what "good ol' Kevin" had told him.

"Yeah, uh maybe. Uh, I don't know. Kevin said that they run combat missions out from bases they call launch sites, so, uh, I guess we will get a chance to go in the field sometimes. It can't be too bad, 'cause Kevin says that he has a waiting list of guys that want to go there."

Yeah, I'm thinking about good ol' Kevin. I'm going to find good ol' Kevin and shove a good ol' fragmentation grenade up his ass as soon as I can get him isolated. Bernie is still pleased as punch. Should I tell him that there isn't any place in this bloody country that has a waiting list, unless it is the airport, and has to do with a flight out of here?

I drift back from my thoughts and Bernie is asking about whether I've ever heard about CCN. Oh yes, I think to myself, and if I share it with you, you're going to shit yourself, you dumb Mick. But I have a sweeter disposition than that. I look at him and give him my best "dealing with a lieutenant" look and tell him blandly, "I've heard a few things. I think Hardy's brother was in CCN or something." I look at him innocently. He cocks his head as he tries to connect the name with a face and history.

"Do you mean that guy in the Seventh that's all fucked up with wounds and is half crazy?" You can see that the thought of wounds and insanity are bringing back bad memories from Korea.

"Yeah, that's him, but I think he got all screwed up on his second tour in some A Camp, like up North. I'm sure he wasn't in CCN when all that bad shit happened." Yeah suffer, you dumb Mick. I knew Bachelor and he hadn't been up at CCN he'd been in CCC (Command and Control Central). Not only was he shot up like the lead dove on opening day of hunting season, he was mad as a March hare as well, and I'm sure it didn't come from his upbringing, even if he did come from Arkansas. And supposedly, CCC was a *quieter* operational area than CCN.

Maybe I will go find this Kevin O'Fuckyou and kidnap him. I dream about making him get out of the chopper dressed in a bright orange jumpsuit and run around with a boom box playing very loud soul music, deep inside Laos. At gun point. That will drive the little pissers into a murderous rage. And he won't be hard to find or miss 'cause I'm personally going to set fire to the bamboo so they know exactly where he is. If he ever gets back, bet he won't screw over a real soldier ever again. This has been another lesson in survival. It is normally someone else's idea that puts you in harm's way, not your own. Never, never hang around with the Irish if you want to keep your skin intact.

About the time I am finalizing the great "sell Kevin to a cannibal tribe" scenario in my head, our pastoral respite is interrupted by the loud entry of eight or so of the shining faced liberators of the oppressed, graduating class. They are resplendent in their Tropical Worsted and berets screwed on their heads, like little molded green hero toppers. They are a bit hesitant about interrupting at first, probably because we are in conference, but I flash them the same ether smile that has the Mick under control.

Bernie talks to them and comes back. "Hey, those new guys right out of training group want to go downtown tonight. They said they'd treat if we showed them where to go. They're real happy to be going with us up to Da Nang and all."

Our aircraft will be in tomorrow. We are restricted to the reception billets until then. To any red-blooded American fighting man worth his salt that is an open invitation to find the nearest hole in the fence and get himself downtown. After all, we are here in "the Nam" up to our eyebrows with all you've ever heard about in Far East exotica. We are separated by a measly wire barrier and a legion or two of MPs. What the hell are they going to do if they catch you? Send you to Nam?

I'm mulling this new possibility over in my mind, one last little fling before they march us out into the arena with the big cats, and at the same time, fighting the inclination to operate on that plan to do something particularly nasty to Kevin. I decide that the idea of being paid for howling, and the prospect of being next to something that doesn't smell like Aqua Velva is better. We will have to borrow heavily from the new guys. Shit, in a month, half of them will be either dead or shot up, so it's pretty good odds on the pay back.

Bernie and I sozzle our way to the shower with a cold one retrieved from the diminishing supply of beer in the sack. I stand under the spray reflecting on the situation and figuring out some sort of scheme to get out of it without demonstrating to all and sundry that I am more interested in breathing than in furthering the myth of *The Green Berets*. I already have all the medals I want. In fact, if I can give a couple back and pretend that I am in danger that will be just fine with me.

The water is hot and the pressure blasts most of the angst from me so that by the time I emerge I am actually feeling quite smug and happy. Fuck it. I might as well have some fun. Saigon is one of those cities where it is a perpetual Friday night. With every possible vice you could imagine and thrills, good food, and ambience to boot. I'm in the place that has shaped my adulthood. The place grows on you.

We get dressed in Tropical Worsted uniforms, or TWs, with all the good stuff, as we say, fifteen dollars worth of assorted ribbons and shiny stuff, then make our way down the hillside to a hole in the concertina wire which will provide entry to our fantasies. Hole is a misnomer. There is a well-beaten footpath out past the bunker line where the REMFs (rear echelon mother fuckers) are pulling their guard shift. The trick is to find the area that isn't guarded by the MPs, but rather by the clerk typists and admin bunnies who are doing their punishment tour. MPs are the same the world over, little self-important assholes who, when given a whistle and an armband, feel it's their duty to fuck with anyone they can in order to prove they have a dick. I hate MPs. It has always been my opinion that we should be joining forces with the VC to fight MPs. I bet they have the same type of road guard assholes in their army. Let's make the world a better place; let's kill all the MPs.

We wind our way through the wire quick as Jack is nimble and flag down one of the garishly lit tricycle buses. I tell the driver to take us to Mama Bic's. Everyone knows where Mama Bic's is. From this bordello-bar-safehouse unofficial Special Forces headquarters, we can get to the rest of what Tu Do Street has to offer. We are snuggled into the pedi-cab like sardines, so the driver flags down another and, after a quick exchange of dollars, four of the guys pile into it. I tell all of them to keep their arms inside and take off the big Seiko watches because the street cowboys will strip them off your arm faster than you can blink. Besides, we can always use them for trading material if the night gets really interesting.

After about 20 minutes we pull up to Mama Bic's. The place is a pulsing shifting tide of GIs and hookers, mixed with the odd construction crew, CIA spook, war correspondent, and a sprinkling of minor functionaries from the embassies. The big dogs don't come here; they have their own set of upscale establishments that sell the same thing with a more sedate face on it. Besides, who wants to be around that crowd? In fact, hanging around with that crowd is a good invitation to get caught by a bicycle bomb. You don't have to worry about that at Mama Bic's. She has paid off everyone who might have a grudge against each other; bombs are bad for business. Also, this is the unofficial meeting place for Special Forces in Saigon, so I can catch up with buddies and scout a prospect for getting out of going up north to be sacrificed on some weird altar of certain death.

As we weave our way inside and find a place big enough to seat our little band, there is a Philippine band rocking out a rendition of "Ploud Mally." My ass hasn't even settled into the vinyl seat when a waitress arrives wanting to know what we want. Eight or nine of Mama's girls imploring you to buy them "tea" accompany her. I've already told the new guys to not waste money on the tea because it costs what champagne costs at a San Francisco cafe and it really is tea. If the little darlings want to drink buy them a beer or whiskey, or if you are a classy guy like me, feed them cognac in the hope they get drunk and are in the freebie mood. Save your money for the more important stuff boys, mainly getting Uncle Nick drunk and laid.

The place is like old home week. Within a few minutes we are safely nestled in our booth with the crowd washing around us like a sea of uniforms, and an equal number of brightly colored, undulating hips of oriental femininity. My lethargy has been supplanted by cognac and coke, tepid, just right for the mood I'm in. Bernie and I hold court with the newbies. I am imparting my vast knowledge of the etiquette of nation-saving graces and how not to get robbed by the flotsam of beggars and Saigon cowboys. Bernie is off in some dreamland of having "arrived," so the world is perfect.

We are indulging in the finely honed practice that follows every army since the boys from the Tiber marched over the Alps, or good old Hammurabi's cousins mounted a chariot and whisked off over the sand dunes, that time honored practice of planting of the seed. Praise Bacchus! Fermented juices to numb the mind are what we need, and to top off the evening, something soft to prove that you are a man. Shit, I'm getting philosophical. Within the space of ten minutes semi-drunk and totally drunk, familiar faces come, stop, and exchange the complimentary "What the fuck are you doing back here?" salutes.

I spend a few moments with each old friend discussing the usual: Who bought the farm? How? What's going on up-country? Who's where? What is open, project-wise? Within an hour I am up to date on the situation in-country, and what I haven't heard, Bernie has.

We are comparing notes and I still haven't told him the royal fucking we are in for when we get to Da Nang. What the hell, he didn't do it out of malice. But, Kevin? Kevin is a dark ember in my heart.

Bernie is still basking in the awed gapes when he tells people that he is going to CCN. Thank God he is so trashed that he can't discern the fare-thee-well looks. The new guys are soaking up the ambience and a couple have already slipped upstairs and been relieved of their pent-up passions. From the looks on their faces it hasn't been a Pearl Buck experience. You quickly learn that heaven has claws. In a combat zone, there isn't any romance about it, just plain old needs to be taken care of clinically for the exchange of dollars. Soon we are back to the only family you really have, your own kind. One of our heroes has the mistaken assumption that fucking has given him ownership rights and we have to drag some 230 pound zoomy off him when he protests the attentions said airman is paying to his recently enjoined spirit.

Mama Bic shows up and starts hollering about me being "numbah ten," me "long time Vietnam no bling trouble," the usual litany of recriminations. The use of the number ten connotes the basement of the scale, in behavior or situation, anywhere in Vietnam. It is all high entertainment. We get the airman back to sanity with a couple of well-placed kidney shots and a good stiff kick to his solar plexus. While he's gasping for air, Bernie stomps on his hands for good measure. You have to love the Gaels; if his hands are broken he can't fight that well. We are out the door and down the street. We stop at a French restaurant and have a sumptuous meal, complete with wines and brandies. A couple of the kids have passed out in the soup, so they miss the excellent duck with saffron rice. By the time we leave we are well within the limit of destitution. We are swaying back and forth like a huge animal, half of which keeps collapsing in derision and an occasional regurgitation stop. We have gathered up other fellow comrades in arms, fellow brothers in our revelry. There are several regular infantry types with us, four or five marines and the odd Navy guy, by the time we begin to start working up the logistics of getting back to the base. Just when I have exhausted all the fresh ideas I had in that quarter, entertainment and transport arrives in the form of three jeeps of Military Police and their White Mice counterparts (White Mice is our pet name for the Vietnamese MPs). Three jeeps and there we all are, needing a ride. We are musketeers; all for one, one for all. I am certain that these fellows will assist us in getting back to the base, all of us. I am sure. This is perfect.

The staff sergeant in charge of this band of society's finest, jumps out and starts demanding passes, IDs, and berating all for shoddy uniforms, all the while babbling threats like, "We are going to arrest you and haul you in, by God." He doesn't even clear the sidewalk before Bernie short jabs him in the face and makes his nose look like a liquid rose. The prick drops like a ton of bricks and there is a nanosecond of shocked silence as everyone freezes.

The "gyrenes" are on the other five before they can react. They go through the MPs like a school of piranha. Seconds later, it is all over and the entire shiny helmet liner crowd is down and out.

The Marines are considered in many quarters as the finest assault force on the planet. You have a beach that needs to be taken, an island to be leveled, some banana dictator that needs to be peeled? Call up the Marines. That's what they are for. And even though there is always intra-service rivalry we have taken them into our little band of brothers and nary a bad word has passed between us. The nearest I could figure is that they were returning the favor by clearing obstacles ahead of our return to base. Besides these were Army MPs, so they didn't count much in their book.

But now we have a problem, actually several, but we do have the ability to get away if we use a little savvy. We need to detain the gendarmes until we can get away and before more of their little companions stumble onto this particular indiscretion. So we get organized and drag them out of sight. After delivering a couple of judicious kicks to make sure we have getaway time, we handcuff them all to a stout drainage pipe in an alley. Their guns go in the nearest canal. We load as many of us as we can into the vehicles and take the back streets to the edge of the sprawling base we had left many hours before. Along the way there is the temptation to try out the sirens and lights, but sanity breaks out. We creep along the outer perimeter of the base's defenses as we try to find the particular hole in the fence we came through earlier.

After what seems like a very long time, we finally find the hole. Actually, we stumble onto the entrance by almost running over a perfectly good staff sergeant who had passed out going into the wire. We get all the lads out, pick up the poor sod from the Ninth Division, and start through the wire. I figure we have probably roused the entire Provost from all of Saigon, so Bernie and I are last going up. In a stroke of tactical genius Bernie suggests that we torch one of the jeeps. That ought to give us breathing room he says; they won't come too close until they figure out if it's an ambush. In fact, he is all for going back and getting some more MPs and leaving their bodies around the jeeps to dress up the scene. This of course endears him to the "Uncle Sam's Misguided Children" crowd. I manage to get him calmed down, but I have to promise him that we will do something particularly nasty to the MPs in the future; I think I also agreed that we would adopt two of the gyrenes as well.

The kid at the bunker is some clerk from Ohio. Bernie and I stop long enough to tell him to keep mum. No problem, everyone has had a bad experience with MPs.

Lingua franca. Everyone hates them. It's almost dawn when we get back to our barracks and we have to catch an early flight. We crash on our bunks and before I drift off in the haze of alcohol and camaraderie, I'm of a mind to let Bernie in on the disaster that waits for us in Da Nang.

* * *

The heat is oppressive. Even with two of the big GI floor fans on me I am a sodden mess. My head feels like someone wrapped it in aluminum foil, and then took a hammer to it. I am drifting in that state that is not quite awake. I don't want to wake up because that would only make me feel worse. There is nothing nastier than sweating cognac and rum and whatever else I may have consumed last night. I swallow and it feels like sandpaper on my throat and there is the distinct taste of something only a lizard would pass.

I climb out of the fog and realize where I am. I look at my watch, trying to get my eyes to focus. It's 5 AM. I lie back onto the pillow and start to stretch. God, that hurts. Why do I do this to myself? I slowly get into the mode of rising and think how good a hot shower will feel. I sit up.

"Gagh!" I gradually force myself into the shower and take a long hot one. I shave without cutting my throat and get dressed in a set of jungle fatigues. The buses will be here at eight to take us out to the airport. We will travel from here to Nha Trang. Good old SFOB (Special Forces Operational Base). At least by the time we get there we can get a cold beer. I go down and roust Bernie from his bunk. He looks like something the dogs have dragged in from an Algerian alley. We go to the mess hall and wolf down breakfast and what seems like several quarts of hot black coffee. By this time we are the most wide-awake corpses in Vietnam.

The bus ride out to the airport is punctuated by the arrival in my life of one more idiot. This is in the form of a certain Staff Sergeant Booth. Right out of Appalachia, about twenty-five, dumb as carrots. He lists off all the dos and don'ts, and a litany of dweeb rules that are meant to impress the privates with how important he is. I am too worn out to cause trouble. Bernie and I can only snicker at the little prick. I haven't got time for this. I am too busy vacillating between a wish to die right now and a wish to regurgitate the horrible slimy weasel that has crawled down my throat.

Our flight to Nha Trang is a short hop. We are on the ground before noon. A short ride to the SFOB and then we spend the afternoon in-processing. We are going up to Da Nang tonight. They must be in a hurry to kill us off. By the time the evening rolls in I have consumed enough aspirin to deaden the San Andreas Fault.

I am in the transient barracks, which is behind the NCO club, with the large floor fan driving a hot sirocco across the room. I hate air conditioning, preferring to get acclimated to the heat. I have shut the air conditioner off in the two-man room and ventilated the place by forcing the window open. Bernie comes in and says we have an 1830 lift to Da Nang. It is about a four-hour wait until they take us to the airfield so we spend the time just kicking back. We have a few beers with some guys coming in for a promotion board from one of the outlying A Camps. I hadn't been in the U.S. long, but it seems to me that the war has taken on an intensity and a frenzy that wasn't there before I left on leave. We hear about some of the leg units refusing to fight. Not good. Of course with the drug problems and all the other breakdowns in discipline, it was bound to happen. The military can only be efficient if it maintains its order.

The regular units are full of draftees and, of course, McNamara's 100,000. These are draftees and enlistees that came in under a program that lowered the IQ and several other inductee requirements. Now even the poor and deranged will get their chance to die for God and country. The results have been enlistees who are unable, and in many cases, unwilling to become soldiers. With the waning popularity of the war comes the concept that, as a soldier, you can refuse to do what you are ordered to do. Sorry boys, this is the United States Army and that particular fantasy is called mutiny. Then there is the new term "fragging" that has become the watchword for NCOs and officers in conventional outfits. Fragging is when someone who disapproves of you rolls a fragmentation grenade into your bunker on a dark night.

I'd love to be in a unit where some loudmouthed creature threatens me with a fragging. I would wait until some dark night when they are all sitting there smoked to the gills and I'd roll a couple of frags in on them. After the smoke cleared, I'd order any that may have survived to haul the corpses out. If a survivor so much as blinked I would cap him. Two can play that game. There are stupid officers, stupid policies, stupid operations, and a host of other stupid situations, which go along with the other rigors of this occupation. That's the Army. Your job as an NCO is to accomplish the mission and get your men back, in one piece if possible. Nothing is more destructive to that effort than one troublemaker who gets away with it. It only leads to more miscreants thinking they can do the same.

Everyone is afraid to confront the problem of fragging head on. Too bad, that crowd will come back to haunt this country later. Of course, the McNamara 100,000 program mostly encompasses the minorities, so you have an even larger pool of the bizarre and the unwilling filling the ranks. Everyone is becoming "sensitive" to the voice of the minorities. I don't see myself as what they call "whitey." I personally had nothing to do with oppressing anyone. And as far as the historical record goes, the attitudes that the races had prior to my being delivered onto this mud ball are just that, history. I was called; I came to serve; and I get the same opportunity to get my ass shot off as everyone else. That is what citizenship is all about. I don't understand this jive about inequality. Not that the problem doesn't exist in Vietnam, but that fight isn't to be fought here. We will settle that when we get done with the job we are here to do.

If someone wants to change all that by refusing, well, kick the shithead out and strip him of his citizenship. You don't want to fight? Good, go to some third world shit hole and live, but you aren't going to enjoy the fruits of my labors. I have watched the Army and the country change over the last ten years to the point where it seems that anyone with a bitch, who whines loud enough, has that spineless crowd in Washington pissing all over themselves. The people that inhabit Special Forces have the same ideals and outlooks that exemplify a volunteer outfit. They've got the same job, the same danger, the same bullshit to put up with, OD (olive drab) green in color. Of course, the people that make up Special Forces are probably not a good barometer for social tolerance, since most would heartily agree that anyone not in Special Forces is a sniveler.

Bernie and I spend the afternoon gathering information on CCN. It isn't rosy. But it is voluntary. It doesn't much matter; we have orders to go and we will go. I have never found anything to be as bad as it is normally reported. Besides, I have always been a volunteer and that's SF—triple volunteers. How bad could it be?

I am soon to find out that I should sometimes listen to the majority. We spend the time at Nha Trang getting processed in and as the day wears on I am actually starting to feel human again. The SFOB has all the comforts of home and is a bustle of activity. This is the nerve center of SF operations in-country, so at some point you see everyone coming through here. We are just faces in the crowd here, just another batch of personnel being moved up-country to an assignment. I have always hated this place because it is too much like the stateside forts. There are plenty of self-important little assholes with their rulebooks clutched tightly to their chests. I am impatient to get where we are going. It's an old adage that the farther from the flagpole, the less chicken shit.

The truth is that any time the Army gets somewhere they can put up permanent buildings or stretch out the tents, there is a hurried rush to make it all neat and trim. This goes with the ordered mindset of militaries. Everything must be in line and dressed in the right dress. This, of course, attracts the worst sort of people, like MPs, staff flunkies, rising stars of the rear echelon, and worst of all, those parsimonious souls that feel it is their duty to instill discipline in those beneath them. Thank God for the VC who trundle out occasionally and drop a few 122mm doses of reality into this place and kill a few. If they weren't out there, this place would be full of REMFs. All the more reason to go to some remote outpost and spend your nights hunkered down in a bunker, shooting rats with a silenced twenty-two for entertainment. None of the aforementioned riffraff out there, it's much too messy.

CHAPTER 2

Keys to the Kingdom

I awaken in the land of the Philistines. I am in a C-130 winging my way to Da Nang with thirteen cherries for Christ's sake, what could be unluckier? I look over at Bernie as we begin our descent into Da Nang Airbase. He is sleeping with his head propped against the pallet on the back of the ship. He looks very Leprechaun-ish, with a line of drool coming out of the left corner of his mouth. Charming. He is probably dreaming of some sort of boiled stew dish and a pint of Guinness.

As we begin our landing approach, we hit thermal turbulence at about a thousand feet. Bernie wakes up and the newbies stir as well. There is nothing like taking a nap on a C-130 to refresh you. Welcome to the answer to insomnia conveniently provided by the US Air Force and built by the lowest bidder.

Bump, bump and the snarling of the engines becomes a crescendo as the crew of highly paid aerial truck drivers reverses the props to slow us down. The plane taxis to the ramp. The crew chief lowers the back ramp with the screaming of hydraulics as a backdrop and a blast of hot humid air replaces the cabin atmosphere. Mixed in with the fetid air is the aroma of burning kerosene. Ah, just right. This is a warm comforting smell.

The bird never winds down completely. It will refuel here, take on more passengers, and then go north to Quang Tri. We grab our gear and file off the rear of the bird. The exhaust from the engines and backwash from the props pushes at us as we walk over to the lee side of the nearest bomb revetment.

The noise of the idling engines is supplemented by the laboring sound of a deuce and a half which rounds the corner of the ready ramp and pulls up next to us. The truck is painted black. There is no canvas top over the driver's cab and on the back are two Americans and about twelve of the most evil-looking Chinese Nungs I have ever seen. They are armed to the teeth with CAR-15s, lots of ammo, grenades, claymores, and wearing some sort of sterile fatigues for a uniform. They also appear to be seriously impaired by the sheer amount of equipment they are carrying. Armed to the teeth doesn't completely describe this crowd. They have a very strange looking set of combat harnesses. What I notice mostly is that six canteen covers have replaced the ammunition pouches, and there appear to be six or more magazines shoved in each one. The two Americans jump down, and as one peels off to go into the flight office, the other directs the Nungs to get all their gear on board the plane we just vacated.

The American that went into the head shed comes back and as he nears us he looks us over like we were fresh steaks at the butcher shop, laughs to himself and says, "Welcome to Chuckle Chuckle North. If you're lucky you will have a bad accident on the way to the camp and get medevaced before you get to Recon Company." Then he walks up the back ramp of the bird. The C-130 closes and the engines wind up as it pulls out to the taxiway. The noise abates and I turn to look more closely at our transport. The truck is so ratty that it looks like someone retrieved it from the scrap yard.

Our driver is dressed in the same style uniform, but has what appears to be a water polo helmet on for headgear. It's bright red with the number 666 in white across the front. He is in his late thirties or early forties and is as bizarre as the team that just departed. He looks crookedly at us, then horse coughs from underneath the biggest handlebar mustache I've seen in awhile.

"You waiting for a fucking invite?" he growls. "Get your gear on board. I'm your duly appointed official greeter, driver, and protector of your sad asses until we get to the camp." With that last bit of information, he pulls out a Thompson submachine gun with a drum magazine and waves it in the air for emphasis. The cherries load their gear hastily onto the back of the truck and I follow suit. The newbies settle into the back while I climb into the cab. All are ready to go, except Bernie, who is standing next to the driver's side of the deuce. The driver is looking over Bernie like a panel of mothers-in-law. He is apparently trying to place the round Irish face with some distant past association. The light must have come on because he sighs and then squints real hard.

"Were you ever in the Eleventh Airborne? Or in the 502n? Yer sad sack Irish mug looks familiar." Bernie looks at him, throws his bag up in the truck and starts to climb into the cab.

"Fuck you, Stevie boy. You always was a loudmouth sorry excuse for a bowel movement. I must have fallen from grace if you are part of this outfit." They both are grinning now as Bernie sits in the cab, squeezing me between them.

Oh great, fallen in amongst the poetic tragedy crowd. The mere act of being with two Irish in a combat zone is a patent solution to worrying about a long and peaceful life. I am trying to remember if the name on the uniform is an Irish name. It doesn't matter, because the name sounds like it has been infected by Gaelic, and that is close enough. As the truck winds through the streets of Da Nang, I find out that Bernie and Stevie, here, apparently had been in Korea together. I also find out that our escort is a Distinguished Service Cross winner from that late, great, police action.

But there is more good news about Stevie. He apparently has a steel plate in his head from wounds suffered in that last one. As a result, he has express written instructions from every exalted medical facility connected to the military that he is never, *never*, to consume alcohol, a fact which the good sergeant has chosen not only to ignore, but to flaunt in the face of reason. I am quickly pulled into the warm embrace of veterans; our escort has kindly brought some beer and a bottle off Bushmill's to make the journey less tedious. The cherries are relegated to gawking at the scenery.

I notice that there appears to be two rules to the good sergeant's driving. They are: go as fast as you can and, if anything appears to be on a collision course with the vehicle, honk the horn. The "horn" is some hurricane powered air horn, concealed beneath the hood. When the scenery gets a bit more open with paddies off to the right, he punctuates the sound of the horn by using the Thompson to fire a couple of short bursts into the air or off into the rice paddies. This gives him great pleasure and after awhile he lets Bernie be the horn honker, which seems to give Bernie a feeling of old home week. Me? I just suck on the beer. I want to stay away from the rye. It's far too early to get into that sort of suffering. I am drifting over the rationale of acting like this in broad daylight. I know what it is like out in the boonies and on the A Camps. This kind of behavior is commonplace with those little rascals, but this is a major metropolis. You could get away with these sorts of indiscretions in the backwaters, but not here.

There is no sense of guilt or apprehension. It would appear he does this with impunity; ergo he must know something I don't. Besides, it is too weighty a problem to worry about in the hot sun. I glance back at the rear of the truck where the cherries are; they are quite obviously flabbergasted by this behavior. Give them a few weeks. This ain't Smoke Bomb Hill. This is the Nam. God, I love a war zone. It encourages the eccentricities in all of us.

We wind over the I Corps bridge and out towards the east. Our driver is droning on as if he were a tour guide in Hollywood. Here is the China Beach Hospital where all the round eye nurses are. That is the German Hospital ship where all the round eye nurses that speak German are. Hmm, German nurses, I like this place already. We make a turn and start south on the main hardball. We come to a wide spot in the road with a rat's nest of shanties to the right. He down shifts and informs us that this is "Gonorrhea Gulch." He drones on as we pass a large American compound on the left, the Eightieth Group where the MPs are. We roar down the highway. In the distance we can see a mountain that seems to grow right up out of the seaside and after about twenty minutes, we come to the front gate of a compound that is right on the beach. To our right is a huge trash dump with hundreds of Vietnamese picking amongst the garbage and trash. The dump appears to be run by Americans and there are several Army skip loaders and a D-7 Cat moving the trash around.

We turn into the compound and go past a machine gun post in a sandbagged bunker. Bru and Sedang Montagnards man it. I recognize them by their bracelets and features. They are short, compact little tribesmen. Their uniforms are a mixed bag but their weapons and gear are all well maintained. This evokes a flood of memories from the past. I am starting to feel more comfortable with the idea of this assignment, mostly because these men are obviously the backbone of the strikers, or troops, that we will be using. I know these people; they are the finest fighters in the country. With that and a heavy dose of karma, we might even survive this tour, that is, if I can get away from this magnet-headed master sergeant. Isn't 666 the mark of the devil or something? It is too hot and my brain is fuzzy from the heat, and of course, the beer. I will not ponder that one any longer than I have to. I decide I don't want to know about the water polo helmet.

The truck skids to a stop just past a PSP (perforated steel plate) landing pad and in the front of what appears to be the Headquarters shed. There are two staff cars and a few jeeps outside. All are painted black. Stevie yells toward the back.

"End of the line, ladies. Get off my fucking truck. Go inside and they will process you in. Get a move on it, because it's hot out here and I am out of beer." He looks over at Bernie, then me, and belches something about catching up with us later. I am already formulating a plan to avoid that, but Bernie looks like he just found his long lost brother, which is a double reason to avoid that particular liaison.

We dismount, pull our bags off, and the truck roars off down toward the beach along a line of barracks hootches, all identical. There is a well maintained trench line that surrounds the camp, with bunkers interspaced every few meters. Lots of barbed wire and an apparent mine field beyond that. All in all, this place has the appearance of a normal Special Forces camp.

Bernie looks around, and spots what is obviously a crashed Cobra gunship just at the edge of the PSP pad, takes in all the bunkers, the wire, and the fact that the place is crawling with armed Yards. He turns to me and blurts, "Jeez Nick, this don't look like no show camp."

No shit you mallet-headed Mick, this is CCN. This is the place they ship you to when you are too fucking crazy to be in any other unit. Well, I don't say it to him, I just think it, but I just can't resist checking to see if his headspace is working, so I ask, "Bernie, what exactly was Stevie boy like when you knew him in Korea?"

"Mary, Mother of God, he was a lunatic. When we were in Korea he was always in the shit except when we were at the front. We were in a Regimental Combat team and…"

I don't let him finish. "Sort of like the Rangers in WWII? The kind of outfit where they sent you out sneaking, peeking, raiding, and generally doing mischief in miserable weather while getting your ass shot off?" I smile at him; well, actually it's a half smirk. He looks at me and cocks his head to one side. His eyes keep darting over to the crashed helicopter that graces the front of the compound like some kind of weird war sculpture. "Well, yes?" He still says nothing. He doesn't get it. I'm going to have to draw stick figures here. So I lean forward to emphasize the next question. "And do you suppose that your bosom buddy would be assigned to anything that might even resemble a normal unit? I realize that we are in Vietnam, but in your mind, think about this for a moment. How long would he last in even a normal Special Forces Unit?" I see the lights go on in Bernie's head.

"Oh shit," he says, kind of sighing. His cheeks puff out and he emits a low whistle. He has this look like the nightmares of his youth just caught up with him. All sorts of memories about Korea and his reunion twin are flitting across his memory banks. He really looks a bit pale.

Our trip down memory lane is interrupted by a new master sergeant who comes out and directs us inside, telling us to bring our gear with us. This one is the normal model, complete with pressed uniform and shined boots. I have been so busy with Bernie that I haven't noticed the few Americans that are standing about the area around the front of the building. They are eyeballing us with the practiced eye of a Roman centurion looking for replacements. Some are truly disreputable looking and more are drifting over from the area around what appears to be a jail compound inside the main camp. It is a fenced enclosure containing one long building. Uniforms seem to be, well, on the ones that look like they are actually field types, they seem to be whatever is thrown together. There are the usual headquarters pukes with their starched fatigues and patches and shined jungle boots. But more and more of the brigand crowd is showing up and giving us the eyeball.

One in particular shows up with a fatigue shirt that is cut off at the shoulders and cut off jungle fatigue shorts with what appears to be a bottle of wine protruding from the pocket. He is blond, tall, and looks like a recruiting poster for the SS. Someone calls him *Dai Uy*, which is Vietnamese for captain.

There is a short, dark looking little Cuban individual who the others call Castro. I notice he has a nametag that says Castillo. Both of them look like extras in a bad "B" melodrama. The Cuban looks us over and snorts; he casually retrieves the captain's wine bottle from his pants pocket as he goes by.

We go inside and are greeted by blessed air- conditioning. It is a normal head shed, with the place bustling with paper shufflers, typewriters, and telephones. Sure enough, a normal looking sergeant major comes out after a while and tells us our assignments. Bernie and I, and all but three of the FNGs, are going to Recon Company. The others are going to what they call a Hatchet Force. From what I can gather, this is a scaled down Mike Force or an assault company. We are fucked. Our assignment is like getting the Order of the Purple Shaft with barbed wire clusters. Bernie and I pick up our gear after we are done and go back outside. The heat hits us like a wall of flame. There is a three-quarter ton truck sitting there and the driver is wearing a Hawaiian shirt and sporting what appears to be a Civil War kepi. It's gray, of course, with crossed sabers, and a really ratty, grease-stained one at that. He drawls a quick, "Load yer gear up," and we get in the back. We whip down the fence line about two hundred yards and pull up outside of Recon Company. There is a white picket fence in front of the crosswalk. A lopsided sign hangs from the upper crossbar, "Nurses Quarters—off limits to all male personnel." It has two bullet holes in it as punctuation. There are chain marks on one end of the fence where it has obviously been wrenched from its former resting place.

The entire camp is built on the sand and we can see the ocean just outside the east wire. There is a barrier of concertina wire with a minefield beyond that surrounds the camp, which lies in front of the main trench line. Inside this enclosure are the metal-roofed buildings that make up the barracks and various buildings like the mess hall, etc.

There seems to be one area for the Americans and a second area for the Yards which are comprised of longer buildings. All have corrugated metal roofs. The ones in the American areas have a cement revetment extending up the outside of the buildings to chest height. These are grenade revetments and, in effect, make each hut a fighting position if needed. All in all, it's pretty cozy.

We get down and our escort points us at the second line of hootches and tells us to report to the Company Commander in the company office. Next to where we parked is a guy sitting in a blue lawn chair, apparently sunning himself. He is asleep and is snoring loudly. There is a claymore mine next to the chair and he has the detonator in his hand. His only attire appears to be some sort of Montagnard loincloth affair and a "Do Not Disturb" sign from the Bangkok Hilton on a string around his neck.

As we walk up to the orderly room dragging our bags with us, our guide drawls something about waiting outside in the shade until the Company Commander has a chance to talk with us. He sticks his head in the door and says something to those inside. He suddenly jerks himself out of the way just as the door bursts open and a body flies out, landing in front of us. The man begins to pick himself up, then falls back face first in the sand. He then manages to help himself up and staggers off toward the back of the company area. We stare at the retreating form wondering what this is all about and then our heads swing up as the door opens a second time. A short, squat blonde captain is standing in the doorway with his fists balled up. Without blinking an eye he surveys us. He looks around as if expecting the body that had preceded him to still be there.

He has all the charm of a bouncer at an orphanage. He sticks out his jaw, apparently in an attempt to punctuate his next statement, but it fails to delineate if this troll actually has a neck. He takes a breath and starts in.

"Welcome to Recon Company. I'm Captain Manes, but you may call me Sir, or Motherfucker Sir, or just hide when you think I am looking for you. I will be assigning you to a team just as soon as I can because we need warm bodies. This is a volunteer assignment. If, at any time, you feel that you can't hack it, all you have to do is come in here and tell me or the sergeant major and we will reassign you somewhere else. Gentlemen, this is real important so I hope you have been picking your ears instead of your ass. If you are too shaky to do this job, you don't need to be out there where you can get someone else killed." He pauses, which is good because I am trying to figure if this is actually a human being. He gulps a breath, his mouth settles into some sort of grimace that slashes across the square features like a water mark and continues. "That is the extent of the briefing, welcoming speech and pre-dark pep talk. Are there any questions? If there are, they better not be stupid questions, because question and answer time cuts into my leisure activities."

I look at the sand where the man had struggled up and walked off and figure, what the hell, I might as well test the waters. After all, as weird as the events that have transpired seem, I am not about to be intimidated by some officer. I have the sneaking suspicion that this particular one probably has the shadows of NCO stripes still on his uniforms. He has all the mannerisms of the recently anointed.

"Uh, Sir?" I say it loud enough to get his attention.

"Yes?" he fixes me with a benign look. This is, I am sure, a veiled sarcasm thing. I know he is a retread now. I use this same stalling tactic from time to time. Fuck you squat bread, I am not about to be intimidated by some kind of alien life form masquerading as a captain.

"What did this fellow here do?" I point at the disturbed sand where the man had landed. I figure that I will give him the double litmus test. That being an obvious question which will either lead to explanations or indicate the level of chickenshit potential in this outfit, if there is any. I don't have long to wait. The captain sets his shoulders and sticks out that bulldog jaw before speaking.

"He came in here and wanted to quit," Chunky hisses as if someone showed him something unpleasant, like his own visage in a mirror. "Are there any other questions?" He glares at the crowd with impatience. A clipped answer of that sort is not what I had in mind, so I press the issue.

"I thought you said this was a volunteer outfit, Sir?" I ask this with a bit more demanding tone, careful not to appear to be disrespectful. He looks me over as if I represent some tedious task in front of him.

"I did say that, numb nuts." He punctuates that with a grimace.

"Then why did you hit him?" As he fixes me with one eye, well, the bloodshot orb that passes as one anyway, everyone is sliding away from me as if I suddenly developed leprosy. Survivalists all, they figure that I am going to be on the shit list and none of the pussies want to be guilty by association.

"What's your name?" he barks at me.

"Brokhausen, Sir."

He looks over his shoulder and calls back into the orderly room to someone. "You hear that you ignoramuses? I have to run into a new guy before someone shows me the respect that befits my exalted status and rank in this here goat-fiick of an outfit, someone that puts 'Sir' on the end of a sentence." He turns and puts his hands on his hips as if he were setting himself for a difficult task. I have already spied a loose iron fence post lying in the sand. I figure if it looks like he is going to swing, I am going to take that post and drop him as hard as I can. He smiles at me and looks right at the post then back at me, still smiling. I am positive now that he is an ex-noncom. He isn't some strutting little martinet. This is merely chitchat for information's sake, sort of an informal mental sparring match. I am starting to have doubts that the iron fence post will be adequate for the task.

"I did say that this was a volunteer outfit. I hit him because he is a whiner. I won't have a whiner around me. He wanted to quit and he hasn't even been on a mission yet. Well, not a real mission, yet. So unless you are a dimwit, a three year old, or just a barracks lawyer, does that explain it?"

"Uh, yes Sir, I just don't wants to be doin' sumfin dat upsets yo." I give him my best Rastus act and shuffle from one foot to the other. There is a collective gasp from the crowd I arrived with, but the captain looks at me and points a sausage-like finger in my direction. Everyone else has taken refuge in the act of trying to look invisible.

"I am assigning you right now, Brokentrout, or whatever your name is. The rest of these gents I will interview this afternoon after dinner. But since you have demonstrated very plainly to me that you are obviously a frustrated comic and wit, I am assigning you to Recon Team Habu. You can fit in with the rest of those degenerate, insubordinate excuses for a waste of taxpayer money. They will appreciate your finely tuned sense of humor more than I will." He turns to the crowd that came with me. "I will be interviewing each of you later, so after you go inside and get assigned to a team, you can drop your gear and stand by until I call for you." He looks at me, grimaces in my direction, and then shakes his head as if he were in on some secret joke and laughs.

With that he stomps back through the doorway of the orderly room and shortly afterwards a head peeks out and points me to a hootch with RT Habu painted on the front door. I look at Bernie and he shrugs and laughs. I figure he is indulging his humor at my discomfort. Well, have your chuckles now, Bernie. I hope they assign you and Stevie together, just for old time's sake.

I pick up my stuff and walk the few meters up the sidewalk to a hut that has a garishly painted skull with a Green Beret on it and the words RT HABU on a scroll above it. I knock on the door and then wait for a few moments. No one answers so I open it and heave my duffel bag inside. It takes a moment before my eyes fully adjust to the light. There are two guys sitting inside. One is bare-chested and looks to be about fifteen years old and has a small patch of hair growing in the center of his chest. Jesus, they are robbing the cradle to fill up the ranks. The other one is positively the homeliest-looking excuse for a human I have ever seen. His head looks too big for his emaciated body and he has ears like Dumbo. Both are drinking beer and quietly cleaning what appear to be silenced pistols. I start to introduce myself, but the short adolescent one stands up and goes over to a small Sanyo refrigerator and fishes out three beers. He hands one to the mutant, then holds another out in my direction.

"Have a beer. I see you have met charming Larry already, and you must have attracted his attention from all the ruckus we heard out there. Let me see if I can follow the chain of events. After you attracted attention to yourself, "the Midget" decided you needed to be assigned right away and that's why you are here, right?" He takes his seat at the table. I pull up a chair and look them both over again. What the hell. I go into the discourse of the conversation which seems to amuse both of them.

I finish up and then ask them, "Is this where they send the fuck ups?" They both look at me with a mixture of hurt and incredulity and then laugh.

The mutant looks over at me and drawls, "No, you are here because you stood up. Larry doesn't respect ya unless ya stand up. If you are timid around the *Dai Uy* he will get rid of you. He also probably sent you over here because he wanted to annoy us with a Yankee. I'm Jimmy Johnson and this here runt is Lemuel MacGlothren." He sticks out his hand and so does the other one and they both say, "Welcome to RT Habu." I introduce myself and get back to the Midget, who is obviously the captain.

"Shit, he swears and looks like a fucking NCO. Is he a retread?" I ask.

"Yep, used to be an E-7, but then they sent him off to ossifer school to keep him from scratching his nuts with the salad fork at dinner, and now he's in charge," the one called Mac answers.

I take another beer gratefully, sit down on the bunk they point to and settle back. This is it, I am home. These two will be my new family and this humble hut will be my new home. We start shooting the shit and I begin to find out what I have gotten into. It can't be all that bad. At least you can run amok apparently, and the commander is as crazy as the rest of them. I think I am going to like it here. One thing is apparent, this unit is what we call "tight" in the military. That means it is competent and the members take care of each other. They may call the Commander by nicknames, but there is obvious liking and respect behind it. We continue to talk as I start to unpack my gear and get it stowed in one of the wall lockers at the far end of the hootch. The door opens and the swarthy looking little Cuban saunters in and snags a beer out of the refrigerator. He looks at Mac and then Jimmy, then at me, then takes a drink and belches.

"You guys got new meat, huh?" he says and swills the beer around in his left hand. Jimmy looks up at him; Mac just keeps cleaning his pistol and reassembling it. As he is screwing the end cap on the silencer he looks over at me then back at the Cuban.

"We not only got a new guy, but he is obviously the cream of the crop 'cause smilin' Larry didn't even interview him before he sent him over here." He and Johnson giggle for effect. The Cuban looks at them and snorts, which is real charming because it causes some beer to shoot out his left nostril. He picks up one of the oily cleaning rags and wipes his nose with it before he comments.

"Sheee-it, he sent him over here because he probably figures to raise the collective IQ in this place to three." Then he turns to me. "Run! Run as far and as fast as you can so you don't get tied up with these two, permanent." He laughs and tosses the now empty beer can into a trashcan and deftly hooks a new one out of the fridge. At just about the same time, Mac finishes assembling the pistol, slaps a magazine in the weapon and pops a cap in the space between the Cuban and myself. There is a "pfffft," and the beer in the Cuban's hand springs a leak about half way down. It doesn't even faze the Cuban; he continues to gab along as if it were an everyday occurrence. The beer is leaking out like the can is pissing.

"Oh that was clever," he says to Mac, then turns back to me. "Don't have anything valuable around these two. If they can't skin it and eat it, they just 'bubbafy' it with guns." He finishes his beer, belches and sticks his hand out. "I'm Bob Castillo. Welcome to Recon." He saunters to the door before I can answer. "See you over at the mess hall. Tonight is steak night." Then he is gone.

Jimmy looks over at Mac and says, "Pretty good shootin', Mac. You drilled that can almost dead center." Mac laughs. "Nah, I was aiming at him. I figure if we wounded him we might keep some of the beer."

Oh, I am going to love this place.

CHAPTER 3

First Blood

There is the crump of grenades to my right and I hear Jimmy and Mac yelling. They are directing the team and training the new guy. The new guy would be me. For the last week or so I have been learning all the finer points of how the team operates. We are on the range again today, practicing IA (immediate action) drills. This is a controlled method of putting as much firepower as possible in a specific direction while disengaging in the opposite direction. With an eight to ten man team we can put a lot of lead out there in a very short time. The team works like a well-oiled killing machine. It has to, since our being able to fight, and fight hard, until we can get some air cover is our only hope for survival.

We are part of an organization that provides strategic and tactical intelligence directly to the war planners in Saigon. They, in turn, relay that information to Washington, and disseminate the information for tactical use by the US Army-Vietnam and their allies. That means we go deep into the enemy's strongholds and battle formations to gather that information. To put it simpler, we get the information by getting out there in what we call "Indian Country." The whole idea of this is to not be seen: sneak around in their base camps, pick up prisoners and bring them back, and call in bomb strikes, if you can, to destroy their troop formations and supplies. That was the program as it was initially envisioned. It appears that I have arrived too late for that program, for it is getting almost impossible to sneak around out there too long before they run you to ground.

The Yards are some of the toughest fighters in any man's war. They are natural soldiers, and their loyalty is to the tribe, to their fellow warriors, and then to whomever pays them. Once they accept you, you become one of the tribe, a fellow warrior, and best of all, in this theatre we are also the ones who directly pay them.

After being here two days Mac and Jimmy take me over to the SCU (Special Commando Unit) barracks, where our little people are billeted. I have been around Yards before so I knew some of the protocol. There is the touching, arm pats, sniff next to the cheek on both sides and handholding. Mac and Jimmy introduce me to the Yards and them to me. The Yards are all Bru. They are short and compact and have somewhat of a bushman look to them, as opposed to the Rhade, who appear to be more Polynesian.

We have Bru, Rhade, Bahnar, Jarai, Sedang, and a smattering of other tribes in the outfit, as well as Chinese Nungs, and Vietnamese. These are what make up Recon Company and the two Hatchet Force companies. Recon Company is, in theory, a group of teams that go out to do reconnaissance; the Hatchet Force companies are strikers who do large scale raids and ambushes. Our team is all Bru, and Cuman, the Yard team leader, is the most powerful Bru in the camp. It's easier if you think of them like the American Indian. Cuman is the War Chief of the Bru Nation. Bong, the thump gunner (M-79 gunner), is a shaman, or one of the medicine men for the tribe. Thua, the assistant team leader, is some other muckety-muck in that tribal structure. They all just happen to be on our team.

These boys are hard as woodpecker lips. Most of them have been fighting for nearly ten years. We recruit new members to fill our losses directly from their home villages. When a Yard is killed we escort the body back to the village with Cuman and pay the widow and family for the loss. At the same time there is a selection. New recruits that want to join the war party are all lined up and Cuman picks the ones that are to go. We never have a problem getting recruits, since the Bru consider it an honor to be able to fight. But I digress.

During my initiation into the team, which started in the hootch, I quickly passed into acceptance. Acceptance was immediately followed by the mugging which relieved me of my GI issue watch, two packs of cigarettes, and of course, some money for the Yards to go buy some beer, to welcome me into the team, along with a chicken and the fixings for later. This is done very politely and it is accepted protocol for me to pay. Mac and Jimmy had watched all the proceedings to see how far I would go. Hell, I've been around Yards before. They are simple, straightforward people. There really isn't a concept of ownership. If I have and you don't, I will give what I have to my brother. The tribe owns you and your possessions. There are rules, but none that most round eyes would understand.

We don't view them as gooks, chinks, slopes, or any of the other derogatory terms that GIs use to tab the general population. Calling a Yard one of these names in our presence is likely to get you cold cocked or capped. Special Forces and these people are family.

The last week has been a flurry of activity. I have drawn my equipment, to include weapons, STABO rig, sterile fatigues, rucksack, etc. Jimmy and Mac have been drilling me with the intricacies of the communications, operational techniques, types of targets, missions, and most importantly what the areas of operations are like. Then there is special information like the enemy tactics, weapons, combat lore, and getting me ready to go out on operations with the team. Supposedly, the team will have about a week of stand down and preparation before being assigned a new mission.

Once we are alerted for a mission we go into isolation, plan the mission, and then move to one of three launch sites: Quang Tri, Phu Bai, and one in Thailand at NKP. The last one is used for penetration into North Vietnam and Laos. Technically we aren't in Laos so the military can say that no ground troops from Vietnam are conducting operations in Laos. This is the Army being cute, and technically it's not a lie because we are launching from Thailand.

We are designated by numbers on the team. The team leader, an American, is a One-Zero, the next American is a One-One; the following is a One-Two, etc. With the Yards it's just the opposite. Cuman is a Zero-One, the next a Zero-Two, and so forth. Most teams only have two Americans, sometimes three, and rarely four. Once you have proven yourself capable of running a team, they move you into a One-Zero slot and give you your own team.

The losses in Recon are heavy and with wounded and normal rotation you can expect to be a team leader in about four months. This is what will happen to Jimmy. He will move and take over a team shortly. I have met the One-Zero of Habu, he's all right but I suspect there is something there that Jimmy and Mac aren't telling me. They seem to be treading lightly around it and I figure they will clue me in before we launch.

Bernie has been assigned to a team with another of the new guys. They are doing the same as we are, dialing up their skills to get ready for launch. Recon is a tight unit, tighter than any I have been in before. The only way to describe it would be condoned insanity.

After I had been here for a few days, I'd gotten my "official" introduction to Recon from Captain Manes. He explained what the mission was and how the teams were structured. He also informed me of his reasoning in assigning me to RT Habu.

"You have combat experience, so I am assigning you to Habu with MacGlothren. He is junior in rank, but that's how we do things here. It is based on experience. He has been running for almost a year now. He will be taking over the team and you will be his One-One. You have any problems with that?" He looked up at me waiting for an answer.

"Does he go out and come back with the same number of people? More importantly, does he come back with all of them breathing, Sir?"

"So far." He looks at me to see where I am going with this.

"Well then, *Dai Uy*, I don't care what rank he is or how young he is. In fact, if he is responsible for getting my hide back here in one piece, I will warm up his bottle, wipe his nasty little ass, change his diapers, and do it with a smile."

"Get out of my office, then, since you apparently seem to have taken a fondness for the little runt, display an admirable trust in my decisions and little or no common sense when it comes to your associates."

This is one scary place. The missions are impossible to comprehend. They are in the heaviest concentrations of enemy that is imaginable. We go in loaded for bear;

hell, I have so much ammunition that I can't carry much in the way of food. I carry 35 twenty round magazines on my belt and another six 30 round magazines in the AK vest on my chest. That makes a total of nearly 1000 rounds of ammunition, not counting the extra bandoleers in my rucksack. In addition, I have 15 mini grenades, three regular grenades, a white phosphorous grenade, and two smoke grenades. I also carry a pistol with silencer, four magazines for it, a claymore, and extra paraphernalia in my rucksack. When I mention the lack of space for chow and sustenance in the rucksack, Mac just says not to worry because I will need the ammo and be too busy to get hungry. Hah, that makes me feel good.

Since I have been here we have lost four men, three on one team alone. If that's the normal casualty rate, by my math I have a life expectancy of about a week and a half. Normally I would be in a panic at this point. Actually I am, but peer pressure is powerful. Can't show that you are scared shitless, besides Mac and Jimmy have been running for 12 months and they are still alive. Habu is a lucky team; they pull the toughest missions and come back with all their people. They might be shot to pieces but everyone makes it back. So in Special Forces math that gives me a fighting chance. I have also gotten to know Captain Manes a lot better, though I am not sure that will be a good recommendation if I ever get to the pearly gates. He is one tough son-of-a-bitch but the people genuinely like and respect him. He is a former sergeant first class, so he has the mannerisms of a gut shot Brahman with the morals of a whiskey drummer. Of course, any normal officer who has aspirations of making the Army a career wouldn't last five minutes as the commander of this band of lunatics.

The good part is that I have found a home. Not the regular Army here. This is a real combat unit; it is what can be called a meritocracy. I have found my niche here and some of the others are even crazier than I want to be. The officers are no exception. The tall blonde SS looking one is Captain Messinger, or fittingly, Captain America. There is Captain Wunderlich, or Lightning, so named because he got hit by lightning. Then there is Captain Butler, aptly named Captain Psycho because he looks like some muscle bound nerd with those thick, black framed, Army issue glasses. He is always looking for new and innovative methods of destroying any humanity he comes across. His running mate is Staff Sergeant Les Chapman, competent, urbane, self-possessed and a dozen other descriptive terms rolled into some serious anger management problems. There is Lieutenant Entrican, or Tupelo Flash, so named because he comes from Tupelo, Mississippi. He is a quiet reserved sort. He doesn't say much, which in my book means still waters run deep, dark, and very murky.

The guy who runs the motor pool is a former One-Zero who evidently, in civilian life, was some sort of mobile chop shop roving the freeways of Chicago. The mail clerk has "love" and "hate" tattooed on his knuckles and some sort of nervous tic that centers on being in the presence of officers. We don't see much of the headquarters staff and support elements because they hang up at the "puzzle palace."

We just got alerted so we are off to isolation. I am getting the team packed up with Jimmy when Mac gets called over to the head shed. He comes back in about an hour and tells us that he has been appointed the One-Zero of Habu. Everyone seems as relieved as I am and there is a lot of cheek sniffing with the Yards. He then sits Jimmy and me down at a table. He tells Jimmy that he is to take over another team and that it will be just the two of us on this one.

Jimmy says that he will straphang, which basically means that he will go along, even though he isn't on the team, but Mac says no, he thinks I can handle it. Jimmy looks at me and says that he thinks so, too. Jesus, I feel like I just got my first piece of ass. All the Yards are doing the cheek sniff, arm squeeze again, only this time it's with me. Mac tells me that we have drawn an easy target and that we will be launching from Phu Bai.

The next day and a half is all mission prep. It's a simple area recon to try and see what Uncle Ho's little cousins are up to just north and west of Da Nang. It is hilly terrain, with sharp ridgelines and a river going through the middle of our operational area.

Early the next morning, I get up and get the team fed and ready. Mac has gone to do a VR (visual reconnaissance) with the Covey pilot, who is our lifeline with the air assets. It is his job to get us in and get us out. Mac will select a primary and two alternate LZs (landing zones) for our insertion, and pick a primary and alternate extraction point. I am in the team hootch with the Yards and we are stripping and cleaning the weapons and magazines before reloading everything. This is a last check to make sure we have all our ducks in a row. It's all pretty much old hat, I have done this many times before, although this is my first time with RT Habu.

Mac comes back around noon and we hear the air package coming in and setting down on the PSP. We both go and brief the pilots with the launch site commander and later the Covey rider comes in and they all start talking nonsense, so Mac and I go eat with the little people. We will launch at 1400. This will give us daylight in case we are discovered after insertion. One would assume that insertion right at last light would be better, but Mac says we need daylight in case we get boxed in. I am not going to argue since he knows the area of operations and the enemy.

Fourteen hundred rolls around and the air package gets warmed up as we file out to the choppers and get on board. There are slicks, or troop carriers, and Cobra gun ships that will cover us on the insert. My rectum is pushing against the back of my throat and I am as dry as the Gobi desert. The usual pre-mission jitters. I am in the second bird with four of the little people. Through the headset I hear the launch signal and we lift off. It will be a twenty-minute flight.

I sit in the doorway, watching the terrain slide beneath me. We listen to the chatter between Covey and the fast movers who are working over the area. Our plan is to insert at the same time they are extracting another team. The hope is that the NVA will think it was only an extraction and all we boogey men have fled the area. It might serve us long enough to get away from the LZ and find a hiding place. We intend to move about five hundred meters and hide up in some twisted terrain for a day before moving out to look for "Chuck."

The Peter Pilot (co-pilot) tells me that we are five minutes out and I get the team ready and on the skids. I see the choppers that are picking up the other team about a klick away and they are having a go at the ground with the gun ships. We are hugging the ridgelines and come in quick onto our LZ. Mac's bird rolls in, seesaws, and then they are out. Now it's our turn.

Same procedure with us, we roll in and I am clear of the skids and on the ground with the rest of the team. The bird lifts off behind me and I see Mac and the other four Yards next to a large tree trunk that has been blown over on its side, its upper branches pointing downhill.

I move my section over to him and we do a communications check with Covey. We wait for about five minutes. I am checking my equipment, making sure everything is tight and I haven't lost anything. There is enough adrenalin in my system that I could run a marathon race and never break a sweat. Mac gives a hand signal and the team starts moving forward. I am near the rear of the team covering our tail gunners and our trail. The Yards move like the little jungle beasties they are; I try to be as quiet as they are and not embarrass myself by floundering around.

The next two hours are a rhythm of move with stealth, then sit and listen, then move with stealth again. We get to the edge of the broken ground and wait for about 30 minutes. This gives the bush a chance to start chattering again. That's how it is; when everything goes quiet you know that something is moving. Once we are sure that we are alone, we move up into the rocks and tangled undergrowth. We find a good RON (Remain Over Night) position and just before dark we move into it.

We set the claymore mines out and settle in for the night. We will sleep in shifts in our gear, so close you can reach out and touch the other guys. We are in a thicket of wait-a-minute vines, vines that impede your progress, and have good neutral ground. We haven't seen any sign that's fresh so we are reasonably sure we are in a safe hide. We give Covey a "team okay" and he turns us over to Moonbeam, the night C-130 command ship that will baby-sit us in case we get hit.

It's a long night, but I am able to catch about four hours of cat naps. Just before first light we all stand to and listen. This is when they will hit you if they know where you are. The Yards are super-tuned and listening. Their eyes work over the terrain around us, but they use their superior bush sense more. Bong suddenly makes a low hand signal and points off to his front. I strain to see something, but everyone else is taking their safeties off the weapons very, very, quietly so I do the same. Then I hear it, a clink of metal against metal, very soft, but also very close. I can see about 25 meters to my front and I realize that I am holding my breath. Metal against metal sounds only mean one thing: there are men out there somewhere. The only other people out here are bad guys, as I am positive that howler monkeys have not taken up arms.

I still can't see anything and I am scanning the limit of my vision in short sweeps ten meters at a time. Then out to my front I see just a hint of movement, like someone's arm or leg moving. Shit, I hope they don't see us. Then it stops. We wait; they wait. Then another movement slightly behind that, and a shoulder and head come into view about 30 meters out. Yup, NVA khakis, some sort of soft bush hat and he looks just like one of our Bru.

I can see he isn't out for a Sunday stroll. He is hunting something and I know what. Another figure comes into focus just behind the first. He is watching and scanning our thicket and the hill behind us. I am trying to keep my eyes on them and see what Mac is going to do at the same time. I wonder if I should cap them with the silenced Walther I am carrying, but figure I will have to let them get a hell of a lot closer to make sure I kill them.

I am flirting with all this indecision when Mac and Cuman make it all moot. They cut the two figures down in a hail of automatic fire. The shooting stops and no one else joins in. Jesus, that is good fire discipline. I look at Mac, he makes a hand signal to me and the rest of the team to wait. We hear one of them thrashing around out there and moaning, then there is the sound of a lot of movement behind where they came from and fanning out to our left and right. Mac is on the radio and telling Covey to get up here fast, that we have made contact and it looks like we are going to need help PDQ.

There is a roar out to the front, then a whoosh and a huge detonation behind me and up the hill. Then it seems like every AK-47 in the world starts to chew up our thicket. I hear someone in Vietnamese calling out commands then, of all things, some sort of gong or cowbell.

I am wondering if this isn't all a bad dream when Mac yells, "Claymores!" All of our claymores are detonated. Mac screams, "Twelve o'clock, one hundred meters!" We are up and running, firing as we go.

I come across four mangled bodies, dressed in NVA uniforms and then I am past them. Our extraction LZ is about two hundred meters ahead. We have moved about a hundred meters when we pull up and take a head count. All four of my guys are there and so is the rest of the team. Everyone checks their equipment and puts a fresh magazine in their weapon. Mac sidles over to me and explains we have about ten minutes and then every little "Ho" in the area is going to be trying to kill us.

The team gets up and we are moving again. We are a little more open in formation so we can use our firepower more effectively. We are moving fast, but as quiet as we can. We have to make it to the LZ, get set up, and hope we can hold them off long enough to get air assets over us. We hear more signal shots off to our rear and then one off to our front about two hundred meters.

Suddenly we are there. The LZ is a cleared area of an old bomb strike. Probably a hundred yards of torn up trees and five decent-sized craters. We make for the center crater and scramble into it, like one big foxhole. It's a good thing, too, because we no sooner get in than six of the bad guys break cover almost right behind us.

I start to open fire when the team opens up on them and chops them into dog meat. Mac is talking on the radio and I get the B-40 and the RPD positioned on my side of the crater. I see two flashes, followed by a roar, then two rockets come our way from the tree line and slam into the fallen timber at the edge of the crater. We open up and pepper the wood line with the machine gun and one rocket round. What does feel good is being able to scream out loud, and I am doing a fair amount of it. I hear Covey come over, and then two of his marker rockets slam into the wood line. Mac yells over that the slicks are about fifteen out, but Spads, or A-lEs, are on the way.

Now we are getting fire from three sides, and I take Bong and Ti Ti over the lip and into the next bomb crater. We have to spread out a little bit or they are going to put so much fire on our position that we can't look over the lip. That's when they will come and finish us off. These boys know they have to slam us real fast before the Air Force gets here with the bad shit. Thua and Bop slide into the hole with us and they have brought the B-40 and four rounds. I put two claymores out on the other side of the tree we are all behind. I figure, as a last resort, if they rush us we can blow their assault into mincemeat.

Good thing we moved, because the volume of fire picks up. We rise and pepper the area to our front and we drop two rockets into the tree line, which is about 50 meters from us, just as the first bunch gets up and tries to rush us. The front of the log starts to get chewed up and we have to get down. I count to five then clack off one of the claymores.

We are chucking mini grenades as fast as we can uncap them, and then we are up again and firing. I hear Mac yell, "Birds are two minutes out," and I'm hoping we are still around when they get here. It is getting real easy to see out to the front as the claymores cut the vegetation down in a widening swath. Anyone in that swath got chewed up as well. I hear the heavy blade smack of choppers and Mac yells again to get ready. I yell back that I am going to clack the last claymore. When one goes off on his side, I follow suit. The guns come in and rocket the area to the north of the LZ, and I hear their Miniguns burping in a steady stream.

The first bird sets down almost on top of the log and the five of us are up and slinging ourselves inside. The gunners are shooting up a storm, as I heave myself into the belly of the cargo bay, landing on top of one of the Yards. There is the feeling of defying gravity, like being on a roller coaster, as we rocket into the air.

The second chopper is right behind and I get a glimpse of Mac and the remainder of the team scrambling aboard. Then we are all up and away. We watch the Spads work the whole area over with napalm and hard bombs, and then we are finally out of it.

I'm checking myself to see if I have any leaking holes, when the crew chief taps me on the arm and hands me a tepid can of coke. Jesus, it tastes like elixir from heaven. I take a long pull and go to give the Yards some when I notice they are already sharing two others. Grins, hand pats, cigarettes. I grab the headset and put it on. I catch the last part of Mac talking to Covey. Covey says something about a bunch of folks on the ground, and that the Spads are taking fire from a truck mounted anti-aircraft gun, then he cuts out.

Twenty minutes later we are on the ground at Phu Bai. We disembark and go over to the mess hall. I am sitting outside on my rucksack, counting my ammunition and notice there are two neat perforations in the left side of my gear. That's why we put the magazines in the pouches with the bullet part facing out. If you take one in the ammo pouch, it's less likely that you will get wounded by your own ammo cooking off. I am mulling over this little tidbit of combat lore when Mac comes up and motions for me to go with him. We go over to the TOC and there I learn the big picture. The first two guys we capped were a tracker team; Mac had waited until the lead man almost stepped into the thicket before he opened fire. He had enough presence of mind to grab some stuff off the bodies as we rushed through them. An anti-recon team of about 30 strong backed them up. We had chopped a big hole in that lot and escaped the noose that was getting ready to strangle our BBs.

By the time we had gotten to the LZ, there had been close to three whole companies coming in to kick our asses. From what Covey said, there were more on the way. Funny thing about combat, you only see your little part of it. I saw probably eight bodies and figured maybe there were a couple of platoons out in front of me, by the volume of fire, etc. Covey, because he has a balcony seat up there in his little aerial sport coupe, can see a lot more. But the trap had been prematurely sprung and our aggressive response had thrown them off their plan. The lack of fire from their side just goes to show you that the NCOs on their side had enforced good fire discipline as well. My hat is off to you Nguyen. I hope you are enjoying a nice canteen cup of rice wine, licking your wounds, and breathing. I made it, that's what counts to this child.

Mac turns to me as we are leaving, slaps me on the back and says, "You did good out there." I am swiping my face with a cravat to remove some of the caked on dirt and grit.

"Thanks Mac, I hope I held up my end."

"You did. The Yards think you are numbah-one and *dinky dau* (crazy); that's what counts." He half chuckles, and I realize we have both broken our cherries. This was my first mission and this was also his first mission as a One-Zero. Good enough, we are officially war whores.

"Do we go home now? I've had all the fun I want for this week."

"Yep, tomorrow we head back to Da Nang. By the way, we picked this target because it's relatively easy if we make contact, and it gives the team a chance to see how you are going to react." He smiles that little southern smartass smile.

EASY TARGET?! I considered this to be a real ass kicker. "What the fuck do you mean, easy target? If that's an easy target what in the hell do you call a hard target?"

"A Shau." He turns and walks toward the rest of the team.

Right then I just want to take a hot shower and hopefully unwind by drinking myself into oblivion, so I follow Mac. We pick up our gear and walk over to one of the huts that serves as our team house at the launch site. The next few hours are made up of cleaning and checking the gear, getting the Yards fed, and then finally ourselves. After all are tucked in and secure and the day closes down, we go over to the mess hall and have a go at destroying a goodly portion of their booze supply. We know we won't pull Bright Light since there are two other teams here. One more is out there in Indian Country and at last light they were tucked in some thicket for the night. Tomorrow we will head over to the airstrip and catch our ride south to Da Nang. All in all it has been an educational moment.

My first mission, I think to myself. I acquitted myself well with my peer; we had, as they say, bonded and on top of that, I was "in like Flynn" with the Yards. It's a beautiful night. That's the thing about survival, through the joy of being alive, the mind soon forgets or shoves all that bad stuff to the back and gets on with the next thing coming up.

Late into the evening Mac and I stumble back to the team hootch and Cuman is waiting for us like a reproving father. The Yards watch as we clumsily shed our fatigues and crawl into the bunks. I am pulling a poncho liner over me, when Cuman comes over and looks down on us, shaking his head and mutters something about my being same, same, *Trung Si* Mac, all the time beaucoup fuck up. I nod in woozy agreement as I drift off into the soft embrace of sleep.

CHAPTER 4

Cold Storage

We don't get the whole five days of stand down; it is more like two and then we go back into the cycle of isolation, movement to the launch site and insertion. Our next target will be one of the DMZ (Demilitarized Zone) targets. That is an oxymoron, the term Demilitarized Zone. The area fairly bristles with NVA. The only thing demilitarized about it would be the lack of any US military in the area for longer than a few hours.

The launch site at Quang Tri is in sharp contrast to Phu Bai. The site is located outside the sprawling Fifth Mechanized Division's base camp and adjacent to the main ammo dump. This means a quick turn-around time for the gunships on reload. It also means that we are isolated from the hubbub of prying eyes. The site is run by an acerbic major named Slatten. He has the same grace that Manes shows, that of a retread. The starkest contrast is the launch site NCOIC (Non-Commissioned Officer In Charge). His name is Budrow. More commonly, he is known by his nickname "Pappy." Actually, he has several nicknames, but other than "Pappy" the rest will get you clocked if you mutter them within earshot.

Most important to us is the fact that he is a former One-Zero. Pappy won't launch a team unless he has the assets to support the teams on the ground. Pappy is our shepherd, he watcheth over us, he layeth us down in green pastures, and *he* shall fear no evil. Those pastures are full of pissed off PAVN (People's Army of Vietnam, aka NVA) and he has the great equalizer: air support. Without it getting there on time and in strength, we'd be just another red smear on the ground and letters of regret to our families. He has our trust. Of course, this imbues him with the charm that comes from big responsibilities and too little sleep.

We no sooner arrive at the launch site than the shit hits the fan. There are two teams on the ground and one at the site to act as a Bright Light. At first light, the first team gets hit in their RON and is on the run. Mac walks over to the TOC for a briefing. The air package arrives a few minutes later with a dozen slicks, and the gunships set down on the PSP strip, throwing red dust everywhere. The reserve team trundles out past us and onto the pad, loaded down with arms and ammunition.

Mac hurries back as we watch the first of the Bright Light team lift off. The entire site has an air of expectant disaster about it. Mac tells Cuman to get the team ready because we are going to launch as a Bright Light right behind the one that just lifted off. Grabbing me, he heads back over to the TOC, briefing me on the way over.

About an hour after the first team got hit, the second team also ran into the NVA, in force. It looked as if the two contacts were related and the enemy was making a coordinated push to kill both teams. The second team was fighting for its life as we waited for the next air package to arrive. We had maybe half an hour to get briefed and loaded up before Pappy inserted us. They had already tried to pull the second team out, but had been shot out of the LZ. The team had gotten split with the One-Zero and four Yards in one group, and the One-One and another Yard in a second group. All had gone to ground to hide from the thousand plus NVA that were hunting them. They were separated by a narrow ridgeline and the One-One was severely wounded. Two little people had been killed at the contact point. The living came first; the dead would have to be left as the NVA would use them as bait. Covey had flown over the ambush site and the two bodies were still laying there, a sure indicator that the NVA were waiting for someone to come in as a Bright Light.

The One-Zero and his group has found a defensive position on a knife-like ridge that will keep the NVA from massing on them. Air support will bomb the snot out of everything around the survivors and pull them out. In the meantime, we will try to get onto the ridge where the One-One and the Yard are. Since that will be the only area on the ground not being pummeled by the air, we will have to fight our way to the two men. The Yard is talking on the emergency radio with Covey when the One-One regains consciousness and begins helping vector Covey to their location. They are hiding in a thicket and so far no bad guys are onto them. We will go in as the air package preps the extraction of the rest of the team. The terrain is steep, but there is a usable LZ a few hundred meters up-slope.

We get a quick rundown on the operation and then we are back out and moving to the hut where the team is. We rig a couple of ring mains that we will use to blow down any trees that might be a hazard to the choppers. We grab extra hand grenades and extra claymores, as well as fill all our magazines and sling several bandoleers of ammo into our rucks. Thus loaded up, we start out the door when we hear the choppers coming in. Mac takes his half of the team and loads on the lead slick; the other half of the team and I mount the second. The whole package winds up; we lift off and head west. I am on the headset listening to Covey talking to the team and directing the bombers. It is touch and go with the team, although the air strikes have slowed the NVA a bit. The One-One has lapsed back into unconsciousness.

We bounce into the small LZ and quickly move downhill. Covey has worked the guns and a set of Spads to our front and flanks, allowing us to move more quickly since we are right on the tail of the strikes. In our world, when you have to work ordnance that close it is called "danger close," but unlike the exercises at Bragg on the bombing ranges we have shaved it to suicidal distances. It works, though.

We work our way through the bomb and strafing debris towards the two men. The Yard is using a mirror and the orange panel in his hat to signal Covey. This allows Covey to direct us so we don't have to search for them. Throwing smoke would be better, but it would give their position away.

Covey tells us that they are under 100 meters from us, so we start moving up slowly so that we don't shoot each other. There is a burst from a CAR-15 and the crump of a grenade in that direction. Then we hear several AK-47s open up and then another grenade followed by a hideous scream. We get up and move forward in a modified "V" formation. Our right flank runs into an NVA platoon within a few meters. They are facing away from us and their attention is riveted on a small thicket that has grown up around a deadfall. They don't even see us. My half of the team opens up on their backs and we chop them into the next world. The few still breathing stumble off downhill, survival their primary objective. We shoot about eight of them. Mac gets the team up to where the One-One is and yells at me to get everyone in a perimeter. Cuman and I have been checking the bodies and pulling anything that looks like it might be of intelligence value off them. Cuman caps two of them who are still breathing. No prisoners today, we have much more pressing issues.

I get to the One-One and look at his wounds. He is shot up pretty bad in the chest and legs with a bad wound in his head as well, probably from shrapnel. He has an expended morphine Syrette pinned through his cheek and his dressings are soaked with his own blood. I get a blood bag started as Mac relays the situation to Covey.

There is no way we can go back up the ridge. We will blow an LZ here and lift out. I rig the ring mains and we set them off. The large trees that were obstructing the view go down along with a considerable amount of flora, blasting us with dirt, debris, and a host of half-roasted critters. The thicket is enveloped in a choking, blinding cloud. Almost immediately there is firing inside the cloud, both CAR-15s and AKs. I see a khaki clad figure and two other shapes come out of the cloud next to me. I open up and all three drop back into the dust. There is the crump of grenades and something hits me in the side of the face. I have cuts and splinters all over one side from the debris. The dust clears and I can see Mac on the radio. There is a dead NVA lying next to him. Two of the claymores close to Cuman go off in quick succession. I can't hear worth a shit because of the ring mains and the grenades, but after the claymores explode the AK fire abruptly stops.

Mac yells at me to get the team pieced together, the slicks are on their way. I hustle around our small perimeter. Our thump gunner is shot bad and two of the others are fragged up. But everyone is still able to fight. There are about seven bodies in and around the southern end of our perimeter, ten counting the three that I hosed. The NVA regrouped after we hit them and when we blew the LZ came in on top of us. It almost worked.

A chopper comes in, its blades slapping noisily. Mac gives me the hand signal and I grab the wounded One-One and signal for the Yards to come with me. I scramble aboard with the One-One and the wounded Yards are thrown in beside me. The gunner on the downhill side of the bird fires a long burst as the pilot pours on the power. I can hear incoming rounds hitting the bird with dull metallic thumps. We are up and pulling away, grabbing for air space. I look back out the side and see a second bird picking up Mac and the rest of the team. Then they, too, are aloft.

The medic on the bird is a kid named Yevitch. He is frantically trying to save the One-One. While I am checking the rest of the Yards, he finally stabilizes the One-One. Next he turns to our thump gunner and starts in on him. The rest of us will wait; we have flash bums and shrapnel, but none of it is life threatening. As we heading east I reflect on what Mac said about the northern targets. If I thought the Phu Bai launch was an ass kicker, it seemed tame to what we had just been through. I still couldn't believe how fast Nguyen had gotten organized and on top of us.

The One-One never made it back. He was conscious long enough to know we had gotten him out; then he passed. We hadn't gotten there soon enough. Now I know why everyone hates this fucking valley. It is truly the valley of death. Only luck and training saved us.

As it turns out, we lose only the thump gunner permanently. The Yards are stoic, licking their wounds and taking it all in stride. Cuman is all full of praise to Mac about my conduct. He doesn't have a clue how scared shitless I was. The next day we are back in Da Nang. We get three days stand down and the first night back is always an alcohol-filled night. This one I feel we more than deserve.

* * *

It is cold and I am freezing and half awake. My body is cramped and I am shivering uncontrollably. I keep trying to climb up through the fog, thinking I have malaria again. I had torn those facts out of my medical records so I could get back over here. I hope what I'm feeling is a hangover. Hell, I hurt all over. I start to sit up and bang my head on a surface not two feet above me. I try to move my arms and find solid hard surfaces as if I am in some kind of box. The walls are too close to be a room.

Oh shit. What have they done to me? As I struggle awake, I know that my comrades are somehow linked to my present circumstances. It is dark, and I am laying on some kind of cold surface. Maybe I passed out underneath the air conditioner we installed in the hootch a few weeks before. There is a strong smell of antiseptic and death, though. I try to connect with a memory that will tell me where I am, but focusing is difficult because my big toe hurts like hell. Don't panic, I tell myself. I hope those cretins remember where they have left me! At least I am not floating on the ocean somewhere, in some insane rendition of a Viking funeral. That has happened before.

It is the cold that bothers me, like I am in some refrigeration unit. Am I in the meat locker in the back of the mess hall? I hope some lame brain finds me before I die of hypothermia. I hear footsteps behind my head. There is a metallic click and I am rolled backwards. The room is neon lit and I am staring up at the tiled ceiling. It is unfamiliar. I am also staring into the horrified face of a black Spec-4 with a clip board in his right hand. I moan and start to sit up. That is enough for the kid. He disappears through the two swinging doors to the right before the clipboard hits the floor.

I sit all the way up, groaning in protest. I am wrapped in some kind of hospital sheet, which has welded itself to the side of my head from the dried blood and pus from my shrapnel wounds. I jerk it free and the pain helps clear my head. I look around, still in a bit of a daze and slowly come to the realization that I am in some kind of morgue. Jesus, what happened? I look at my toe, which still hurts like the dickens. I groggily pull it up on the opposite thigh so I can read what appears to be a tag wired tight to it. The tag reads "Killed in Action," then "Bomb Concussion." Bomb concussion? Dead? Have I returned miraculously, like Lazarus, from the dead? More importantly, can I get convalescent leave?

My memory is coming back. I get snatches of hysterical laughter and a jeep ride. I am sure now that those little shits, my friends, are responsible. I am going to kill them when I find them. I hurt all over and am nauseous. I am half standing now, leaning on the tray that has been pulled out from the wall. I am hopping because the wire on the toe tag has caused my big toe to swell up twice its size. I manage to get the bloody thing off and almost faint from the pain of the blood returning. The doors burst open and a gaggle of medical people come rushing in. They have a gurney and, uh-oh, a fib (defibrillator) machine. All of them have that serious look that the sawbones profession screws on when they are trying to save your ass. I hear murmurings of "calm down" and "we're here to help you. You're in Da Nang hospital. We are here to help."

I get the tray between them and me, and pick up the clipboard, swinging it like a broadsword to keep them at bay. They screech to a halt, but I know they are looking for an opening. I am talking as fast as I can and trying not to slur my words. I am all right! Step back! That sort of thing. I can't slip up or this crew will be on me like a pack of Saigon hookers on a cherry boy. The doctor is a baby-faced captain and next to him is a nurse who seems less enthusiastic about making medical history.

I motion to them with the swish of the clipboard as punctuation. "I am all right! Don't try and touch me with those paddles, or I will kill you!" That really brings them up short. My mind is racing. First things first, survive the medics, and then get some hardware to get even. The combat pygmy, Mac, is involved for sure and I will bet my britches that the weaselly Cuban is, as well. My memory is coming back. I remember a wild night of drinking a homemade concoction called "bandit brandy" and trying not to pass out. The unconscious invariably end up as the butt of some crude joke.

Bandit brandy is a concoction originally invented by our illustrious forefathers, Merrill's Marauders. I had stumbled onto it in an old book about the Burma campaigns in World War II. The Command had pulled them off the line after the capture of Myitkyina Airfield. By that time all of them had malaria and most were walking wounded.

The command dosed them, deloused them, gave out some few rations and supplied the officers with liquor. There wasn't enough for everyone, so the boys resorted to a native concoction as a bypass. They took several fuel drums and, using sand and fast moving water from one of the streams, scoured them shiny clean. Then they added all the tropical fruit they could lay their hands on. When all the drums were about eight inches from the top, they threw in some yeast and poured in a bottle of whatever liquor the platoon leader drew. They topped the whole brew with the leaves from the cannabis plant; the area abounded with it. Finally, they capped the drums with black plastic and set them out in the hot sun. Soon the tight drum toppings blew out into balloons of opaque gray. All they had to do was slice the plastic, scoop out the mold and cannabis, and voila! Bandit brandy.

We had duplicated the process to perfection. Now I know why there was a General Order signed by Wingate, himself, prohibiting the ghastly stuff. All this is running through my head as I am keeping the medical staff at bay. I go along with their story about how I had been brought in by our medical staff, supposedly dead from a bomb concussion.

"Don't you nitwits check for a pulse?"

"Oh," they assure me, "there was no need. Dr. Cottrell had signed the papers already."

"Cottrell? A doctor?" I may have had a bad night but this much I know, Cottrell is another One-Zero, and if he is a doctor of anything, it's mayhem. Yes, George Cottrell. I now have one name for my get-even list. Impersonating an officer and a physician, I am going to cook his nuts over a slow fire.

The paddle crew backs off and escorts me to a warm room where they wrap me in a blanket. Someone comes in and gives me some hot sweet tea. I have my shaking down to the occasional tremor when they come in and tell me that the unit is sending a senior NCO to pick me up. That's great. They are the worst of the lot. I get some hospital scrubs and get dressed. I want a cold beer. My big toe is still on fire. My ride shows up while I am plotting my revenge. It is Stevie. Just what I need, a wild ride back with "metal head."

As I have mentioned before, he has a plate in his head, and in my foggy state I can't remember if it is from Korea or if he was just one of the misanthropes from *The Island of Doctor Moreau*. And he is a seriously deranged person without all that scrap metal floating around. Basically, he is not the kind of person that the Army wants wandering the highways and neighborhoods of Main Street, America. So they humor him and allow him to stay in Vietnam. Of all the things that I have observed about the Army, this is one of the saner decisions they have made. It approaches the logical which means it is an oversight, not a decision.

There is a rumor that he has been here so many times that he knew Ho Chi Minh's mama and that General Giap is his illegitimate son. That can't be true, because the Sergeant Major would have had to approve it, and Billy doesn't approve anything unless you volunteer for one of his "good deals." God help the western world if Stevie ever procreates.

Regardless, he has come to pick me up and he has been doing the one thing that the entire staff of Walter Reed would have a come-apart over, he has been drinking. With Stevie, no one wants to get close enough to do the sniff test because on a good day he looks like a deranged wolverine. But I know. I don't even have to assume. He probably has some other pharmaceuticals running around in his system as well to counteract the steel plate in his head, or he starts to twitch like a frog leg on an electrode. The mere thought that Stevie is there leads me to believe that all of Recon, including that deuterium midget, Manes, are involved in this little cover up.

I go along with it because I don't want to be delayed in getting back and getting my hands on some serious firepower. We spend the ride back babbling about how boys will be boys, and ain't them buddies of mine the proper rascals and me plotting horrible retribution for that very sin.

As we pull into the compound there are Captains Manes and Butler standing by the bunker that is the redoubt for the second gate past the primary wire barrier. We stop next to the twin pillars of discipline, and I figure this ought to be good. Manes will be full of cheap commander tricks and to back up whatever logic he is going to use to somehow put the blame on me, he has Butler with him. It makes sense in a way because Butler is a textbook when it comes to the consequences of psychotic behavior.

Stevie lets me out of the vehicle to stand there in my hospital scrubs. After he drops me off, he drives down to Recon Company. Left alone to receive the "ass-chewing with deluxe finger wave," I am a study in calm resignation. This is all defensive action. They know that as soon as possible I am going to get some hardware and declare hunting season open. Around here that could mean something as simple as gunshot retribution to burning down the shitter with the evil little miscreants inside.

As Manes starts in, the theme is, since it was my idea to make the bandit brandy, I am personally responsible not only to what I have been through, but every other imaginable sin that has ensued over the last four days. I am not at all surprised that, according to the Midget, I am fortunate not to be charged with all that has ensued. There is a whole litany of accusations, including the kidnapping of the Lindbergh baby, Josef Mengele's medical experiments, and last but not least, the bad smell that this country has. Oh yes, I endure being professionally counseled by the "heavy gravity planet" and his side-kick.

The two of them look like a couple of ghouls in Quasimodo's holding pen. This is just an attempt to make sure no one gets so seriously injured that they can't run a mission when it comes up. I understand, it is simple personnel management and

I limp down the road toward my hootch, under the direct supervision of Captain Psycho, himself. He is chatting with me, just out of reach. Lucky for him. I want to off him just to stop the inane chattering, but I know he is there to drop me if I go for any kind of hardware, so I smile sweetly and suggest that we go to the club. I change and we wander over. It is still going full tilt. Evidently I lost only about ten hours.

With typical aplomb, after leaving me for dead at the meat locker, they all came back here. No problem, I give my best oh-shucks-you-rascals-got-me-good act, and study each face for the guilty looks of those who might have been directly involved, which isn't hard since they are all guilty of something. If I came back here and chained the doors from the outside, soaked the place with jet fuel, and lobbed a hot torch onto the roof there wouldn't be one innocent victim in the lot. I have patience though. I will get even today or next week. Or maybe I will wait 30 years to get even. I will write a book some day when they are all gray-haired and masquerading as pillars of the community. I will expose them all for the horrible, twisted, little monsters they are. There is a black spot in my heart for the source of all this abuse that has been heaped on me.

Mac comes over as the litmus test and, as we are drinking together, informs me that we have two days of training starting tomorrow, and then we are getting another target. A couple of rounds later I have calmed down enough to see the wisdom of that.

Fine, I am ready. I just hope we draw something other than a Phu Bai launch; the place has got me spooked. It could be that the NVA are getting stronger out in that AO and probably are getting ready for another major offensive, but all the teams getting shot or lost are coming out of that particular launch site. I already hate the assholes that run it.

In my absence, Mac hired two Bru as replacements for our injured team members. They will begin their training with the rest of the team tomorrow. In the morning, I will have to take them up to the S-4 and get them equipped. Retribution and angst flow out of my system like the lifeblood of some fearsome beast as the ordered discipline of continuity takes over. Somewhere in the depths of my secret heart, though, is the challenge of one-upmanship that must be fed with the carcass of one of my friends. Fair is fair, and with yin must come yang. Yang will hopefully consist of a Cuban, a few of the indiscreet and the other half of my soul, Mac. Throw in a few hapless pedestrians for good measure and all will be balanced in my world. We all exist and survive to become victims in the end. It is like Yosarian in *Catch-22*, all seems very logical now that we are part of the landscape in a war zone.

We finish up and go back to the team house around 0100 and I drift off into sleep dreaming about being in a life raft floating in the Pacific with a case of cold beer and no opener. There will be plenty of time to start plotting revenge tomorrow, besides, my toe hurts like hell.

CHAPTER 5

Buffaloes Can Dance

It's Tet, the traditional New Year. It is also hot, muggy, and my head feels light from the hunger pangs that are gnawing at my stomach like a couple of divorce lawyers chewing over the respondent. We are at Quang Tri again and have the good luck of being weathered in. Covey has been up the last four days and our target area has been completely socked in each day. There hasn't been a hole in the cloud ceiling long enough to insert us and keep air support over our heads.

The area that we are going to run is called DM-10. You are considered lucky if you can stay on the ground longer than a few hours and it's miraculous if you are there overnight. The last two teams that ran it were not even lucky. One managed to get off the LZ and make it about five hundred yards before they were mauled by at least two companies of hard core NVA regulars; the other team just disappeared. Nevertheless, we have drawn the target and they are intent on putting us in.

I'm sitting in the hootch that serves as the Americans' watering hole, and contemplating eating a PIR (Patrol Indigenous Ration) which is the indig version of the LRRP (Long Range Reconnaissance Patrol) ration: dehydrated fish and rice, or salted shrimp and freeze-dried *nuoc mam*, instead of beef and rice or chili con carne in the American rations. I can't stomach the American rations, too heavy, too greasy, but I love the PIRs because they are tasty and light. There is, however, some kind of processed sausage that resembles a pair of mini nun-chucks, which I avoid.

We all eat the PIRs so when we sweat we smell oriental instead of like some meat-eating gringo. It's another trick to staying alive. The camp is on iron rations because we can't get a resupply in from Da Nang. We scrounge for fresh rations for the Yards and ourselves. To the civilian, that means we steal, barter, and extort wherever and whatever we can for fresh food.

It has been a few days since we moved the launch site closer to the destroyed pagoda and next to the old Pacific Architect and Engineering compound. In our present location we are essentially outside the perimeter of the sprawling Fifth Mechanized base camp. This is fine with us because we pull our own security, meaning that our personal safety doesn't rely on the fact that someone might be smoking dope until he can't remember what planet he is on. To ensure that someone will actually be awake and see the sappers, we also have a platoon from Security Company pulling night duty, so sleeping is an actual concept here.

We relocated because the NVA got sappers past the so- called security and blew up the ammo dump next to our original site. Man, you want to see a fireworks display, watch a division size ammunition dump go up. The initial explosion started with a tremendous boom and continued to crescendo for the next eight hours, like Mount Vesuvius waking up Pompeii. Our launch site, however, was situated much closer to the dump than Pompeii was to Mount Vesuvius.

The explosions had blown the old camp down, literally, from the concussions. During the steady downpour of ready-to-explode ordnance, we evacuated the launch site. Initially, we reorganized and counted heads at the airstrip until we realized that we had made another tactical "oops" because the rally point was located right next to the refueling station. This resulted in a hurried dash out of the impact zone. CONEX containers, twenty feet long, shot out of the center of the inferno and into the sky like huge, rectangular ballistic missiles. Some were full of artillery shells, others with 17 pound rockets. These would sometimes cook off and the sky would be filled with awesome bursts like the ones seen at Fourth of July displays. If one had airburst in the wrong direction we would have been toast, because these babies showered thousands of steel fragments all over the countryside. Mac and I hopped into a jeep and were frantically trying to dodge our way out of camp while all of our Yards and another team followed, hanging onto a deuce and a half.

Tired, scared shitless, and still smelling of cordite, the next morning we look for a new location. Vowing that never again would we be so close to that much stacked ammo, we settle for a more sedate neighborhood. We finally find the right place comfortably tucked between the shell of a destroyed Buddhist temple and the sprawling base camp of the Fifth Mechanized Division.

Pappy Budrow decides, after we string concertina wire and build fighting bunkers, he'll have us connect the bunkers with a trench. This allows us to spread the line out where we can and to move between the bunkers and the TOC. I suspect his Gallic gene pool is bubbling to the surface and he's attempting to build a mini Dien Bien Phu. He gets an engineer outfit to come out and excavate the trench with a crawler and a backhoe. The trench eats up most of I Corps's supply of sandbags, so only about half of it has sandbagged walls and floor. Now with the rains, we don't have a trench anymore. We have a moat inside the wire. We are thinking of coordinating inner tube races around the perimeter since the movie projector is down again due to the humidity.

This move had also precipitated the arrival of our new antagonist, who we have taken to calling the "Chuggin' Charlie Express." Somewhere out there in the warrens of the old trash dump, way out in the salt flats, marsh, and destroyed bunker lines dating back to probably the French, is a VC Home Guard cell. They must have gotten their hands on a mortar because for the last week or so that's what they have been lobbing at the camp.

It's easy for local yokels to find or steal a 4.2 inch mortar. Since the troop cutbacks began, American units are fleeing the "Great Swamp" and burying anything that isn't on the books. We watched an engineer outfit bury two dilapidated dump trucks, a road grader, and an engineer tank out in the marshes the last time we were up here. If it isn't on the Table of Organization and Equipment, it just disappears.

Scrounging is so rich that Mac and I have even gotten our hands on an M-48 tank. We put it into the revetment we built for it, so it can protect the end of the perimeter facing the old PA&E compound. We will get plenty of beehive rounds from the engineer ammo dump in trade for a brand new jeep Mudhole Waters stole from some medical outfit. Besides, as a result of the "Mount Quang Tri Eruption," there is plenty of relatively intact ammo for it scattered all over the countryside. You just have to be willing to tiptoe around all the stuff that can, and will, go off for no apparent reason. We hear daily explosions out in the swamp when some poor deer or hog, or maybe some poor VC militia private, does the wrong thing at the wrong time and ends up a fine red mist. In spite of the danger, however, the VC Home Guard starts using its ingenuity to harass our base camp.

These "heroes of the Revolution" hide until it gets nasty, weather-wise, or dark as the inside of a weasel's ass. Then, they trundle out with a mortar and whip ten or fifteen rounds at the huge sprawling base camp to our west. A Division size base camp is so large that all you really need to do is point the barrel, rapid-pump rounds down its throat, pack it up and be gone, and you will still manage to hit something. It's easy enough to do with the US 81mm or the Russian 82mm because charge calculation isn't that critical, just crank the barrel higher, subtract a few more charge bags from the fins and you drop closer. To get farther out, reverse the procedure. Pretty simple, you can even teach lieutenants how to do it.

Now a 4.2 inch mortar isn't like the 81mm. The four- deuce has two elevation settings and you get your range from adding or subtracting charges that screw on the round pipe at the base. Unlike the 81mm charges, they clip on and look very much like American cheese packets, you know, that stuff kids love, flat, yellow orange, turns to ooze in the sun. These have the same look and feel, except they are a nitrous-compound.

With the 4.2 there is a whole set of charge tables that explains how many charges to put on to push the round so far. It takes real math to figure it out, and most lieutenants can't fathom it. If they can, they are transferred to the artillery where you have to know this shit, but apparently the Oriental mind is able to grasp this without much trouble.

All this considered, I don't think this particular group has a four-deuce mortar. I think that they are using a length of five-inch diameter pipe that they welded onto a piece of flat iron or steel, with a nipple for a firing pin. They have probably reinforced it with bamboo and wrapped the whole thing in wire. This is how they made cannons in the Middle Ages and works if you aren't looking for pinpoint accuracy. More importantly, the wire and bamboo will hold the little beauty together and keep it from eviscerating yon gun crew when the charges cook off.

There is one small wart in this big scenario, and that is our hootches are directly in the flight path and on the gun target line. This means that whenever Nguyen miscalculates charges, we end up with his short rounds landing somewhere on us. Usually they impact around the PSP on the chopper pad. When there are no helicopters on the ground, the only thing out there is sand and steel plate. You can hear the big fuckers coming in though, they chug.

Now as a school-trained heavy weapons man, that sound is what leads me to believe these guys haven't got a rifled barrel and, more importantly, whatever they are using is oversized. In a four-deuce the barrel has lands and grooves just like a rifle barrel so it makes the round spin-stabilized. At the base of the mortar shell is a copper/brass ring about a half inch wide. When the propellant explodes as the round hits the firing pin fixed to the bottom of the tube, the hot gasses make that ring swell and that is what engages the rifling. The chugging sound that we hear as the rounds pass overhead comes from the fact that there is no rifling in their tube and the round is tumbling and yawing in the air.

There's not a lot to do around a launch site when you're not running operations. Therefore, scientific speculation is a form of entertainment. I consider myself brilliant and explain my theory to Mac and Mudhole, but I might as well be speaking Mayan. Cretins! Peasants! They get this blank look on their faces and wander off on some prurient interest concerning their gut, their dick, or their brain. It doesn't matter because with Southerners all those parts are interchangeable. I also explain it to Pappy. He fixes me with a baleful eye, listens to my brilliant theory, and then tells me to get the fuck out of his TOC. As I swing out the door he shouts at my back that if he's lucky he'll be able to put us into DM-10 tomorrow. With even greater luck we will get captured, and in that case, we would become some NVA sergeant major's headache.

So for the last three days at about this same time, "Ol' Chugga Lug" starts in, lobbing eight or nine rounds, most of which go over us and hit the Fifth Mech. Good for the staff flunkies, they can write themselves up for the Combat Infantryman's Badge. But it has been bad luck for us because one was short and hit the reefer where we had all the good chow like real meat and reconstituted milk. If they had hit the hootch where I am sitting, they would have blown up the beer and booze supply. In that case, we would be out there in the rain tracking down their atrocity- committing hides to kill them.

I see two figures running towards the hootch making giant splashes every time their boots make contact with the red pudding masquerading as the ground. The figures make a beeline for the awning under which I am sitting. As they near the 4.2

inch mortar pit, which is about 25 yards from me, they begin to slow down because the mud is thicker. Bloop, bloop, bloop, bloop, chug-chugga-chug: here come the rounds. The first one heads left into the compound; the next one hits our latrine. A sharp crump, an orange red fireball erupting with black angry smoke, and then there are wood splinters and shit paper raining down everywhere. The remaining debris of the structure and the two sawed-off 55 gallon receptacles for the feces, and their contents, land with a dull thud next to the TOC and sit there steaming. The next round doesn't even register until the mortar pit suddenly erupts, just as the two figures are abreast of it, and a wall of mud engulfs them both.

I am waiting for the fourth round, which by the pattern would mean that it would fall to my left rear. It doesn't quite make it. Should be 50 yards to the west, but instead it plunges through the cook shack in the rear and destroys the sink and one of the refrigerators that holds, or at least used to hold until we ran out of food, the fresh vegetables. It doesn't explode; it just mangles everything.

The two figures are completely covered in mud from the bottom of the pit. They haven't got a scratch on them because the water and mud were deep enough to absorb the impact of the big shell which also had not detonated. They come up quick, stopping under the awning with that panting, "Oh shit!" look of people who have just escaped being in front of the Big Guy explaining why they used to play with themselves so much. It's Mac and Mudhole, from what I can tell.

About that time the Chinese cook comes in from the back and is rattling about the refrigerator and the sink, yelling all the while about, "He no bomb fixee!" and "We go now, takee bomb and fixee!" Mac and Mudhole realize that I am bone dry, clean, and unscathed, and of course, in some bizarre way responsible, because I had some sort of theory about the fucking mortar and who was doing it.

Events are taking a bad turn here. The Chinese cook is now looking at me like I am at fault. The three of them have fixed me with their evil eyes and are standing there as if I am going to have some sort of answer for the whole mess.

Now I, like the others, have a black spot in my heart for whoever is out there in the swamps with his cousins, thinking their little innovative engineering scheme is somehow detrimental to our war effort. I'm searching for some flippant remark to make in self-defense when the remains of the cookhouse door gets another shove and there stands Budrow.

Oh, this is good. Budrow, who on a good day has all the charm of a Jurassic raptor, is at this moment clean out of charm. He yells to all of us that since we don't appear to have any brains, then one of us should take the mortar shell out of the scrap heap in the back, just in case it decides to go off and destroy more of his camp.

Again all the eyes are looking at me. Fuck! I want to go into DM-10 right now. Launch the birds! I might just fucking "*Chieu Hoi* (give up)," and come back here in charge of the little rice-fueled shits and their five-inch pipe super-gun. At least, I'd remember to put a fuse on it! We all go back into the cook shack. Sitting in the wreckage is a mortar round, still smoking. Yep, there's no fuse, just a shipping plug. Marvelous! Mac and Mudhole help me get it to the door and, at that point, decide they have done all they are going to do for democracy. I drag the bloody thing over by the berm and leave it and that's where it will sit for a couple of months until someone finally takes it away.

When I come back to the awning, I see that the mud twins have hosed themselves down and have stood in the rain long enough that they no longer look like a couple of bubbas looking for night crawlers. They have pulled up a couple of chairs and are drinking beer. Mac looks at me and says that we are probably not going to be able to launch for another day or so, because the weather over the target is really thick. We need to get the little people some chow. We are mulling over the possibilities of whom to steal from to where we can get the raw materials that Yards run on: fish, cabbage, rice, peppers. We have taken their PIRs from them, because one thing a Yard will do if he has chow around, is eat it. All of it. They are children of the moment.

It stops raining hard, so we decide to get a couple of the birds in the air and go deer hunting, none of this noble, stalk-the-shaggy-beast, deer slayer, Hawkeye bullshit. Take the bird up and fly about 100 feet off the ground over the marshes. If you see something moving, and it isn't wearing clothes, blast away. If it goes down, go back and load it on the chopper. Bring it back, let the Yards dress it out, and bada-bing, we have fresh meat for dinner. We've done this before; the area fairly abounds with feral pigs and roe deer. We rouse us a couple of the crews and explain what we are planning. When dealing with aircrews, one has to remember that they all still think of themselves as aviators, you know, those dashing fellows with the silk scarves and lady killer looks. They don't see themselves as we do: big balls, small brains, packaged in Nomex, and smelling of kerosene and urine. There is a hurried conference about ceiling, barometric pressure, hydraulic intersufferation, or some other science bullshit they seem so fond of. They should have let Jeep design the fucking whirlyhoozit. It would have had a military starter switch, on/off, clutch, throttle. You wouldn't need four guys who look barely old enough to drive trying to explain an aerodynamic Frostee Freeze to us chimps.

We all go out to the pad and find yet another four-deuce round cratered next to the fuel truck, no fuse again. The crewmen all start getting skittish about vibrations setting the thing off and Mac looks at me and says I should go do the Budrow Activation Test on it. So I get out a pair of binoculars, walk up to it, adjust the binos, view it from several angles, then give it a swift kick and tell him its all right. "The pizo-electric crystals must be in stasis, because it's not clicking." Take that, you silly aerodynamic chopper nerds.

We get the birds wound up and I'm thinking about the last round we just found. I hope we see the assholes out there. I would probably get a medal from Uncle Ho himself if we caught them and capped their asses. This level of incompetence cannot be tolerated. Why let this kind of shoddy performance go unpunished? No telling what sort of degraded state both sides will fall into. Yes, it's our duty to find these slipshod fuckers and kill them.

We can send the two unexploded rounds and pictures of their shot-up carcasses north with the Navy when they are having one of their little jet jockey conventions over the Rue de Kickass and they can drop them right on downtown Hanoi. We will even put a nice letter in the package, about keeping the whole thing quiet if they will take Budrow and keep him until long after the war is over, sort of a quid pro quo. As we sit there warming up Bell's collection of spare parts and green tape, I am lost in my little fantasy.

We lift off and start zinging our way out over the marsh and broken ground to the east. As we go along, I am trying to calculate where the gun might have been located when the other bird sights a deer and Mac and the door gunner are chewing up the flora. I see it go down. They hover, and Mac and the crew chief get out and load the thing on the bird. I am watching them when the door gunner on my chopper opens up with the "60." I look out and see a sow with about eight nice sized piglets, tails up, pushing through the knee high grass. I open up with my CAR-15 and see three of the piglets go spinning ass over teakettle. The gunner gets Ma Schwein with a burst. Ahhh, visions of plump, roasted, suckling pig are dancing through my head as we slip over to where the piglets met their maker. The rotor wash pushes the grass down, and I can see two of them and parts of the third. The rounds have torn him apart. We lower down and I jump out, rounding up the succulent little corpses, and get back in. We lift over to where the sow went down as Mac's bird joins us. We will have roast pork tonight!

We see the body of mama pig and are sliding over to it when a burst of green tracers blasts past Mac's bird. Green tracers, that's bad. Our tracers are red. Most chopper pilots have reflexes somewhere between Superman and a used car salesman on a slow night. This one is no different because suddenly we are jinking and swerving, and before you can say whirlyhoozit, we are several hundred yards from our pork roast feast.

Well, we found the VC, but they gotta be nuts to be shooting at us, since there ain't no cover out here. We get stable and I look back trying to find the gun position, when I see three Nguyens running around like crazy in circles. They are blasting away with their guns, but they aren't shooting up! They are shooting into the grass, first here, then over there, then over here, but not up! I hear the pilot say, "What the fuck?" over the headset, and then I see the biggest, meanest-looking water buffalo I have ever seen in my life, break cover.

He snorts a mist of blood, deftly hooks one of the gallant foes with a horn, tosses him about fifteen feet with a snap of his head, then stomps over and turns him into strawberry squeeze with his hooves. There are more bursts from an AK, and the two survivors are frantically trying to run away.

The buffalo is leaking from about a dozen wounds, and is one pissed off hombre. He catches up with Nguyen number two, who has forgotten about everything except getting away, but you can't run in that muck out there. Well, skinny little rice burners can't, but buffaloes can and do. The bull tramples and gores him into a red, muddy spot, bellowing the entire time. "Ooo doggie! That is one pissed off buff," comes over the headset, I think from one of the door gunners. We all are stunned, so much so, that no one has even thought about shooting at the three hapless assholes.

The buffalo doesn't get a shot at the title with the third hero, though. Nguyen number three, his legs pumping, arms swinging, is practically flying across the marsh. His hat and gun gone, escape has become the prime objective. The bull slows, then stops, snorts a few times and looks up at us with a red-eyed, murderous glance, punctuated by another snort of blood-stained mucous. He pauses a moment then turns and lumbers off into the cane and bamboo. We swing back over to where the sow went down and load her on, while keeping one bird up higher to keep an eye out for the buffalo.

The surviving VC? Well, he got away. I hope they were the mortar squad. It was perfect retribution for being inept. We surmise that the door gunner's burst must have winged the buffalo. Buffaloes having a brain that is mostly wired for anger and instant retribution, acted out in common buffalo terms. He started looking for a victim.

When we hovered over the pig, the rotor wash must have blown the VC's scent to him. Once he got the whiff of humans, away he went for some bad-tempered ass kicking, that only water buffaloes, grizzly bears, and fat women with attitude understand. The burst that went past the windscreen was their first panicked attempt at killing the water buffalo.

When we get back, we make the victory loop over the launch site. As we pass over the Yard hootch I drop one of the piglets, and it lands next to the fire barrel. The Yards are all giving us the thumbs up and we circle in to land. We haven't even cleared the chopper, when the Budrow shows up. He looks at the carcasses, then at the aircrews and us, mutters something in Klingon, and then stomps off toward the mess hall to get the Chinese cook. Our pilot looks at his retreating back.

"If he had bullet holes in him, and was leaking, I would have sworn that buffalo followed us back."

CHAPTER 6

The Coolest Man Alive

The weather has cleared overnight and it's bright, sunny, and hot already at 0600. We are saddling up, making sure that we have all the ammo and ordnance we are going to need. We move the Yards and our equipment out to the helicopter pad and wait for the choppers to come back from the fuel and arming point. Mac and I are huddled in the TOC with Pappy Budrow, Major Slatten, and the lead pilots from the guns and slick packages. The birds will fuel up and be back in about ten minutes. We listen to Covey as he reaches the orbit point and gives us a last minute report on any activity in and around the target area. He and the trail FAC are working a pair of fast movers at a road intersection just about eight klicks from our insertion LZ. They have found a truck parked up under the canopy. This is normal activity in the DMZ and we are hoping that we can increase the bombing activity and slide our insertion in as a side bar. Maybe we can keep them so busy that we go unnoticed.

Covey comes up on the air again. We had ordered two sets of Spads with cluster bombs and hard bombs on one set, and napalm and hard bombs on the second. They are in-bound to the orbit point and should arrive about the same time we do. We have the team on two birds, and three spares which will stay at the orbit point in case a one goes down and we have to try to get out in a hurry. One of the spares has a chase medic onboard. We have SF medics as chase medics because they can do miraculous things that a normal medic wouldn't and couldn't do. They do things that ensure you make it to the evacuation hospital.

We get the last word from Pappy and confirm that the contingency plans for shot-down bird, team separated, team emergency, escape and evasion routes, and day letter codes are understood by all. One of the good things about launching out of Quang Tri is that both Pappy and Slatten are old hands; Pappy has been a One-Zero before. In fact, he had been a One-Zero so long ago that it was rumored in those far back times they were wearing furs and used a club as their basic weapon.

Pappy is totally devoted to getting a team in and, more importantly, getting them out. If he doesn't have enough birds to lift the team and anyone else that might have gone down, it's a no-go as far as he's concerned. This is real important to us, since we rely on him as our umbilical cord. Slatten backs him 100 percent. When someone once complained about the huge number of air assets we used and had on hand, the two of them told the parties complaining that if they had a gripe take it to Chief SOG. End of bitch.

I look at Mac, who is all One-Zero at this point. We have been together long enough now that we work like a well- oiled Swiss timepiece. He does his tasks and I cover the bases. We hear the choppers coming in and everyone finishes and gets ready to mount up.

"Hey numb nuts." We turn, thinking that Pappy has some other forgotten detail for us. He is standing by the radios monitoring the Covey channel and says, "Well, I finally have a plan to make sure you don't disturb the tranquility of my camp." He grins evilly, reaches up and turns the radio off. "I don't know why I didn't think of this before. If I can't hear you sniveling, I won't be bothered about having an attack of conscience, and sending perfectly good aircraft and crews out there to get all shot up trying to rescue you."

He's still grinning as we go out to the pad and get into our equipment. Real funny guy that Budrow, but at this point it fails to relax me. I've got a knot in my gut, like every time we get on these choppers. No, let me correct that, I get a knot in my stomach when we go into isolation in Da Nang, and by the time we are at the launch site I look all twisted up like a strychnine victim. I don't care how many times you do this; the fear is a gripping, gnawing, animal eating at your insides. It's how you handle it, and then force yourself to keep going, that determines if you can make the mission happen. By the time you get to this point you are so chewed up inside you want to get in and make it happen rather than live another day of this gut-wrenching anticipation of disaster.

We are lucky. Sounds crazy, but it's a fact. We have stayed alive a long time. We have what only combat veterans can explain, and only to their peers, because it doesn't make sense to a layman. We are lucky. That luck is based on the fact that the team is competent beyond comprehension. When we do make contact we react like a single-celled organism. Our only hope of survival is that we can maul whoever is unlucky enough to run into us so bad that they back off and gasp long enough for us to find terrain we can hold and work the air cover. The enemy is just like us. You hurt them bad enough and they have to get their balls back before they come again. Down here at ground level it is reality, the mechanics of war that make the rules. It is a bunch of guys in different uniforms; all with one prime directive, survive.

Cuman and the other Yards have been fighting for five, six, even ten years. I have come to know them and respect them as the finest combat troops in the world. Hell, Bong, who is in his late forties, had originally fought with the Legionnaires in Force 36 during the Indochina war. It's amazing. His English is good enough, but he speaks German better. Most of the B.P.E. of the Legion had been Germans trying to escape persecution after WWTI. France took them in by the hundreds.

Five years in the Legion and you got French papers, clean slate. So Bong had learned German when he had been a teenage striker with them.

I have Xaung and two others on my ship. Xaung is our tail gunner on the team and, though only 15, is a seasoned fighter. He has an ESP about when we are going to get hit. He reaches out and touches me, usually just before all hell breaks out. He looks at me now, shrugs, reaches over and pats my arm, then grins at me. He knows that I am getting skittish about his habit of touching me and the usual consequences that ensue, so he is having a laugh at my expense. Comics surround me today.

I put on the headset as the bird gains power, then the nose drops and we start lifting forward and up. I can see Mudhole's team coming up to the pad. They will be our Bright Light if we get in a world of shit. We are rising and banking to the left, accompanied by the first four sets of Cobras, who will prep the LZ with nails and hard rockets, then cover us until we get clear and are moving on the ground.

As we pass over the TOC Budrow leans out, grinning like a Cajun looking at a crawdad, and makes the "turning off the radio" motion again, then gives me the thumbs up. I wish I had enough bile left to throw up on him.

It takes about 30 minutes to get to the orbit point. As we come up on it I am listening to the radio chatter as Covey is working over the area to the south and setting the stage for us to drop in and insert. Mac has arranged that we will go in and flare at the base of the old calderas. He will then throw out a Nightingale device. This is a three-foot by four- foot device that looks like a wire gate with bumps inside, like little spiders. The CIA came up with this one. It is made out of slow burning fuse and when you ignite it the fuse bums around the perimeter and down to the little clusters. These are firecrackers and M-80s, which will sound like a firefight when they go off. It actually sounds like AKs and M-16s and grenades going at it. I look over through the port side as we dip and see a pair of Cobras roll in behind a pair of Spads who drop their CBU load off to the southern end of our target box. They must have spotted something on the lower slopes. I make a mental note of the location. Never go into an area where they have dropped CBUs. Nasty little buggers, not all of them go off. They get hung up in the foliage, and just sit there until something disturbs them. Then they go off.

There are a hundred little explosions as the CBU canister spills its little babies over an elliptical pattern. Then the Cobras let loose with mini-guns and a brace of rockets each. We descend and flare out. Mac tosses the Nightingale device and we lift out and up.

Covey comes on and says we are taking ground fire from lower on the slope. Another set of Cobras drop on that location and start working it over. Our plan is to lift up the slope to where a trail cuts through the rim of the calderas. With only one set of Cobras, we will set in using a rocking horse motion so it looks like we didn't actually set down, and the team will bail in that split second when the airspeed bleeds off just before it picks up again. It's so effective, that if you don't actually see the action, it looks and sounds like the birds never stop. The Cobras and air package will appear to the ground observers as the normal protective coverage for one of our extraction packages coming out.

The Cobras and all the other birds will linger and make a show of working over the area where the Nightingale is cooking off. This little aerial display might give us the edge. We had picked the LZ area because it gave us the high ground, where we could actually see the target area. Also, there is enough cover for us to hide, yet still be able to see. It will give us a good view over the junctions of the trail system going south. Intel said that a division, plus, was moving through the area. We hope to catch them with their pants down. Allow a few hours for the area to quiet down, catch them moving, and then call SPECTRE and a host of other air assets in on them, without giving away the fact that the air was being directed from the ground.

As we lift up the side of the mountain, I can see into the bowl which has eroded into a saddle between two peaks about two hundred yards across, sloping up to their tops from the trail in the center. It looks good from here: no ground fire. Everyone must be concentrating on the phantom team below. We know they have trail security elements. Covey spotted one of their bunkers at the far end of the saddle and the Cobras worked it over coming in. Yep, there it is. All that remains is a smoking hole in the ground with torn up logs and parts of a human body lying just outside the burned area.

Mac is going in. I see the lead bird touch with the back of the skids, As it rolls forward, the nose dips and by the time the front of the skids are on the ground the back is already lifting. I see Mac and the four Yards with him bail out both sides. The last one leaves the aircraft about six feet in the air because he was slow, but they are all on the ground. Then it's our turn.

We aren't even on short final when I hear the pilot screaming, "Abort! Abort!" I look down where Mac landed and get sick to my stomach. He is lying on his back and right next to him is the trap door to a bunker concealed right at the crest of the trail. He has fallen on it and plugged the door.

There are two NVA trying to crawl out of a side entrance and the Yards shoot them. Worse yet, I can see about fifteen other likely bunkers up-slope on the opposite side. I am standing on the skid and I feel the ship start to gain power. I instinctively know that they are going to abort and pull up, which will leave Mac with too few men to save himself. I slam the barrel of my CAR-15 in the back of the pilot's helmet and scream into the mike, "Put this fucking bird down where he is, NOW!" He chops power. We slam into the slope and we all jump or are thrown clear. I land heavily. When I hit the ground my ears feel like I just ripped them off. I still had the headset on when I jumped. The bird screams loudly as it winds up and is gone.

Immediately I get the Yards in some sort of fighting perimeter where we can at least hold on or fight our way to better ground. I run up in a crouch and Mac says, "Why did you land? I told them to abort."

"There are bunkers all over the hill to our right and eight of us can fight a lot harder than five," I yell back.

He grabs the radio handset. "Go tie in the team and let me bring in some air." I work my way down-slope when I see Xam Pot stand up and fire methodically six times like he's on the rifle range. He is standing upright, just like we did at the range; it is almost amusing, because he looks like a poster child for the NRA. I think he's shooting at nothing. He is new on the team and this is his first mission. I yell at Bop and Thua to see what he's firing at. A grenade goes off over by where Thua is and he yells at the team because he thinks one of the team has thrown it and it fell short. I run over to where Xam Pot is and down the trail I see the crumpled bodies of three NVA with a whole shitload of canteens on bamboo poles lying amongst their bodies. They had just walked up the trail; he just stood up yelled something like "Hey!" and dropped all three. That's pretty good discipline, or he just got lucky. We are starting to take ground fire now and the tempo is picking up. I run back up- slope. Well, I trudge up-slope. I need the team to tie in closer and I am working my way back up to where Mac is beside the bunker.

Nearby I can see a group of NVA in green khakis break from cover by some rocks to his left front. They start to try to flank him. Cuman and Bong drop all but three, who make it into a small wash below Mac. Cuman throws a grenade down into it just as a stick grenade comes lofting out of the wash and lands where Mac is and explodes. I hear Mac scream, "God damnit!" Panicked, I push to get up the hill. I can't see anything lying on the ground, and I'm trying to get everybody in tighter. I get to Bop and he is firing the grenade launcher uphill at what looks like a platoon, plus, group of NVA setting up to fire and maneuver down toward us. I dump three magazines at them and between the two of us we make them go to ground.

I have to get to the radio. If Mac is down I'm going to need to get Covey in here as fast as possible and get us some air. I get to within about ten yards of Mac and I can see him. He is on his back with his pants down to his knees and he has the handset cupped in the crook of his shoulder. I can't see any blood, but he has his genitalia cupped in both hands. The little pervert! This is the coolest and craziest man I have ever seen. We are in a world of shit and he is *masturbating*?

I get up to him and he looks up at me and yells that I am drawing fire. Is there some reason I am walking around? Right. We've got more problems than my running around in plain view while you worry about damage to your nut sack. I can see that he is bleeding inside his left thigh. Obviously the shrapnel from the grenade had nicked him. He looks at me like, "Well, I'm wounded…" as if that was an excuse to have his pants down. I take the handset from him and I can hear Covey asking for a sit-rep. I yell into the handset that we are in a hornet's nest, but they will have to wait because my One-Zero is busy playing with himself and it looks like they shot one of his balls off. He grabs the handset, frowns at me like I told on him, and starts giving Covey the situation whilst trying to pull up his britches.

We both look up-slope to our east and the platoon we had driven to ground has been joined by about ten more stalwart lads and is getting ready to assault us. The Yards are dropping them like they were ducks in a shooting gallery, but the small arms fire isn't slacking off at all. We are getting heavy fire from both slopes now and I can count at least six bunker openings with muzzle flashes. Some of them are only forty yards away. Mother McRae, this is bad, bad, bad. We are tucked into a wash so they can't really get at us, but if they can lay enough fire on us they will be able to make us keep our heads down. Then they will hit us with B-40s and rush us. That will be the end of RT Habu, the end of my dreams of becoming President, and any dreams I have of ever becoming a porno star.

Mac yells down at me, "The guns are on the way and the slicks are about ten minutes out. Hang on!" Oh no, Red Ryder, I think I will just give up. Maybe they won't put me in a tiger cage with someone who is more interested in his future as a breeding stud.

Crump! Crump! The high explosives go off to the west about 50 meters. Oh great, someone brought a mortar to the party! How novel, now we are really fucked. They can reach us in the wash with that. I'm trying to figure some great tactical wizardry that will allow me to get out of this alive, but all I can come up with is becoming invisible. I look over at the torn bodies of the two NVA we shot coming in. I am wondering if I can fit into one of the uniforms and slip away in the crowd.

I remember reading how some plainsman had escaped from a war party of Sioux by crawling inside a horse carcass and concealing himself. I look around. Nope, there aren't any horse carcasses here, but there are plenty of pissed off Indians and they are starting to get organized. I hear the unmistakable "brrrrrp" of a Minigun, and the slope in front of me erupts, causing bunches of the green khaki tribe go down. Rockets and 40mms start hitting the slope to our rear.

I have my URC-10 emergency radio on and I can hear Covey talking to another ship that has been hit and gone down. The crew is out and slicks from the package are dropping in to pick them up. The Cobras bank up and to the right and a pair of Spads come in, guns chewing up the real estate.

"Get down! Nape!" Mac yells. I didn't see the canister drop, but then a rolling fire storm erupts in front of us and envelopes any of the survivors of the assault force who were splashing into the bunkers. There is a blast of heat behind me and I can hear someone screaming. It is too far away to be one of us. Fry, you little rice-eating ant. Napalm sucks oxygen out of the area making it hard to breathe. I don't notice because when I'm scared shitless I have a tendency to hyperventilate, so oxygen is not yet a problem. The mortar has stopped so maybe we got lucky.

Mac yells out over the ground fire, "Choppers coming, short final. Take the first bird, get everyone on. Covey says there are a lot more of them moving up the slope behind us. We gotta go." Now that is an understatement.

The first slick comes in and slams down about ten yards from me. I run toward it and start throwing little people onboard. I am about to dive in when it is suddenly up and gone. I stand there, momentarily, with feelings of despair, betrayal, and a big "oh shit." However, I haven't got time for hurt feelings. I have to get back to where Mac is or they will leave me here and all these pissed off people will blame me for ruining their lunch hour. I run over to Mac and the second bird slams into the ground almost on top of us. We dive inside, Cuman lands on top of us, and we start to lift.

The door gunners on both sides are burning their guns out on full auto and they have plenty to shoot at. The NVA are trying to get right on top of us because the guns and the Spads are killing everything except what is about twenty yards from the chopper we are on. You can feel the rounds hitting the chopper, a staccato metal thunk, thunk, thunk. From where I am lying on the floor, I can see an NVA officer running at us with a pistol and yelling at his men. Shit, this boy must have watched too many war movies. I wonder how he can run that fast, having such big balls. I can't get my gun up because I'm half laying on it, so I just pull the trigger and let it rip. We are lifting and I can't see if I got him. A grenade flies in. Mac kicks at it and it tumbles out the side of the bird. Another grenade bounces off the gunner's helmet and falls out. The gunner swats at his face with one hand, like he was shooing away some nasty bug, but keeps burning up the gun with one long, continuous burst. The engines are screaming up to full power and I can see rounds chewing up the overhead and the inside of the bird. Then we are up and away. There is another sudden rush of hot air from ordnance going off real close, and the chopper jumps up from the concussion. But we are still gaining altitude, pulling free and getting some sky, getting up and beyond the 12.5mms and all those other weapons trying to pull us back down.

I look back and the mountain is alive with explosions going off. In the distance you can see more jets and aircraft stacking up for their chance. Every fighter jock in Southeast Asia that has both ordnance and fuel is coming over for a drop. Some of them are down to minutes of airtime so Covey is working them first. As we get farther and farther from the battle, I look back at the half moon shape of the caldera we had been in. It is getting pasted from the air by everything from Cobras to F-4s and Skyraiders. The zoomies will need a couple of extra hands each to tell this story at the club tonight. There is enough aircraft zinging around up there to create a traffic jam.

I am half-lying on the floor with my back braced against the stanchion behind the pilot, watching this entire tableau recede. Mac has the headset on. All our people are out. We hear Covey say that they got the crew of the gunship that was knocked down and they are starting to get secondary explosions in the calderas and the surrounding area. Marvelous. Blow the whole bloody thing up.

Forty minutes, plus, and we are sweeping over the Fifth Mech base and then wallowing into short final until we are down. We had been on the ground for about an hour and change. The first person I see is Mudhole and he is sitting under a brightly colored beach umbrella. He is naked except his boots and a panama hat, beer in hand. Then I see Pappy and Slatten heading our way with the medic. They grab Mac and the medic is trying to look at his wound. I vaguely hear Slatten saying, that's it, good job, and that we will be going back to Da Nang tomorrow.

Mac is calm, cool, and collected, like always. Pappy hands him a beer and holds out two steel ball bearings, big ones. "Here, you might need these. Your One-One says they shot your balls off." That's right, pamper the little gator excrement. While we were out there about to get turned into victims, I distinctly heard Mac, the Combat Midget, on the radio. At the height of every pissed off Nguyen in the world shooting at us, Covey was asking if we were declaring a Tactical Emergency. Mac's response? "How does it look from where you're at?" I'm going to shoot him.

I see some Air Force light colonel with Slatten and he's staring at me and the rest of us as if we are aliens. Then I remember I'm wearing Uncle Otto's German helmet with the SS runes on the side. I remember that we had joked about it maybe giving us a couple of extra seconds if some NVA saw me and pondered whose side the Germans were on. Hey, it might have worked.

Actually, if we ever have to go back there again, I am wondering about the feasibility of getting our hands on a full dress, Russian General's uniform, or even a 55 gallon drum of vanishing cream.

I snap back to reality when Budrow instructs us to get our team chowed down. The operations are closed for the day; we are lucky more rain is moving in. I snap my heels together and scream, "Zu Befehl! Herr Scharfuhrer!" and march off in my best Prussian manner. The Air Force guy looks me over and then looks at Budrow and Slatten. They shrug as if to say, "Don't pay any attention to him." I hope that guy is the weatherman; I'm going to get drunk and see if he wants to buy some good war stories.

Mac comes plodding up and grabs my arm. "Well, we got out of there, didn't we?" I love the little Alabama gator bait. Talk about the master of the obvious. I hope his balls swell up; maybe we will get an extra couple of days stand down if they do.

Mac continues. "You have to quit walking around like that when you are under fire or someone is going to think you're brave or something. You know we have been able to convince Captain Manes that you are too dull-witted to take over a team by yourself, but if they mistake dimwitted for brave they are going to break us up."

Yep, that's the Mac, always looking out for me. I see him doing the same thing, walking around in the middle of a firefight, at least when he isn't tripping over something and falling down. But the latter part of that statement is indeed true; I've caught Manes eyeing the two of us with that look. We'd better be careful.

We go by and see the Yards. They are out of their gear, and we get the usual nose touch, cheek sniff, pats on the arm, accompanied by grins. The mugging follows this, where we give them cash to buy stuff like beer, cigarettes, etc. They have the fetus of the deer we shot yesterday cooking in a pot already and we are to come back and eat with them.

Then it's drop the equipment, and go over to the mess shack/club for some cold beer. Mac looks at me and says it's a good thing we got out when we did bud, because he was down to about eight magazines. Same here, it had been real close. The good thing was that we had made it and wouldn't draw that target again until at least someone else ran it. The next mission in there would probably be a Bomb Damage Assessment mission. They would probably carpet bomb the whole area then send in a team to see what was still walking around.

We close out the night with the Yards, mildly drunk, eating the venison. Once you get past how they cooked it, the entree is delicious. They make fun of my skills as a hunter as we prepare the blasted piglet and what's left of his siblings. The Yards tell me to take a crossbow next time so there will be more meat. Ah, life is good; I am alive and I'm with my tribe of little head-hunting killers. I love them. I am drifting with contentment, almost dream-like, when I realize the little shits have been cooking with herbs again.

CHAPTER 7

Polite Society Meets Reality

Two of the Yards and Mac have wounds, but they are minor, so the medic has swabbed and bandaged all of them. We will fly back to Da Nang and have Doc Wang, the Project Surgeon, do any major stitching and repair at the infirmary. We have a better care facility than anywhere else in Da Nang for the indig. If we take them to the Vietnamese hospital they would leave them untreated, and in some cases would mistreat them, so we have built a complete hospital and recovery ward right there in the camp with our own surgeon and nursing staff. Unless they're shot to pieces, most guys prefer going to Doc Wang, although he is a bit strange.

The traits of "extremely talented" and "eccentric multiple personalities" should be a harmless combination in most people, however, with the doctor you never know which one in particular you're talking to. Two questions come to mind: One, which personality is working on you at the moment, and two, is this the one that actually graduated from medical school? The Doc changes personas like stations flashing by on the express run. It's like watching a wheel spinning inside that inscrutable egg he calls a head. It's rumored that at least three quarters of the possible personalities were insane, but only a few were violent at the same time. It's a crap shoot as to who is going be there for you. Apparently, they all can cut and sew; it is the recovery you have to watch out for. You might get Florence Nightingale, angel of mercy with the demerol, or you might get Colonel Akira, head of the bio-testing laboratory in Manchuria.

In any event, the weather is spotty so they have no need for us to stand by for a possible Bright Light requirement. Mudhole is scheduled to launch into DM-5, and the next team up from Da Nang can be his Bright Light.

We get over to the airfield just as the C-130 from Da Nang touches down, and rolls off the taxiway to the offload point. They leave the engines running and the rear ramp comes down disgorging one of our teams and two *very* pissed off Donut Dollies. This is the nickname given to Red Cross volunteers, who are here ostensibly to cheer up the troops. The Dollies are complaining loudly to some Air Force major about the unseemly conduct of those "people," as they put it. They are very upset about some sort of unwashed sub-humans, and apparently the bunch is still on the airplane.

One of the Dollies is rather mousy with butter churned hips. The other, the taller of the two, is a redheaded horse-faced lass, who, by her accent, must come from some Midwestern farm burg. She complains loudly and indignantly about one of these "people" exposing himself. The major rolls his eyes and tries his best to keep a straight face. She keeps up this nagging, shrill demand for social justice all the while they are walking to the cool refuge of the operations hut. I can see that the major is probably the aircraft commander because he is wearing his Dr. Denton flight suit.

The redhead and her dumpy friend shoot us a snooty look of disdain. Horse-face informs the major that she will make a full report to someone with commiserate rank. She plans to have something done about this outrage. I'm tired and dirty, as we all are, but this little drama is at least an interesting momentary distraction. She gets abreast of me and says, "Well here's some more of the filthy bunch," like I was some training aid for a venereal disease lecture. Obviously she has had her sensibilities offended by someone. What is more obvious is that they are connected with us.

I am aghast that anyone in his right mind would even let two Red Cross dainties even near us, much less lock them up in a plane with any of us for an hour. Then the answer comes strolling down the ramp, at least the who, if not the why. It's Rick Hendrick and his team of Chinese Nungs. On a good day they look like thugs in a Chinese propaganda film, but today they are bristling with weapons and gear common to SOG. They are loaded for dragon slaying, with knives, pistols, and other assorted mayhem devices, and garbed in a mixture of sterile and NVA uniform parts.

Rick is actually not the giant of the crowd. Although he is almost six foot, two of the Chinese are as big, if not bigger, than he. He can't get their names straight so he has nicknamed them after a couple of Donald Duck's nephews, Huey and Dewey. Huey speaks colloquial American as well as any of us and he is obviously amused by something.

We greet each other, exchange news and gossip, and find out that their target area will be the northern A Shau Valley. He shakes his head at the backs of the two Red Cross witches and the hapless major, making their way off towards the operations building. We ask him what got their panties in a bunch.

Oh, they had all sorts of complaints; the Nungs smelled like garlic, were obviously low-life gooks, all the usual round eye superiority crap, and figured that none of the Nungs "parlee any Englee." Rick was forward chatting with the flight crew when Huey looked at the two Dollies and, in his best American English, informed them that they smelled like cheap hookers on the rag, and that at least he and his fellow Nungs had the decency to bathe. Of course with Huey, once he was on a roll he liked to give you the whole show and full depth of his vocabulary in English. Short of capping him, there was no way to stop him, so he had informed Horse-face that he was curious about the rumor that was all over Vietnam about Donut Dollies making a fortune being hookers and selling pussy on the side. This had brought the inevitable shocked silence to the scene. They were in complete and utter outrage, which provided him both opportunity and encouragement to compound the upcoming insults by delivering them in a calm conversational tone, as if he were inquiring about their families or the weather.

Hendrick, their One-Zero, is not exactly adult supervision by any means. Try to imagine a seemingly soft spoken, giant ogre with a shock of red hair, and the ease and grace of a Serengeti Water Buffalo. The Chinese admire and follow him because his joss, or luck, is exceeded only by his intense love of breaking things. This, of course, negates any hope of Huey going inscrutable.

Huey continued on in a conversational tone, smiling all the while, that this Donut Dollie story completely amazed him because he personally owned a whorehouse in Nha Trang and he was certain that he couldn't demand more than five dollars a trick for the two of them unless they had something special to offer, like doing it with a dog, or on a trapeze with a wolverine. Well, he might get ten for the two of them, but not from any self-respecting Chinese, perhaps from some lonely Spec-4 shoe clerk. That was the clincher; it launched them into some kind of toxic reaction. They went through all the phases, from first standing there red-faced and embarrassed with mouths open, then realizing the full impact of what he was suggesting, and finally igniting the raging response.

While Huey was demonstrating his command of English, the loadmaster had quietly slipped off to hide behind one of the pallets, to relay the ugly turn of events to the flight crew and probably look for a spare cargo net to throw over the estrogen kitties if it got really ugly. Good man, think of the aircraft first. The crew had informed Rick of the bare essentials and he got up and headed back to the cargo area, arriving right at the end of the wolverine suggestion.

The women looked at Rick and demanded he do something about these horrible creatures. He looked over his crew of cutthroats, then turned to the charity twins and laconically suggested that maybe they ought to try and put a calm face on everything, and do what they do when they are around American troops. All the while he was thinking that it was impossible that these two had ever been in the presence of words like hooker, pussy, cash, and tricks. This was going to require all of his skills at putting a pretty face on an ugly situation.

He starts out by saying that he is sure they have misunderstood Huey and perhaps they can appreciate the fact that the troops are bound for a dangerous mission. They need morale improvement as much as any unit they might have seen up to that point. Perhaps they could dig into their little Red Cross kits and come up with something that would make everyone more comfortable, like "Name that State," which is a game where the doughnut crew holds up paper cutouts of states and when the troops guess correctly, they get a donut and a beaming smile.

Smiling, and solicitous, he continued. "Swell, let's guess this one." He deftly unbuttoned his fly, pulled out his John Henry and said, "Well, well, lookee here; it's

Florida." Like I said, he used all his talents at compromise and negotiation. There hadn't been much there to begin with.

That had shut them up, but they spent the rest of the flight sitting on the tail ramp bending the Air Force loadmaster's ear. The crews that fly these hops know us, so he listened and nodded while trying not to laugh at them.

The major comes back from Operations and tells our team to load onboard, as Rick and his team move off and load onto the deuce and a half that brought us from the launch site. We walk through the hot wash of the port engines' exhaust to begin loading. The smell of a C-130 burning aviation fuel is distinct from a Huey. Each has its own set of memories and triggers. A C-130 means traveling with no one shooting at you, a Huey's smell will give you an anus tightening for the rest of your life.

Going home. The tension begins to flow out like water through a tap. We get up the ramp and the Yards sit and stack their equipment under the seats. Everyone has unloaded and checked their weapons so we don't have an accident. It makes the Air Force real testy if you shoot a hole in their bird, although it amazes me because some in the inventory have more "100 mile-an-hour" tape than rivets holding them together. Not entirely true, the C-130's are fairly well maintained; it's the Caribous that are all taped together. We sit down on the red nylon jump seats and buckle in.

The loadmaster hits the ramp control, lifts the ramp, stops it just past horizontal, and we begin to taxi away from the pad in front of the Operations Center. The loadmaster comes by with his headset on, coiling the long umbilical as he moves forward. He makes eye contact with Mac and me, grins, and starts to lean over to say something, then stops and begins talking rapidly into his mike. Ignoring us, he goes over and looks out and up through one of the forward port windows. We are turning and suddenly come to a stop. The crew chief goes back and lowers the ramp. He gets out and walks to the port side of the plane, trailing the intercom cord with him. A few moments go by and he comes back in and he just gives us the thumbs down sign, nothing more. We are rolling again and it appears that we are going back to the pad area.

Mac gets up and goes back to talk with the loadmaster for a bit, then comes back and leans over and tells me that they have red lights on the number two engine. The plane will be grounded until they run down the problem. Shit. That means we will probably have to stay at the launch site another night, which means if someone launches we could end up getting sucked into a Bright Light. No! Uncle Nicky has had enough fun for the week. You know in your heart, that if it happens you will go because it's your buddies out there. At the same time, you hate a fickle God and you find yourself making inane promises to the Big Guy like, "I swear I won't touch myself that way again," and "I'll even go back and confess to stealing the underwear out of the girls' locker room in the ninth grade, just let me go back to Da Nang."

The aircraft stops; the ramp goes down and the loadmaster jumps out pulling the wheel chocks by their ropes with him. The engines feather and then shut down. That's it, no more "go flyee" today. We get up and swing into our gear as the flight deck crew comes down. There is a major, and a captain and a first looey. Well, well, that makes it a pat hand.

The major we know. He grins and shrugs and tells us he's sorry, but they will be staying overnight due to technical problems. He explains that there is a Caribou coming in. The Air Force is going to put us on it and send it back to Da Nang. Thank you, God. I swear I'll keep those promises just as soon as stand down is over.

The major has his hand on Mac's shoulder and says, "Look you might want to make yourself scarce over there in one of the revetments." He says he'll have the Operations Center send a jeep over when the bird is about fifteen minutes out. He points to an area about two hundred yards from the Operations Center. "That will give you time to get over there where the aircraft will set to pick you guys up." He confides to us, "This is for your own good. That redhead," meaning the taller of the Red Cross troopies, "was on the phone with my boss, which won't do her any good because he has more important things to do, but she is just the type to take this to someone who will want to ingratiate himself on their charms. I know you guys didn't do anything, but if she gets the right set of ears they could cause you to miss your Caribou."

I hate Donut Dollies at this point. All the memories come back to me of being forced to attend their inane little shows when I was a private. They would always come around to boost the morale of the troops, prancing themselves around like they were raving beauty queens, when the stuck-up little snots wouldn't give a lowly enlisted man the time of day. All of them were looking for some officer to marry. Well to be fair, I have met two or three that had real charity in their hearts. It didn't mean they were going to hand out any shorts to anyone, but there were a few who actually seemed to care about what they were doing. I doubt Dumpy and the redhead are playing on the same team.

They will probably come screaming back here with some Lieutenant Colonel of the Manners Police. We, the innocent, will get hauled in for questioning because those types of twits come with a platoon of MPs and Cadillac Gauge Armored Cars, all of them full of regulation self- righteousness. We are totally innocent, but they will screw us out of our ride back to Da Nang, sure as Davy Crockett liked bear pussy.

This kicks in the tactical side of my brain, which is the side not directly responsible for body functions and pornographic images. Let them come, we have enough ammo left with the B-40s and the claymores and all the other stuff we didn't fire saving our asses that we can probably kill a couple hundred of them. I have the CAC codes from yesterday. We can get on the radio and lie to Covey in order to get some air assets with some napalm and some CBUs. Yes, and get that worthless shit, Hendrick, and those Chinese bandits of his to flank them. It is their fault we are in this mess. Let him and his star English student work for a living.

If we can get enough fireworks going, we can make the world a better place. I check my gear and plot the lay of the land. Let me see, I can put Bong and Bop over here by this concrete wall, and the rest of us can take the Operations Center, give us a crossfire that way. Yeah, we will take over the TOC, that way we can call them on the radio and tell them that we are hiding in that little building over there. Then we can suck them into a spot where we can catch them with their pretty little whistles, sirens, DR books, and shiny little helmet liners. And massacre them. Perfect, I'm going to move Bop up on the roof of the Ops Center that way he can lob 40mms down on them. I'll strip naked and paint myself with camo-grease and take my SOG knife and personally chase that snooty, redheaded, dream-destroying, miserable, Midwestern, bitch from hell down and cut her heart out. I am actually enjoying the fantasy of retribution. I can see it as clearly as if it was actually happening.

"Nick. Nick!" A voice jars me back from all my mental preparations. I come out of tactical la-la land and realize that Mac is talking at me. The major gives me this queer look, like he just saw a bad dog. And Mac, who has some sort of Alabama swamp ESP, somehow knows where my head just was and shakes his. With the buzzing in my ears all I hear is "… team … there … wait … in shade … until bird … here." He enunciates every word slowly, with a long pause between each.

You know, don't you, my fearless leader? I was plotting our escape, just doing a One-One's superlative job. That's what I am here for, emergency planning. We could do it, and we could win. I hate Hendrick and his horrible little horde. Why can't he keep his peepee in his britches without involving us in the clean up? The major looks me over real careful-like, shakes his head and gives a nervous laugh. He tells Mac before he walks off that maybe he ought to think about getting a leash. I wonder what he meant by that?

A half hour later we are lying under the Quonset of the revetment, baking in the heat. I've got my shirt open and am in that somnambulant state of baked boredom and fatigue that the midday heat brings on. The humidity is crushing and I am half-awake when Mac shakes me and says there is a jeep coming. I pop awake because I just know it's the long arm of society on its way, but I am wrong. I look up and the jeep swings into view. It is being driven by an airman first class, with ears the size of cab doors and so many freckles he looks like Howdy Doody. He screeches to a stop and yells over that our bird is coming in and that we will load up as soon as it gets here.

"The colonel says you better get right on, Sirs, because Sirs, there is a major from I Corps Provost Marshal's office coming and he will take your ride away, Sirs." This is all done in one long breath, and then he hops in and squeals out in the direction of the Operations Center. I haven't heard that many "Sirs" since the night we got caught skinny-dipping in the town's drinking supply back home and my brother thought if we were real polite the nice policeman would cut us a break. Must be some sort of Air Force, Pavlovian experiment, thing.

We saddle up in a hurry and start to file over to the ready ramp as we hear the big props of the DeHaviland reversing down the runway. I have my German helmet on and am tucked down, hoping that we can get on the bird before Twinky Command gets here.

The Caribou swings into view, a big ugly, twin-engine job with a high tail. It's slower than a C-130, but it is our ride home. As it taxis up, the ramp is coming down and we run up from behind and climb up the ramp. Mac and I dump our gear and go to the side of the aircraft facing the Ops Center. The ramp comes back up and the Crew Chief makes a circling motion with one hand then thrusts it forward, signaling that we are moving out. We are rolling, and then finally turning onto the runway. The bird hasn't been on the ground ten minutes before we are rolling for take-off. As we flash by the Operations Center, we see an MP jeep, actually three of them, outside and a gaggle of pissant MPs standing about. My ambush would have been perfect. I don't see the charity twins. Then we are gone.

The plane climbs and turns south and everyone begins to drift off into sleep. We are flying about 6000 feet over the South China Sea. They have the ramp partially open to let a breeze in. Caribou crews are usually earthy people; this isn't the glamour girl of the inventory. I am safe so I drift off into sleep. No worries, we will be in Da Nang by late afternoon.

"*Trung Si*" Shake. "*Trung Si*" Shake, shake. I see Cuman's face floating over mine. "*Trung Si*, wake up!" It is Cuman. I ain't dreaming. I sit up, my mouth tastes like someone stuck a jock strap in it and I have a crick in my neck. I rub the sleep off my face and take out a canteen, take a swallow, then pour some on my head and dry off with my cravat. I am soaking with sweat on the side that had been on the seat. Cuman is sitting on a rucksack like it was a chair, peering at me intently. He has a concerned look on his face. The engines are droning along. Everything seems to be happy in our little Air Force world. Why does he look so worried? The rest of the Yards are real close, too, and they are all looking at me intently. They all have the same worried look, so the mugging for cash can't be the reason they woke me up.

"*Trung Si* Nick, ooush, numbah ten, *Trung Si* Mac," Cuman says to me. What? Has the little crapper fallen out of the plane? I'm half irritated; I'd been dreaming about getting laid. Where is Mac? I look around and notice Herr Combat Pygmy isn't anywhere to be seen.

"Oush numbah ten!" There's that "numbah ten" thing again, which means bad, or bad thing, or bad is gonna happen, or just plain bad, bad, bad. Everybody uses it. With the Yards it can mean a thousand things, depends on how they say it. Cuman has this "I don't approve of something" tone. That means that Mac is doing something that is upsetting the boys or liable to get us all blown to hell. Now what? Can't I just pass out? Will the little people let me go back to sleep? I test them. I let my eyelids droop. Wrong move, shake, shake. Whatever it is, it must be serious.

I look at Cuman and ask him what is wrong with *Trung Si* Mac. Is *Trung Si* Mac dead? Is *Trung Si* Mac touching himself? This doesn't humor him at all; he is obviously upset about something, and I, in his eyes, am acting irresponsibly.

"Oush! *Trung Si* Mac beaucoup fuck up," he starts out. At last we are getting somewhere. "*Trung Si* Mac no be flybing airplane. *Tahan* no like *Trung Si* Mac fly. *Trung Si* Mac, beaucoup *dinky dau Tahan* no like *Trung Si* Mac fly airplane!" Okay, now I'm awake. Where *is* our fearless leader? I notice one of the flight deck crew stretched out on the jump seats. Whoa, who's flying this thing? I distinctly see another stretched out and I'm doing finger math. Let's see, there were four crew members on this airborne junk heap when we left. So, there is the assistant loadmaster asleep, co- pilot asleep, assistant air wing asleep. I bolt forward to the flight deck. Before I get there I hear the unmistakable humming, the twang of South Alabaman, the Mini Mac, talking Air Force-ese. He has the headset on and he is flying this lumbering crate. I knew I couldn't leave him alone. What the jaspers blue blazes were these zoomies thinking? Don't they know he is deranged? The fact that there is one of the flight crew up there with him is absolutely no comfort, because the first thing I notice about him is the troubling indication of casual ignorance, like the drool coming out the comer of his mouth. He is half asleep as well.

No wonder the Yards are worried. I am terrified. How long has this deranged little prick been up here flying this crate? With his sense of direction, the odds are that we are probably over Hanoi and there are probably SAMs (surface to air missiles) by the hundreds pointing at us right now.

I'm looking for the "compass direction/anything meter" and also for the fuel gauge. I can't find the right gauges but we are going south according to the sun. My panic level stops and starts to fall slightly. Mac leans over and says something to the ingrate in the other seat, who rubs his eyes, then swings into the jump seat to the right rear of where Mac is sitting. He grins at me and waves a hand, indicating I can have the seat he just vacated.

As I get in the left seat, Mac motions for me to put on the headset. I put it on and his voice comes over. "You want to fly for a while? I know the crew and I've got about a hundred hours in these." Sure you do, and I am a donkey that can solve trig equations. The real flight person comes on and says go ahead. I look back at him and he has this bored look. What the hell, why not? I ease up and he is giving me instructions and lets me get the feel of the thing. Mac acts as if he is in total control, and I have to admit that he seems to know what he's doing. This is all a ruse I am sure, since I am absolutely certain that southerners invented stock car racing and spectacular crashes on the same day. But because you don't need the fingers on either hand to count the number of brain surgeons in my family, we are soon chatting and I am full of the feeling of flying.

The flight officer says we are about 45 minutes out. We are at it about 20 minutes when he says, "Go down and wake up the crew, will you?" I get up. I've been having so much fun I forgot the Yards. As I turn to go back down the ladder, I see eight little faces staring up at me. Cuman has a disgusted look on his face. I come down and shake the crew awake one at a time. I watch as they stretch and shake their nap off. Cuman looks at me with that disapproving father face, but I just go about getting to the back and sit down and smile at him.

"No sweat. *Trung Si* Mac fly all the time." He looks at me then turns and says something to the rest of the Bru. They all shake their heads and sit back down. Mac comes down a couple of minutes later and we both light up a cigarette and start mapping out the stand down. We will pay the Yards, send them off to Mai Loc, and then the two of us will either go to Nha Trang or stay in Da Nang. Party time! We get three days if we are lucky, a couple of days to train ourselves back up, then back into isolation with a new target. As soon as they see that the conversation is not going to include any major explanations, coupled with the fact that both of their lunatics are now back here with them, the Yards are satisfied that all is well in their world.

This doesn't mean that it is over. Sometime in the next three days I am sure that our loyal little band will troop into our hootch and Cuman will give us a long speech about how irresponsible we are. He, as war leader of the Bru Nation, is responsible for all the *Tahans*. He will be eloquent, and forceful, and remind us that our dicks are not the thinking organ. This will culminate in the issuance of a fine of say, a pig, four or five chickens, and some cash for the *Tahans* to buy beer and cigarettes. The opportunity to extract a mugging will be too good to pass up. It's a good thing Captain Manes doesn't stumble onto this equation. No, it wouldn't work for him. We would just be broke, and then have to borrow money until we owed so much he couldn't risk the chance we might get out of it by dying.

The time winds down and soon we are slipping into descending traffic going into the sprawling airbase at Da Nang. We roll down the runway and taxi up to the parking ramp. As we wait for them to shut down, a black deuce and a half pulls up to the rear of the aircraft. It is one of ours and Jesse Thompson is driving it. We offload and get the Yards on the back. I get on with them, and Mac climbs in the front with Jesse. Jesse looks up at me and says, "I hear you guys got shot out of DM Ten. They say they are going to put Eldon's team in or Murphy's after the B-52s work it over." He lets the clutch out and we are motoring out of the airbase.

Once past the front gate, the ordered, neat, manicured facility gives way to the teeming metropolis of Da Nang City. This means the sickly sweet aroma of the Orient, and packed streets, a mixture of Honda cycles, garish buses, and military vehicles snaking between the close-knit, haphazard architecture of "build-as-you-grow" on both sides of the road. It takes us about an hour to negotiate our way to the I Corps Bridge which spans the river. There are machine gun posts and military checkpoints on the western side, matched by their twins on the eastern side. It is a big structure and from the back of the truck I can see the German hospital ship, the Helgoland, berthed with a multitude of other ships that bring in everything that keep the war effort and the economy going. The wind feels good. The Yards are laughing and making suggestive comments at the numerous pretty girls that we pass along the side of the road.

The bridge road narrows into a two-lane blacktop. There are six lanes of traffic trying to squeeze into it, but it is moving fairly quickly. However, Jesse shouts back to have the Yards stand to. The favorite trick lately has been to have some poor ARVN veterans who are double amputees roll out in the roadway to stop traffic. Of course, the average GI from "Scrubbed-Face America" will stop, then, bang, there's a gun in the face, he's hauled out and beaten up, then the vehicle and the load taken. They tried this on one of our trucks about a week ago coming back from the airfield. The Viet driver merely downshifted, poured on the gas and kept going, turning a couple of them into red spots on the road. Because our vehicles are painted black, they give them a wide berth if they see one coming now.

Just before we get to the corner, traffic slows but doesn't stop. There is a five-ton Army semi stopped at the corner, and the MPs are there. Curled up under the left front wheel well is a jeep with two very dead GIs in it. It is a bad accident. We notice it is one of our jeeps. Jesse says, "Don't worry. It isn't anyone from Recon. It's some cherry lieutenant from S-4 and that asshole from Security Company that was afraid of his own shadow. You know, the E-7 that wouldn't go outside the wire unless he had ten strikers to go with him." The five-ton was driven by some leg with a pick stuck in an Afro big enough to be a helmet. He is so hopped up on heroin that you can tell it from here.

The MPs have him leaning against one of their jeeps. He will probably get drug rehab for this little mishap. I suggest that we ought to stop and cap the little drug-fucked prick just for good measure. Mac says no; let's get back to the camp. We turn right, and head back south. After about a mile we come to the infamous "Gonorrhea Gulch." This is a collection of ramshackle hootches off the side of the road. It's a baaaad place, full of bandits and shooting galleries where the junkies from the Ash and Trash support outfits shoot heroin until they think they are big, bad, "Night Warrior Muthas" and stumble back to their bunkers to sleep it off. There isn't any real order to the layout of shacks and ghetto housing. The place just sort of winds around with dozens of blind alleys and pitfalls for the unwary to wander into. It has a seedy, decaying quality, a twisted rendition of bayou burg and maze, all in muddy earth tones perched at the edge of the paddies. There is the scent of human excrement permeating every pore of the layout as well.

The place is full up, just like Da Nang itself, with the trash of the deserters. There are about 500 in I Corps, mostly junkies, who make their living robbing and stealing from the depots and hooking more of their brothers on that shit. One of our guys got jumped in there. They beat him up pretty bad. He came back with his Yards and a couple of satchel charges and did a little urban renewal. The black truck with us perched on it has the same effect here; they give us a wide berth.

On past the gulch we pass the prisoner of war camp on our left, and then it's our own little patch of heaven. Our camp sits right at the base of Marble Mountain, a collection of martial order laid out on the glaring white sand. The highway is on the west, the South China Sea on the East. We slow down and turn in, with Jesse showing off his dexterity at downshifting. The two Yards at the outer gate wave us by, and then we go up and past the chopper pad to our right, to the bunker line and the second gate. As we pull through, a jeep is coming out. It's Captain Manes. He stops and yells at us.

"Hey! You two numb nuts had better not destroy anything while I am gone. I'm going to the safe house and I don't want to see you riffraff coming down there, either." Then he pops the clutch, and the jeep starts to head back out the gate from which we just came.

I am incredulous; he's driving our jeep! I can't help my outrage over this obvious breach of etiquette. I scream at him as he pulls away. "Come back here! You thieving shit. That's our jeep! We stole it just before we left."

He flips us the finger and yells back, "That's 'you thieving shit, *Sir*' you enlisted swine." He laughs in a cackle and then adds insult to injury. "Besides the only thing you two are good for is getting me new jeeps." Then he is gone.

A fine welcome home this is. Now we will have to steal someone else's jeep, and the thing will snowball until someone doesn't have a motorized seat. I realize that this is a good idea because that situation can quickly turn into a night of foraging to see who can come up with the most original theft. This, of course, will be a glut of jeep and other motorized inventory appearing by the morrow, resulting in Captain Chunky eventually having to go to the Provost Marshal's office for explanations and recriminations. I would love to see his face when he tries to explain why he is driving the I Corps Chaplain's vehicle.

CHAPTER 8

We Few, We Happy Few

It's late in the evening and I am in the Recon Club. I am way beyond redemption. "We are so very few," a line from King Hank comes back to me, the speech that Henry gives to his dispirited and outnumbered troops and peers of the land. They are fleeing before the French, a "retrograde action" as they say in the military, a fighting withdrawal. He and his army pause next to an obscure French village. They are weak from lack of food because the French Dauphin has ordered that the countryside be laid to waste, so there is no forage to be had for man or horse. His men suffer from dysentery to the point that some of his Irish foot soldiers will fight naked from the waist that day. They must stand and fight, or be cut to pieces by the swelling army of the French. Weighed down with baggage and loot, Henry turns to face his adversaries. It is St. Crispin's day and he begins his speech with "We few, we happy few. We band of brothers…" That is us, "we band of brothers," peers in a horrible dance with death.

The club is our private place. It's where we keep our grip, and if you are an outsider, you do not come here, regardless of rank. Everyone here is Recon or Hatchet Force, and everyone has paid his dues, or is paying his dues, in that small little world that is ours alone. We have guests that we bring in, like the pilots that fly our air packages; *they* are welcome because they are like us, different, but like us. Other project guys drift through from time to time, but if you're not invited don't come here. You can die here and you can definitely get hurt here. We do it to each other. The rules are simple, but we often get too jagged or someone says the wrong thing, and then it is face-off time.

This is also where we come to mourn. This is where you get your wake, your send off into the shade. As you ride Charon's boat across the river Styx, this band of iron-hard men, who are your closest living relatives, will gather here and drown your memory.

Oh, the Army will send your earthly remains back and they will, if possible, make the carcass look presentable. This is done out of courtesy and respect. There will be an honor guard and a trumpeter, and the honor guard will hand your closest kin the folded

American flag that drapes the coffin, fire the salute before the mechanics of burial come, then fill the hole and place the headstone over the cold dead thing that was once you.

Here at the Recon Club you are *remembered*, remembered by men that will talk all night and relive all your ribald antics, your amazing balls, your supreme fuck ups, your smallest kindnesses. This is done out of love. They will curse you; they will regale your exploits with sharp wit, and they will openly cry for you with no shame, because you were one of them. You were special and now you are gone.

The club is not the most swank place on the compound. The officers have a club up at the other end, and there is a senior NCO club for the staff. The hatchet companies have their own hootch reserved for drinking. But officer or enlisted, if you are on a team, this is where you drink, play cards or shoot pool with your brother misfits. There is an abundance of alcohol. You can also get burgers here and fries, chili, that sort of thing.

The club manager is usually some shot up recon type who is either convalescing or is too injured to run anymore. There is a lot of money that flows through here, so it has to be one of us. None of us would even think of cheating the guys, money-wise. We have the best booze, the best of everything, even a slush fund so that if you ever get an R and R you can get a money assist if you are broke.

Certain teams run together, like Habu and Crusader and Indigo, and Python and Mamba. The One-Zeroes and One-Ones are inseparable. Mac and I are like that. If you make the mistake of going after Mac I will kill you with no question, no hesitation, no thinking it over. He is my twin, the other half of my being.

We spend a lot of time comparing notes about tactics, both ours and theirs. New things, like if you run into trackers, are they Indian, Yards, and how many? What did they do when you fish hooked? Did they pick up on it? Everything about the situation in the targets gets gone over here. It's kind of like a think tank except about half the tank is loaded up on something, and we all are armed. Pistols, sawed off shotguns, knives, mini grenades, you name it, it's here. It is normally loud, and depending on how many teams are out, it is usually packed.

Tonight we are holding a wake. Two teams have been virtually wiped out. Only one American and a couple of the Yards survived on one team, and a couple of members on the Bright Light that shot their way in to rescue them are down as well. The second team is gone, not a trace. They came up, gave a "team okay" after they got off the LZ, then zip, nothing for four days, no emergency radio, no distress codes, nada. They are gone, swallowed up, fini, dead.

We know that the NVA have standing orders to "impact interrogate" us if we are captured and then to execute us immediately afterward. They prefer to kill you in some horrible way to encourage the morale of their own troops. We are hurting them and tying up manpower; we are the ghosts who walk, the boogeymen.

The teams that went down were friends. The team that disappeared consisted of old guys, guys with their second tour up here. Their numbers were up, they ran into something new or unique. They were not careless or sloppy men. Worse yet, it happened in the northern A Shau and we all run it, so we are trying to piece together what happened. But there is not enough info. They just vanished.

Walt, the One-Zero, had been an old and experienced hand. I say "old" because he was in his early forties. This is a young man's game, you don't find old guys running on the ground. There are a few like Billy, the sergeant major, but he is an exception. I liked Walt. He had been a quiet, deliberate man and we both liked woodworking. I had trained as a cabinet maker before I joined the military. He had a woodworking shop back home in North Carolina. We used to talk about working with wood, the smell of the shop, what the wood felt like when you sanded and shaped it, how it felt like a living thing and creating things from it was clean and honest, a good thing. The Lord Jesus was a carpenter who took to saving souls, and we took to dispatching them, an odd parable.

There is a group of us sitting around sharing information about what we'd heard about their disappearance, and listening to Roger, the One-Zero of Mamba, who had been the Bright Light designee. Roger had been in the TOC when the team inserted and had listened to their exchanges with Covey. They got off the LZ, moved about a klick, and set up their RON. Covey came back up in the morning and flew over the target area, but got no radio transmission from the team.

Covey had flown the long axis and gunned his engines to let them know he was up and listening for them. If their radio had been down they all carried emergency radios, so someone should have come up on the air. If they had been jumped in their RON and all were dead, even the NVA would have tried to get on one of the radios to try to make us believe that they were one of the Yards, in hopes of luring in a Bright Light. This losing an entire team was weird. It only reinforces my heebie-jeebies about running out of Phu Bai. The place has a jinx on it. Better to go to Quang Tri, even if it's hotter targets.

The other team and their Bright Light had also launched out of Phu Bai. They had run the southern end of the A Shau, with a plan to establish a defensive position on an old fire base where they could watch the truck and river traffic at the junction of the trail and the river. They had gone in heavy and had gotten set up, reinforcing the decaying sand bag revetments, and tying them together into a hilltop fortification.

Old fire bases were perfect for static positions. These were the leftovers from the division-sized movements a couple of years ago, and were on prominent hilltops with steep slopes. Usually they were built around a battery of 155mm or 105mm howitzers. The trenches and bunkers were old and falling in, but if you had enough daylight you could work feverishly and make them into something that ten or twelve of you could defend. More importantly, you could go in with a mortar and heavy machine guns, which would give you some punch if it came down to a fight.

The choppers had dropped the team off all right. They secured the hilltop and the extra birds brought in additional equipment: sandbags, mortar, mortar ammunition, a .50 caliber machine gun and plenty of ammo for it, plus a couple of 60mms with even more ammo for them. They spent the next two hours working to tack a perimeter in, to get the mortar set up, and to put the ammo for it under cover. As they worked, the weather started to sock in, with heavy ground mist and rain covering the valley floor.

The thing about this type of mission is that the NVA knows you are there, no sneaking and peeking about it. As long as you are on top of that hill, anything moving in your area of observation is choke-pointed. The hope is that you get some air assets in and work them over. If that doesn't work, when they come to kick your asses off the hill they have to mass and you kill a bunch. Then the idea is to pull out, destroying the mortar and anything of value that you can't shag in a hurry to the birds. Not real sophisticated but it works. We have been having some success with it ever since Captain Psycho Butler and Les Chapman chewed up about half a thousand of Uncle Ho's children with the same tactics. You have to admire the dynamic duo. They are, at least, innovative.

The team had used the Butler tactics. Slightly after dark they started getting probed and caught a squad moving into the few bunkers they were not occupying, those that were part of the old perimeter the artillery unit had constructed. They called Moonbeam and asked for a Spectre on station, but before it could get there the weather really turned nasty and they were in deep trouble. They were getting pressed by at least a battalion, and the NVA had started dropping mortars on the top of the hill. They had obviously registered the hilltop because everything was hitting the mark. The first or second barrage had taken away their 292 antenna so the team was only able to talk to Covey on the whip, and the atmospherics were screwing that up. Around 0200 the team started dropping flares from the 81mm they took with them and the mist below them started to clear. They saw company sized elements moving into position, so they started working Spectre on them when another barrage came in and wiped out the mortar and about half the team. At that point they couldn't hold the perimeter so they tightened up and got to the high ground.

By morning everyone is wounded. Two of the three Americans are dead, and the only reason they haven't been overrun is that Spectre has made their hilltop the only safe place for a two kilometer circle. Daylight and the weather breaks and they are able to get fast movers in along with the Bright Light. The hilltop looks like some cat clawed it up. There are dead NVA mixed right in with the team.

The Bright Light was able to get the survivors out, then bag the others and lift them out as well. They blew up the .50 caliber machine gun with a thermite grenade, but they said it was no good anyway because the barrel was burned out and shrapnel had sliced through the receiver. Then the Bright Light started taking fire from what they thought was a Chinese recoilless rifle and heavy mortars, so they backed off. It was a bad mission, just too many folks and bad weather. They have caught on to what we are up to, so now when they see us moving in, they immediately come to kick our asses.

We talk with Tubby, who has been up to the hospital and talked to the surviving American, to get a clearer picture of what happened. The kid is going home; his right hand is severed at the wrist and he has lots of shrapnel wounds, plus two AK rounds in him. He is lucky to be alive.

Apparently, the surviving Yards drew back to where he was and they made a last ditch stand at his position. They got tucked in as best they could and he told the fast movers to lay it right on top of them. That broke the back of the last assault.

Wesley comes in. He is down from flying Covey and has a mini grenade in his left hand. "Hey, you heroes!" he shouts. He lifts up the grenade and the spoon flies off as he rolls it across the floor. There is instant panic and shock. Eight of us are trying to hide behind the same cigarette pack. Murphy runs into the john. One of the other guys has grabbed the chaplain, who had come to console us, and is using him for a shield. Five seconds go by. No explosion. We all start to get up. Someone has found the grenade, the pin and spoon still in place. The evil little shit had palmed another and flipped it so you heard that distinct "pling" when it hit the floor. Everyone stares at Wesley. He stares right back and yells, "You want to live forever? I can hear you ladies crying and weeping all the way over in Recon Company! Let's get drunk and send those guys off right!"

The place goes back to an even higher level of hubbub. He's right. They would do the same for us. We are all now creatures of the moment, but they will live with us forever, so they aren't dead. The chaplain is pissed, aghast that he was used as a shield. He finally gets too annoying and someone shoves a pistol in his nose and escorts him to the door, telling him to go back up on the hill and pray for souls that want redemption. I think it's Jimmie Reeves; he always gets poetic when he has a gun up your nose. He also has a reputation for being a redneck, mean drunk with a hair trigger. The sky pilot flees off into the night, his duty done.

Jimmy Johnson is playing pool and trying to use an M-67 baseball grenade as a cue ball. He is telling some new kid it's only fair since in Mississippi he is known far and wide as the best pool player in the land, so he has to use a grenade as a four to one handicap. He can't hit shit with the grenade because the spoon gets in the way. Someone suggests he cut the spoon down. There is always some technical whiz. The kid looks like he wants to be somewhere else. You either hang or you quickly find out what your tolerance for insanity is. The club manager comes out, walks over and picks up the grenade off the table and yells that is enough grenade shit in the club. "You guys wanna play with your 'go boom boom' toys, take 'em outside."

There is a huddled conference about going back and getting some M-79's and loading up some CS rounds to lob a few into the POW camp to the north of us. There are about 1500 NVA and VC POWs there and occasionally we drop a few gas rounds on them so they don't get too fat. More importantly, there are MPs there who are our natural enemies, like lions and hyenas—they are the hyenas.

We have recruited a few of the POWs as strikers. We have one on Habu. He used to be a Sapper Company Commander with the NVA. He is Bru, and testament to the fact that tribal loyalties are deeper than all the political indoctrination you can imagine.

The POW camp idea is rejected and instead we contemplate going by Gonorrhea Gulch and lobbing a few in amongst the warren of thieves and junkies just to make them miserable. I am getting really jagged and the Green Hornet I took an hour ago isn't working. I decide to slip out and go over to the little peoples' hootch.

I stumble through Recon Company. It is beautiful out. I walk down past the Yard barracks and go out to the bunker line facing the beach. There are two Bru from the Security Company in one of the bunkers with the watchtower on top. They see me and I walk over and lean up against the tower, letting myself drop to sitting.

The moon reflects on the waters of the bay and I am content to watch it ripple into shore like some silver- fringed, rolling blanket. I drift off into a dreamlike state thinking of wood and working with my hands. I hear more figures come up and there is an exchange of Bru, then gentle hands helping me up and carrying me. It's four of the little people. The Bru on the bunker had sent one of their number back to the team hootch and gotten Cuman. They told him that *Trung Si* Nick was out on the wall and needed to be looked after. He sent the team for me. They carry me back to their barracks and deposit me in a hammock, where I will spend the night. One of them will go over and find Mac and tell him where I am. I am safe here; they all smile and take turns patting me on the arm, then go back to their card game. The place smells like home to me. They are cooking something; they are always cooking something. I drift off to sleep, listening to them talk as they play some kind of poker game where the loser has to wear a helmet. The warm feeling of home compresses time and angst into a sphere that shrouds my dreams.

CHAPTER 9

Luck is a Fickle Mistress

We are in Laos. I can hear the choppers fading off into the distance. The bush goes into a brief freeze-frame and then slowly resumes its normal balance of sights and sounds. We have picked this LZ because it is so unlikely a place to set down. We don't believe that the NVA have trail or LZ watchers in the immediate area, so while the bush is still on pause we are moving and trying to put some distance between the small clearing and us. We cover our track as we go. Our plan is to try to loop towards the south and pick our way carefully into the Hotel-5 target area. Because we haven't tried to run this area for some time, we may have lulled the NVA into suppressing the density of their watches on likely LZ positions. Our target area lies on both sides of the border.

RDF (Radio Direction Finding) and imagery indicates that there is a major base and logistics center in this area to the south and east of us. We have come prepared to do a variety of missions. I have a wiretap with audio cassettes, in the event that we come across a coaxial cable or major landline, and we have special demo and silenced weapons in case we are able to isolate and take a prisoner. This is reconnaissance, much different than running the DMZ, or the A Shau valley proper. No LZ prep, we're truly trying to deceive the enemy into believing that nothing has transpired. We have birds out seeming to land when, in fact, they are embedding seismic sensors. These are long tubes with synthetic branches and foliage. They are normally air dropped so they plant themselves into the ground and activate. They work on seismic vibrations that relay a signal to a passing aircraft, or some other space cadet stuff the Air Force has. We also know from the past readings that the NVA came and looked, but found only the sensors. They would have cast around and found no sign of a team landing, so we hope that they will assume this was another such implant.

All the guns and other birds stay at the orbit point in case we get into trouble. So far, so good. We move about two hundred meters and sit down to listen again. Soon the bush returns to its normal sounds, birds, and some monkeys yowling at each other to our north. No alarm howls from them and that means good news. It is entirely possible that we have not been seen.

We squat down in a line. Xaung has been covering our back trail and I have been covering him. Bang and Bop are directly in front of me. Bang and me are covering left and right rear. Bop is right flank, next man up will be left flank, and so on until it gets up to Mac in the front with the point man. Our normal procedure is to move for twenty minutes, then sit for twenty. But the terrain and the target zone really dictate how fast you move, and how long before you change intervals.

We are lucky. We have been moving now for a couple of hours, stopping to make sure we are not followed, reading and interpreting the lay of the land. We are making our way so that we use the terrain where someone else would not normally be moving, thus preventing anyone discovering the small signs of our passing. It is slow, laborious, and hot. The forest is always a dank and wet place. The smell of decay is a rich sweet odor. Mac and I have been on indigenous rations for a week so that we don't give off that rank smell Americans carry with them. These are the small details that you are concerned with. They can lead to alerting the enemy, because just a hint sometimes leads to discovery. The Yards communicate with each other making calls that are natural in the wood; small monkey barks and songbird calls are our communication to stop, go, wait, and listen.

Mac and I are able to do some of them with a small degree of perfection. Well, Cuman says that with our limited proficiency we could probably hunt with the boys in his tribe. I am indignant at Cuman's assessment of our *Wild Kingdom* expertise, since I personally think that my male howler monkey with a hard-on grunt is sublime. No matter that it only evokes howls of laughter when I try it out on the Yards back at the launch site. They say I sound like a monkey "with bad stomach." Talk about primitive arrogance! Just because they have existed in these forests for a millennium or two, what do they know? It sounds pretty good to me. Mac says it sounds like a possum that ate some bad fish.

Move, wait. Then move again. It's a rhythm. Mac is *so* good at this. It is as if a mental cord connects him and Cuman. Move. Wait and listen. Move. Wait and listen. We are making slow but even progress. I am covering Bong and Xaung as they disguise and hide our passage. So far, we have found no sign of human intrusion, no wood cutters, no wild tribe hunters, nothing. This is good, but it won't last; although if we can walk into the target box without being discovered we might be able to ever so slowly move around and get a look-see.

By now it is almost twilight. We stop and pick a thick place to hide up overnight. For an ideal RON we will find a thicket in an area that is not right next to the ideal camping spot, one that is so thick that you don't want to walk through it after dark. This is so the bad guys don't come along and bed down next to you. That type of situation gets real heavy. We are the masters at using neutral ground. Mac comes back, gets real close to me and whispers where we are going to lay up, how we are going to lay out claymores, and where the rally point will be if we get hit. The Yards get the same information and we move into the RON just as it gets too dark to see clearly beyond six or seven feet. We set the claymores out close, with a tree trunk, berm, or something solid behind them to absorb the back blast.

We leave our rucksacks on but loosen them up, the same with all our gear. Get comfortable, but not too comfortable. We will sleep in shifts; there will always be at least a third of us awake. If you are prone to snoring, you gag yourself with a cravat. It doesn't work all the time, so there aren't a lot of people with adenoid problems in recon. The night settles in, and with it the chill. It's naturally damp down here. The first night isn't bad, but after five or six nights you are so mentally and physically exhausted that you chill easily. I carry a jungle sweater that I put on at night. It doesn't take long. Each man does it with a buddy watching out for his sector, never all at once. The night goes fairly easy. The first night is the most jagged, because you are not quite in tune, yet. There is no eight-hour beauty sleep here; you sleep in bursts, just enough time to get some alpha waves, but not too long.

Just before daylight we are all awake. As the darkness peters out, we can see for the short distance that the foliage allows. We wait and listen. Pull the claymores in; camouflage the forest floor where we have disturbed it. We are up and moving again, same as yesterday, working our way into the box. We descend about 500 meters along a lateral and stop. Mac comes back to tell me that we have a high speed trail ahead. The trail looks like it is traveled fairly often but not a heavy volume of traffic. The team positions itself so we can cross: put out flankers; get a few across; spread flankers on that side; make a box. Then they come back, signal, and I pull up stakes with the rear, and camouflage our crossing with Bong and Xaung. Mac and I have a short conversation about maybe finding a spot where we can rig an ambush and grab a prisoner. But, we will need time to find the right spot and a place we can extract from. The trees aren't that thick, which means we can blow an LZ. The trail is a communications trail so there will probably be runners on it. We agree to move ahead and see if we can gather more intel because we are just inside the upper northwest corner of our target box.

After moving in about 100 yards, we sit and listen. Mac gets Covey on the air, gives him a team okay and tells him about the trail. It appears they don't know we are here so we want him to stay out of the air above our box. No sense advertising.

Again we move. It's been about four hours since we found the first trail and we have covered maybe a kilometer. We have just crossed our second trail, where we are able to get a boot count, and there appears to be cart tracks or the big balloon tire reinforced bicycles the NVA use to haul equipment. Recent too, the impressions are not more than 24 hours old. They are moving south, deeper into the target area. The tracks are deep so both men and the vehicles are laden with equipment. Voices. They seem to be about a couple hundred yards to our southeast.

We move in that direction, very slowly and deliberately. We can hear them every once in a while but not enough to make out the words. The tone isn't of alarm, but rather of people involved with a task. We haven't gone far when we hear a truck engine start up and the noise of metal on metal and more shouts. We move up and soon are looking down an open slope from the edge of fairly thick undergrowth. Off to the right we can make out figures moving, but no definite shape. There must be a road below because we can hear the truck down there with them. Suddenly the truck, or at least the top third of it, drives out of the brush and stops, obscuring our vision. It is definitely on a road bed. There is an NVA standing in the back with his shirt off; he calls to someone behind the truck. Cuman is listening and tells Mac that it is a party repairing a section of road which has been washed out. There is a sergeant down there yelling at the troops to do it right or they will be here all day.

We decide to move down a little closer, so we carefully pick our way down until we find a spot where we can actually see them. They appear to have no security and we can vaguely make out the shape of a Csepel, the Soviet version of a '58 Ford, ton and a half truck.

Working with it is a crew of about 14 privates and a sergeant putting in a road bed where the rain has caused a landslide and washed out the roadway. The bloody thing is marvelous, a real piece of work. By the way they have laid it out, looping here along the hill, it looks like part of the natural watershed. I bet they repair this every time they get a heavy rain. The road bed should be located up another 50 yards where the runoff won't wash the hillside out. But, then you would see it from the air.

As we watch, about ten bicycles laden with 50 pound rice bags come out of the forest to the right and turn past the truck toward us. Mac has the camera out as the troops will pass about 25 yards beneath us. There is a cut-off to our left. He takes about eight pictures of the truck, and then another series of shots of the bicycles and their porters. There are three soldiers traveling with them. They are carrying the Chinese Type 56 version of the AK with the rust brown, plastic stock and fore grip, and each has an AK vest.

All are dressed in blue-green khaki with pith helmets. They move down the trail to our east, and we continue to watch the work party for about another 20 minutes. They load up on the truck, throwing their picks and shovels and baskets they use to haul dirt into the back with a clatter. Then it, too, passes our position and moves off to the east.

We have stumbled onto some very serious traffic. All the soldiers were regulars, though the work crew had green khaki fatigues so they are probably from two different outfits. This is not uncommon but, more importantly, it points to their being part of a larger complement of troops in the area. We listen to the truck as it labors off, winds for awhile to the northeast, then works it's way back south.

They are about four or five hundred meters to our east- southeast when the truck stops again. This time it is joined by the sounds of two or more truck engines starting up. They stay in the same general area for about ten minutes then all three shut down.

Mac and I look at each other and we are both thinking the same thing. There is a truck park over there, and probably a way station. They are dotted all along the trail. Some are simply huts and cleared areas under the canopy where they can't be seen. Others are more elaborate with underground parking. Either way, we want to get a look at it.

We still have daylight. The question is do we go look now and rush, or hole up another night up-slope and come back to watch the trail early in the morning to see if we get a pattern. There were about a thousand pounds of rice that went by. That will feed a bunch of Uncle Ho's children. We opt for a RON site that will put us back here early enough so we can watch the trail for a couple of hours. Then we will move down and see if we can find the truck park in the early afternoon when it is *pac* time, or we'll try to follow along parallel with another bicycle convoy. As lax as these dudes are, they will probably stop and talk to any trail security they see along the way. That will make it easier for us to move. Damn! I wish we had brought some NVA khaki and a couple of AKs. We could have our point in them, which would give us an edge if we walked up on an OP (observation post) on our side of the slope.

We find a nice briar bush thicket and lay up for the evening. We are about 200 yards from the road. About 0100 we hear two or three trucks moving on the road, coming from the west and moving east. They stop at the same point the others did yesterday. They must have a truck park over there and an engineer outfit that repairs this section of road. They apparently haven't a clue we are in here, so we head back to our thicket for a few more hours.

Before dawn, we check in with Covey and have him do a relay on where we are going to try to move, telling him to make sure we get air if we get into trouble. We move down to where we were yesterday and watch the trail. After about an hour, a young NVA comes down the trail. He looks like he is about 16 years old. He is swatting bushes with a switch as he walks, looking like a kid on a dirt road anywhere just lollygagging along. Except this one has an AK slung over his back and is wearing the same green khakis as the work crew. We take his picture as he passes. Oh, my little friend, if your sergeant saw you walking along that way with your head up your ass, you would not be so happy.

We are so lucky. They still have no idea we are here. Fifteen minutes after the kid goes by, two guys walk up the trail from the east. These two, however, are not loafing. They are checking the road and the sides of the trail. They are all business and we will be in trouble if they spot us. Everyone gets down real low and tries not to look at them. The Yards call it not looking at the monkey, but at the tree. The monkey is still there, but you look at the area he is in and not directly at him. After about five minutes they are out of sight around the bend. Okay, that means they have a regular security outfit that walks a set distance, either one direction all day with a return in the afternoon or a couple of times a day if it's shorter. They didn't get off the road, so that's good. We can parallel the road to the truck park. We just have to be careful about trail watcher stations.

Now all this sounds simple on paper, but in reality you have a great big lump in your throat and your ass is so tight you couldn't drive a needle up it with a sixteen-pound sledgehammer. There isn't any relaxing your guard out here, because the smallest slip and you're dead, or if you're lucky, just in a world of trouble and about to be dead.

Another five bicycles come by and they are weighed down with either artillery rounds or 122mm rockets, judging by the tubes lashed to their bamboo reinforcing.

This group has no escorts and is moving slowly and easily. We let them pass and then pick up and start moving parallel to them. The ridge stays the same, with the road about the same distance down from the slope on which we are walking. We occasionally see, through breaks in the foliage, the bicycle convoy slightly ahead of us intent on pushing their load, no looking up or enjoying the scenery. They probably have to make so many kilometers a day, so it's a job, not a walk in the forest. All that food yesterday had to be going somewhere, and that ammo has a home as well. We know they are building up to something over here and it spells bad times for someone down the road. We get about halfway to where we estimate the truck park to be when Mac holds us up. He signals three men at 50 meters, walking, and gives the direction. Not good, they are moving across our front and going uphill.

I slide up to him and we lie close enough so he can tell me they just saw three guys with AKs going uphill about 30 yards to our left front. I am looking up-slope when I catch some movement up in the tree tops. I look at it closely and see a 12.5mm position on a platform about 50 feet up in the canopy camouflaged really well. I nudge Mac. He sees it too, and so does Cuman. We are all looking around in the trees now, and pretty soon Thua points out two more. Uh oh, base camp. Something major is down in here and it isn't just a truck park.

Now that we have stopped we can see that there are clear lanes through the brush in front of us. The lower branches have been cleared up to about six feet from the floor in some places. This can only mean bunkers. The cleared brush is for firing lanes, sighted from the apertures on the bunkers. You won't see them until you burst out of the bush thinking you are on a trail and suddenly you run into a machine gun.

We back off through the trees and start working our way higher. We need to move very slowly. It will take us a number of days to work our way around the whole thing, but there is an easier way. If we can pull it off, we can grab a prisoner. We figure that the green khaki bunch is probably a permanent party here and the blue khaki bunch is a larger unit passing through.

After a couple hours of moving real cautiously, we get back up-slope and, on the way, we find another high-speed trail like the very first one we found. What's better, we find a place that is masked from those guns, a place where we could get strings in and get extracted. We can set up on this trail and grab the first likely green-clad lad that comes panting down the trail. More than likely he will be a runner, but we might get lucky and get an officer. These are communication trails away from the logistical trails that get bombed. Political commissars, tactical officers, runners, paymasters, etc. use these trails. If he is a high-ranker he will have an escort with him. The NVA have a complete traffic system down here to move their troops, logistics, and ash and trash details. The only thing missing are traffic lights and signs. But they have the equivalent of signs, if you know what to look for. Simple things like a couple of cut bamboo lengths at the side of a trail saying, "Go this way after dark" or a triangle of small twigs arranged at an intersection, that means the trail is booby-trapped. There is even graffiti sometimes, carved into the tree trunks by some bored rice burner, on his way south. Eldon found one once that said, "Born in the North to die in the South."

We look the trail over for 100 yards, not too far from our extraction point. It has plenty of boot tracks and some are only an hour or so old. This is a communications trail, probably linking the integrated parts of the base camp with the satellites. We find a series of "s" bends and start to figure out how to set the ambush. To keep it quiet, we will go for no more than three. Mac will take the one we want and shoot him in the legs with the silenced 9mm, and I will kill the other two with the other silenced 9mm. We will jump the prisoner, tourniquet him, shoot him full of morphine, and run like hell for the extraction LZ. We call up Covey to tell him our plan and that we will need the choppers on station before we grab our duck. The challenge is that we want to shoot him to immobilize him and then get out quick. We are too far out for those choppers to be at an orbit point too long, so we have to make someone use this trail when *we* are ready.

We come up with a workable solution. We will have them act like they are inserting a team to the south of where we think the bulk of the camp is. You can bet your ass someone important is going to come down here to see what's being done, or at least, important messages will be streaking up this trail. They are smart enough by now that they stay off the radio. I wish we could find a commo line and tape a day or so of traffic. That would be better than a prisoner. But so far, there have been no obvious lines. Sometimes they actually lay them in bamboo pipes underground. There is a coaxial cable down here somewhere. The size of this camp, coupled with the overhead gun platforms and the truck park we suspect to be in here, suggest something more than a regimental hidey hole. Problem is, can we last long enough to find the cable? It would take us a month to crawl around this place and, inevitably, some private out to relieve himself would be our undoing. Besides you have to be real careful with a wiretap; they have guys that walk the line every day checking it for load loss on the line. One slip putting it on and someone's gonna come around from Hanoi Bell. As tempting as it is, Mac is right, a prisoner or even two is a better solution.

It's late so we plan the thing for the next morning. We are going to have about 40 minutes from the time traffic gets in the area until we have to come out, prisoner or no prisoner. We hit the jackpot with this target. If we grab the right guy, we can get some good intelligence out of him when he's interrogated. Stick with the plan: shoot him in the legs, or foot so you don't hit an artery. He can't run off; shock and pain make him easy to handle, and he is easier to interrogate if he is wounded.

It all boils down to gas. If we leave the choppers orbiting around too long as decoys, we run out of fuel and don't go home. Besides we have confirmed what they suspected, there is a whole bunch of these liberators running around in this area.

Worst-case scenario, the Air Force can load up those lumbering, flying, warehouses they call B-52s and scoot over here. They can drop enough ordnance on this little health spa to level some major terrain features, and be reasonably sure they got a return on the taxpayers' investment. This is after we are gone, of course.

We find a safe area to RON, away from where we want to ambush. Again we hear someone moving on the trail a couple of times before dark, and after we move into the RON we see faint glimpses of lights through the trees. They must be using it at night with a flashlight or a carbide lamp to illuminate their way. Another night in paradise, but this one is different because tomorrow we are going home, or we are going to be in a fight for our lives and wishing we had picked door number three.

We are up early and get Covey on the horn. The birds are about 45 out, so we get into position. They are going to come in with fast movers and guns and work over the false insertion point, and then send a few birds in like a team is getting dropped off. We relay where the guns are and tell him to make sure the choppers stay away from our area.

The birds are about ten minutes out of the orbit point when the fast movers and Covey get over station and start working over the false insertion point. The scream of the jets and a couple of sets of lumbering Spads are the backdrop to the bomb strikes. Their concussions are almost continuous as Covey lets the boys in blue work the area over. There is a secondary explosion and then another; they must have hit an ammo dump or a truck. When Thua signals three coming up the trail, everyone tenses. Mac is next to a fairly large teak or some kind of hardwood tree and I am slightly below him against another giant.

I will see them first, and hopefully I can make out shoulder or collar ranks; or, if one of them has a courier bag, I will target the two that don't. There is enough separation between Mac and me that I can make a hand signal—one, two or three so he knows which one to shoot in the legs. The Yards know if I miss my targets, kill the other two. Then we snatch and grab our victim and run like hell through Bong and Xaung, who are our rear security facing the direction of the LZ we intend to use.

Covey calls in that there isn't anyone on the extraction point as of 30 minutes ago and no sign of the opposition there. We are going out by STABO, so everyone is already in a harness with the leg straps buckled. I see our quarry; they are about 40 yards away, and no rank, but two are obviously young and raw, trailing slightly behind one who looks to be about ten years older.

I make a "one" signal to Mac and he nods. We have already decided we will wait until they are directly abreast of me before I cap the escorts. The two are real young and carry themselves like privates in any army. I glance back at Mac and wait. We have already agreed that, no matter their ranks, I will take the forward one first and the back one last. We are lucky the one we want is in the lead, so I don't have to shoot past him.

They get closer. None of the trio is talking, just walking fast. The first guy is intent on the trail, like he is thinking about something. He gets past me and is about four steps from Mac, when I step around the tree and raise my gun it in one fluid motion.

The first guy is about six feet from the end of the silencer. I am looking right at him as he realizes the awful truth and I pump two rounds in the center of his chest.

I don't watch him fall because I am swinging to the left, slightly, to take the one behind him. At the same time that I am lining up on the third guy in the group, I hear a "pfff" from Mac's gun. My two shots on my second target take him a bit low in the right chest. He exhales a bloody froth, and as he slumps to the ground his AK falls from his grasp. His hands reach for the gun as he lays on his side looking at me. He sighs and says something that sounds like "brother" in Vietnamese when I shoot him in the head. I check them quickly; both are dead.

Behind me, I hear a sound like someone slamming a side of beef with a hammer and turn around. The one we want is down and out, a hole in his lower right leg and bleeding from a cut on the side of his head where Mac has slapped him with his pistol. He lies in a crumpled heap. Mac and I are all over him. I strip his belt and sidearm, both good signs that he is an officer. He also has a set of binoculars and a canvas case, which also gets tossed into the pile. We rip through his pockets, look around his waist, and secure him with plastic handcuffs. Before starting first aid, we get him off the trail. The round hasn't hit an artery so we apply a compress and carefully shoot him up with morphine, then tie a cravat around his mouth as a gag. Three of the Yards drag the other two off the trail and strip them naked. The two were carrying rucksacks and the Yards throw everything inside them and sling their weapons, while a fourth Yard takes a branch and covers the scuff in the trail. There wasn't much blood; in seconds the trail is clean. The two bodies are stuffed under a bramble and we are moving.

I have the prisoner with Thua and we are carrying him between us. He is dead weight because he is out cold.

When I notice he is continuing to bleed, we have to stop and put a tourniquet on his leg. Mac is on the radio and the choppers are on the way. We can hear the fast movers and the air assets working over the area where the diversion was planned. They are starting to get return fire from the tree platforms as they work their way over towards us. The sounds of the jets and the exploding ordnance are covering our movement, but this works against us as well because we can't hear anything moving until we get right on top of it. In a case like this, we still have the element of surprise; they won't expect to run into anybody on the ground not on their chow roster. That will give us just enough time to smash them into casualties and get to the LZ.

A pair of Cobra gunships flashes by to our front and lets loose a barrage of rockets where I think the LZ is. Jesus, I hope no one is there ahead of us. We get to the extraction point only minutes ahead of the pickup choppers. I loosen the tourniquet and check the prisoner. He has stopped bleeding, but I cut his pant leg clear, pour some water on the wound, put another compress on and tighten it. The first bird comes in and five strings drop down. Mac yells down that the choppers will have a hard time picking up a heavy load, so I motion Thua, the prisoner, Cuman and two of our heaviest Yards to go out on that one.

They are up and away, and within minutes the second bird comes in and takes Mac, two Yards, and me. The strings tighten up and I pull my crotch straps away so I don't get squeezed, all the while looking around. I keep my gun ready in my right hand as the chopper peaks power and we lift out. The fast movers start working over the ridge. Hopefully, the NVA will think that it is a target of opportunity and for the next four or five days they will be busy looking for a team that isn't there.

Snap links hook us together so we don't spin around. I pull my crotch straps down so I can sit better. It is blessedly cool up here and the tension leaves my body. We are going home, and we have a prisoner, which means stand down and a cash reward for everyone. All the Yards will get the equivalent of one month's pay and we might be able to wrangle a trip to Taipei on the CCK flight. I am one happy son-of-a-bitch and so is Mac. Yelling over the wind, we try to talk to each other as we have ended up almost face-to-face. We grin like fools.

The other chopper is about a mile ahead of us. We are still grinning like two Cheshire cats when we see what looks like a rucksack break loose and plummet towards the ground. Then it grows arms and legs and we realize someone has slipped out of his harness and fallen to his death. After 20 minutes, the choppers put down at an old firebase and we both run over to find out which one fell. There are our four Yards. No prisoner. End of trip to Taipei, no bonus, and we are going to have to explain what happened. Mac and I look at each other in dismay, with the realization that it is our fault. We know better. I think it is standing policy to always have an American with a prisoner. If there isn't a policy, there will be. Sending the live, kicking, cash bonus out with the boys to even the load is no excuse.

Cuman's only answer is, "*Tahan* no need bonus! *Tahan* no need stand down! *Tahan* need only kill VC!" A big chunk of his right cheek is hanging loose and looks like shit. We put a compress on it while we talk to him.

Apparently, the prisoner had come to and realized where he was. He managed to get the cravat gag loose, and the swinging motion under the helicopter slammed him and Cuman together. Since he was handcuffed and bound he hung on with his teeth to the nearest thing he could find, unfortunately, Cuman's face. Cuman punched him until he let go then reached up and cut his rope. Not that you could blame Cuman, reactions that saved you in a firefight sometimes worked against you. Besides, this was a guy who'd seen his wife and three kids butchered by the VC.

We saddle up and get the birds aloft, floating dreamily back to Quang Tri. Bad luck on our part, however, from our observations, we should be able to lay out a map. That will allow the Air Force to come back and administer an Arc Light enema.

The birds set down as dusk falls. I am totally relaxed now, and just want to bathe and grab a cold beer. We do a quick debrief with Pappy and a cursory look through the captured material, enough to see it looks like good stuff. In all honesty, I wouldn't know good stuff from bad as far as linguistic interpretations, but I see a tactical map with markings on it, and no porno pictures.

We had bagged documents in the canvas case and in the rucksacks. The contents later proved that there were two divisions in the area. Saigon suspected that they were getting ready for a major offensive. No shit, Batman. The papers we took off the two privates proved that, in fact, they were brothers, both from the Haiphong area. That rang a bell in my head, for it explained what the one said as he was dying. I felt bad about that, but not bad enough that I wouldn't have done it again. If we'd had time we would have brought their bodies out so that someone could autopsy them to see what kind of physical shape they were in, how they had been eating, if they had malaria, intestinal parasites, etc.

The prisoner who took the long plunge was a senior lieutenant with the coveted "American Killer" decoration. It was found in his little soldier packet they all carry, along with pictures of his family. I never looked at that stuff; too close to home. That's why I carried a picture of John Wayne around with me, signed "Love, Dad." Let them figure that one out if they capped me. Among the lieutenant's other effects we found a Zippo lighter engraved with the name of a Spec-4 in the 101st who had been killed in 1968.

Tomorrow is another day. The best part will be telling Captain Manes that Cuman cut the prisoner loose because he was trying to impress him, so he could be just like *Dai Uy* Manes. Yeah, Cuman wants to prove that he is just like the *Dai Uy*, you know, tough, far-sighted, the hawkeyed killer elite. Have to be careful pissing on Larry's shoes like that, though; if he thinks you're messing with him he could hurt you.

We are in the hootch discussing our good fortune. Because we are at the end of the schedule, we will be going back to Da Nang. No Bright Light, unless someone gets their tit in a wringer. They are going to launch a team in the morning if the weather holds, and as soon as they either get shot out or manage to get off the LZ, we will release and go to the airfield. They have three teams here, plus us, so we are the reserve reserve. I can't wait to get back to Da Nang. Tomorrow is steak night and I intend to be sitting there as they come off the barbeque. I also intend to be well-oiled.

Mac and I can't believe it; we actually lasted in the target area for a couple of days. That has to be a record. Usually, it is shoot your way in, stir them up like a pack of rabid wolverines, and make them talk on their little Peking radios so that the Air Force can locate the signals. Then shoot your way out and come back here to see if you have any leaking holes you might have overlooked during the adrenalin jag.

This was almost like real recon. I could get spoiled doing this. I fired five rounds the entire time out there and they were through the can. Usually I am sixty pounds lighter from all the stuff I have fired, thrown, cooked off, or set fire to, to stay alive for a measly hour or so in the DM targets. If this kept up I might take to running around out there naked, with only a tomahawk and a squirt gun.

Mac shakes me out of my daydreaming with the news that Manes thinks we did so well that he might move me to a One-Zero slot. Not good, not good at all. We start plotting on what to tell them when we get back. We will tell them that I was the one on the strings with the prisoner and that I forgot to tie him in or something really inane. After all, I am supposed to be dimwitted. He is a captain; we need to make him think that moving me into a position of responsibility could ruin him. Nah that won't work, he doesn't have a career. Whatever it is it has to interfere with his leisure time or, better yet, ensures his having to write a report about it or something. That's the one thing that smiling Larry hates: writing reports.

Something like this, where the blabbermouths are all whistling and congratulating each other on the airwaves about having a real live NVA snatched from his bed by commandos, is probably all over Saigon by now. They are probably sending the General's jet north to Da Nang to pick up the prisoner and Captain Chuckles to take them back to Saigon. News like this doesn't have a lid on it, neither will the unfortunate conclusion. This might work in our favor, since something like this is probably a potential 400 page report, plus appendices and indexes. If I am the root cause of that he will gladly leave me on the team, just in case I do something else that would force him to write another report.

This sounds crazy to a layman or to someone with ambitions beyond breathing for another day, but suffice it to say that when you are lucky, *you stay with a proven formula*. We have the whole thing worked out. In fact, we start to have some fun with the idea, like maybe we will tell Manes I was roughing up the prisoner and stealing his watch when I let go of him in order to hang on to the watch. Or maybe that I insisted on tying him in with a knot I had learned in the Sea Scouts, called a sliding granny, because I forgot the extra rig we carried for prisoners. I had to use an old length of rotted rope that we found out there because I needed the room in my rucksack for candy bars or, better yet, beer.

We are yukking it up and having a good time with the whole disaster, when I get this feeling, call it bush ESP, that something isn't right. We both get it, because we stop talking at the same time and start rubber-necking into the shadows. That's when we notice Budrow in the comer of the hootch. He's sitting there drinking a beer, smiling at us like a possum that has stumbled across a three-day-old road kill. He snickers in that way only senior NCOs can with both scom and derision.

"You two ladies better hope that Manes never has a reason to ask me for a favor, or I might be tempted to tell him the truth. The only thing that is saving your asses is the fact that if they give dimwit here a team," he points to me with the hand holding the beer, "that would mean that one of you would be here twice as much as you two are now. And, that would give me twice as much gas, as your presence here disturbs my tranquility now." He heaves himself out of the chair and finishes his beer, tossing it into the trash can before heading out the screen door into the dark. His voice floats back to us in a cackle, "I may just have to start charging you money for my silence."

CHAPTER 10

Blue Eyes

We are in the isolation unit at the upper end of the compound. All of the operations that would normally launch from the Phu Bai site are being run directly from the TOC at Da Nang. RT Habu and RT Indigo are both crammed into the isolation compound and we both have targets that are west of Da Nang. Mac returns from the TOC and says that we are saddling up for a Bright Light mission with Dave "Dirty Dick" Daugherty. We will be going after another team that had tried to insert earlier this morning and had gotten chewed up, losing three aircraft.

One of the choppers had gone into the river that snakes through the highland escarpments that comprise the leading edge of the target zones. We will be launching in about 30 minutes, as soon as the birds that made it out refuel and rearm. We grab our gear and make last minute adjustments, like throwing out food packets and replacing them with extra bandoleers of ammunition, extra grenades, and claymores. Everyone grabs an extra B-40 rocket. There is nothing like the Russian B-40 or RPG-2 when it comes to slam power in heavy contact. It's a simple dry propellant rocket fired from a tube that looks like a water pipe with a handle on it. The whole thing is modeled after the WWII German *Panzerfaust*. It is simple, easy to operate, and we have plenty of munitions for it thanks to recovered caches and captured war stocks.

Bong is the new rocket carrier. He is the best, next to Bop, with the weapon. I watch as he readjusts his load on his STABO harness so he can manage the B-40 as well as his CAR-15. Cuman, the team leader of the Yards, and Thua, his Zero-Two, are making sure that everyone has what they need to fight our way in. Cuman is fussing around Mac and me, making sure we haven't forgotten our dicks or something essential, until Mac says, "Let's go," and everyone gears up, shouldering their rucksacks.

The rucksacks aren't for carrying sleeping gear and rations. They have what we need most; that is, all the extra ammo, grenades, mines, and rockets, for shooting your way in and out. We'd pack a bloody nuke device if they would give us one, something, anything, that would give us the punch we are going to need.

We walk out of the isolation area followed by Dave and his team. We are both heavy teams, with ten men each, heavy also in our armament. Everyone has a CAR-15 except me. I am carrying a Russian RPD machine gun with the barrel sawed off just in front of the gas port. I have 1000 rounds of ammunition for it in preloaded drums. The Russians use a non-disintegrating belt made up of metal with half moon-shaped links, so you can reload the belts, unlike the M-60 where the belt comes apart as the round is ejected.

Every man on the team, in addition to their own ammo and equipment, has an extra 50-round belt for the gun and 40 rounds of AK ammo in case we really get screwed and have to reload. I like the gun for missions like this. It's compact, half the weight of an M-60 and you can rock and roll with the puppy. In close quarters it will chop a platoon up and break the back of an assault lickety-split. With the barrel sawed off, it shoots a green-yellow flame out the front that is terrifying to the guys you're shooting at, and reassuring to you if you are knock-kneed terrified like I am.

We go out the inner gate to the PSP pad where the helicopters will come in and pick us up. About half of the air package is there from this morning, four slicks, and four Cobras with their rotors turning. We hear the sound of more choppers coming in from the west. I look up and see five more coming in, two of which, a Cobra and a slick, are smoking and slewing trying to stay aloft. The gunship makes it as far as the outer wire and crumples into the ground, breaking off a rotor as the skids collapse. The launch crew and Fish Smith head their way with the fire extinguishers and start to pull the two crewmen out as the engines wind out and the rotor freezes up.

The remaining slicks come in with the one that was smoking in the lead. As they land, we all drop our gear and run over to start helping what's left of the team out of the slicks. Two of the slicks are the command and control with one having the chase medic onboard. The chase medic has two little people onboard that are seriously wounded.

The bird is shot to pieces. The windscreen is gone on the right side and the pilot is dead; his body tipped against the door, eyes wide with that surprised look the dead have. It looks like a machine gun or a whole bunch of AKs had chewed up his side of the aircraft. The co-pilot is busy shutting the bird down and doesn't realize that his partner is dead until we start to haul him and the other three team members out of the aircraft. In the back there are the two little people and the team's One-One, all wounded. The One-One is able to move under his own power. Miraculously, the gunner on the left side is unscathed. The other gunner is shot to ribbons and dead as a Christmas duck.

The whole inside of the aircraft looks and smells like a charnel house, blood everywhere and pieces of bone, intestines and part of the gunner's brains are stuck to the walls and pads on the ceiling. The machineguns are smoking and the smell of kerosene and urine and feces is overpowering. It's amazing how much waste your body voids when you die. They don't show that in the Hollywood versions. We pull the wounded out and medics are there trying to patch and save, then get them away from the aircraft, which is still smoking. Someone douses the inside and the engine ports with a fire extinguisher, getting white foam on the dead gunner. He looks like a macabre Christmas ornament with white frosting.

More people are streaming down to help and we start to pull the dead gunner and the pilot out. I pull on the door and it comes off in three pieces, it's so riddled with bullet holes. I reach inside and unbuckle the pilot's straps. The left shoulder strap is shredded and he falls over limp and leaking. We get him out and about 15 meters away, while three guys pull the gunner free and lay him beside his buddy. Both still have their flight helmets on. The bird doesn't torch, but it is toast. This baby isn't ever going into the sky again.

I get back over to Mac, where the One-One is sitting in a jeep from the TOC. He's groggy from the morphine and has two wounds from an AK in his left leg. His face is pocked with pepper shrapnel. He's hanging onto Mac and telling him that the One-Zero and two Yards were in the bird that went in near the river. He doesn't know if anyone got out. The chopper took a rocket just behind the engine and the tail boom broke off just before they cartwheeled into the trees on the bank.

The slicks had been almost side by side coming out, just a matter of luck that the lead ship got the rocket and not his. He had seen his One-Zero hanging onto a Yard, and trying to fight the centrifugal force to jump free before they hit the trees on the river bank. They were only 30 feet or so above the water. He is telling Mac that he saw splashes in the river. It could have been them, or it could have been big chunks of the aircraft. Then a machine gun forward and to the right of the bird, had opened up from below, and chewed the length of the bird he was on, killing the pilot and the gunner. He had been lying down on the floor, so all the rounds hit above him. A couple of rounds had been low and knifed through the fuel cells in the floor wounding him. He had fuel all over him, mixed with his and the door gunner's blood. Good kid, trying to be concise and give us impact information, and wanting to believe his One-Zero and some of the rest of the team made it.

The co-pilot is in the first stages of shock and the other crews are grouped around him, trying to get his helmet off. He keeps swatting at them. He can't accept that his right-seater is dead and keeps telling nobody in particular that we should go make sure that Steve is alright, "He had been hit pretty bad, you know."

The launch site commander and the TOC people signal for the choppers to shut down and the crews start going over their birds to see if they are flyable. The medics give the co-pilot a shot, and he sits mannequin-like as they drive off with him and the other wounded. The team One-One is yelling that he is fine to go back in and not to leave without him as they cart him off and up to the surgery. He keeps trying to get out of the jeep, until Graham, one of the commo guys, cradles him in a bear hug like you would a hurt kid. Graham is a big man and so black that he is blue; it is like being wrapped in the Congo.

Fish comes down with a big dump loader that he had stolen from somewhere and carries the wreckage of the slick over to where the Cobra sits looking like a broken child's toy. Soon we are bustling again. The slicks are getting refueled and the guns make the run over to 80th to re-arm. Mac, Dave and I are over by the edge of the field where they have a jeep set up so we can listen to the Covey that is still orbiting the crash sites. From him, we learn that they have at least two people on the emergency radios, one of which is a Yard. Every time Covey makes a pass near the downed slick they are taking automatic ground fire from at least two heavy machineguns.

The Launch NCO comes back and wants us all up at the TOC, so the four of us go up to the TOC, leaving the Yards. They sit down on their rucksacks and try to grab as much shade as they can next to a couple of the trucks. The bodies of the pilot and the gunner are still lying there, and I see Cuman take a poncho and go over with Bop to cover them up. No sense looking at dead bodies; makes you cognizant of your own mortality. Dave has a team of Rhade, and as we go by them they are all fingering their Buddhas and popping them in and out of their mouths, like "Oh shit, this is going to be a bad one."

We get out of the jeep and go inside where the TOC is alive with the radios talking to Covey and the air packages. Very faintly we can hear the emergency radios talking back to him. I ask Mac if he knows who is flying Covey and he says it's Wesley. That is a relief; at least we have someone upstairs who has had plenty of time being the dummy on the ground.

The pace is quick because Covey needs to start vectoring any survivors to an area where, if possible, they can link up and hold out until help arrives. Before he starts dropping bombs from the air packages to keep the bad guys off them, he has to determine where they are and if there are others that may be alive, but haven't got a radio. On the other side, they are working quickly, because the enemy wants to capture the guys that survived and they are pushing hard. Covey is using his Willie Pete rockets to keep them off, but it's more show than effect. He also is going to reach his fuel cut-off point in about two hours.

The Launch Site Commander and his Senior NCO come over and we start laying out what we know from the survivors and Covey, about how many we think are alive, where the birds are, and what we have for a reception committee. I never liked these two assholes, and I like them even less now. The Site Commander is a careerist and a pretty boy and has a reputation for putting teams in when he doesn't have enough birds to get them out if more than one gets into trouble. His NCO is an E-8 that I wouldn't use to wipe his own ass with, a real ass kisser. The feelings between us are mutual. I am sure that they know we often take Quang Tri targets, which are in a hotter area of operations, because we don't trust them.

The LSC starts telling us how we are going to go in when Mac drawls that if he is going in as the One-Zero then he can do it his way, but as long as it's our asses, he can shut the fuck up and give us what we ask for when we ask for it, because those are our guys out there. The LSC takes a big gulp of air and gets this pissed-off, "You can't talk that way to me" look. We hear a quiet voice behind us ask him would he please come over there. I glance over my shoulder and see Colonel Donnie, El Supremo himself. He takes the officer outside to have a "chat."

Now it's just sergeants, so I get my two cents in. "We are going to need everything that can flap in the air," I direct this at the launch NCO. "That means no more missions until we get in and get out. And just so you know we are serious, someone from Recon Company is going to be in this TOC the entire time." We already knew Manes would be up before we launched, and we would make sure he knew we wanted him to ride herd on the assets.

Covey comes back up and says he has three round eyes at one location, and one of the Yards with another American at another, but the American is wounded and the Yard can only repeat the team name and that he is okay. Covey has located them by flying a cross-stitch pattern over where he thought they were, and having the Yard say "mark" on his radio when he was right over top of them.

He is ordering up the air packages out of Gunfighter in Da Nang, and we eventually have four sets of fast movers and four sets of Spads. We are going in on both sides of the river. Our team is going to take the west side and search for the downed slick, then move up to where the Yard and the wounded American are.

Dave is going to take the east side, go in on the two birds there and attempt to get the three Americans from the slick crew out. So far no one knows if any of the Cobra crew made it, or if the wounded American with the Yard, is the One-Zero or a crewman. Plus we have missing Yards. We have a possible thirteen people on the ground and the bad guys are hunting them.

Covey begins to work the area over with on-call air assets, hitting all the approaches to the area in the hope he can keep the NVA from flooding in with more troops. We find out that the team was going in on a prisoner snatch in an area where they thought a Regimental Headquarters was located. The air packages had reported that there were flak corridors to the east of the target, so Covey is avoiding that area because a 57mm had opened up on both him and the slicks when they did the insertion.

Manes comes in and we brief him on what is going on. You've got to love Larry. Despite his having run recon back in the stone age of 1968, his depth of experience is our bulwark against the idiots. He is short and compact, as befits his nickname as the world's largest midget. Fiercely loyal and tough as nails, we love him. Still, no one wants to drink with him because when nursing a bad hangover he has a tendency to take exception to weird things like saying "Good Morning" or some other deeply insulting slur.

Right now he is all business. He tells Mac and Dave and me that there are two teams who have their Yards out on stand down, but there are Americans here, reasonably sober, who want to go along. Additionally, he informs us that he has two other full teams gearing up and moving into isolation to be our Bright Light and a company from the Hatchet Force is gearing up to reinforce.

We don't want the Hatchet Force going in with us, at least not initially. It takes too many birds and they aren't used to reacting with the speed we can, but we want them ready to go in case this turns into a major pissing match. In that case, we are going to need the Marines and their H-34s, so they start ordering up additional air packages in case they have to lift the hatchet mob to come save our worthless hides. Our plan is for the two additional recon teams to come in on-call, if we can get to the downed birds, grab any survivors, and need help to get the bodies of the dead out. Also, if we run into more than we can handle with air support and what we are carrying they will come in and secure a hilltop about 400 meters from our insertion point, turn it into a redoubt and we will fight our way to them. The Hatchet Force will reinforce us all if we get to that point, or insert to the west and make a bigger target to bleed off some of the NVA and take the pressure off us. At some point we will have to chew the NVA up bad enough that they cut their losses and back off. This is all grandiose, and will probably get us nowhere because getting that many aircraft and people organized is a complex operation. As it is, we have three heavy teams of about 30 people in the bull pen as far as a ground force going in.

Manes assures us that he will watch the launch site so someone doesn't start playing "further my career" with our asses hanging by a thread. We go out and find four guys from two other teams geared up and ready to go. Mac and I take two. One is another experienced One-Zero with a One-Two who hasn't been on the ground yet. What the hell, if you are going to bust your cherry this is as good a mission as any to learn on.

Dave takes the other two. Now we are 24 people. That will give us twelve on each side of the river. We are going to need the extra brawn if we are going to muscle the dead into body bags and get them out. The heat and adrenaline sucks up your energy at an alarming rate. And two more Americans will help us in either case. I take the cherry and the One-Zero goes with Mac. His name is Davidson, but everyone calls him Dave, as well. It won't matter because everyone has a number so they won't get confused with two Daves on the ground. I have their radio so we have plenty of commo. I let the kid carry it and tell him to glue himself to me. We all get in a three-quarter ton and ride down to where the birds are sitting, rotors turning. We grab the Yards and load onto six birds. There is a crowd there from Recon and the TOC. Everyone has emptied down to the pad. If I wasn't scared shitless, I would suck up all the attention.

I get the kid and three Yards on the number two bird, then I put Bop, Xaung, our tail gunner, and Xam Pat on the last one with me. Mac, Davidson, Cuman, and another Yard get on our lead bird. Daugherty's team loads on his slicks and we start winding up. I get a headset from the crew chief so I can listen to Covey as we are joined by four sets of Cobras loaded with nails and hard rockets. Then the whole armada lifts off and heads west.

We have about 25 minutes to the target. I look around at the interior and everyone is bracing himself for the insertion. It never escapes me that these crews think we are some kind of legendary bad-asses, but they have the real nuts in our family because they come in and put you down and come back through unbelievable fire to pick you up. The door gunner is chewing gum as if he thinks that chewing fast enough will make him either bulletproof or invisible, preferably both. I'm wondering if maybe he has something there, when I hear Covey through the earphones. Xam Pat and Xaung are looking at the scenery and grab-assing. They are amazing, these Bru. They are their best when the shit is about to hit the fan.

Covey has located another American and vectored him to the Yard with the wounded American. He is on the emergency radio that the Yard has been using to talk with Covey. It turns out that the Yard is with the One-Zero. The team leader is alive, but drifting in and out of consciousness.

He and the Yard had made it free of the chopper before it crashed in the trees. The Yard had pulled them both from the water, but they lost the One-Zero's weapon. He dragged and carried the One-Zero until they were about 200 meters north of the bird. They had bad guys all around them, but they weren't under fire, yet.

The four Americans on Daugherty's side of the river were not quite so lucky. They had stripped the guns off the bird and were hunkered down in a bomb crater, but were getting pressed from three sides by what they thought was a company, plus.

We are about ten minutes out and I can see the air packages stacked up over the target area and catch the darting, agile, shape of the Covey plane, as it rolls out from marking something with a WP rocket, so the bombers can hit it. I watch an A-IE flip and roll in, and as we get closer, watch the concussion whip out from the bright orange splash and dirty black smoke that is the signature of what looks like 250-pounders. I can see another set of Sandies roll in to the south and east of the river. As they pull up and hang on their propellers, you can see the forest light up with multiple concussions over about a 400 meter square, the unique mark of cluster bombs. It registers in my mind that Covey must be working over troop concentrations or he is going after any AA that might be out there. I glance out the right side at the area where they had reported a 57mm. The ground and forest are smoking and torn up, so they must have already eliminated that threat.

We start to drop into the gap between the two hillsides and the pilot says we are about two minutes out. Before I take the headset off I hear a frantic voice talking to Covey that there are bad guys less than 50 meters from him. I see a Spad drop down and watch the puffs of smoke coming from his guns as he slews past us on the left.

I'm out on the skid, half-in half-out, with the wind tearing up my eyes. I see Mac's bird go in and set down just briefly, then it's up and gone. The second bird is starting to short final when the crew chief on my side opens up on full automatic.

The team darts from the bird and goes to ground. Then it's our turn. As we are coming in, I can see green tracers coming from above us, but the gunner is not leading us properly so they are going high and behind. The crew chief is burning up ammo trying to get the gun. They must have the gun up in a tree platform. Then we are there and I'm bailing out, crouching and running for where the rest of the team is beside the remains of a large hardwood tree that has been shattered by a bomb, creating a natural fort for us.

I can hear the firing now. It's starting to kick up splinters from the tree we are all hiding around. Mac signals me to extend the line out, so we aren't all in one place. I get up and start pushing and pointing, but the Yards are already moving, seeking nooks and crannies that they can fight from. The cherry is wide-eyed, but he's bushy-tailed. I have to grab him because he is following me so close. I tell him to stay put, down behind the bole of another tropical hardwood and jink myself over to where Mac is. He is talking with Covey and laying fire on the two guns that are trying to chew their way into where we are. He yells "Get down!" and everyone eats dirt as the Spads come in and drop a couple of hard bombs about 200 meters up-slope. The concussion blasts our ears, and those of us who have been around an air strike before remember to open our mouths so we aren't deaf afterwards.

The guns stop and, with the exception of a few sporadic bursts from AKs, it's relatively quiet. The east side of the river is another story. They are bombing and strafing all around where Daugherty and his team went in and I can see green tracers coming up from about a dozen places on the hillsides trying to lock on the Cobras and fast movers.

I am just thinking how lucky we are, when an RPG-2 rocket launcher goes off about 100 yards from our position and the round hits the bank to my left rear. Two more follow in the blink of an eye and suddenly I realize I have been standing up. Both Mac and Dave are laughing. Mac asks if I am satisfied now that I've gotten them to pay attention to us, too. Wiseass. The Yards open up and Bong fires a B-40 at the same area; I see maybe two figures crumple and thrash around and that's the end of our rocket serenade. Mac tells me the downed bird is about 75 yards from us. We are going to check it and see if there are any survivors. We get up and move in stages; he takes half the team and moves out in a modified wedge formation and the rest of us cover them from the trees. Seconds later, I get up and make the short plunge into the tangled mass with my half of the team. We're in a column, so we look like an arrow moving forward, and we are moving fast. The brush is thick, but relatively easy to move through and visibility is about 15 yards.

The air is permeated by the stench of burning kerosene and plastic, and over the top of that you catch the whiff of roasted pork, that unmistakable smell of bodies burning. It isn't quite pork, but it's close. Mac stops. I close up the team, and suddenly I'm at the crash site. The trees and brambles are chewed up like a giant weed cutter went through them, courtesy of the main rotor blades. I'm looking at the ravaged upper branches of the trees, and I see one of the crewmen stuck to the side of a tree. He is way too close to it to be breathing anymore and his body has that knobby broken look that tells you that his flight suit is all that's holding him together. His left leg is turned around and a stark white spear of bone from his broken tibia is jutting out and up, pointing at the rest of his body. He's about 15 feet up and I work out the logistics of getting his body down. I direct two of the Yards to drop their gear and they shimmy up the tree. They do some hacking with a machete and the body tumbles down.

We are shoving the remains in a body bag when Mac comes back to me and tells me they found the rest of the crew and one Yard in and around the bird. The chopper is barely recognizable; it is a twisted mass of wreckage. The fuel cells had burst with the violence of the impact and then burned, so the forest on that side is all burned and charred. Dave is standing next to the main part of the wreckage.

He calls down to both of us, "You better come up here. One of them is still alive." If he is, then God is kind, I think. That is, until I get up to where Davy is standing next to what had been the left rear of the chopper. Then I change my mind.

The thing that is melted into the remains of the aircraft is inhuman. Plastic padding and bits of strap are melted into the charred figure and the twisted remains of an M-60. The body is so burned that the hands and most of the forearms are just blackened bones. It is the same with the lower torso. This is deep tissue damage all the way to the bones. The only thing left is the torso, and it is a mass of water blisters and charred flesh. The only clothing is a flight helmet and one boot, everything else is burnt, fried, melted. His face is gone but he still has one eyelid, or at least part of one, and it's blinking, once in a while. His eyes are so blue. I look at Davy and Mac and we all know he shouldn't be alive, and we aren't going to be able to keep him alive. There is no way they can put him back together. Jesus, most of the body can't even be viable tissue. There is nothing here to work with. I look at this poor pitiful thing that had only hours ago been full of life and expecting to survive this pisshole. I take out a styrene of morphine and go to jab it in the neck area.

Mac stops me. "Don't waste the morphine. We may need it later." We all stand and watch as the light fades out of the eyes. Mac looks at me, and so does Davy. I know I started to do the right thing, and would hope that someone would do me if they found me in that shape. They just nod and we start packing the bodies. Mac goes off with three of the Yards and by the time he is back we have the bodies ready.

The team is fairly safe in here: the river is about 20 yards to the east and there is a long sand bar we can use to extract from. But, leaving the bodies, we decide to get to the ones still alive. They are about 100 yards from us, according to Covey, and he gives us a direction. We take off and move towards them, with Mac talking to Covey. He tells him to tell the Yard we are coming up on them. I am not worried about the Yard shooting us, but the chopper crewman and his .38 caliber revolver is another matter. We move quietly and cautiously; they haven't had any close-in movement, but better to be safe than sorry. A lot of times the enemy will use the evader as bait, then ambush you coming out. We get up another 50 yards and then the Yard stands up and we move up and around him. The crewman turns out to be one of the Cobra crew, who had actually gone down across the river, but he swam across because he had too many bad guys in his area. He is happy as a puppy to see us. Just by a miracle he had stumbled on the Yard, who had enough sense to flag him over so that he could see the wounded One-Zero. He is dehydrated and Dave gives him his two-quart canteen, which he gulps from greedily and then hands to the Yard.

We are in a perimeter that is probably 25 meters across and a little bit longer. The hill slopes up and away from us, and the undergrowth thins out on the southern end where it slopes down toward the river. The Yards immediately go into defensive mode and I signal two of them to put out claymores toward where the guns had been firing at us as we came in. I have them put another one toward the south and pointed west, facing in the direction of the downed chopper.

I do all this as a matter of habit because Mac is busy talking to Covey and trying to order us up a ride home. The choppers have gone back and refueled and re-armed. Covey had been replaced because Wes had run out of fuel. I make my way up to where Davy and Mac are and they are working on the One-Zero, who is conscious now. His shoulder is dislocated, he has shrapnel wounds from when the chopper took the rocket in the back, and one of his fingers has been shot off. But re-hydrated with a blood bag and some water, he has come to.

He is coherent and able to sit up and, after a while, we are able to get him standing. He's weak but at least we don't have to carry him. One of us can stay with him as we move. Boy, does he look bad, though. His face, and actually his whole body, is swollen and starting to turn blue with the bruises. He had managed to grab the Yard and jump free in the seconds after the rocket hit, and they had both pancaked into the water. He doesn't remember anything after that. He looks like some advertisement for body bruising. Davy takes his knife and slits the swelling around his eyes so it will drain and he can at least see, then bandages it up. He looks weird, like he has olive drab horse blinders on. We give him the pump shotgun and the ammo for it, while the pilot looks longingly for something other than his popgun. No way, he is baggage at this point.

We can hear the battle on the east side of the river. It isn't in the category of a firefight anymore; they are bombing and strafing the other side continuously and the shooting never stops, although it appears to be moving east and up the hill. I remember on the way in I had seen numerous garden plots and hootches along the hillsides camouflaged under the upper canopy of trees. They would be impossible to see unless you were right on top of them. This spelled bad tidings for us. We were in the middle of a major concentration. If the NVA have been there long enough to build garden plots, and there weren't any villages near here, this spelled lots of troops and they knew we were here. They would want to pin us down and kill us, if possible, to keep away the bombers that were sure to come. It would give them time to get out of the area or go deep underground. As long as they had us occupied, they could keep the big stuff like Arc Light raids from saturating the area.

We follow the progress of Daugherty on the other side of the river. They had picked up the four survivors of the chopper, but had been unable to get to either wreck site and had run into stiff resistance. We still have one crewman from the Cobra and two Yards missing. Our Cobra crewman is sure that the front-seater is dead. The floating gun sight in the chopper had caved-in his face on impact. Our guy had only a few moments to get free before the bird went up in flames. But Daugherty will try and get to the crash site and confirm.

They have been working the bombers on both flanks and to the front, while fighting their way up to some high ground where one of the recon teams from Da Nang had inserted and was ready to receive them. Most of the air package was enroute. The plan was to pull us out as soon as the two teams linked up, and then follow up to bring them out. They had managed to steal a couple of Marine H-34s to pull them out, so we were to go out on the slicks.

So far, Daugherty has been lucky; they have sustained no casualties. The decision is made to abort trying to recover the body of the front-seater in the burning Cobra. No sign yet of the two missing Yards. If they are out here and able to get to us, we will take them with us. Everyone is looking for them. We are going to move back to the wrecked slick to retrieve the bodies, then dogleg to the river and get picked up on the sandbar. I describe the lay to Mac, Davidson and the wounded One-Zero, who, with the morphine in him, is feeling like fighting.

We are having this little war council when Cuman starts making hand motions. I don't need to interpret them because it sounds like a couple of companies are coming in our direction. Everyone gets ready for the contact we know is going to come, when Covey comes up on the air and says he has people all over the wreck and wants to know if it's us. Mac tells him no way and asks how many. He comes back with, ten or fifteen that he can see. About that time the claymore we had laid out facing towards the wreck goes off and the Yards on that end open up on full-auto. I hear the crunch of hand grenades and the gunfire is mostly ours.

I head for the end of the perimeter and Mac yells, "Screw the bodies. We are getting the living out of here. It is time to start heading for the river." By the time I get to the north end of the perimeter I see a dozen green khaki figures moving to my left just breaking the edge of the tall trees. The Yards on that side drop them and Mac makes the hand motion that we are moving out to the river. I crouch behind the tree where Xaung is. He has the clackers to both the claymores out to the northwest. When the team opened up the first group of NVA was mowed down like they ran into a thresher, and now you can hear some of them screaming and choking and thrashing around.

I have the lid open on the RPD and am feeding another belt into it, not forgetting to pick up the old one and stuff it in the claymore bag I carry for that purpose. Too long, I am taking too long! Before I can snap the top down, the entire forest in front of me erupts and the foliage around and above me starts to shred and fall amongst us. It becomes a solid cacophony of AK's and CAR-15s. I know they are going to charge us and look for Mac. I spot him; he is calm as can be and talking to Covey. Over the rifle fire I can hear the sound of Spads rolling in, then the forest in front of me begins to shred as the wing guns chew up the real estate. We get a nanosecond breather out of that and I hear Mac yelling IA drill and to move 50 meters at 9 o'clock. He is always at 12 o'clock, the direction we were facing when we stopped.

Ten odd NVA break clear of the chewed up area and start towards us, shooting and screaming as they come on. I signal Xaung and he blows both claymores and the NVA dissolve in a wall of steel pellets and chewed up foliage. The Yards and the newbie peel past me. Dave, Xaung, and I are the last to leave the perimeter. We dodge and weave through the brush and eventually make the riverbank. We can hear the NVA NCOs, over the moaning and screaming of their wounded, yelling and shoving their men into position.

We drop claymores, every one we have, out to our front and get ready to take them head on when they come. We have the river to our back. The sandbar is out about 40 feet from the bank. We are taking light fire on our rear from a stand of bamboo on the other side. Cuman grabs Bong, and they fire a B-40 into the cluster. Bad move, Nguyen. Bamboo bums like it was made of flash paper. Sure enough, within seconds the whole stand is a blazing inferno. The Yards drop a couple of shrieking, burning, figures that make it out.

I can hear the choppers coming. If we can last the next ten minutes we will get out of this. I look to the gun, removing the drum and putting in a fresh belt. I've gone through almost five hundred rounds. Everyone else is doing the same: reloading. The gunships are rolling in hot and the NVA are going to try to get right on top of us to get out of that death storm. The first slicks are dropping down circling in from the southwest. A Cobra goes across our front and you can hear the "brrmrrp" of his Minigun just as he banks off. Here they come, lots of them, the bmsh above and around us getting chewed to pieces and we fire back. Just as the first slick drops down on short final, Mac blows his claymores, I blow all of mine, and we are up and running for the slicks. One gets loaded and up; two gets loaded and up. I'm in the last one. I'm diving into the bird and trying to twist around so I can shoot. The gunner is firing full-auto at the river bank and we are up and lifting. Where we were is nothing but chewed vegetation. Here and there, stretching back for about 100 yards, are clumps and individual bodies. Lots of them.

The guns are having a field day on the way out. There isn't any ground fire as we get higher, so they must have knocked out all the 12.5mm positions. I'm looking to the southwest and I can see fast movers working over a hilltop. On a slightly higher hilltop, an H-34 is hovering and you can see our folks getting aboard. Please don't let any more aircraft go down. I do not want to go back there.

The crew chief hands me a headset and I hear Mac on the other end. He says we got everyone out, no birds down and that was it for the day, calm as if he had been on a Sunday walk. That's why I don't get the radio, I have a tendency to scream and shout hysterically when my asshole is tighter than a gnat's wallet.

As the warm air wafts in past the slipstream I slide up to Xaung and he pats my arm and grins. The gunner hands me a pack of Marlboros and I take one out and give the Yards the pack to pass around. He nods and smiles when it comes back eight light. God, does that taste good. A cigarette coming off an adrenaline rush is sex. It's starting to get late. I look at my watch and realize that it has only been six hours and some change since Mac had walked into the isolation area and said we were going on a Bright Light.

I am dog tired and I have that sour stench of sweat and fear all over me. When we get back to Da Nang, we come in low over the trash dump and land on the PSP. All of Recon Company is waiting for us as we come in. I have a cold beer shoved into my hand as we get all the Yards out and assemble the team. Everyone is around us, and the entire milling swarm moves over as they load the wounded One-Zero onto a gurney with the surviving Yard for the trip up to the infirmary. The Cobra pilot is getting the same reception from the air package.

Despite the beer, I am drained. We load on the deuce and a half and go up to the isolation area just as Daugherty and the other team come in. They have four wounded little people and all look like they have been 30 days on the western front: haggard, slack jawed, and happy to be alive. The debriefing begins as we all come into the isolation area. We put the Yards to work cleaning their gear and get them chow. The Americans go to the far end and we start the information flow to get all the details while they are fresh. How many machine guns? What types? Where were they? What kind of ack-ack did you see? Were they bursts or just explosions when they hit something? What were the NVA dressed in and what kind of weapons? It's a play-by-play of what happened after we got on the ground. What about the bodies? Could we recognize them? Where were they around the wreck? It's the forensics and autopsy of the mission so they can figure out what went wrong and how bad it was. It doesn't get much worse than this unless you go in and everyone is dead. We have a few small victories. We got some of them, most of them, out alive. None of us say anything about the badly burnt crewman, just that he died before we could get him out of the aircraft.

We hear about Daugherty's ordeal. Some of us are starting to name the place the "Valley of the Jolly Green Giant." There were fields everywhere under the trees, and there had been more and more troops pouring in from all the hillsides. We wonder how they managed to fight their way nearly half a klick to the static position established by the third team. That one we are calling Little Cemetery Ridge, just like the one at Gettysburg. But Daugherty had made it and into the waiting arms of the other team.

The Air Force is ordered in with a nine ship Arc Light that night. Another team will be inserted to see what's left, after the ground cools down and there is enough oxygen to sustain human life. It is a bad place. Some staff twit asks if we thought there was a regiment in there and Mac looks at him with contempt and says, "Well if there wasn't, then we wasted a lot of good men and equipment."

Larry appears and breaks up the interrogation. I can see that he is burning inside. Someone screwed up and big time. We learn that they had confirmed the existence of at least *two* regiments before the team had been inserted. This had been no prisoner snatch, it had been a deliberate move to make the enemy climb down from the hills and kick some ass. The snatch operation had been bait. Oh, they got all the confirmation they wanted, but someone had not told the team about the radio intercepts in detail. If they had, they would never have picked the bend in the river as the insertion point; they would have picked someplace where they could claw a protective perimeter if they were hit.

Someone had blindsided the team. What's worse, they did it deliberately, and we all know who that career asshole is. Manes comes over and The Old Man tells everyone else to leave. They both stand there and Manes tells us straight out. They know who is at fault and they are going to handle it. The guilty parties are, even as we speak, being taken care of. Don't be getting any ideas about shooting some asshole because he isn't worth the rest of your lives. Coming from Manes it makes sense, but just barely. The Old Man finishes up, telling us that we get two days stand down and that we are out of isolation if we don't get stupid. Nods all around. I feel as if someone has made me work like a mule all day in the hot sun.

We gather up our gear and ride the 300 yards to Recon Company. I drop radios and other stuff on the floor that won't do so well in the Recon dunk we are about to take. Mac runs over to get two six packs of beer. By the time I am done, he rejoins me and we walk down to the showers. Still wearing all our gear and guns, we each grab a lawn chair and set them under a shower head, sit in them, and pop the first beer with the water washing the day off us. It's amazing how dirty you get, especially around all that high explosive. It grinds into your whole body. The water running down the drain is muddy, filled with bits of chaff, and sometimes red from the blood where we had handled the dead.

Mac leans back after our third or fourth beer and looks over at me. We both look like a couple of drowned rats, but the water has stopped running brown or red. He holds up a squeeze bottle of dish soap, which we liberally spray all over each other and the equipment. I stand up and turn the water on so it is hot. "Now comes the rinse cycle, ladies. Watch carefully that we don't get dishpan ass."

We rinse everything off and stack it at the back of the shower, guns, ammo, magazines. Don't forget those mini grenades, get them rascals clean. When we get back to the hootch, which will be in about two beers, we will strip everything and clean it, then oil it all down. By that time we will be two little oil pissers, so we will come back here and take another hot shower. By the time we return the second time the web gear should be almost dry enough to put all the stuff back.

By this time, Mac the combat pygmy has regained his droll sense of humor, complete with this kid brother look he always has. He kind of smirks and says that as long as I owe him money would I please not go running around in the middle of a firefight making house calls with my machine gun, unless it is real important.

Gator breath. He does it as much as I do. You want to stay on the ground, God knows you want to be in a hole, but you can't see if you're down all the time, and you certainly cannot fight from there. I feel really old. The face of the kid with the blue eyes keeps flashing in and out of my mind.

"Mac, the kid, the door gunner that was all burned, do you think …," I start out, but he doesn't let me finish. He knows what is going on inside my head.

"He was already gone, Nick. All that was still going on in there was nerves, refusing to shut down. As far as I am concerned, you would have wasted the morphine." He turns to start picking up his gear. "I was about to do the same thing." He shrugs and helps me up out of the lawn chair. "But, I didn't think of the morphine; I would have used the pistol." Deep down, I know he is right. Save the medicine for the salvageable.

CHAPTER 11

Operation Afrika Corps

We are back in Da Nang and are on our second day of stand down. The grand operations that require the fiery intellect of people like our fearless leader Captain Manes don't concern us because we are in the middle of "Operation Afrika Corps." Mac, Jimmy Johnson, and I are staking out the 1st ARVN Field Force from across the street because the prize of my life is sitting outside the gate. It is beautiful. It is baking in the hot sun and it was meant for me.

It is a White M-3 half-track. The ancient beast is in working order and freshly painted OD green. We chatted up the ARVN sergeant in charge of it and found out that it belongs to some high ranking general with the ARVN, who uses it to tool around town and to review the troops, all that silly pompous stuff that staff gets such a woody over. They have completely refurbished the thing, including a new canvas top for both the crew and the cargo area. It even has the metal roller mounted on the front that was designed for rearranging French hedgerows.

I had seen this prize about a month ago on the streets of Da Nang, and followed it back here. Two things happened after I saw it: my larceny genes started working overtime and I fell in love with it. My dad had bought one back in the late fifties and when I was a kid I used it around the ranch, so I was intimate with all the systems. I'd strolled over and talked to the driver of this one, who was an ARVN staff sergeant. The larceny potential went up a notch when that I found out that the sergeant hated the bloody thing because it was his job to keep it ready all the time. He spent most of his time sitting in or around it, baking in the sun and waiting for various field grade pukes to demand he drive them around town with their floozies. Consequently, to him it was like some great albatross suspended around his career. The General had ridden in it possibly twice in the year that the sergeant had been in charge of it.

Now a half-track requires some special handling skills, and in the narrow canyons that are called streets in this metropolis, it is a bitch to maneuver. And of course, when it gets dirty you have to clean it because general officers can't be seen driving around in a mud-splattered vehicle, unless it's a photo op. Lately, a certain Major

Nhu had become the bane of this poor fellow, demanding to go everywhere in this chariot. This resulted in the sergeant having to clean the bloody thing four times a day.

We have agreed to relieve him of both his bane and the vehicle, at no risk to himself. Additionally, because we are all sergeants, we have agreed upon a little stipend on the side for his troubles. His task in this enterprise is that he will tell us, correction, he will signal us when the major is taking the halftrack himself, with no driver. This auspicious occasion is normally when Major Nhu is visiting his mistress. The flower in this romantic tryst is a mere two years older than the major's own teenage daughter and he has installed her in a house near Papa Joe's, the Algerian Legionnaire's restaurant. This area is a maze of side streets and house compounds. In fact, it is the district that our own safe house is in. It is just the perfect place for hiding a few nefarious activities, which is the reason that we picked it. With a few judiciously placed payoffs on the monthly expense bill, we control the Vietnamese police and Ruff Puff military checkpoints.

The sergeant will signal us when the major is about to take Daddy's wheels for his afternoon tryst by simply putting a chalk mark number, for the time, on the back quarter panel where we can see it. Now that we know where the lovely little flower of the orient lives, and the major's usual route, we have done our recon on the route and have set up a wonderful ambush for him. Da Nang is awash in deserters, as I have mentioned before, so to throw the heat off us we have stolen two MP jeeps. We have also enlisted the help of our own evil rendition of Shaft, in the person of "Spearchucker" Hauser. Spearchucker is one of the very few blacks in Recon, and is as twisted as the rest of us bleached models. There are no color barriers in Recon, because you have to be rejected by your own kind as horribly stunted socially just to qualify for the brotherhood. So Spearchucker is one of us, heart, soul, and twisted little mind.

Jimmy has his team dressed as "white mice," the Vietnamese MPs. They are adroitly perfect for this job since his team members were all petty criminals that he recruited out of a Vietnamese prison. Lovely fellows, they are all "ex-cowboys," the term for the Vietnamese underworld. In fact, they play the roles of cops better than the real models do.

The agreement is that we will make the good major's day into a nightmare of being captured by the underworld and sold to the VC, then abandoned in such a way that his little love nest and unauthorized use of the general's toy are blaringly evident. I get a half-track, and the good major gets canned like a tuna to be shipped off to some outpost where they get mortared every night. In return, our gallant allies get the benefit of no longer having Major Nhu and the general's shiny wheels as an impediment to getting the job done. Ah, sergeants, what would any army do without them? If you train us and encourage us to commit acts that require great skill, cunning, and mastery of deceit, don't be surprised when we start using it to better our quality of life.

Anyone can steal a jeep, but stealing this will make us legends. I have already arranged to have it painted black and have made a stencil of the Afrika Corps with the swastika and a date palm in the middle of the trunk. This will be my crowning achievement. We are ready, willing, and able. It's about 1600 when the major comes sauntering out, actually about a half hour early. He stops long enough to inspect the vehicle and stands our co-conspirator at attention, waiting while the little guy runs into the guard shack and comes back with a rag to wipe down the tan leather seats so Major Nhu can sit his portly ass down on clean leather. Once this degrading act of arrogance is completed, he climbs in and settles into the seat.

The major fires up the beast, and waits until the sergeant salutes before he pulls out into traffic. This guy is just like those naval patricians we are infected with. We pull out in our jeep and as we pass the sergeant he gives us, at waist level, the thumbs up signal. No doubt they won't miss this arrogant fat little staff major around the sergeant's mess.

I'm on the radio; we are using a KY-38 scrambler encryption model that was originally designed as a secure voice link for us to use in the bush, and which weighs in at seven pounds. No one I know wants to carry one willingly, because 15 pounds of extra ammo will fit in the same space, and I'd rather have that and so would anyone else. KY-38s make great sea anchors and they are perfect for things like this, to keep some ASA (Army Security Agency) radio surfer from listening in. I get Jimmy and his gangsters on the line and tell them that the turkey is on the way to the oven.

We are about a cycle length back from his rear bumper and just before he gets to his "house of love" an American MP Jeep, with Spearchucker all done up like the main MP, is waiting and flags him over to the side. The major starts to ignore him when one of Jimmy's gangsters, dressed as a QC (*Quart Canh*, South Vietnamese Military Police) and standing in the back of the jeep, cocks the M-60 and swings the barrel in the direction of the half-track. The major comes to a screeching halt and before the track quits rocking back and forth, three more of the boys step outside and walk up to the driver's side.

I love these guys. One of them is dressed in the preferred uniform of the South Vietnamese Internal Security Department, a pale blue walking suit with aviator's sunglasses. No one on the sidewalk wants anything to do with this scene. In fact, you can almost see the cloud of amnesia taking the crowd. The major leans out of the driver's window and with a pompous look starts to say something when our fake ISD guy whips out a slapjack and slaps him alongside the head, all the while screaming, "Traitor, deserter to the communists!" That kind of stuff drives even those with less than average intelligence away from the area, lest they be caught up in the dragnet. This is a black market economy, most are bound to have something incriminating on them, or in their house. The civilians on the street vanish. The boys drag the fat major over to the jeep and two of Jimmy's guys sit on top of him.

The one to whom I've been giving driving instructions on half-track operations, gets behind the wheel.

The major is handcuffed and blindfolded, and they roar off down the street, after shouting for all and sundry to hear that they are going to search the house of his mistress, "Mademoiselle So-and-so at Rue de Dragon's Breath" or wherever.

We take the half-track and the good major to a warehouse down near the port, where the half-track is painted in about an hour. All the while the good major is sitting in a back room tied to a chair, still blindfolded, stripped to his underwear, which turn out to be blue satin with "L'amour" stitched in bright red thread.

This toad thinks he is a real stud. Spearchucker and Jimmy's Zero-One are carrying on a conversation right next to him, so he can't miss one word. Spearchucker is going on in half Vietnamese and pidgin English about how "This ain't the general, but I gets my money anyway," and the Zero-One playing the part of the local VC cell leader is countering with "The Popular Front doesn't pay for some worthless supply puppet of the running dog lackey regime in Saigon." The dialogue is right out of the movies. This goes on during the hour that the vehicle is being painted with our livery. We figure they won't miss fat boy, or the half-track, for at least a day. Our plan is to wait until it gets dark and then head for the other side of the river and home. It is best to get this baby back to CCN, where we can hide it until the storm blows over.

The major's day gets worse as the physical intimidation starts, all hearts and minds stuff, followed by a few head twisting slaps. They begin to force the major to drink gin. He has already pissed himself, but other than the bruise where the slapjack caught him, no one hurts him too bad. He is babbling about how he always admired the Viet Cong, that he has personally known about cell members and never turned them in, that he is secretly a sympathizer of the cause, that he could be a real valuable asset to them if he went back to his job at headquarters, etc. It is the pathetic litany of a toad trying to save his own life. Pretty soon he is babbling out some kind of espionage plan that will hopefully gain their confidence, and get him back in. He even names who the ISD people are and where they billet. By now he is drunk as an English lord. He is ready to serve the cause, and in perfect shape for the next phase of our plan.

We have to ensure that he doesn't come back to haunt our gallant allies in the ARVN Sergeants' Mess. He keeps lapsing off into unconsciousness, so we remove him from the chair and return him to the back seat of one of the stolen QC jeeps, still wearing nothing but his passion shorts and black nylon dress socks. He is handcuffed, but we don't need the gag anymore. We get packed up and make sure we have an incriminating tape of his "confession." Once we have him in the stolen MP jeep, with two of the former gangsters driving, we take off for the other side of the river. The cassette is taped to the small of the major's back. He doesn't know; he is so drunk that he can barely remain conscious. We could have taped a sex-starved porpoise to him and he wouldn't know.

Traveling in convoy, we weave our way towards the I Corps Bridge. About a block from the main Police Headquarters we leave him and the jeep sitting on the side of the street, where they are bound to find it. I would love to be there when the good major tells his harrowing tale about being kidnapped and mistaken for the general and then how he was threatened with being sold to the VC, and furthermore, how he apparently escaped. The scene will get much better when ISD listens to the tape and plays it back to him, just before they hook his genitalia to a field telephone and start dialing for dollars. It will serve him right, the fat slug, safe and warm in a rear area, making sergeants' lives unbearable just because he has the power to do so. I hope they cripple him before they ship him to one of the prison islands.

We are off and tearing across the I Corps Bridge, mixed in with the night traffic. Turn right at the crossroads, and then the dash past Gonorrhea Gulch, and we pull up to the front wire barrier. The Yards see it is our good selves, smile, and flag us in. We are home free.

We motor down to Recon Company after first making a tour past the Yard barracks. I am standing and driving; I have my German uniform on, complete with the Iron Cross and the high-beaked *Wehrmacht* officer's cap at a jaunty angle. Mac is beside me wearing a long overcoat with "P.O.W." in bright yellow letters on the back and my German helmet, giving the "*Sieg Heil*" to anyone we see. We pull up to the club and honk the horn. I discover the thing has a siren so we give that a blast or two. It sounds like an air raid siren, which empties the club and everyone comes out to admire our wheels.

Anyone can steal a measly jeep. We have our own, one of a kind, vehicle. It's so COOOOL! We take it for a few turns around the compound, with about 15 of our fellow miscreants hanging all over it. Jimmy and his hoodlums and Spearchucker are still in their police regalia, following us in the one remaining MP jeep as we pass the Yards standing at the door to their club. All the Yards are caught up in our exuberance, and start cheering, giving the thumbs up. Even Cuman is smiling. He waves, then shakes his head and goes inside. Now we have but one small compact little problem, a problem that is sometimes insurmountable, and comes in the form of Captain Manes.

By this time, we are good and roaring, and are working out how to protect our new beauty from the rest of this thieving mob, so we go up to the motor pool and wake up Fish to get a long length of chain. We drive back to Recon Company and run over the fence in the process of backing the half-track between our hootch and RT Indigo's. Then we chain the thing down, running the chain all the way around our hut. Next comes the padlock. It is one of those military issue Greenleafs. I take one key and so does Mac. We put them on our dogtag chains. We give each other a couple of high fives, collect Spearchucker, who has fallen asleep in the back, and then it is back over to the club. We are mighty, we are kings!

But even in paradise, there is always an ill wind blowing somewhere. We have settled down to bask in the warm adulation of our twisted peers when the club goes silent. Our foul wind gusts in, in the form of the heavy gravity planet, his hands on his hips and lips pursed to the point where they have all but disappeared. The place is quiet enough to hear a mouse pissing on a cotton ball.

"Which one of you fucking criminals ran over the colonel's car?" Car? Did we run into a car? I remember hitting a few things, but I don't remember a car. "That's right, you bunch of morons. You have really done it if you are involved, because someone wrecked the back of the staff car. So, naturally, HE comes and gets me and interrupts my peace and tranquility because it has to be you hoodlums." Messing with Larry's drinking and thinking at the same time, that's bad.

"Now the stupid motherfucker," referring to the colonel, obviously, "said it was some yahoos in a tank. I explained to him that we are a ground reconnaissance unit. We got helicopters, we got jeeps for going to the whorehouse, we got guns and mines, even special use of Spectre, and of course, we have all that to keep you morons busy and occupied, but we haven't got no tanks." Pause. Stare.

"I can see by your bovine faces that none of you heroes is gonna 'fess up to the crime, so I am going back up there and tell him that it ain't Recon Company, and not to bother my drinking again." He spins on his heels and lumbers out the door, and we all are about to split a gut laughing. It is about two seconds later when we hear him bellow.

"Who wrecked my fence?" There is a short silence, punctuated by the sound of pieces of the fence being thrown around, then an incredulous, "What in jaspers-blue-the-fuck-blazes is this?" I am out the back door and moving in a crouch with all the other conspirators and fellow thieves. It will be better to sleep in the Yard huts tonight. They will shoot the horrible little dwarf on sight. We will tell the Yards that *Dai Uy* Manes is a witch. The Yards are real spooky about witches. That'll fix him.

As we round the back side of Recon Company I see Larry standing there beside our new wheels, just looking at it, dumbfounded. It's a good thing we chained it down. No telling what might be spinning through that skull of his. Yes, it is best to just stay with the little people tonight. Wait and see what the morning brings.

We get over to the little people's quarters and Cuman is waiting for us. He gives us the fatherly finger wave about how we always get *Dai Uy* Manes mad. "Why do you make *Dai Uy* mad? Oooush! Numbah ten!" Mac and I just look at him and tell him not to worry, because *Dai Uy* Manes is always mad, and we can't understand why he thinks we are the ones who make the *Dai Uy* mad. This of course makes us both break into the giggles. Cuman tells the other Yards to make room for us. The boys rig up a couple of jungle hammocks for us. It takes us several attempts to get in them, even with Cuman presiding over the operation. Finally, we are safely tucked in, and I am drifting off into dreamland, something about blue silk shorts on a mouse.

CHAPTER 12

Selection Process

After a couple of days, Larry got over the ripple in the time-space continuum that had disrupted his delicate experiment of consuming all the good scotch left in Southeast Asia. This was intended, as he put it, as a mission so that it didn't fall into the hands of the heathen communists.

Larry gives us the usual, "I am saving your asses from the colonel who wants to have you court-martialed and then have you shot" speech. We suspect this is hogwash because Colonel Donnie loves us. Without us, he would be back in Des Moines playing golf and working in some dead-end ROTC slot. Besides, if he had us shot, who would run these missions for those weenies at the TOC? I suppose they could cobble together an ad hoc team of shoe clerks and drive them aboard the choppers at gunpoint. Right after they ice skate down the main street of purgatory and ring Ole Scratch's doorbell, that is.

What the captain really means is, "I want to confiscate this half-track from you and drive it around myself." No one is driving it; primarily because it is on the list of the top five hottest vehicles in Southeast Asia and anyone caught driving it will join Major Nhu, who is busy turning big rocks into pea gravel on Skull Island.

I want to go tooling around Da Nang in it, myself. I have had some special uniforms made up for the Yards and ordered six German helmets from some mail order outfit in Spain to complete the ensembles. What a turn of events.

Chuckles has been instructed to turn our half-track into something that "will contribute to the camp defense, rather than our continued delinquency." Our Captain Manes has taken time out from his busy schedule of covering our social and tactical indiscretions to order that the half-track be converted into a mobile gun platform for use by the security weenies in case the camp gets overrun. The last time the camp had been overrun was in 1968, and they swam in from the sea, cut their way through the wire, and proceeded to satchel charge everything in sight. So his argument about why it was needed was pretty skinny. A case like that called for a big tank with a flamethrower. We have reached a compromise, however, in that we will convert it into something, but it will stay in Recon Company. I would rather burn it than let it fall into the hands of those security weenies. If there is going to be something neat in this camp, Recon is going to own it.

Fish, a mechanical genius, and the Filipino armorer have been working on it. We have it all rigged up with four long whip antennas on the back, each with its own little pendant. Larry has this thing for whip antennas, the long ones that go to a VRC-42 radio that look like Marlin fishing rigs on Hemingway's canoe. He doesn't want the radios. Nope, that means having to talk to someone and, more importantly, being able to be located. No sirree, Larry just likes the antennas, so when he starts or stops they whip back and forth like the bullwhip on a borax train. He figures the more whip antennas the better. I guarantee if you steal a jeep with a whip antenna on it, Larry will confiscate it fast as you can breathe sarsaparilla. I suspect he was planning to turn the half-track into his personal whip antenna farm as soon as he laid eyes on it. It's our saving grace and the reason we still have our little *Kampfwagen*.

Fish and his boys are going to trade some of our surplus jeep parts to some AA outfit for a quad fifty, and install that on the back of the half-track. It should be done in about a week. In the meantime, my baby sits forlorn and locked up in the motor pool, and we are in need of transportation.

In a moment of weakness, because we thought we had the half-track, we had given our other transportation, a jeep, to Mudhole and Murphy. They had an unfortunate accident with theirs when they got drunk and drove it into the surf during a storm. Near as we could tell, it was somewhere offshore acting as an artificial reef. Now we had to get another one.

In the original Table of Organization and Equipment, CCN, it stipulated something like six deuce and a halfs, four three-quarter ton M-37s and six jeeps. Practically every team in Recon had a jeep stashed somewhere and some of them had two. There was a veritable host of broken down, nearly broken down, and new jeeps all over the compound.

A hot jeep had to be able to get past the MPs at the checkpoints, so we kept phony logbooks. We had even taken to changing the numbers on the frames, since the MPs had become more persnickety in their inspections at the roadblocks. They had started checking the numbers on vehicles and matching them with their master list of stolen vehicles. This began after Pee Wee stole the Provost Marshal's jeep in order to get the fancy red siren. He is a Texan; they get soft in the head about sirens down there.

So now we are in delicate negotiations with Fish about building us a jeep like his. Fish started in the automotive business as a freelance salvage source, you know, those guys who, when you ran out of gas on the freeway, stripped the temporarily abandoned car down to the frame. His own personal chariot is a doozie. By all intents and purposes it looks like any other typical M-151, A2, but this little baby has a small block V-6 in it, a solid rear axle, a Hearst four on the floor, drag shift, and a big, four-barrel carburetor. The thing will outrun anything on the road.

We are heading down to the airbase to see if we can locate a staff car with the right engine in it and the rear axle we will need for our new jeep. The Air Force has a cornucopia of such toys. Fish already has a 151 body tub that is reasonably new that we can dummy the papers on. We calculate that we can separate the staff car from the Air Force in one night, allow a week for fabrication (provided that we can swipe everything we need before we get our next mission), and by the time we come back from the launch site we should have our beauty ready for us.

On top of all the finagling with Fish, and getting all the parts, we have to ensure that the whole affair is kept from Chuckles. More importantly, we need to keep our peer group from finding out about our new hot rod, lest they steal it from us.

As we walk down the hill we notice one of the two and a half ton's pulling in and there are seven or eight new guys onboard. We are the closest, so we will get first look at the new cannon fodder. Maybe we will see someone we know coming back and we can snag him as the One-Two on the team or, by some remote chance, we might see some guy that has promise. Someone with a court martial or a prior felony record is a good catch.

We divert our meandering and go right to the head shed as they are piling off the truck, all with new jungle fatigues and jungle boots, duffels and tired faces. It will take about two hours to process them in. Most of them will be carted off to the Hatchet Companies or Recon, with the odd simian who can turn on a radio or has some clerical skills getting assigned up here in the administrative section. There's not an old familiar face amongst the crowd, but a couple are wearing combat patches, so we are eying them over.

The admin sergeant major comes out with his clerk. They read off the roll and he welcomes them to CCN. He gives them the rah-rah, the "this is the toughest assignment in the Army" crap as he looks them over. He notices us and chooses to studiously ignore us. By his reaction, I am sure that someone has sent for Laughing Larry and Sergeant Major Waugh, who are the *official* Recon greeters. There are two that will positively go to Recon; they have that smart-ass look that only the multiple Article 15 holder has. I look at their faces; yep, bet they both were staff sergeants before. I wonder who they pissed off to get sent here.

Mac nudges me, points at the group and says, "What do you think of that one?"

I'm looking at all of them. "Which one?"

"That one there, by the tailgate." I look the guy over. He is in his twenties, olive-skinned, or very tanned, and hair, black wavy, curly hair, everywhere. You can tell he has to shave two or three times a day. There is hair peeking out at the neckline. He is sharp and very military looking, complete with neat fatigues, and oh God, a Ranger tab. The guy is all soldier on the outside. He has what appears to be a line of hair that composes a single eyebrow, and is scowling as if this was an unpleasant place. Other than that, he is prettier than anyone in Recon. Everyone else looks like they had slept in their fatigues, but the one that Mac has taken an interest in looks as if he had been freshly laundered. That is all except the five o'clock shadow of a beard shading his face. Here we go with the "feeling" thing again.

Every Alabaman personally believes that he is the considered expert on firearms, horseflesh, hunting dogs, women, and, last but not least, "fighting men." There is no sense arguing. I sigh in resignation, because the Mini Mac has already made up his mind that he is going to have a look-see. He saunters over to where the guys are and starts chatting with the uninitiated, calm and deliberate, very even-toned. The Ranger eyes him suspiciously, and doesn't say anything. By his obvious look of suspicion I think that he might be all right after all. At least he can smell a rat.

I'm leaning on the colonel's jeep smoking a cigar and picking my nose, when Chuckles rolls up with Billy. The two of them slither out, and I snap to attention and scream, "Good afternoon, Sir!" Then I whip him my best knife-edge salute. What makes this somewhat less than military is that I am wearing sterile fatigue pants unbloused over jungle boots, a Rolling Stones World Tour, tie dyed t-shirt, and a cravat made from a remnant of a pirate flag, with a short-billed boonie hat called a stingy brim or "catch me, come fuck me" hat.

Manes scowls at me and snarls, "Get away from these fine young men you disgrace to the *Wehrmacht*. I ain't having you and the rest of that riffraff fucking up their standards before I can take them under my arm. Where is that Alabaman dog-robbing partner of yours?"

"And don't ever salute me in public. I don't want anyone to know you belong to me." Waugh doesn't say anything, with good reason. Dracula is a day person compared to Billy, who has been surviving on adrenalin so long that his system could probably metabolize nerve gas as a vitamin supplement. He already has something like nine years in Vietnam. Billy is lean, hard, mean as a snake, and on an insane quest to collect the Big Blue, the CMH (Congressional Medal of Honor), our nation's highest. The sergeant major won't ask you to do anything he wouldn't, but then he would go into the devil's own toilet if he thought he could get "the Medal." Since we are on stand down, it is fairly likely that he also has enough Crown Royal in his blood stream on an average "off" day to kill a marine platoon. He looks just like Heinz Guderien, the German progenitor of the Blitzkrieg. I am not kidding. The resemblance is spooky. It is best to not spend too much time with Billy, lest you get hooked into one of his "good deals." These are special missions that involve daring, audacity, and a heavy dose of insanity. Rumor has it that General Custer was on one of Billy's "good deals" up in the Little Bighorn valley.

Mac makes himself small and they don't even notice him as they go inside. Now comes the screaming match between the Head Shed and Recon. We lose so many in the field that we need new bodies. The whole place exists to support Recon. We have priority, but the Hatchet Companies, et al, have people standing in this crowd tagged to go to their companies. Recon is a volunteer assignment. Of course, the fresh meat doesn't know that.

The head paper shuffler comes out and tells the newbies to go on down to the mess hall and get something to eat. Mac grabs two guys and the Ranger and says, "Why don't we give you a ride?" We walk over to the jeep that the sergeant major and Manes just arrived in. Like I said, ownership is a transient thing around here. We pile in and head for the mess hall. We get down there and let the new guys go in first.

Mac drags me aside and says the new guy that he wants is named Cook. He also found out that Cook is supposed to go to B Company. "Do you want him on the team?" It doesn't matter what I'm going to say, he is already plotting on how to get him. The kid looks okay, good shape, but he is always scowling. I heard him talk, and from the stretched-out syllables have properly identified him as another aficionado of grits. Not a bad situation, if you like round-the-clock hunting stories and practical jokes. Why not? We are going to have to get someone someday. The question is, will the Yards accept him, and is he lucky?

We go inside, get some chow, and wander over to their table. We make chit chat for a bit before Mac asks Cook, "Are you coming to Recon?"

Cook looks at him and says, "'Fraid not. I'm assigned to B Company. That's where the army is sending me and that's where I reckon they need me."

God help us all, he sounds like a Ranger commercial. The boy is really intense. Mac kind of looks down like he's feeling sorry for him. I get it, and butt in, "Yeah? No shit. Geez, that's too bad." And then as if to emphasize my sympathy, I look down at my food. The other muffins are all ears.

"What do you mean? Is B Company a bad company?" Cook asks us, his face taking on an even more serious slant.

Mac kind of rolls his eyes and says out the side of his mouth, "Well no, but they got chewed up pretty bad on that last operation. They lost quite a few Americans and a bunch of little people." He turns to me, and with choirboy innocence he asks, "Where was that, Nick?"

I look up from my food and chew what I had just shoveled into my mouth before answering. "Up in the A Shau, I think. Yeah, they got mauled by an NVA regiment. Lucky any of the survivors made it out." I look over the faces of the new guys, and you can see that now all of them don't want to be in B Company, all except Cook who is showing not one wit of apprehension. Let's just see how uninterested you are my furry friend.

"They will probably be done recruiting new strikers, and with these new guys they should be almost up to strength." I look over at Cook, smile, and go back to my potatoes.

"Yeah," Mac wheezes. "If they get a full complement of Americans they should be ready for that big operation with the ARVN army. It shouldn't be too bad." The minute you say ARVN, everyone immediately cringes. This is because the normal ARVN Regiment needed a spine transplant. There were horror stories by the score about advisor units being wiped out to a man, because of some ARVN perfidy. It was 90 percent bullshit. Most ARVN units were hard chargers. There were a lot of crooks, VC sympathizers, and blackguards, all generally with bad people skills in hopeless situations. But this is a war zone; nobody is perfect.

Cook is now a bit more interested in a possible alternative, and begins by asking just what it is that Recon does. We lie like a couple of snake oil merchants. We tell them we go out and sneak around like Roger's Rangers and when we find the enemy in enough concentration, well, we get extracted. But it is only after we are safely in the air that they put in those poor guys from the Hatchet Companies to fix and hold the NVA until they can bring in enough air strikes to kill a bunch of them. Naturally, they take some horrendous losses though, because they always have an ARVN commander on the ground.

I put the icing on the cake by telling the crowd that a bunch of those guys have got two or three silver stars already. Hard-core. I look them over. There are one or two medal hunters who are almost sexually excited at the prospects of the "impossible mission." I look at Cook. He has the pragmatic look of a survivor. "I'm glad I'm in Recon," I continue. "It's all stealth: get in, take a look, then get out. In the Hatchet Companies, there are too many targets for the enemy to shoot at and you're bound to get hit by mistake, so they send them where there are sure to be a hundred to one odds."

By the time we are done with our lunch we have Cook talked into coming down to Recon. No sweat, we tell him, we'll fix it with Larry, the commander, and get you assigned to our team. Furthermore, we tell him that he only has to tell the head shed he wants to go to Recon, and we will do the rest. We take Cook and the other two back up to the head shed just as Manes and Billy are walking out. We are lucky; we just turn off the jeep and get out as they come out and point at the two new guys and say, "Get in the jeep, men. You are going to Recon."

Cook starts to say something and we give him the "not now" signal. He goes in and comes back in about ten minutes and says with a smile. "Well guys, looks like I'm in Recon. You know those guys asked me three times if I was sure that's where I wanted to go?"

Oh, I like this one, level-headed, good on the uptake, and almost as stupid as we are. We take him down to the club and introduce him around as our new One-Two on RT Habu, buy him a couple of beers and go over to the Orderly Room. Actually, we stake it out. When Manes and Billy come out and head over to the mess hall, we go in and grab Frenchy, hand him Cook's packet and tell him, "Larry said that the new guy, Cook, was supposed to be assigned to Habu. He will talk to him tomorrow." Frenchy enters him on the morning report as being assigned to RT Habu, takes the packet, and voila! Cookie is ours. By the time Manes realizes we have a new guy on the team, it will be history. Besides, we can probably convince him that having a super soldier like this guy will probably rub off on us, for the good of the Army and all that. You have to be careful with Larry; he has a hair trigger with a stiff arm behind it to make up for any supposed lapse in his thought process. He is lovable and cute if your taste runs to Tasmanian Devils as house pets. But he is, sigh, our commander. There isn't another officer in the Army that would take this assignment. We are a careerist's nightmare.

Now you could say that we were deceitful, rather like the story of how I got bamboozled into recon by Bernie. However there is also the fact that Recon is supposed to be voluntary, but voluntary has many different shades. Can I help it if, in the wisdom of the Army, the Recon assignments have become more of a question of will you stay after you get here, or be less in the eyes of your peers?

When we get back to the club, the Cookie is looking at us like we just raped his baby sister. He is really scowling now, and he has several empty cans in front of him. Shit. I identify the problem immediately. Castillo! The Cuban sees us come in, gets up from the table with Cook, and snickers as he skitters across the room, tossing an "Ooh, you lie, GI," at us. It is apparent that the rest of those lying, thieving, back-stabbing, don't-lose-a-chance-to-inflict-misery assholes have told him the real story. As if that isn't bad enough, they have laughed at him as well, and now he is pissed.

We pull up to the table and he has that single eyebrow pulled down tight. He looks at us and slides his chair back while standing up and balling up his fists. We don't even get a chance to try and put the ether mask of lies on him. The fight is on. He packs a punch like a mule that hasn't been laid in two frosts and suddenly sights the widow's mare. He not only knocks the piss out of both of us for a while, but a couple of others as well. While he is busy with them, we pistol-whip him and he goes down. This boy might just be handy in the A Shau. An hour later we are pouring whiskey on each other's scrapes and loose teeth, and Cookie is officially ours. He is so serious, though. We are going to have fun with this one; he is the perfect straight man for our act.

We start to take him over to meet the team, but I suggest we shave him first, lest the Yards mistake him for a rock ape and try to cook him. We stumble into their hut and introduce them to him. After we see that he is comfortable with them, and they are with him, we start back to the club. It is already dark out.

Cuman grabs Mac before we leave and asks him, "He no beaucoup fuck up all the time like you and *Trung Si* Nick?" Mac grins that coon-dog grin at him and we go back to the club. Cuman just shakes his head. The Yards are happy. They have relieved him of his Ranger watch and some cash to celebrate his coming.

When we get back to the club we stagger through the door. I am last and as I come in something that feels like a slab of bacon slaps me in the side, and then sausage-like fingers grab me from behind. Either a gorilla has escaped from the zoo or it is Manes. I hope it is a gorilla.

I turn around still hoping it is a gorilla. My luck is holding at bad and real bad, as usual. It is the captain himself. He has his trunk-like legs planted firmly on the cement and has me anchored by one mitt. With Larry it is best to play the blithering idiot. Any semblance of intelligence in your eyes and he is on you like a cheap flower print dress on a fat woman.

"Whazzish ssshit that fugging frog tells me you got a cook on Habu, my man?" Oh just perfect, Frenchy has mistaken Cook, the name, for cook, the occupation. That idiot could screw up a dirt casserole. And, to make it better, our illustrious leader is more than half shit-faced. This is good, in one respect, because if we are left alone long enough I could possibly convince him that Frenchy insisted that the Cook be assigned to us. That would piss Larry off; he would go find the frog and pull his head off like a chicken. But here in the middle of "snitch central" I am cooked.

"Oh?" I smile blandly.

He shakes me like a rat terrier to emphasize his point. "Anybody going to get a cook around here as his personal chef it's gonna be the Commander. That would be me, to you degenerates."

I see the Combat Pygmy, Mac, grinning like a boar coon at my discomfort. I am getting ready to put his tallywacker in a vise with Manes by blaming it all on him when I hear the Cook yell out, "Hey Mac! Who's that sawed off, little, ugly, water buffalo-looking, piece of shit that has our One-One? Tell him to let loose, or I'm going to kick him so hard in that wide ass of his that his breath is going to smell like Kiwi." Cookie is moving through the crowd, which is parting like the Red Sea for Moses. Manes has a shocked, then pleased look which suffuses into pure malevolence as Cook comes into sight. Mac intercepts Cook, and hog rushes him out the side door leaving me alone, ensnared in the Midget's ham-like paw. That's right you fucking ingrate! Save the new guy. Don't give a rat's ass for the guy who has been saving your ass for the last four months.

I keep waiting for Larry to let go of my shirt. At least then I could get to my Luger. Perhaps if I wound him I could make it back to the hootch and get some dwarf- killing heavy stuff and finish him off. But now he is in the conciliatory stage. He drags me over to the bar and gets two drinks, one for him and one for him, looks at me and says, "You know I do everything for you degenerates. Why would you want to steal my cook?"

I think I will demand that we must have a warning flag that has to be flown anytime Squatty is in the Club. Green means it's safe to drink; yellow means he's here, but not pissed off or loaded. Red means he's both, and they threw him out of the Officers Club.

I get back to the hootch and the Mini Mac is sound asleep. The Cookie is cleaning his weapon. God help us; he is not only cleaning his weapon, but it appears that he is cleaning ours as well. He is putting that worthless LSA lubricant on them.

I take them away from him and tell him, "Never, never, touch our weapons with this shit again."

He looks hurt, so I explain that everyone has their own quirks. One of the taboos is, don't touch anyone else's guns, knives and assorted mayhem tools. Then I explain why we don't use the LSA. WD-40 works better and holds up to the heat better. As he is sitting there, he asks me about, as he puts it, that wide-ass cretin that was giving me a hard time. I look over at my little Alabama hunting partner and inspiration hits me like a rush of cold air. I tell him Manes is one of the mechanics and he owes Mac a lot of money, but Mac is afraid to push him over it since he is related to the colonel.

Best just to let it drop, I add, and don't say anything to Mac about it, because it is kind of embarrassing to him. This ought to be good entertainment for later. Who knows he might shake a few bucks out of Laughing Larry, just before Manes drop kicks him through the goal posts of life. I wearily crawl out of my fatigues and between the sheets. Cook goes over and turns off the lights. I wait until he heads back, and then I tell him to turn the lights back on. He mumbles something, and then the lights pop back on. I hear him gasp. The place is already crawling with the prehistoric looking, two-inch long versions of cockroaches that inhabit every wood structure in Vietnam. He looks around wide-eyed as I tell him we always leave a light on since it keeps them from crawling all over you while you sleep. He takes it pretty well.

CHAPTER 13

Bright Light

My head is pounding from the heat at Phu Bai. I am sitting in the small relief of shade next to one of the Hueys, breathing the sharp smell of the oil that they have sprayed to keep the dust down on the chopper pad. I am drinking water and sweating it out as fast as I consume it. We cannot break for the coolness that the huts offer because we are waiting for the word to crank up and load.

We arrived here two days ago to line up for a mission to find a pipeline they believe the NVA are extending down from the North to carry fuel for the next big offensive. Our air superiority has kept their logistics interdicted, or so everyone thought, with the minimum of supplies getting through to the units down south. For 90 days now, the Air Force has been killing more and more trucks on the main hardball of the trail. Many times the flashes of secondary explosions indicate they hit vehicles carrying fuel or munitions.

Of course, the Air Force chortles away saying that they are diminishing the enemy's capability to wage a major offensive and that they have destroyed his ability to project his force outside his strong points. If you are to believe the zoomies, it should be safe to assume that we will be able to retake most of the Central Highlands and sweep north and secure the northern provinces of South Vietnam, safe enough that one can go for a stroll in the A Shau and never see anything more dangerous than the odd hornet or two. Not the case. We, and our counterparts in Kontum, are getting pressed every time we try to get into the target areas.

Our targets that are normally hot are becoming impossible to get into. There is more and more heavy stuff being thrown up at us, not just 12.5mm, but multiple 37mm and 57mm anti-aircraft guns are being used, as well. To a slow moving helicopter there is only one way to get away from it and that is to get low and hug the earth. And that puts you down where the 12.5mms will tear you into Grandma's ribbons.

We had tried to insert yesterday and were flying nap of the earth, right off the tree tops, and it looked like a steady stream of green tracers coming up from at least seven different gun positions at that level. There'd also been a couple of 37mms tracking the fast movers as they tried to silence the guns and blow a hole that we could maneuver into before the enemy could fill it with hunter-killer teams.

All the way in we watched the air battle. The Cobras were jinking and trying to provide the slicks with cover, barely keeping up with the wall of lead that was being thrown at us. As soon as they would nail a gun position, another would open up somewhere else.

When we got set to flash into the primary LZ, the ground fire got even more intense. We aborted to try the secondary, which was a small clearing about 1500 meters higher up the ridge. Same story, too hot to get in. Every bird took hits; two barely made it back through the keyhole before crashing in a riverbed and we had to use the chase bird to pick up the crews. There is nothing that smells quite as bad as when the bird that you are on is burning somewhere in its innards. There is nowhere to go, and if the fuel cells ignite the choices are fry or take the long plunge.

Mac and most of the Yards were on the lead slick and the Cookie, two Yards, and I were on the second. As we popped up to abort on the secondary, the lead slick got pinned by a 12.5mm and the force of the slugs hammering into it caused it to slew sideways. The pilot broke right and the enemy gun crew couldn't catch up. Then the pilot of our bird did a roller coaster dip that left my stomach hanging where we were, and the gun overshot us as well. The next 15 minutes were the worst I have had on one of these inserts. We were constantly slewing, dipping, and jinking around in the air as we tried not to fly in formation. That way, if they shot at one bird and missed they wouldn't get the next one by default.

The pilots must've been connected to one central nervous system because we barely miss about ten midair collisions and then we are out of the heaviest of it. A Phantom got nailed coming past us dropping CBU on the slopes to our port side. There were a series of airbursts from a 57mm gun and the F-4 erupted into a rolling ball of wreckage that splashed the side of the ridgeline. It was horrifyingly beautiful as we watched the bright, almost white center of the burning comet blowing out into angry orange-red petals of burning fuel and aircraft, just before it made impact with the lush green hillsides.

We passed the wreck and everyone is screaming in the headset, asking if anyone saw an ejection or chutes, but it all happened so fast. It was a great, sleek, fast-moving bird of prey one instant, and in the next it was a bright phoenix before it became a greasy black scar in the forest below. The rest of us limped back to the launch site. Mac's bird didn't quite make it and had to set down about five klicks out. We spent the rest of the day pulling everything back together.

Since then, there has been no sign or word from the F-4 crew and it is assumed that they splashed in with their aircraft. If they did eject they were only about 700 feet above ground level. Not a lot of time between your chute opening and being skewered on the trees. Everyone who is connected with SAR (Search and Rescue) is listening for someone to come up on the emergency frequency. So far no one has come up. The air over the target is too dangerous to linger so they have Moonbeam offset, listening. Until then, the decision has been made that no Bright Light will go in on the crash site or area. If we know they are alive we will go back and risk as many as it takes to get the poor bastards out, but not until there is some indication that we have a live one.

We started this fiasco because of all the assurances from space command that they were crippling the will of the enemy and their ability to wage war. Nguyen shot that story to hell in a hand basket when a trail FAC caught three T-54 Soviet tanks crossing the Song Ba on a submerged bridge in broad daylight, well, just before dusk. They opened up on him with their turret machine guns, and then columned right into a heavy stand of triple canopy on the other side. In the brief moment in which he was able to get a good look at them, he managed to get an oblique shot of them with his camera. Saigon initially denied that the FAC had seen "mediums" this far south and said they had to be PT-76's, but they developed the film and, sure enough, they were T-54s.

Another thing came to light from the film: there were no external fuel drums on the 54s. If they weren't carrying the 55-gallon external feeds, they had to have a fuel dump close enough to get to in their regular tanks. That meant fuel depots, or something else. These babies were so far off the map from the main hardball that could support their weight that someone came to the conclusion that while the Air Force was chasing trucks over in one area, the other team had built a totally separate road system to the east of it.

If the trail FAC hadn't caught them at just that moment, no one would have been any the wiser. The fact that these were medium tanks and were this far south was bad news. The increase in anti-aircraft coverage over the target areas was making all the analysts start to scream what we had been surmising for the last six months: things are going to get a whole lot worse.

We had been trying to insert teams all over the suspected concentrations, with very limited success. The type of activity that we had come to expect north and west in the DMZ was now becoming commonplace further south. I loved the target briefs that we were getting: "It is considered that the likelihood of denser concentrations of enemy units can be expected in these target areas." No shit, Sherlock. When these boys had something they didn't want you to get at, they threw A A on all the high points. And if they started layering it by caliber, then go back to your organizational charts, Nerd Control, and see who carries 57mms around with them.

This wasn't the Home Guard. This was a buildup for a full-on push, to sucker punch us right on our can. Those of us who had survived the '68 Tet were wont to be a little leery of believing that the countryside was pacified. The Air Force, for all its wonderful "you don't have to clean it after" weapons, wasn't going to stamp out anything, but possibly VD infections in Salinas, California.

But back to the basic equation: tanks have to have fuel and if they aren't getting it from dolly carts with drums, then they have to have it piped to them. The pipeline is something that the Air Force can interdict if we can find it. But with all these clanking pill boxes wandering around, you can't just grab the nearest high ground and call in air to chop up their formations. No, with tanks they can set back and direct-fire your rosy red ass into tea biscuits and letters of regret. And with tanks come troops, lots and lots of angry, hard-core, well-led, let's-kill-us-somebody troops. Tanks. I hate tanks.

We try every trick in the book, offsets, false insertions, and walk downs. None do any good. If someone gets in, they are shot out. If a team gets on the ground, within a short space of time they have someone on you, and then it's the dance. They pour more and more troops in and start to canalize you. Soon you run out of terrain and stamina.

Once a team goes to ground and gets static, they bring in more people and you're dead meat.

There are three teams here now and two on the ground. The three of us waiting for a shot at the title are running Bright Light for the ones that tried to get in, or are trying now. One team got in this morning and is already running, and another is being inserted or trying to insert as the first team extracts. We are standing by to go in and pick up downed air crews, or if we have to, fight our way in to rescue one or both teams. I hate this; I have never seen such willingness to give us birds.

They must have every ash and trash bird that can be scraped up, either here, at the refueling point, or out over the target. That means inexperienced crews. These are people that have never flown our type of missions, and more importantly, people that are *soft*. We normally get our Phu Bai air packages from the 101st or from the Marines. We have composite groups here, patch-together units with maybe one crew from our normal package, and two or three crews that have probably been flying Donut Dollies and club runs.

We are lucky in that the one crew, in the lead position with each of our lifts, has taken the riffraff aside and tried to explain what to expect and how to fly the envelope. I can see that they are just as apprehensive and disgusted as we are. The other crews range from attitudes of "no way Jose," to excitement about being in a real combat situation. Neither is good; both will get all of us killed when reflex experience means life or death. This is insane, but we have people on the ground, our people. If they get slammed we will go, and these flying clusterfucks will get some real quick OJT (on the job training) on what it means to fly into the tiger's mouth.

This is why I hate Phu Bai: good Coveys, bad missions. The Saigon pencil-necks don't know how to say "no." There are far too many of us up here, and their answer is more choppers. We could fly these with a Chinook from the Marines. That means one bird instead of three. If they were going to do anything, why not get more gunships instead of more inexperienced slick drivers? The Chinook will take a lot of punishment before it falls out of the sky. And, if you go down, everyone is in one area. You get three slicks down; that's twelve crew in at least three locations, plus whoever was on the bird with them.

But the idiots want dispersion because of the AA and ground fire, which is another thing. Want to find the pipeline, suppress the ground fire, and see what's on the ground? There are enough prime indicators like heavy flak and fire, tanks, and in-depth dispersion to know there are a lot of folks on the ground. So pull us out, ring up the mighty Air Force, and have them dust off a couple of 12 ship Arc Light missions from Guam or NKP. They can fly at 25,000 feet; get a pedicure en route, and open the bomb bay doors over the targets. There won't be enough oxygen in the air for 30 minutes to resuscitate a frog. Then they can turn around, get back in time for cocktails at the "O" club and come back and do it again.

This is a waste of good men's lives and we know it. Somewhere, up the chain, is someone who is using us to further his career. We are stretched to the point of murderous despair.

The one good thing that has come out of all this is the Cookie. He is perfect, cool, calm, hard-core, and easy to be around. He loves the Yards and they love him. He has taken everything in stride and has wedded himself to us and become part of the "animal." I don't have to worry about where he is and what he is going to do. And this boy can throw an M-67 baseball grenade like it was shot from a cannon. Our only problem is going to be convincing Manes that both he and I are too stupid to be left alone so we can all stay together, which is another part of the case of red ass I have about this whole fiasco. If they lose teams they are going to want to start making One-Zeroes out of those of us who have been here for a while. I know I can do it, but I am at home on Habu. We never turn down a mission; we always go and pull our load, so we are always running.

We get the crank up signal. Shit, here comes more bad news. They are cranking up two lifts. The Operations NCO comes running over and grabs us. We go to the TOC shack and we can hear the radios squawking the situation both in the air and on the ground. My intuition when the call came in to get cranked up is correct. The attempt to extract one team and insert the other had gone terribly wrong.

Just as the ships were inbound the team on the ground had been hit and hit hard. The NVA had been shadowing them with trackers and had finally brought up enough anti- recon forces to jump them right on the LZ. They were pinned down in a bomb crater and four of their little people were dead. Both Americans were wounded, with the One-One wounded so badly he wasn't expected to make it.

The second team had come in behind the gun sets, lighting up the LZ with rockets and nails, which had driven the NVA to ground. They had become a Bright Light mission at that point and had managed to start getting the first of the wounded on the lead ship. As the second ship came in preparing to land, the first started to lift. It never cleared the ground. Hit by heavy ground fire, it was lying on its side with the rotors busted all to hell and they had no way to clear it off the LZ. The second ship veered off and gained altitude. Now they had the original team and half of another one on the ground. In addition, two of the chopper crew were seriously wounded. This left three Americans not wounded, two of whom were air crew, plus six little people to care for four seriously wounded. Not good math, they couldn't move those people to another area and fight at the same time. The other half of the team was too small to act effectively as a Bright Light, so we were going to try and make a "hail Mary" play and get them out.

The plan is brutal and simple. Covey thinks he can blow us an LZ near the original one to insert on and then extract from. He will lay a set of fast movers in with 250-pounders and blow down enough flora to get a halfway usable LZ in place. The only other area that can be used for an LZ is over a klick and a half away. That is much too far away for us to fight our way to the team and then extricate them with their wounded. They are working the area over around the team and have taken the pressure off, at least for the time being. The survivors are in a good spot, most of them in two bomb craters, with no way for the NVA to get direct fire on them. The four dead little people are only about 20 meters from the larger of the two craters. We want to have Covey bring in the fast movers and blow a patch of slope below the team clear, so we can insert and make our way up to them. No sense having to drag wounded uphill. Between adrenalin and stress, we are going to be shagged by the time we get to them, anyway.

They are in a good position to have the planes work the ordnance that close. Most of our guys have called stuff in on themselves as close as this before. I'm sure for the survivors of the flight crew it is going to be an eye opener, though. If we can get the Air Force to be precise, we will have a usable flat piece of property that we can hover over and do what has to be done. We are rigging the choppers with ladders so that, if necessary, we can climb down or hook in on the way back. This will save a lot of time. The bombs will shatter the trees but not blow them completely down. There will be huge shattered trunks sticking up like spears, so we prepare for any contingencies in that regard.

The other team is getting fired up as well; if we get into trouble they will be our Bright Light. It's Jimmy, who is from the swamps and bayous of Louisiana and his running mate, a full-blooded Sioux, Fred. Both are tough, competent sergeants, if not a bit odd.

We organize the rescue by drill. We will go in after they prep and create the LZ. Covey comes on station to say that they are blasting a hole for us to use and it's about 100 meters down-slope, almost where we designated. We are going to go in and move as quickly as we can up to where the team is using the gunships and air assets to pound the area around them.

Our plan is to have the gunships do 360-coverage around and on the LZ, and work the area over well between the team and the LZ. They have 17-pound rockets and nails, which should kill or wound anyone stupid enough to try and get in-between.

The NVA are going to try and get right on top of the team to escape this fire or they are going to withdraw. Covey says the team is taking fire from the northwest, which is beyond our line of march from the LZ to the two craters where the team is holed up. Mac and I will handle the tactical movement and the fighting; Cook will organize getting the wounded ready to go and keeping them in the center.

After we assess their condition and get them ready, the Americans will handle the American wounded, as far as carrying them, and we will use the Yards not on our team to fill in. We will use the two aircrew members to help carry the wounded. We have enough manpower to take the Yard dead out with us. We get lucky and get one of the chase medics to go on the ground with us. He can patch and save, which gives us more brawn to get the wounded the 100 meters or so to the LZ.

In about 15 minutes we are rigged and lifting. Nervous grins, a couple of thumbs up, and we are off. Mac has the lead bird again. We will move like we always do, him at the head, me at the tail, the chase medic and Cook in the center. There are all kinds of aircraft working the AO (Area of Operations), you can see them stacking up over the orbit point. There is a pall of smoke, the dull gray-black of HE (high explosives), and there are white scars amidst the green of the bush. That is the bomb strike; the white is chewed up trees. We can see a long pattern of old pock marks that denotes an old Arc Light scar. About midway is the shattered wreckage of the Huey, and near it are the two craters sheltering the team. There is a fresh scar slightly to the left of it, and that is our LZ. It looks pretty good; they must have laid two racks almost on top of each other. There is a shattered and mangled patch of forest cover about 30 yards wide and 100 yards long along the east-west axis of the ridgeline.

The climb uphill is going to be a ball-buster. The terrain is not steep, but it is uphill and the LZ is a jumble of shattered tree trunks and collapsed portions of the upper branches all enmeshed together. The best area is right next to two slate gray holes about 20 feet across. Whoever did this was thinking. The blast pushed most of the debris down-slope so we don't have to pick our way through it. Mac will have to keep the guns working this area because if the bad guys get in there we will have to fight them in that twisted mass of wreckage.

Mac's ship settles in, and they jump at about six feet. The slick can't set down because there is a jagged spear of a tree about ten feet high that makes it impossible. The shattered tree is about 15 inches in diameter. I have four, five-pound ring mains of TNT spread out amongst the team just for that situation. As soon as we land we will set those and blow them as we move off so that when we come back we can load the wounded on and not have to hang on the ladder with them.

My slick is last. We come in and flare, and everyone jumps. There are a few rocks, but the ground is torn up and there's not very much debris so everyone makes a relatively soft landing. We are down and the ship moves off, while the guns are working the slope between the team and us. Mac points at two jagged stumps and yells over at me to get them down. No sweat. I run over with one of the Yards, place the TNT on both sides by sliding it down the knot of detonation cord that connects the two, wrap it with a parachute line to secure it to the tree, and prime it with a claymore detonator. I use the same procedure with the other. It's a little tight on the second one, but it ends up where we can all get down behind the remains of a large tree that is on its side. We tell Covey we are going to torch it and to get all the guns to lay off. Mac gives me the signal and I blow them. The whole thing is over, from placing the charges to blowing them, in little more than five minutes. I look up and we now have an LZ where the birds can set down.

Mac gets on the horn and says to keep the Pink Team on us as we move up. I have to give it to the guys that fly the Loaches on a Pink Team; they can make that little bird do wondrous things. It is ahead of us right at tree top level, slow hover forward. He is trying to draw fire if there is any, so the two Cobras above and behind him can deal with it. The rest of the guns are taking "targets of opportunity" as Covey calls them up.

Laboriously, we move as fast as we can, expecting a fight as we move up-slope. The Loach opens up with its Minigun and then fires a white phosphorous rocket about 60 yards up the slope to our left. The radio crackles and Mac signals three guys, machine gun. Then the guns roll in and they paste the area over. We get the "all clear" and start moving again. The area ahead of us is chewed up by the guns, but Cook sights three bodies and a gun, and points them out. We can hear the remnants of the first team, firing an occasional burst, answered by a few bursts from AKs uphill and beyond them, but the gunships are working everything over.

We have Covey tell the team we are coming in, and when we break out into the old bomb scar, some 20 meters ahead, there they are. We quickly move up and form a perimeter. The medic goes to work on the wounded. It's bad, three of them are too shot up to walk and the One-One is dead. That's five bodies and three wounded. We pull all the bodies into one hole where the medic is working on the ones that can make it. We are pairing up the Americans to get the wounded out. We drop the wounded on a poncho and make a sling-carry so we can piggyback the worst wounded of the helicopter crew. We will use the chopper crew for that. They won't be of any use in a firefight, so better to use them to mule the wounded.

Cook and I move over to the downed Huey, and try to jimmy open the hatch where the secure voice equipment is. It is gone. We run back over to the team and find out that one of the crew has pulled it already. It will go out, also. The Yards from the other teams get the bodies. We call the guns back and move downhill, keeping pace with the slowest man.

There is solid gun work by the fast movers and Cobras. They keep the enemy out of our corridor and flanks. Just before we get there, a fast mover napalms the LZ and we move down through the smoke. The choppers are coming in.

The wounded get thrown on the first bird with the chase medic. The next takes the downed crew survivors and two Yards from the first team. The third comes in and takes the half of the first Bright Light. The next takes the dead and one Yard; another Cookie and me and the three Yards from our end; the last takes Mac and the remainder of the team. We are lifting and pulling free of the trees. As Mac lifts off, the ground fire picks up and his bird takes a number of hits, but stays in the air. We start east to the launch site. Covey tells everything that hasn't got fuel enough to stay long on the target area to drop their ordnance on the downed bird.

We come slipping back into Phu Bai and we are down. Everything winds down and the team goes back to the huts. That's it for the day. The kid that didn't make it and the dead Yards have to be taken care of. We always have our people strip the bodies of equipment and make them ready for the medics to take to the morgue. The Yard dead are put in a freezer. They will get the customary trip back to the home village, accompanied by the surviving Yards and someone from Recon if none of the American team members are able to make it. It is the last measure of respect from us to their tribe and to them. These were all Rhade, so someone will be going to Ban Me Thuot with the bodies. Cook and I go over to the hospital and are stripping the One-One of his equipment and all operational papers. The kid had a silenced twenty-two on him when we rolled him on the bird, but it isn't there now. The helicopter crew wouldn't take anything off our dead; they are like us and that's a "no-no." If they wanted something like that, they know all they have to do is ask, at least that's true of all the normal packages. You don't know about the plug-ins. Maybe one of them took it.

Cookie goes ballistic, grabs the head orderly of the morgue by the throat, and tells him all the terrible things he's going to do to him if he doesn't produce the pistol. The guy is pissing his pants and swears he hasn't touched anything. The hospital staff knows they are to wait until we get there.

We make the ride back to the launch site with me driving, two Yards in the back, and the Cookie Monster fuming and inventing some really innovative profanity dealing with ghouls the whole way back. We get to the launch site and the jeep isn't done rolling before he is out and headed for the helicopter package. Mac, Jimmie and Fred look at me. I just shrug. If those guys thought the mission was tough, they are in for a real ass-tightener. Best to let the Cookie work it out of his system. He is a Ranger after all; they have some sort of mechanism that sets off their release valves. They are kind of like Marines on denatured alcohol and too much testosterone.

This has been one bad day all around. The problems will start all over again tomorrow because the mission to find the elusive fuel supply is still a priority. The new administration at Phu Bai has actually pulled all this together quite well. I still don't like the place. It gives me the heebie-jeebies. I hope we can move it to Quang Tri. At least there Pappy will be running the show, and we might have a better chance of surviving. Well, surviving the mission. Pappy is still pissed off at us for our last foraging foray. We stole a Conex container full of canned sauerkraut, and now he has to use it as the main entree for three meals a day. If we go north we'd better do some judicious trading with the Navy or someone, and show up with steaks, or the Buffalo will find some way to insert us by bicycle.

The Cookie comes back and he has the silenced twenty-two with him. Along with him is a rather sheepish warrant officer. He is from our regular air package. We get a very sincere apology along with the promise that the crew member that had taken the pistol will never do anything like that again. I guess the Cookie pretty much beat the snot out of him, and in the process scared the shit out of everybody. The gun doesn't mean crap to us; it is the thought that someone would ghoul the bodies. The guys that normally fly with us feel the same. This had been a patch crew; they just didn't know any better. The guy saw a neat bit of kit and lifted it, figuring no one would care.

CHAPTER 14

The Anthill Mob

We spend another two days at Phu Bai with no better luck. Saigon finally decides to Arc Light the target boxes, and see what they come up with. Since that will require only two Bomb Damage Assessment teams as a follow up, we are sent back, leaving two teams there and one that trades places with us. We have an amazing four days stand down coming, which we might be able to stretch into six if we get in a couple of days training.

Back in Da Nang we enjoy a new brand of insanity. Everyone has been stricken with "prisoner" fever. It has infected the entire command structure. Of course, capturing a prisoner is the supreme way of satisfying the intelligence requirement. It's like being a burglar: why stumble around in the dark trying to find the hidden safe when the owner is upstairs sitting on the john? Just go up there, stick a gun in his nose and get all the info you want. Only here he is hanging around with all his little *nuoc mam* messmate buddies and they hate people tip-toeing around their back yard.

Eldon had gone out with his Nungs. He was doing some good recon inside his ten by ten area, when they stumbled upon some NVA lieutenant. Now, the lieutenant did what any sane person would do. He took one look at "Mayhem Incorporated," and ran. Hell, if I came upon Eldon and his Chinese cutthroats I would run for cover, too. They, on the other hand, saw a golden opportunity to grab some real intelligence, make a primo cash bonus, and get back to Da Nang all in one fell swoop. So they ordered him to halt. Panic set in. The NVA did the high sneaker and carry, and they were forced to shoot him in one leg. He went down.

Then he struggled to his feet and took off again. So they shot him in the other leg. They bagged and tagged him, the SOG shuttle came in and picked them up, and they got back to the launch site where they rushed him to the hospital. The doctors were upset because we wanted to interrogate this guy while they worked on him feverishly.

It is policy that if we get a prisoner back to camp, one of our people acts as guard. The team sends the perfect guy as guard, Bob Castillo. He comes back late that night with the news that the prisoner died. Most people don't realize how septic gunshot wounds are. The dirt, and every other nasty bug around, gets pummeled into the tissue on impact. There is some cauterizing from the bullet, but in general it's a messy affair. Infection, massive and systemic, sets in and eventually the guy has tubes running out of his chest and is in real bad shape. The prisoner looks at the docs as if to say, "Fuck you. I'm going to die." and does just that. Now Eldon is upset because he is one of those perfectionists and has a professional attitude about what we are doing here, unlike the rest of us who are here in penance for our sins elsewhere. I think the Beaner killed the guy, probably because he got tired of having to sit out a really dynamite celebration party for Eldon and his pirates, or perhaps the guy recognized him as a Cuban advisor. There is also the possibility that Castro capped him because he wouldn't give him his sister's address in case he ever got to Hanoi. At any rate, the only thing they get out of the poor sod is curses.

And now, to top off the epidemic of prisoner fever, we have ringside seats to what will become known as "The Battle of the Anthill." Castro and I are sitting up by the front gate sipping beer, watching the show. The choppers are cranking up to take a composite team out with the primary objective being to bust the commander's cherry. For some insane reason the commander of CCN, Colonel Donnie, has decided that he will be part of a band of intrepid lads that go to a "Free Fire Zone" and bring out a live one.

Now they call these areas Free Fire Zones because there aren't any friendlies out there, ergo anything flying around is free to light up anything and anybody they see. Admittedly, if you want to find a prisoner, that's a good place to look. The place is crawling with potential candidates. The Air Force calls it a "target rich environment."

The colonel is of a mind to be one of the lads, and actually earn his kudos. But his dream team won't be going out to the A Shau to waltz around for a couple of days. Where they are going is a relatively quiet area, just to give The Old Man a feel for running a mission. That is, the area would be "quiet" by our standards. There are still plenty of folks running around that would happily blow them out of their Bata boots. Still, he doesn't have to do this. Is this an act of courage on his part? Nah, the real act of courage is not in doing this, but in risking the puzzle palace in Saigon finding out about it. The colonel must be planning to run for the Senate sometime in the future. Something like this will work real well in conjuring up the image of a steely-nerved, patriotic leader, with a Capital "L." We need to stay alive, just in case that is his plan, so that we can blackmail him into giving us cushy jobs in the Public Works Department. As they trundle down to their rides, Castro and I are arguing over whether there is a slot we can invent called the "Undersecretary of Fun."

I think I should go get my camera for before and after pictures. I have to admit the colonel looks good right now. I want the "after" pictures, though, just in case they get into something that resembles, in a small way, one of our normal days in the A Shau. Now those pictures would be worth a fortune, at least worth a director of something at the state level.

You have to hand it to Colonel Donnie. Not many commanders would mount up, put on the harness and go out there, even in a quiet area. However, it is only confirming our suspicions that Colonel Donnie might be suffering from "medal hunter disease," a sure-fire scary program, because in the equation you eventually become a throw-away pawn. It is also possible that his cheese has slid off his cracker, which is not a good situation either. I've seen a number of senior officers over the years who have flown over an area where troops are engaged on the ground, and then had their aides submit recommendations for all kinds of valor awards for themselves. We call these types of awards science fiction ribbons.

The fact that Manes is agreeing to this insanity brings up some disturbing questions. Larry must owe him money. I can't see Squatty agreeing to this insanity without some sort of payback. I love to think that Colonel Donnie is making him do this. Ooooh, what I wouldn't give to know what he has on Manes to affect that sort of obedience. We have to investigate this further.

Of course, one can't send the commander out with us degenerates. Captain Metal Cube, the human Conex container, wouldn't allow that. Perish the thought. We might display conduct unbecoming of an officer or slip up and mention something horribly ungentlemanly. Something like his girlfriend coughed up a tapeworm longer than a plastic grade school ruler and it might be a good idea to put French kissing her on the back burner. Perhaps the officers simply recognize the fact that we just aren't as interested as they are in the big picture, like the potential for someone's future political career. I'm sure the captain has his very own and very good reasons for leaving us poor cusses behind. Perhaps he wants to prove that he still has the old magic. I can tell you we are impressed.

Anyhow, to satisfy the commander's desire to "see" combat, this composite team has been thrown together. Oh, there are some recon superstars on it. There is Noel Gast, Captain Laughing Larry is the One-Zero, Colonel Donnie, and of course Andre Smith. No little people, just the boys. They have planned mightily and laid on the best of assets, including a Pink Team as cover when they spring the ambush. This is to keep any of the gazillion other heathens from interfering with the Lord's work.

Actually, it is a good plan and they have some good people with a lot of experience going out to do this. If I wanted to straphang on my first real mission, this is a team I would want to be on, with the exception of Andre perhaps, because he wants medals and fame too much for my liking. I have a finely tuned survival gene, which makes me avoid hanging around people like that. They have decided that they will go in dressed as NVA, with pith helmets and tan khakis, which intelligence says the units in the area are currently wearing. They are replete in AK vests and Bata boots instead of our jungle boots, and carrying Sov-bloc weapons as man jewelry to complete the fashion ensemble.

Everything is perfect, right down to the belt buckles. Anyone seeing them at a distance would think, "Hey! Look, it's a bunch of our guys. Let's go over and share a few rice balls with them and see if they have any captured imperialist pornography." But up close, there is no way to mistake them for part of the greater Asian gene pool, because they are big guys. All kidding aside, Andre is over six feet and so is Gast. Manes looks like a tank with a head on it, and both he and the commander are blond. Since none of them speaks Vietnamese other than "Halt, or I will blow your nuts off," there is no chance they will chat someone up and convince them they are Russian or East German advisors. Sneaking and peeking should get them by if there is enough vegetation to hide these minipachyderms.

Even Castro finds this amusing and comments that if it he were some poor NVA and had been living on rice chaff and dried minnows for the last twelve months, he would shoot them just out of suspicion that they were stealing his rations. Andre looks the weirdest with his 255-pound frame and Fu Manchu mustache. We are in agreement that the pith helmet they have screwed on his bullet-like head ought to confuse all those rice converters for about a nanosecond.

It's a funny thing about the motivation behind doing things that could be viewed as courageous. The act is all in the eye of the beholder. If and when Chief SOG and Saigon find out about it, they will have a come-apart. This is good for us in the respect that we can probably wrangle that particular anonymous phone call, and maybe juggle a few blackmail points, for use in a future pinch. The bad thing is that if something unfortunate happens we may have to go haul these four behemoths out of the jam they get into.

As the dream team files by, there are the usual "good luck fellas" exchanged. Castro yells to Manes, "While you are gone, is it okay to have a party, Dad?" which gets him the usual obscenity-laced threats from Captain Larry and a baleful glance from Colonel Don. We continue our harassment in the form of jokes about the very largeness of the bodies being shoved into the NVA uniforms. Noel Gast and Andre ignore us. They are thinking mission. I mean to tell the colonel to keep the three slabs of beef in Bata boots between him and the source, if they start taking fire, but I miss the opportunity.

The choppers are winding away as the lads mount up and the package gets airborne within minutes. They head west into the AO. The colonel is probably as nervous as a virgin in a lumberjack camp, but at least he has good experienced guys around him. We are taking bets that they will fly around until the colonel is disoriented then land somewhere south of us. They can run around for three days, act all *kotuku* scared, and then extract in a withering hail of cover fire. All of this will be very dramatic, with lots of noise and tempest, but not really dangerous. They continue to head west. The only areas out that way are truly free fire zones. Maybe Manes does owe him money and they are going out there to snuff the colonel. The possibilities are getting better for us to have some real dirt on the Deutrinium Midget.

Murphy, God bless his thieving Irish heart, has bought a Mule from some Marine. It is a flat affair with an air-cooled engine mounted in the rear, with a seat and steering wheel on the front left side. It looks like a motorized coffee table. Neat little package, and we are enjoying the novelty of driving it hither and yon, whilst waiting for the boys to make it to the LZ. We make a quick detour to the club and pick up some more cold beer. Captain Butler flags us down and mounts up in a swim suit and carrying a lawn chair. To the flatbed we rig a brightly colored umbrella that we have stolen from some downtown cafe. We inform everyone lounging around Recon Company of the progress of what we are calling "RT Screw," then head back up to the TOC to listen to the radio traffic. Castro makes a quick trip to his hootch and returns with some pilot's helmet that he had collected at some wreck site and is demanding that he drive since he has the helmet.

We sit there arguing about it until Butler pipes up from the back. "I don't care who drives. Just put the thing in gear. This beer is getting warm and I'm losing the sun for my tan."

"Yes, you are the deep well of humanity that we have come to love and respect, Jim," I say. "Your colonel and your partner in crime are out there risking their lives for democracy and you here, concerned about uneven tan lines." He turns to me, belches, and makes some sort of imperious hand signal, indicating it is time to go.

When we get back up to the trailer they are using as the launch TOC there are a bunch of people standing around.

Some of the crowd is from Recon Company, but most of them are staff, or head shed types. The crowd is evenly divided between those that hope that the colonel gets a 7.62mm through the gluteus maximus and the ones, like us, that think this is insane.

The radios are busy with Covey talking to the lift package, sending them from the orbit point, to station, and eventually release. The team gives a team okay and they are moving. We have three experienced One-Zeroes and the colonel out there. To us it has entertainment potential if we don't have to get involved. Despite the situational humor, this is dead serious business from this point on. I decide to go back for more beer and take a shower. I am drenched and want some relief from the sun, besides, how much trouble can they get into in the area they're in?

I go back to Recon Company, take a long cold shower, then stop by the club to see what is going on there. As I round the comer of the Company shack, I see Pee Wee and he has a serious look about him. I start to say something, but he asks me if I have heard anything about the colonel and Captain Manes. I tell him no, only that they made it in and got off the LZ, and that was about a half hour ago. I tell him I'm going to pick up some beer, go get Castro, and maybe later go down to the Pink House downtown. I have more important things to worry about than what Squatty and Colonel Donnie are doing in the "dry hole of the month" area.

We have another day of stand down and then pick up another mission. We will probably spend tomorrow doing IA drills, getting our tone back and shaking off the edge before we go into isolation, so tonight will be the big blow out. We grab a jeep that is behind one of the hootches and go over to the club to get some beer. We walk into the club and it is deserted. That's strange, and disturbing, because it can only spell disaster somewhere, or we are about to become victims in some practical joke. I see one of the guys from Mamba come in and he is looking for Davidson. I tell him I haven't seen him and ask him where everyone is.

"You guys haven't heard? Manes and them are in a world of shit," he says. A world of shit? What could possibly have happened? That area is safer than passing out in the Recon Club for Christ's sake. We all hustle out the door and pile into the first jeep we find, of course having the foresight to grab some beer and throw a book of chits on the bar. We pour on the gas and streak up to the TOC area, where there is a milling and grim crowd. Everyone is listening to the reports being whispered back from the front row. The news isn't good.

Larry and the guys moved off the LZ and into a relatively open area, trying to cross quickly to get in amongst the few clumps of forest that ringed the edges. As they were crossing, they heard helicopters and assumed that it was part of the package. More annoyed than concerned, they kept moving. They came across an area with several tall termite and anthills dotting the landscape, and had been surprised to see a Loach skirting them off to the east about half a klick away. Then, out of nowhere, a Cobra gun ship fired them up. Just by sheer luck no one was injured on the first pass, and they screamed on the radio to cease-fire. They had the KY-38 secure voice system and should have had five-by commo with the birds. Nada. The Pink Team rolled back in and fired a salvo of nails at them. Fortunately, they took cover behind a fallen tree and a couple of the concrete-like termite colonies, which absorbed the lethal portion of the attack.

As we join the crowd, Covey is screaming at the birds on the guard frequency to back off because they are firing on friendly troops. He realizes they are not part of our asset package and swoops in to try and put himself between the birds and the team. His appearance confuses the Pink Team just enough that they don't fire on their next pass. They are setting up for another run when he finally manages to make contact with them.

They are still talking when our gun package shows up and takes matters into their own hands. They listen to Covey trying to tell the other birds that these are friendlies, but the errant Pink Team is not buying it. Our gun package senses that their counterparts are getting ready to fire again because, with no direction from Covey, they fire right across the front of the other birds and tell them if they attempt to open fire they will blow them out of the sky. This gets the Pink Team's attention PDQ.

Meanwhile, both Larry and Noel have been hurt in their respective derrieres and the other two have shrapnel wounds. One of our gunships comes over, hovers over them, and faces off with the other Cobras. There is a hurried aviator, "oh-shit-we're-sorry" conference, and then the slicks come rattling in to gather up the team. From that point, all goes fairly smoothly, and we listen to the progress report as it happens. Quick thinking on Covey's part, as well as the balls of the gunship guys, stops this from being a bloody fiasco. As it is, all of the team members are wounded to some degree, and two of them won't be running for a while. Well, at least the colonel tried; he wanted to get a taste of how bad it is out there.

Now the staff pukes have this horrible suspicion that Colonel Donnie is thinking about turning every pencil-pushing one of them into a special home guard recon outfit that he will personally lead into the bloody fray, an idea, I might add, that we have nothing to do with as far as fanning rumor control. It's not a bad idea, but let Laughing Larry be in charge of the death lottery once a month. That way, we can choose a lucky composite team made up of shoe clerks and stay-behinds, get them all dolled up in death gadgets, and then drop them in the A Shau. Guaranteed CIB, Silver Star, and DSC (Distinguished Service Cross), all that pretty shiny stuff, to the ones that make it back to the chopper. Hey, maybe we can get the losers air conditioners. I mention the whole idea to Castro, but his mind is on the virtues of a steam bath with a massage.

Manes has to listen to crude jokes about Noel and him having two of the most humongous asses in Southeast Asia. We ask that that particular Pink Team never be part of our air package since they can't hit a target that wide. He takes it with his usual good humor by knocking the dick string straight of some idiot from up the hill who repeats what we said. Then, of course, he comes down to Recon and blames us for him having to resort to violence through our insolence and disrespect.

Mac and the Cookie come back from Da Nang as the whole thing is winding down. They enter the club as everyone is yukking it up over the debacle. Poor Noel, he is like Eldon in that he takes it all in a professional manner. I am sure that he would just as soon forget he drew this one. Mac wanders over to where Castro and I are arguing with Lamar about the relative merits of hiding behind termite mounds. He pulls up a chair and Cook shows up with a couple of beers.

"What's been going on?" Mac drawls.

Castro looks at him, and in mock surprise asks, "You didn't hear?"

"No, I didn't hear. Would I be asking if I heard something?"

"The Colonel, Andre, Gast, and Manes went out on a prisoner snatch. That's what happened, you dimwit," Castro admonishes him.

"So, what happened? Did they get lost?" Mac asks.

"Nope, in fact they got themselves a prisoner. It was a horrible battle out there, with guns blazing, grenades going off, B-40s coming in. They even got jumped by helicopters." Castro is leaning forward in his chair and is almost whispering, as if it were some secret that had to be kept quiet.

Mac figures it's all bullshit. "Yeah, sure."

"No shit, Mac, they went out," I said.

He looks at me, figures that I am in on it, so he throws the curve question. "The NVA ain't got helicopters this far south, so who did they capture, some private taking a shit?" Then he giggles into his beer. Castro just looks at him and shakes his head as if Mac is just too thick to appreciate the gravity of the situation.

"Nope, they grabbed a high ranking member of the rebels."

"Who?"

"Robert E. Lee." We laugh and tell them the real story. In the end, they are having as much fun with it as we are. We have squeezed just about all the humor we can out of the situation when a hush falls around us. We all turn and there is Manes, his ass all bandaged. He is limping through the front door. When he gets inside he glares at everyone.

"The first one who says anything about the mission, my wounds, or why I got them, I am going to knock his dad-blamed dick string straight. The next one who mentions it, I will personally put in the A Shau with a bicycle and a slingshot, and leave him there!" He limps towards the bar.

He gets just past us when Castro weighs in. "Someone buy that captain a drink. He's been wounded in the brains!" The whole place breaks up. Soon Larry is telling us his side of it. Pretty funny, but at the same time lessons were learned, like when you run around with an NVA kit on, more than likely an aviator is not going to notice you are oversized and will fire you up. Another sobering point is that not everyone out there has a secure voice system in his bird, so if you are trying to tell them "please don't shoot us," they might not hear you.

Still, I wish we had gotten pictures.

CHAPTER 15

With Texans Expect Bumps

I've got dirt in my mouth and I hurt like hell. I try to open my eyes, but I can't get them to open. It's like trying to come out of a deep sleep; I want to wake up, but I can't quite get there, flopping around like a fish on the bank of wakefulness. One thing I can do is get this dirt out of my mouth. I am trying to figure that out when my hearing starts to come back.

I can hear the muffled sounds of someone screaming and the crump of shells landing nearby. Above all, there is the almost continuous rattle of small arms fire. Coming through the haze are two voices; I try to figure out who they belong to and what they are saying.

"Is he alive?" the first voice asks.

"I think so," the second replies. "His eyes are open, but he isn't registering. Let's get him up." Are they talking about me? Who the hell are they? I can't register. I wish whoever is screaming would stop; it's confusing, and it's scaring me. Hands pull me off the ground where I have been face down. There is a moment of gyrating scenery; I see churned up soil, a glimpse of sandbags, and then part of a leg from the knee down, clad in sterile fatigues and a jungle boot. There is a vision of sky, smeared with dust and black smoke. But out there, somewhere, during that brief spinning view, I had seen beautiful blue sky. The image of that leg, though, panics me. Is it mine? And why can't I shake this off? I can't seem to get a clear thought through my head. I am trying to feel and see if both my legs are intact. Everywhere I touch hurts and I can taste blood in my mouth. It's mixed with the leftover grit. A face looms in front of mine and looks at me intently. This person takes a canteen and sloshes some water on my face, then wipes it with a cravat. I can see a little better now. I know that face.

The face turns and yells off to his left, "He's alive, but he ain't gonna be on no quiz show." Then he turns to me and kind of smiles as he gets up and takes his weapon and runs off to my right. He moves too quickly for me to follow.

The man disappears over by a remnant of a sandbag trench line and what looks like a bunker. I am propped up in what appears to be another bunker, but there isn't any overhead cover. I can see who was screaming before. It is a Yard. He is beyond screaming now. He is eviscerated and lying there, clutching his abdomen, trying to hold in his entrails. His shirt, what is left of it, has been ripped apart. Around his abdomen is a combat dressing, which he is clutching to the wound, desperately, as if it will stop the process of dying. It is soaked with so much blood it seems to be part of the mess that is poking out around it. I look at his face. He is staring, but not seeing, and his whole body is trembling. I know that tremble; it's when the body is in so much pain and agony that the nervous system short-circuits and that's all you have left. There is a morphine Syrette pinned through his cheek. It's completely used. Someone has done him right, since we all know that the Yards can't take a full Syrette; it'll kill them. From the shape he is in, he doesn't have many moments left. We're told not to give morphine for a stomach wound because it masks the symptoms. Whoever dreamed that one up has never had to spend much time with someone who has been ripped apart.

I hear a machine gun firing off to my left and I turn to look. I spot the leg again and it's lying in the trench to my left front. It is incongruous; there are no other body parts. Is it mine? No, I can see both of mine. I pan left and see two Yards manning an M-60. They are burning up ammo in long, controlled bursts, down and away. The gunner is intent and he is switching the gun position as he fires. You can tell he is dialing in on a new target each time he moves.

There is a rhythm to it, a five or six round burst, the gun barrel moves, five or six rounds and it moves again. I try to lift my left arm to swat at the place where an expended round from the 60 has hit me in the head, but my arm and hand are all floppy. The casings come out in a steady stream, hitting the left side of my head and the sandbags I am leaning against.

I lean to my right to get away from them. I see the other Yard, who is feeding the gun, stop, reach back, and jerk the pin from a grenade. As he does, I hear a couple of AKs open up, firing in long bursts. The sandbags in front of me kick with each impact, as sand and soil spurts out where the rounds hit the tops of the bags. Someone is trying to knock out the gun. The gunner is firing to the left when the other Yard chucks the grenade to his right and down slope. He swings back and does the same with another grenade. There is the crump of the first one as the second is lobbed in the same direction. There is another sharp crump and someone starts screaming. The AKs stop firing, but the M-60 never ceases. There are a couple of discarded ammo cans lying at their feet. The second Yard pulls a full one out of a pile of about six more, snaps the top off, pulls the square box out, and then hooks another belt to the belt that is already in the gun. He repeats the process, making sure the belt feeds at an acute angle to the gun, guiding it with his left hand. He has his CAR-15 leaning against the trench wall and the barrel is smoking, the heat cooking the oil out of the metal.

I am so groggy I think I am drugged. I run my hand along my cheeks and then my lapels to see if there is a morphine Syrette stuck there, to show that I have had a shot. No Syrette, so I must be groggy from wounds or concussion. There is blood all over my left side, and what looks like small pieces of meat near my knee. I feel no wounds, so it must be someone else's blood. My mind is telling me that I need to get back in this fight. I still can't remember where I am or what we are doing here. I am looking for my weapon, but it is nowhere near me. I reach back and the movement sends stabbing pain down my back. I finally locate the little sawed-off twelve-gauge I keep in a nylon pouch slung across the small of my back. I give it a couple of tugs, but it won't come free. Then I remember to loosen the length of elastic that loops over the butt. I get it out and reach up to find the pouch where I carry 25 rounds of double aught buck and slug and take two out.

I break open the shotgun. There are two already in it, a slug in the left barrel and a double aught in the right. I look down and I have one of each in my left hand, just like I pack them. I do this so I don't have to look when I am reloading. I am still shaky as hell, but I need to find my CAR-15 and I am not going to crawl around looking for it without something to protect myself with. Not here. There are obviously a bunch of folks trying to kick our asses, wherever we are. I am looking at the Yards, as the gun slacks off. They aren't from my team. Who the hell was that face I saw? I know it, but still can't get a cognizant thought going. The Yards look at me, and then back down the slope.

There is more automatic fire from over the hill. There is the sound of a variety of weapons. I can recognize several CAR-15s and at least one M-60. There is also the unmistakable sound of a few AKs. The AKs sound as if they are farther off and their fire diminishing. Then I remember who it was who'd been leaning over me. It was Davidson! I hate Davidson; he has more bad luck than that little guy with the cloud over his head in "Li'l Abner," Joe Btfsplk. Davie gets shot at more than a duck in a shooting gallery. The man is a veritable bullet magnet. What in God's name am I doing with Davie? Where is Mac? Did we commit some great sin that as punishment we had to go on a target with Davidson? If we are on top of some hill with him, we are in deep kimchi.

I am trying to get up. I *have* to find a gun now. I get as far as my hands and knees. I cradle the shotgun. I just know the yellow horde is going to come busting over the berm line. I hear running behind me and roll, bringing the barrel up just as Eldon slides into what's left of the bunker. I could almost kiss him. If Eldon is here, I'm safe. At least I'm not up here alone with that whacked-out, little sawed-off runt, Davidson. Eldon pushes me back into a sitting position and looks me over.

"Are you alright?" he asks, peering at me intently.

"I'm fine." Only it comes out, "Ooom firrlm."

He shakes his head and holds me by the harness. "Don't try to talk. Just nod if you can understand me." I nod. "We got choppers coming in. We're going to put you on the first one with the other wounded." Wounded? I'm not wounded; I already checked. Did I miss something? I start looking myself over again just to be sure. Eldon just squats there, looking at me like I had my pee-pee out in public. Don't just squat there staring at me, you fool. With Davidson on top of this hill we are probably about to get shot at by some sort of super secret weapon the NVA are trying out for the first time. Get out there and find him, hide him, bury him, throw him off the mountain, anything, but get him away from us or we are doomed. Such are my thoughts, but Eldon just continues to stare at me with concern.

"Do you understand?" He is looking at me intently, evidently not liking what he sees. He yells over in the direction where the firing is not so heavy. I hear scrambling, and Davidson comes tumbling into the hole. He turns to Davie. "Stay here with him. He's still not all here. When the first bird comes in, get him on it and the Yard from on the other side of the sixty, okay?" That's Eldon, all business. I am so glad to see him that for a minute I forget what he has said. He is going to leave me here with the fucking varmint.

"Don't leave Eldon! Just shoot me. Finish the job, for God's sake. If you leave me here with magnet-ass, I am as good as dead." I try to yell my concerns to him, but all that comes out is weird mumbling. The nagging thought about wounds is still at the back of my mind. Then it dawns on me. I am being sent out. "Wait guys, I can still fight. See, I got my twelve-gauge. If you send me home all the other guys will think I am a pussy. You can't do that." I try and tell them I am not leaving, but it comes out in some sort of alien language that sounds like Iroquois.

Davidson looks at me and says to Eldon, "What the hell is he speaking, Martian? Boy, that explosion really screwed him up. Ya think we should let him have a weapon? He might shoot himself by accident." He grins and Eldon sort of smiles. You two goobers just try and take this gun from me. I'm gonna shoot both of you.

Eldon listens on the radio for a minute and then says to Davie, "They are about five minutes out." He pauses and then continues, "Get him on the first bird and we will load the two we got on the other side at the same time. After that we will load you and your guys out; then I will bring mine out last." Davidson nods, and Eldon gets up in a crouch and runs across and over the hill. Davie yells at someone over to our right about getting the wounded ready. No, Eldon! Don't leave me here with Yosemite Sam! Everyone from The DMZ to the U Minh Forest knows he is a magnet for anything fired from a barrel -except they never hit him. They hit everybody else. Davie reaches down and plucks the twelve-gauge from my hand, and shoves it back in the sheath on my back. He smiles at me with that feral little smile of his and tells me everything is going to be fine.

Yeah, I'm going to be alright, as soon as they lift me out of here. If you're not on the same bird, that is. If you are, sure as a bear uses the forest for a latrine, we will get shot down. I suspect that whatever and wherever this explosion was, he was right next to me when it happened. I am willing to bet money on it. I can hear the choppers coming. I see a Cobra flash by and as he goes out of sight I hear his Minigun open up. I can't hear any enemy fire so they must be suppressing any thoughts of continuing the attack.

There is the familiar flap, flap, flap, of a Huey rotor slapping into short final, coming closer. Davidson and one of the machine gun crew grab me and half carry, half drag, me to the bird. A Yard who is shot in both legs is loaded on my side first. Then I am lifted and shoved inside as two other Yards are shoved in from the other side. One is shot up pretty bad and the other has what looks like shrapnel wounds to his back. The crew chief is looking everyone over. All the others are obvious, but I appear to be less injured except for the blood all over my left side.

He looks at Davie and asks, "Where is he hit?" I guess in case he has to check my bandages on the way back.

Davidson says, "Keep an eye on him, he's been drinking." Then he runs off as the chopper lifts and banks off the top of a narrow ridge. I can see the ruins of what appears to be an old bunker and trench line. There are at least two teams of our guys spread out amongst the bunkers. There is a black spot to the rear of where I had been. The guys are bagging one body, or maybe more, in and around the area. There are about half a dozen bodies clad in khaki down slope to the right. I get a brief glimpse of the fight; then we are gone. The crew chief keeps looking at me with a bemused look on his face. Yeah, real funny Davie. The crew chief probably thinks I am drunk. I wish I were drunk. What in the name of God was I thinking? Even with the positive karmic aura of Eldon around, why would I go anywhere with that runt from Waco? Maybe I *was* drunk and that's how I got here. That has been known to happen. You have something that I need to run a mission, but you won't give it up? Give, or next thing you know you are a kidnap victim and we take you along. I did that to Castro once. The Yards onboard look at me with the same mixture of pain and relief that I am sure I have. I make the universal, "Got a cigarette?" sign to the crew chief. He nods and hands me a pack of Camels with some GI matches. I light one up, hand it to the Yard that is propped up, and he leans over and puts it in his buddy's mouth. I light another one for him. He takes it and smiles. I try to light mine, and am going to light one for the Yard on my side, but my hands begin to shake so bad I can't. The gunner reaches over, lights both, gives one to me and puts the other between the Yard's lips who is lying between us. The Yard reaches up, pats my leg, and gives me the "Everything is okay, *Trung Sĩ*" look.

I look out the door at the terrain. I am still woozy in the head and I have no idea what happened, or where we have been. The area isn't ringing a bell and I don't trust myself to talk. The crew chief motions to ask if I want a headset and mike. I shake my head, no. I don't trust myself to respond in anything that won't resemble gibberish, which will confirm his suspicions.

The sprawling military camps, of which CCN is the last one, and the cobalt blue of the South China Sea loom into view. We are descending rapidly and the air gets warmer as we do. We flash over the trash dump 100 feet off the ground. I can see the trash pickers scurrying around, and then we are flaring and setting down on the pad. Figures run up to the chopper and gentle hands take the Yards off. Someone starts to help me and I shrug them off, with the intention of getting off and walking. My legs fold under me and I collapse on the ground.

I am lifted and placed on a stretcher, then it's onto a gurney and we are moving slowly towards the infirmary. I see Doc Wang doing triage as we go along, and recognize the concerned faces of guys I know as they each loom into view, and then disappear as another face appears. I still can't hear all that well so most of it is muffled comments that I can't understand. We are taken up to the infirmary.

The Yards have I Vs in them by the time we get there. I am taken inside where one of the nurses and someone from the medics take my harnfiess off and begin to cut my clothes off, checking for wounds as they go. Doc Wang looms into view. I feel a sharp prick in my arm and drift off into never-never land.

CHAPTER 16

As Through a Glass Darkly

I am drifting on Lake Minnewaska with my kid brother and we are crappie fishing. It's a hot summer day and the lake is as smooth and placid as a duck pond. I can feel the heat of the aluminum boat radiating from the sides like a convection oven. One foot is draped over the side of the boat and the waters of the lake are cool and refreshing. I am lying back on an ice chest and have a t-shirt on with a pack of Marlboros rolled up in the sleeve like James Dean. The crappies are nibbling at the line and every once in awhile it vibrates and jumps a little, but nothing like a solid hit. Hell, it's probably perch, I hate perch. My little brother is sitting in the back of the boat and he is intent on fishing. That's Ron, slow and deliberate, all ears and freckles. He turns around with that goofy little smile of his and says ....

"Hey, asshole! Nick! Nick! Hey asshole, wake up!" Huh? My little brother fades away and I am swimming up through the fog. The cool waters of the lake and the summer breeze are gone, replaced by the smell of antiseptic. Someone is shaking me and it hurts, damn it. My whole body is sore, even my tongue. I slowly open my eyes, peering through watery vision. The first face I see is the Cookie. He notices I'm coming out of it and stops shaking me. He backs away as I try to put the who, what, and where together. Another face comes into focus. It is Castillo. I recognize our ward at the infirmary. There are about seven or eight other beds occupied by wounded Yards.

Castillo leans over and with boozy breath declares, "Rise sinner and be healed." As he places his hand on my head, I hear a chorus of "Amen brother, praise Jeeezus!" and there is Charley Jay, Davidson, Pee Wee, and Jimmy Reeves. All are grinning and obviously heavy into the Jack Daniels. In fact, they have a whole medical tray full of Jack Daniels in glasses, what Florence Nightingale would bring if it were hell. Cook comes over and tells them all to shut up and give me some room. I'm confused, solicitous conduct from the Cookie? Surely, I have died and gone to the twilight zone.

But I am soon back to reality when he grabs the front of my baby blue hospital pajamas. He twists the front of them, drags me to a sitting position and shakes me.

"You awake now, Stretch? You have been out for two days. Doc says you should be coming out of it. Well, if you are out of it, then you are going back to the hootch, because I am tired of the team coming over every hour on the hour, wanting to know how you are," he grimaces. "Every time they come over, they con me out of something, food, beer, money, my watch, you name it. So, unless you are dead, which is the other alternative to stop them from coming over, you are going to the Yard hootch so they can see, smell, and touch your little malingering ass."

Then I see the devil himself. Davidson! You little cockroach, I don't know how, but somehow you are responsible for my being here. He gives me that weasel-like smile he reserves for the uninitiated and holds out a glass of bourbon with one hand while the other holds the bottle it came from.

"Wansome?" Oh great, they are all in bad shape. And they are going to take me out of here.

Doc Wang peeks in and I see salvation. "Make sure someone returns those blues back here. I only got so many." He disappears down the hallway. The little Chinese quack! I am going to make it a point to survive this war and track him down and destroy his career. He may be able to bullshit the entire world into believing that he is some kind of necromantic surgery messiah, but right now he has violated the Hippocratic Oath. You little Chinese weasel, do no harm, my ass. What do you think these drunks are going to do, treat my sacred vessel for what it is? I don't think so. That's why that fucking medical badge has two snakes on it. One wouldn't have been enough to cover this betrayal.

The wolf pack closes in. I am stripped naked, then roughly hauled out of bed and someone gives me a fatigue shirt with the slurred admonition that I shouldn't be seen by the Yards in an undignified state. I am still at a loss as to how I got here or how many days I've been out. A Demerol-induced hangover is all I'm sure of.

I am hauled, moaning and bitching, out to a waiting jeep. We make the short ride down to the Yard barracks and I am manhandled in front of my team with Cook officiating in the delivery of the prodigal son. The Yards are obviously glad to see me and have that childlike mirth about the fact that I am naked from the waist down. Cook is beyond compromise in his assurances to them that I am fine. "See, he is here. *Trung Si* Nick, in the flesh, back from the dead." Cuman makes a sour face and informs him and me that I have no pants on. You have to love these little throw-backs; they are masters of the obvious. They are examining my bruise. I say bruise because there is no end to it. My entire back is one massive hematoma.

One of the little people comes in with my clothes. Cuman obviously thought it was beneath the dignity of the One-One to walk around with his bullwhip loose and had sent one of the team to fetch me some proper clothes. As for my rescuers, they are talking among themselves and jabbering like the simians that they are. Cuman sits me down in a chair, and from him I learn what exactly happened. Well sort of, it is part sadness, part regret, part recrimination, a speech directly from the tribal chief to his *Trung Si*.

"*Tahan* no like *Trung Si* go out wib out *Tahan*. *Trung Si* almost die! Make *Tahan* beaucoup sad. No go field without *Tahan*." We stay for about half an hour with each team member coming up to touch me and then say something. It is all kind of primitive, a rekindling of the spirit. You see the same thing at the football stadium with the butt slap. It's a guy thing.

I am feeling really good right about the time the horrible horde decides that all this primitive stuff is enough. We have to go to the club where the rest of the demon crowd is waiting. Cuman takes my hand and walks me to the door. He looks at me as if I was his kid brother and tells me I should sleep here tonight. He says he will send *Tahans* to find me later bring me back. I know they will, so I say okay. We walk from there to the club because the jeep won't start. I suspect Cuman had it disabled for my protection. We arrive and there is the usual tumult of "Here let me get you a chair and a cold beer," then "Okay, we're bored," and they go back to their shenanigans. Davidson and Cook shoo everyone else off and we sit at a table.

Eldon comes in and pulls up a chair. He starts talking and everyone defers to him. He has that quality about him. You know, the leadership trait, epitomized by the calm, even tone of his voice and his presence. The whole package is punctuated by the sight of a .45 stuck in his belt. Besides, he has been there a long, long time. Eldon is one of the most experienced guys in Recon. He starts in by asking me what I remember. I don't remember what planet I am from.

So he begins on the day when he came down to see if we wanted to straphang on a mission that would involve his team, Davidson's team, and the remnants of Habu. Mac had gotten a sprained ankle from practicing rappelling, which left Cook and me in limbo. In order to cover the big lie, the one in which I am too dimwitted and slow to be a One- Zero, we sent the Yards off to Mai Loc and blamed it on poor foresight by Mac after they took us off the ready list.

Cook was slotted for One-Zero school and would leave in a few days. That left me, and Cook, if he wanted to go.

The plan was for a two-team insertion onto a ridgeline that overlooked two key logistic routes. One was the extension of the trail system coming out of the tri-border area and the other was a major river artery. The ridge was juxtaposed in-between a prominent height overlooking the area and had excellent observation. In addition, there was an old firebase for a battery of 105s; the last time it had been used was two years ago, and it was deemed defensible. We would insert at midmorning and get in position by digging into the hilltop and bringing in some heavy weapons so that we could interdict the river traffic and cover two parts of the trail. We were going to bring in a 106mm Recoilless Rifle and an 81mm mortar. With enough fire power and air support we could hold the position and bottleneck their flow. Sooner or later they had to come and kick us off the hill. When they did that we would book and get the mighty Air Force to come in and carpet bomb the area, maybe catch a couple of regiments in the valley and the surrounding hills. But the brilliant part was that while we were digging in, Eldon and his team were going to slip away after dark. All eyes would be on us pesky little varmints on the ridge. They would set up a prisoner snatch in the confusion and get extracted to the west. If that didn't work, they would mine the roads and either make it back to us or get out separately.

Things had gone smoothly in the beginning. We managed to get everyone on the hill and were throwing ammo and the big stuff out. I was putting it all in place and handling the nuts and bolts of defending the position. The far end pointing towards the river was narrow and very steep. Davidson was standing there with one of the Yards and the M-60 machine gun that he was going to lay in. One of the birds bringing in the last of the ammo gusted on takeoff and applied the power just as he was over Davie.

The rotor blast blew him off the ridge and he tumbled down the slope about 75 yards. Davidson managed to keep the M-60 with him, and when he got done rolling and sputtering obscenities he stood up and looked right into the faces of about 15 just as startled NVA regulars who had been working their way up the hill to observe our movements. Quick as Jumping Jack Flash, Davie hosed the group down and started backing up the hill at a slant. The Yard on top of the hill heard him firing, saw the figures and chucked two grenades in quick succession, scattering the survivors.

In the meantime, I was over by the old bunker line with my back to the bald top of the ridge. I had just started for a line of bunkers and the old trench with a case of grenades when one of the Yards behind me started to pick up a box of ammo from among the boxes lying around one of the old gun revetments. Only this box wasn't one of ours. And it was booby-trapped. I don't know why I hadn't seen it when we came in. You usually sweep for that kind of stuff. You find it, tie a rope to it, get behind cover, and pull on it.

Well, we had missed it and the Yard on Davie's team was new. He picked it up and it blew him into a cloud of red mist. It also blew the man next to him off at the kneecaps and eviscerated a third. It threw me ass over tea kettle down the hill into the trench line and two of the shells had hit the top of the bunker next to where the third man and I landed. The blast from their detonation took off a comer of the roof and shredded him again. His body had saved me from the brunt of the blast.

Davidson had made it up the hill by the time the NVA came back with a whole bunch of their buddies. The enemy had organized quickly, and their first assault tried to run up the long slope in front of where I had landed. The Yards had seen them and immediately got the machine guns laid in on them. This broke the back of the assault before it reached open ground about 45 yards to our front. That's when the NVA started trying to get a couple of squads close enough to flank the guns so they could rush us. This was apparently about the same time I woke up and started floundering around, and Davie ran over to see if I was alive. I don't remember anything except an intense red flash. That's it.

We spent about two hours in the club, drinking and talking, trying to work over what had gone wrong. The bottom line was that it was just bad luck that we missed the case of ammo. Who booby-trapped it? Probably the ARVN outfit that had abandoned the hill last. But it was also good luck when Davidson fell down in and amongst the enemy and discovered they were right there.

The guns and the ammo that weren't used saving our asses were rigged and when they got everyone and everything out, they bombed the top of the hill. I had been out for two days since. Cook was leaving tomorrow for One-Zero school and wanted to make sure I got to say good-bye before he went. Of course, convincing the rest of the crowd to come help took about a nanosecond.

I look up for some reason and out past the front door are two small squatting figures. I know they are from my team and they have waited there for me because I will sleep in their hootch tonight. I will be in their longhouse, a brother. I get up and tell Cook I will see him in the morning. Come over and wake me.

"Wake you, my ass!" he says. "One of those Yards is here for you and the other is here for me! Cuman says we both stay there tonight. You and I too much fuck up together without *Tahan*" He mimics Cuman. We both laugh and I stumble outside. Ti Ti is there with Bop. They rise, grinning like the Cheshire cat in *Alice in Wonderland*. There is another figure. It is Bong. He is squatting next to the jeep and smoking his little brass pipe. He stands and says something to the other two; they squat back down to wait for Cook. He takes my arm gently and we begin to walk back over to the Yard hootch. Before we climb the stoop up to the sleeping quarters he stops and looks into my eyes as if they were windows to my soul.

"Did you visit with the spirits, *Trung Si*? You were in the spirit land for a long time. They wanted you to stay, but the *Tahan* called you back. You are not ready to go to the spirit land, *Trung Si*. Your journey has just begun." He turns and opens the door for me to go inside. I will make sense of this tomorrow.

CHAPTER 17

Saltwater Therapy

Our camp's eastern end is on the beach and we have a gate there with what we call the beach house. When you want to go to the beach, normally it is an involved process that you won't see at Laguna Beach or any of the upscale resorts in California. Our pre-beach preparation includes notifying the guys on top of Marble Mountain to keep an eye out for anyone who might be wandering around with a long rifle. Next comes the security sweep which involves two or three guys with mine detectors doing a cage pattern and marking off the clear area. But now we have "Fish" technology.

Fish has salvaged the hull of a 175mm self-propelled gun carriage and stripped the gun off the top. He has made a dolly that attaches to the front that has two rows of 55 gallon drums attached in parallel that act as rollers. These we fill with water to give them weight. Behind the hull is an old-fashioned drag assembly like you would see on any mid-western farm. The idea is that the rollers have enough weight to detonate any mines above the tidemark and the drag follows to pull any mines to the surface that may be defective or have too much sand in the firing mechanism to work.

Simple, efficient and, so far, we haven't found any mines. We started sweeping the beach after a toe popper mine mangled some Yards a couple of months ago. But the old solution took several hours to complete, so teams quit going to the beach. Now that we have Godzilla, as we have named Fish's contraption, we can clear the beach in about twenty minutes. When it's done, it looks like the manicured beaches of Monaco, or it could resemble one of those Japanese stone gardens with all the lines going in one direction. We take it all the way to the water. The dolly assembly and drag are wide enough, and since she is a track, there is no chance of getting stuck. That's one thing about Fish; given a mechanical problem, the boy can build anything.

Waiting for Godzilla to finish its magic today are about forty Americans, dressed in everything from outlandish Hawaiian shirts and trunks to cutoff jungle fatigues, or a simple Montagnard loincloth. There are the ever-present coolers and lawn chairs, bright canopies, Murphy's Mule loaded down with more booze and the newly fabricated 55 gallon drum barbeque grill. We are going to have a beach party. The

Yards are in their usual assortment of fatigues and put-togethers. A few are wearing Rolling Stone T-shirts or homemade tie-dyes that their Americans have bought for them. They are rigged for food. They don't give a hoot for the fun and frolic, these boys are hunter- gatherers and they have every assortment of gaff, spear, and net that you can imagine. They have also brought along a couple of buckets full of what we refer to as "Dupont lures," better known as hand grenades.

Fish has brought the deuce and a half with the back full of inflated inner tubes. There are twenty or so of them to use to float and even body surf the waves. Fat chance of being able to use the inner tubes, though, until every edible thing along the coast is foraged. The Yards have dibs on them first. It is considered unhealthy to be in the water when four or five grenades go off. If you are, you will come floating to the surface like everything else. Hopefully, the Yards won't mistake you for something edible. In that event, one of your buddies will pull you out of the way so someone can revive you, and the Yards can go back to high-speed gathering mode.

Godzilla comes rattling back through the gate, and Fish smiles with the pleased look of a craftsman. He steps down from the track and peels off a pair of gloves to the accompaniment of cheers and rude remarks. He is stripped down to a pair of bright red swim trunks and glistens with sun lotion. My guess, knowing Fish, is that it is a light covering of diesel. Godzilla leaks diesel like a Tiger tank. The entire crowd surges forward and onto the beach.

The Americans are setting up sunshades made of bamboo poles and ponchos, and bright cafe umbrellas purloined in the past. Soon it looks like a beach anywhere in the world. Well, anywhere there's a war going on. Everyone has brought a weapon of some sort.

I look around. There are people out everywhere just having a good day. We don't get many of them. Everyone is decked out in their finest, the more outlandish the outfit, the better. I hear splashing footsteps to my right and I turn and squint. It's my two teammates, Cook and Mac. They are stripped down to Yard loincloths and are both carrying three-pronged bamboo spears. Impaled and vibrating in death throes on the end of Mac's spear is some sort of fish that looks like it should be in the Mesozoic time slot. It is about two feet long, has spines and weird looking tentacles, and is bright red with dark brown spots. The two of them look like extras in a *Gilligan's Island* episode. They have made themselves headdresses out of beach flotsam. There is seaweed, shells, and what looks like the decaying head of an albatross mixed in the creation that Mac has rigged up. Cook, being more civilized since he comes from a state farther North but not yet at the Mason-Dixon Line, has opted for looking like some drowning victim in the Potomac. And they have this thing on the end of a spear.

Cuman, all done up in yellow swim trunks, is following a safe distance behind. I scramble to my feet lest they have some idea of throwing the carcass at me. "Oooga, oooga gwan cookum big squillum fishy, damn," Mac blurts out and does some rendition of what appears to be a Cajun wedding dance, making big splashes.

Cook does an equally gyrating, arm-waving rendition and, for good measure, takes a couple of practice jabs at me with his homemade frog sticker. "White man come, hab plenty good cookum by damn," he chants. I hop out of range and ponder the distance to my CAR-15 up the beach. If I can reach it, I can hold them off long enough to come up with a plausible defense for killing both of them in the surf line. This thing they have caught is obviously nasty. The Yards won't even touch it. Cuman is staying way clear of it. Thoughts from survival training come flooding back to me: Red in the head you're dead, red sky in the morning, all that stuff about nature giving you fair warning that bright red things are hazardous.

All this seems to have escaped the notice of my two stalwart friends. For Christ's sake, these are Southerners. If it looks like it will fit in a gumbo pot, they will boil it for days to remove any kind of natural poison and then add enough hot peppers to melt a steel boiler. I am dancing and weaving and cursing at both of them, which they find hilarious. I will never make it to the gun; they have already figured out if I get there I will at least wound them. They will gaff me the minute I make a break for it. Then I have a stroke of genius.

"*Trung Si* Mac hab beaucoup money for *Tahans*, and *Trung Si* Cook get all *Tahans* new boots," I yell at Cuman. The mere mention of freebies starts a chain reaction of Yards lining up to get their gifts. Naturally, the Americans would never lie to their *Tahan* brothers. If one of you says it, and it involves you giving and them receiving, well then it's the truth. The Yards don't make promissory statements without living up to them. Just as a capper, I remind them of the really neat swim togs that *Trung Si* Nick already gave them and add that Mac and Cook have big surprise for all *Tahans* for beach day. This draws the two of them up short. Ha! You assholes get out of this one. Cuman is already making the move to find out when. The two of them shoot me murderous glances. They won't have a moment of peace all afternoon and, on top of that, they will have to give up something. I wade out into the surf to enjoy the water. Suddenly the fish, and the spear it was attached to, hits the water just behind me. They are lucky I didn't mention the care packages both of them had received from home or the Yards would be on them like a pack of feral dogs.

I drift down the beach about 20 yards offshore and watch what appears to be some sort of brawl. It isn't. Hendrick has organized a football game. He has his entire team of Chinese thugs on one side; the other team is a mixed bag of Americans and some of the Vietnamese cowboys from Johnson's team.

Rules? Well, the number one rule in this game is, never, ever let anyone give you, toss you, or hand you, the ball. If you have the ball, pray you can make a clean shot for the two bamboo goal posts before anyone gets near you. This is what football would be if convicts had invented it.

One of Rick's Nungs gets the ball. He immediately turns and punches the guy on the other team closest to him, knees another in the groin and hands the ball to Hendrick, as the murder squad closes in, grinning. Rick puts his head down, big legs pumping, and becomes a red-headed freight train. He is knocking guys down left and right, punching his way through the line. Rick's definition of finesse is that little frilly stuff on better quality panties. He gets about 20 yards when rule number two takes effect. This rule is: any nearby spectators who disagree with the play of the game are allowed to interfere. Two guys from the sidelines try and blindside him but all they manage to do is get bruised and they only slow him down. One of Jimmy's criminals uses a piece of driftwood across the solar plexus like a war club to bring Rick down, finally, with a 25 yard gain. Not safe to go ashore here. I drift a little farther down the beach when there is a stinging thump in the water and all the beach partiers start shouting and pointing out to sea. I think "shark" and start heading for shore. Before I get there the rescue boat flashes past me with two guys in it.

By the time I wade in, the crowd is laughing and pointing. I catch my breath and turn around to see the boat slowly coming back in. It is crowded. As they get closer, I see that they are towing the other boat that was fishing out there. All of its occupants are drenched and on the rescue craft. They get the boat up far enough that a bunch of us can push it in. It breaks almost in half, so we pull the motors off and manhandle the wreckage up on the beach. Maybe Fish can repair it.

Murphy had had the bright idea that something was wrong with their fishing technique. They kept seeing schools of fish, but they weren't getting many. The grenades weren't going off close enough to the school, which scattered as soon as it felt the splash.

Since this obviously called for innovation, they had gone up to S-4 and gotten a 500 foot reel of detonation cord, and cut about a hundred foot strand. Then they attached a concrete block to one end and for good measure, a claymore detonator with a couple of electric blasting caps properly taped and secured with fifty feet of wire to the other end where the clacker was. They circled over a school of fish, dropped the block overboard, and spooled out the cord until they were at the end. Then they detonated it. Oh, they had fish. They had all kinds of fish. They also cracked the boat hull open like a watermelon at a weekend Baptist revival. On top of that, every shark within miles came cruising over and started grabbing anything floating or splashing.

Murph and a few of the others were killing sharks with their guns to try and save the haul when someone realized they would run out of ammo before sharks and fired a couple of pen flares, finally getting someone's attention. The guys on shore looked out and all they could see were the guys, standing in what looked like waist deep water, no boat. Then they started to see shark fins and that was when the rescue started.

They manage to save a few fish, even one nice specimen of about 40 pounds. It had been a 60 pounder, but some communist shark got a big chunk of it. The Yards and some of the guys go to work filleting the catch, and Murphy gets ready to go out again with the only other boat not there for rescue. He is going to prime the whole thing non- electrically this time so they can get clear first. You have to hand it to the Irish. Given enough time and explosives they will provide first class entertainment. They get busy loading the boat, which has been pushed down into the water.

The football game goes into its fifth or fortieth quarter, with the wounded limping off for cold beer or staggering down to the water to rinse off the sand, blood, and sweat. A couple of fights break out and guys beat on each other until someone gets bored and clocks one or both miscreants. This particular task falls to the "Grand Kahuna," a huge Hawaiian named Wheeler, who, if he had never studied martial arts would still be dangerous. Unfortunately, he has studied martial arts. If things get too out of hand and you disturb his peaceful day at the beach communing with some shark god, you will end up face down in the surf like Captain Cook.

Absolutely nothing could ruin today. Wrong. A laboring engine comes from behind the bunker line and then a jeep appears and skids to a stop with the unholy trio in it. Oh thank God, the recon "ossifers" have come to provide us with adult supervision, and dressed up in their beach togs, too. The Midget is in a pair of swim trunks that defy human eyes to stare at them for too long. They are fluorescent blue with the Marines landing at Tarawa in bright orange slashed across the front. Some kind of parrot is on the back, in the same color scheme. He is wearing all his gold: gold watch, gold bracelet, and gold chains with 24-carat Thai gold gewgaws. He looks like a Spanish shipwreck.

With him is Butler, with his usual aplomb that borders on the atmosphere of a bank heist in Harlem. He is tastefully decked out in cut-offs, a fatigue shirt with the sleeves cut off, and a shoulder holster. Nice shades, though, wrap around black-rimmed jobs that make him look like the senior police advisor to "Papa" Doc Duvalier. Uncoiling out of the back is Keith Messinger. Keith looks like the poster boy for the "master race," six-foot, blond hair, blue eyes, and perfect teeth. He's the perfect picture of Nordic manhood. Good on the ground, but even more useful if you are stalking nurses, because if you take him with you the women fall all over him. This gives you a chance to un-velcro the ones he doesn't want or maybe they will give you some shorts if they think you are tight with him. Hey, you have to play the hand you're dealt. Keith, my man, let's go to the nurses' quarters tonight. I feel lucky. On the other hand, taking the human tree trunk and the psycho with you while hunting the fairer sex is like going down to the church social with your dick hanging out.

Larry chugs through the sand over to where they are cooking the day's catch and a few steaks. He reaches over, fishes out a steak and chews on it, gazing at his command. I wonder what he is thinking. No matter, if it is running through his mind, it has to be a short trip.

I backstroke so I can get out farther. Keith wanders over to where the guys are still playing football, and watches the game while talking to his One-One. Meanwhile, the "Captains Courageous" are standing close together near the barbeque, both now have a steak and are gnawing on them, licking the barbecue sauce off between grunts. They look like what they are, fun-spoiling predators.

I get out about 40 meters and start swimming down the shore away from the scene, intent on getting back and drying off, then going home for a shower and a night in Da Nang. Good food at Papa Joe's, a dash to the Korean Officers Club for some cheap drinks, then over to the China Night for some cognac sipping. A short walk over to the Korean steam bath for a late night steam and cream. Then either back here or I will crash at the safe house. Maybe I will go over to the Helgoland for some wine and a try at getting some Teutonic biscuit.

As I am lazily steaming south, I see the ugly twins, Mac and Cook, still in their getups heading down the beach. They have speared some other evil-looking denizen of the deep. With luck it's a sea snake and it will bite both of them and maybe get Manes and Butler, too. That will leave the way clear for me to get past everyone in the excitement and go back, clean up, and go downtown. Otherwise, I have to sneak back through the wire and hope no one has planted any new mines.

I get to the shallows and wade in, the salt water leaving an oily feeling as it dries. I am getting burnt. I get a towel and dry off. All the Yards are sitting around half-awake from eating. Their little bellies are distended. They gorge like a pride of lions when they have a food source. They have all kinds of fish wrapped in paper and tropical plant leaves for eating later. I tell Cuman I'm going back to the camp. He waves lazily and grins, half asleep. It is around 1500 and more guys are starting to drift back.

I join the exodus making its way back to the camp. The football game has finally wound itself down. I guess Wheeler had enough of breaking up fights and just took the football. He probably ate it. Manes is standing with his back to me looking out to sea. He is studying the new Murphy fishing expedition as it tries to haul the tons of fish that float to the surface after each detonation. Actually, they are trying to get it onboard before the sharks come rushing back in. The sharks have learned to associate the block hitting the water with "boom." A few dull-witted, slow movers end up being part of the catch, but the majority goes out beyond the reef and then comes slicing back as soon as the explosion reverberates. Pretty smart, these sharks.

It has been a good day; I make it through the gate and am trudging down the road with Roger from RT Mamba. His team has another two days of stand down as well, so we are going to go downtown together as soon as I can find out if Mac and the Cookie want to go. We turn the corner to his team room and his Sedang are squatting next to the front door, painting a puppy bright red with a can of spray paint. All the tribes seem to find this particularly entertaining. You see green ones, yellow ones, and red ones running around all over the place, as well as the normal tans and blacks and spotted.

The Yards fatten them up for the cooking pot. They love dog meat. Hey, our ancestors didn't domesticate the canine to bark when the cave bear came around, either. They were a food source. No one has successfully explained why the Yards paint the dogs, though. Ask one and he just smiles and shrugs. It's kind of like Christmas tree bulbs, I guess. As we are standing there admiring their handiwork, I see Mac and Cook come staggering up across the sand. I guess they have had enough fun in the sun. It's best to get back before they get mischief in their heads. I say goodbye to Roger and start around the comer past the showers. God, I need a shower.

I almost run into Baby-san Loi, our tail gunner. He is wearing jeans, a blanket "poncho," and spurs made out of wire with what looks like C ration lids for rowels. The get-up is complete with a hog-leg .38 slung gunfighter style and a boonie hat with a large brim. He straddles the walk and says, "Draw Pudnah!" in his best English and flips the blanket back over one shoulder a la Clint Eastwood. We had gotten one of the spaghetti westerns in and the Yards loved it. They will imitate anything they like. They are still a little confused as to why the cowboys don't like the "American Montagnards," but we told them it was a long time ago and we are now friends with the Indians. Now I tell him to get the hell out of there or he is going to get into trouble again.

Yesterday Billy, the SMAJ, had come out of his hootch to find Loi standing in his best gunfighter stance with that old .38 Cook had given him. Loi had whipped back his blanket serape and told the SMAJ he had 'til sundown to get out of camp. Of course Billy came by later to give us the "I Am Not Pleased" speech. Cook thought it was hilarious. It will pass. Maybe the next film will be a space movie and they will all be running around with fishbowls on their heads. I am mulling all this over as I head for the showers. In the process, I am thinking about the ire of the command structure and how this will affect any planned revelries.

It's been a bad two days. The Old Man is pissed off because someone screwed over a new captain and the guy is screaming bloody murder. We, the enlisted swine, are suspect from the get-go. But I know for a fact that the miscreants are Captains Psycho, Messinger, and the supreme Squat himself. It seems this new captain comes in from being an advisor to some ARVN Ranger outfit and makes the mistake of drinking in the Officers Club. He also has the misfortune of running into Butler, Manes, and Messinger, who are on their way to getting really toasted.

This captain starts telling all and sundry how he is going to run his team and the new training program that he is going to have the enlisted go through, which he has perfected as an advisor. His head is full of Sherman, Sun Tzu, Frederick the Great, and a host of other legendary leaders like himself. He has a very low opinion of the Yards, and anyone not captain or above is basically to be used and abused. The unholy troika tries to tell him this is a totally different outfit than he has ever been in or heard about, that this is a meritocracy. Both Messinger and Butler were One-Ones under relatively junior NCOs until they learned their trade. But Captain "Brass Buttons" is aghast that this sort of thing is allowed. It goes against everything the Army stands for. So they listen to this pompous ass for a couple of hours and ply him with spirits, all the while being politely agreeable. By the time the moon is up, they pile his now unconscious body into a jeep and drive down to the Recon area, collectively searching for some stroke of genius to get rid of this asshole before one of us is charged with homicide for doing a public service.

Finding themselves over in the Yard barracks area; they drive out behind the Yard latrine, which is a "four-holer," that is, four seats with a flap door in the back to remove the sawed-off 55 gallon drums that act as waste receptacles. These are removed religiously every morning and the contents then soaked with fuel and burned. They take the captain and stuff him head up in one of the barrels so he can't get out.

As an afterthought one of them gags him. Then they shove him and the drum back in the slot, close the flap and go sleep it off. About 0900 the next morning the bum detail arrives, opens the flap and finds a hysterical wild-eyed captain covered in the remainders of a hot pepper diet. They rush him to the hospital, and last word was his mind had gone elsewhere. Pity? None from us; we didn't even know the details until later. Justice? You bet. Did he get off light? Well, it's better than dead.

I pass Billy and he mumbles something about looking for Manes. I tell him that he's on the beach and he starts down that way. I get to the hootch and the ugly twins are stripped down to towels and shaving kits. I do the same and we head for the showers. It's China Night tonight; we've got partying to do. The Pink House is out because we are all burned from the sun.

Upon return, I collapse in my bunk and soon the other two come traipsing in. They are barely settled when there is a knock on the door and Cuman, along with the rest of the team, files in. They look at Mac and then at Cook and finally me. I just smile broadly and look innocently at my two teammates. They have nowhere to run. Both their care packages are out in plain sight as well. I get up and start getting dressed, whistling as I draw on some fatigue pants. The Yards are all over them. Soon they are handing out some poncho liners, a few pairs of boots and small gadgets. It does them no good. They eventually have to surrender a smoked ham from the Cookie's box and some peppers from Mac's. I turn and give Cuman a thousand piastres, before the two mugging victims can rope me in. The Yards, finally satisfied that is all there is for today, head out for the shed where they can buy beer and whiskey. Mac and Cookie stare at me in sullen promise. Serves them right interfering with the One-One when he was resting his tactical mind. Life's a beach.

CHAPTER 18

Monkeyshines

We are getting ready to go to Monkey Mountain. There are two teams of us. Davidson and his team will be on the eastern end and we will be on the southern end. We both have new Yards and want to break them in before we go out to play in Uncle Ho's garden. We use Monkey Mountain because the terrain is an ideal model of most of our target areas and it is a place where we can fire our B-40s and mortars just like we do when we are out in the bad places.

Monkey Mountain sits on a peninsula jutting out into the bay and its mass protects the harbor from the howling storms of the monsoons. It is wild and rugged, and the only installation on the peninsula is a Marine unit. We have to let them know we are going to be there, and in what areas, so they don't suspect us as VC and fire our asses up with their artillery. Here we can practice virtually all of our drills, including demo ambushes and using the mortars to lay the hammer on someone pressing us.

There is another reason for using Monkey Mountain and that is the presence of rock apes. Actually they are gibbons; we call them rock apes because they use sticks and fist-size rocks to defend themselves. They travel in troops, usually 20 or more, formed around a big alpha male. They are so territorial, and their senses so finely tuned, they raise holy hell if anything is in their area. The males will form a rearguard and hold territory, whilst the females and young escape. The peninsula is overrun with them. It's great for us, because if we can sneak up and ambush them, we are doing everything right to keep ourselves safe in the bush. And after the ambush the Yards descend on their favorite meal, rock ape barbecue.

We leave CCN and take the ten minute ride out to the mountain and set up on our prescribed LZ. During the morning, we are going to practice LZ insertions and extractions using ladders and strings. We have half a dozen or so locations picked out that have the types of terrain and growth we have encountered before. The birds are going to alternate between Davidson's team and ours so we both get plenty of practice. The first ladder insert goes well but a little slow, so we do it two more times. The three new Yards are getting the hang of it.

The helicopters move to the east to work with Davie. Mac wants to move down the slope of the mountain and use some claymores to blow an LZ. Moving quietly through the undergrowth, we practice changing our line. The gibbons can be heard to our southeast. We won't pull an ambush on them until tomorrow just before we extract and return to base. Today it's all movement and drills, like fishhooking on our trail and covering our tracks. It is slow and easy because this is a safe area.

Occasionally, the VC use this mountain as a staging area. One of our teams was out here about six months ago and stumbled onto a VC sapper unit that was getting ready to attack ships in the busy anchorage and harbor within the bay. They shot three of the sappers and found rafts and explosives indicating there were more on the peninsula, so they sent one of the Hatchet Companies out. The Hatchet Company bagged two more sappers before the rest had gone to ground.

Consequently, we are alert and looking for signs for running into the odd VC. Running into them would be great; we could use them for training aids and maybe bag a prisoner. The added bonus would be a few more days of stand down. There are no friendlies here. The coast is used by the fishing fleets; an odd sampan or two of fishermen might put into one of the little bays or sheltered lees. They may be in a horrible war, but people still have to eat, and the average citizen quickly finds out where to go and where not to go. We aren't out to fire up anyone we see, but if they are up here where we are training, they aren't fishermen.

Traveling down, we cut back and forth across the ridge. We come across a couple of old trails, but can see they aren't being used because the jungle has taken over. Trails are recognizable because the undergrowth is shorter and they follow a line. Nature doesn't follow straight lines. A couple of the trails have reverted to animal tracks. Both the wild hogs and the monkeys use them because they forage on the ground; we find scat and tracks indicating a troop of 30 or so gibbons in one area.

At 1200 we stop for the noon meal and some *pac* time. It's cool here under the canopy. The offshore winds sweep up from the sea and make it hot, but not quite the muggy hell that it would be farther inland. We get a half-assed perimeter set up, and Mac breaks us out of a full tactical situation. Cook, Mac and I kick back, fix PIRs, and talk softly among ourselves about what we have noticed during the morning of training. Some ideas about what we would like to cover in the afternoon are discussed. We decide on IA drills. Because the terrain is mixed, we can do flat to sloped uphill movement, run downhill oblique, etc. just to get everyone on the same page. We know there is an open area to our east and we will use that to employ the minimortar. There is a rock outcropping that we can have the guns on, both the thump guns and the mortar. Everyone will fire them. I am glad because we have been humping the extra rockets and mortar ammo, in addition to our own ammunition, all morning and my shoulders could use the break. We won't fire it all, but it will definitely make us lighter. The new Yards are working fine. We will drill with them on the guns to watch them and see how well they take being around close fire.

With three extra bodies, our team is slightly larger than a normal infantry squad. Having almost the same numbers is the only similarity. Unless you have been on one of our teams and experienced what we are able to lay down in front of us during a firefight, it is impossible to explain to a layman, or for that matter, to a normal infantry type. We carry three to six times as much ammunition and grenades as normal infantry, and each man carries an extra 60mm HE or WP round, and a RPG rocket for the B-40. Team members carry a claymore and usually two homemade mini claymores. And our grenades are different. We have two or three normal M-26 or M-67 baseballs, and usually ten or more V-40 mini grenades per man. None of the Yards have WP grenades, a lesson learned about how far Yards can throw the heavy thing. Finally, we carry smoke grenades and CS grenades, plus the odd assortment of pistols and a couple of shotguns as backup weapons. We are armed like the family of the bride at an Armenian wedding.

In a contact, our immediate reaction is to maul the other guy so bad that he goes down. We kill or wound as many as we can. Our little group, with the training and the techniques we have developed, can kick the bejesus out of a normal company and make a battalion back off and seriously wonder just how many people we really are. To do that, you have to have the right terrain and you have to be super-aggressive.

That's why we are here: to get these new guys up to that level and to fine-tune ourselves. We finish chow and get ready to do our first IA drills. We will use the CAR-15s, RPGs and the M-79, with a few judicious grenades thrown in. Mac starts the drill. He fires a full magazine then breaks, the next guy dumps a full magazine then breaks, and so on down the line until the thump gunners are at the head of the line, dropping rounds until they turn and break. The fire chews up the underbrush and sets the forest denizens to shrieking. Then it goes quiet.

Next we decide to do the one drill that Habu is really good at. Mac takes out some examination gloves which we blow up like balloons. They look like heads with rooster combs. Cook sets the team down and Mac, Cuman and I go out and set the balloons up—some at ground level, some at waist level, and some at head level. Instant bad guys. We go back and tell the team how we are going to run this next set of drills, and tell them to watch to their left and right. We warn them not to walk into their own grenades, explain how we volley grenades and then move forward in the assault. The idea is to smash into the enemy and go through them because they will break with the shock of our assault. If not, we chew them up so bad that anyone still alive wants to wait for reinforcements. The balloons will help us focus and make sure that we are looking for, and engaging, targets, not just spraying the area. We run that drill for a while until we are satisfied with the team.

The choppers are called and we move off to the area where we will blow a hole in the canopy. The new guys will practice coming out on strings with one of us along to calm them down. The rest of us will do it by ladder. They will drop us in the open ground over on the finger, and we will do a couple of drills at that location, with the B-40 and the 60mm added to the other guns of the team. Combine that with our normal firepower and the effect is devastating.

We do the same thing, putting inflated gloves in areas where a man could hide, and do the drills again adding in the heavy stuff. The team is functioning like a well-oiled machine. Mac is happy with the results, so are Cook and me. We pack it in just before dusk, and get on the horn to contact Davidson, telling him where we are, approximately. This is to ensure that we have hill mass between us. No sense getting wounded by overshot, if he is doing any night firing. We go into the normal RON drill, wait until just before dark and move into position. Mac gets everyone situated. I close up the back door and everyone puts claymores out. There we will stay 'til morning. Try and do it just like you do out there. The only difference is that our asses aren't so tight that our mouths are dry.

We pass the night, disturbed only once by a hog rooting around. We think about killing it, but decide not to because Mac wants to practice being hit in the RON just before dawn. We sleep every other man, making sure, however, that the three new men are asleep. Just before first light, Mac blows his claymore and the others go off seconds later. Everyone is up and moving towards the rally point we picked out before we moved into the RON. There are only two weapons that fire, and they both belong to the new guys. When a RON is hit, we want to blow a hole with the claymores and not fire so the enemy thinks someone stumbled onto a booby trap or mine. Either way, they have people down and we can move out in the confusion. Daylight comes and Cuman lights into the two who fired. It's the Yard rendition of "Hey, stupid!" They sit in subdued silence. Cuman is like a war chief among the Bru. Strength and reputation as the leader make the others defer to him. Mac, Cookie, and I are his wayward children, but we are the leaders above him. We, however, always defer to him in matters dealing with the other Yards. They are his warriors.

We go back to more drills and work our way down the mountain during the morning and scout out a couple of troops of gibbons, looking for the springs and rills where they water, and the trees and shrubs that produce the fruit they feed on. They are not total veggie eaters; I have watched them chase down small game. We pick a troop that has a large red and black alpha male as its leader. We had seen them yesterday on the top of the ridgelines and know they will forage and then sleep during the noonday heat. At dusk, they will be around a spring that seeps out of the rocks about halfway up the mountain. We will move up there and set up a demo ambush to try and catch a mob of them around the seep. It's good prisoner snatch practice.

The placement of the claymores has to be just so in order to stun some of them with the back blast. An understanding of the effects of shock waves and air density is necessary to do it right. The heavier and moister the air is, the farther apart your claymores have to be because the shock waves will be heavier. Pick a trail where there is big, thick foliage or a solid structure like a hill mass. Place the claymore mines so that they throw their pellets down the long axis of the trail, both forward and backward of the zone in which you want to stun the prisoners. That way it kills everyone in front of, and in back of, the prisoner, while the back blast from the mines knocks the prisoner out.

We test it by setting up on similar terrain before we do one for real. Lay out the mines and put an ammo can in the center of the knockout zone. Then place a standard light bulb, just like the ones at home, in the center of the can, and another one just outside the can. If the distance is correct between the claymores, the back blast will break the one on the outside but not the one on the inside of the can. Voila! This is war science at its best. There is enough pressure to knock out your victim but not kill him. Run out and collect the prisoner, go home and collect your money, then tell everyone lies about how you had to kill his three seven-foot Chinese bodyguards armed with only a can opener and bad breath.

We spend some time picking a couple of sites and doing our demo magic, and then practice the actual snatch, using one of the Yards as the dummy. We should have brought Lamar out here. He likes being unconscious.

We work our way down to the shore on the south side of the peninsula where there is a beach with rocky breakers on the seaward side. The lagoon is green and the bottom is fairly shallow. We will set up a small bivouac and spend the afternoon kicking back. The Yards can fish and forage for a couple of hours and we can take a dip in the lagoon. There is a small shelf that produces a waterfall, about the height of a man, on the far end where one of the streams dumps out from the mountain. This time of year it is still flowing so we can rinse off and fill our canteens, etc. We set up and the Yards go to foraging. Actually, they have been picking things up as we have been moving since Mac told Cuman it was all right to do so on the way down. They have gathered fruits and tubers and all kinds of jungle plants to make dishes they are familiar with. When we reach the beach area, they "Dupont" some fish up from one of the tidal pools on the east side where the rocks are. We post a couple of lookouts and build a small cooking fire and they begin to prepare the midday meal. The menu consists of fresh fish, cooked on a slit stick out at an angle over the fire, and some kind of snake or eel, I don't know which because it's skinned and spitted. PIR rations with fruits, wild peppers, and tubers. It is amazing. They cook everything in natural containers made of leaves, bamboo, and tree bark in amongst the coals and everything seems to come out on time.

Around 1400, Davidson comes up on our squawk box and says he is about half a click out and coming down to the beach. He gives us the direction he is coming and requests that we please not fire him up. Cuman yells up to the Yard closest in that direction and we wait. I am fighting the temptation to drop a few mortar rounds over to his right flank, just to see if I can drive another troop of gibbons into a murderous rage. They might just swarm down on that stunted runt from Waco. God, I would love to film that fight. He is about the same size, but the females would probably carry him off and Lord knows what kind of stinted, bandy-legged mutants would emerge from the forest in a few years time. Best to leave the order of natural selection alone. We have enough trouble with the fact that he is backstroking in *our* gene pool.

They come wandering in off the ledges to the east and join us on the beach. He has been doing what we have, except he has six new people and is going to stay tonight and do some more drills, and then come back in late tomorrow afternoon. He has arranged to be picked up by our fleet of powerboats and ferried back across the bay to the camp. He, too, is planning on a gibbon hunt. The camp will be permeated by the smell of cooking monkeys and the sight of glutted, happy Yards.

We are getting ready to move up to where we can lay an ambush for the monkey troop, and tell him where we are going. There is an extraction point that we can use to get the birds in with no problem and we won't have to lug the meat too far. We plan on having monkey enough for all the Bru back at the camp as well. The Yards are in a frenzy of anticipation now. They are out for some monkey butt.

We start moving to the ambush site and as we move we stop, as we normally do, to listen and let the jungle quiet down. As we sit, a troop of gibbons moves in on top of our position. The temptation is too much for Ti Ti Loi. He pops an M-79 at a big male up in the trees, hits him dead center in the chest, and the bloody monkey explodes.

As Loi walks over to where the monkey landed, Cuman yells a warning and all hell breaks loose. About 12 males and a couple of females break cover from where they have been foraging on the ground. They swarm out from the undergrowth and are all over Loi like a cheap suit. He tries to get a canister round in his weapon and a big male knocks him down and two or three others hit him with rocks and sticks. This is one pissed off group of monkeys. He manages to get his pistol out and drills one that is trying to get at his crotch, and all but a big male scatter. The rest of the Yards open up and monkeys are going down all over the place, up in the trees, on the ground, you name it. Two big ones come crashing out of the trees. Everyone is trying to drill a monkey. We are so wrapped up that we have forgotten about Loi. We look back and the big male has him by the left foot and is running toward the trees with his catch. I guess he figured that he would finish him off in seclusion. Loi's head is banging on the rocks as he is being dragged along to the big monkey ass-whipping. One of the Yards sees he is in bad shape knocks the big male for a loop with a pretty good shot, considering that it's hysterically funny. The male tries to get up and manages to get another whack in on Loi before they drop him. We run down and pick up Loi. He doesn't have any broken bones, but he is beaten to a pulp, scratched, and pissed. He goes around and personally finishes off any of the wounded gibbons. The rest of the Yards let him work the steam off.

We call for the helicopters. It is only about 100 meters to the LZ. What the hell, we have monkeys; let's go home. The radio comes back and it's the Operations officer for CCN, some twit of a major. He says that Operations is busy right now, "Negative on the extraction, we will pick you up tomorrow when we come to get the other team." Mac tells him we have an injured Yard and want a medevac. The major comes back with questions about whether it's a gunshot wound, can you stabilize, etc., etc. I can see that Mac is getting pissed.

Who does this guy think he is? The colonel must be away and left him in charge. After all, we are only training so he is exercising his command prerogatives. I know this major, he has been with us for about two weeks. He hasn't had a chance to get dialed in yet on what babysitting the command means when the colonel is gone. Mac looks at me and I see the light come on. He tells him that we have sprung an ambush and have seven, garbled, dead NVA monkeys, garbled and one VC, makes more squelch noises and mumbles "monkey." You can hear the scramble in the background. My God, Cedric, they have a prisoner!

The pinhead's voice comes back on the radio net. "Roger, understand you have seven enemy dead confirmed, and one live prisoner. Your extraction LZ is ..." and gives the coordinates we picked. "Please confirm count."

"Roger, we have seven ..." Mac makes static noises through his nose, "confirmed killed ..." more static noises, "and one straw hat wounded." The major is beside himself. He tells us they are winding up and he will be on the lead bird to take charge of the POW. You bet, asshole. I can almost see him composing his valor award and commendation that will be presented by Westmoreland personally. We get busy sorting the monkeys out. We take the biggest male and lay him on one end of a poncho. Three others get piled with him. Then we roll up the poncho like a body bag. We take Bata boots and put them on the feet of the one at the bottom and a pith helmet on the head of the big male. The rest of the monkeys get bundled up to make four more "body bags," and we sit down to wait for the choppers.

The first chopper comes in. We load half the team with Loi onboard and three of the body bags. This bird is carrying the staff lizard and he is full of himself. In his mind he is leading the choppers into a desperate situation. The chopper gains power and lifts off, with the major in the back with the Yards. He is trying to ask the Yards where the prisoner is, to no avail. The Yards go into "No speakee Englee" mode.

The second bird comes in and we load on along with two body bags, one of which has the helmet-clad monkey sticking out of the end of it. We lift off and the crew radios to the other bird and they tell the major that they got the rest of the team and one that looks like he ain't dead. The crew chief on our bird leans over and takes a look at the face under the helmet and says to Mac, "That's the hairiest VC I've ever seen." Mac grabs a headset and starts talking to the crew, and pretty soon they are all laughing their asses off.

We take the long way home and by the time we get there the major has his reception party waiting for the bird to come in. Manes and the colonel are there.

Perfect. They have returned just in time to catch the finale. The little pinhead has probably put himself in for a Silver Star for flying in on the lead ship.

Colonel Donnie runs over to the bird. "Where's the prisoner?"

"Well, he died, Sir, but if we get him down to the Yards, we can eat him tonight," Mac replies. Manes comes over and looks at the corpse, then at us. We're grinning like a couple of bubbas with a litter of bluetick hounds.

Then he looks at the major. "Well, you did real good. I hope you didn't forget to call Saigon with the news flash. You might get a verbal reprimand if you're lucky."

The colonel looks at the major as well, and as we unload and walk off he is dispensing a little ego deflation. Manes accompanies us back to Recon. The Yards don't care. They think the major is a bad person because he didn't even look at Loi to see how badly he was injured. Not showing proper concern is a bad move.

Loi is up at the infirmary. Mac and the rest of us go by there first and see that Wang has him pretty much patched up. He has to stay overnight. By the time we get back down to the company the Yards have a roaring fire going out on the sand and have thrown the bodies of the monkeys on it. When the monkeys cook enough that the abdominal walls sever and the intestines swell out so they look like balloons they will be ready to eat. Every Bru and Sedang in the camp is there, licking his lips in anticipation. They will scoop out the brains and a few of the choice cuts of the big one to take up to Loi so he doesn't miss out.

We hang around for a while and have a few bites with them, then head over to the company to shower and make sure everyone knows about the "great monkey hunt." Ah, it's a fine day. Manes sees us back in the Company and comers us, wanting to know what happened. After he hears the story he just shakes his head and tells us not to worry about it; the colonel thinks it's funnier than hell. Of course, the Midget warns us that if we ever try and screw up his career with some similar scheme, it won't come out the same. No matter what happens in the end, even if they rift him, he will be a master sergeant and can legally beat the shit out of us every day, not just when we need it.

As we head over to the club later, there is still much jovial goodwill emanating from the direction of the Yard barracks. They will feast until they bloat, and sing songs well into the night about Ti Ti and the big monkey. I know the team wants us to come back for more monkey meat. I hate cold monkey meat, though. It tastes like wet hair. In self-preservation I send over a couple of cases of beer and a couple of bottles of that horrible excuse for whiskey they like. They will gorge themselves and forget about dragging us back. I am safe for now.

CHAPTER 19

Isn't Science Wonderful

Lucky us. We're getting another DMZ target, but this time it is a bridge and we are going to try out a new technique. The Air Force has been trying to bomb a rail bridge that spans a gorge very close to the northern limits of the Demilitarized Zone. We will try to place several beacons so that the aircrafts' computers can vector in on the target. It is supposed to give them a pickle window that allows the bombs to be released with up-yer-bloody-arse accuracy. Theoretically, anyway.

We get a briefing from some colonel from the "something-something space command" who brings the little boxes with him, and two tech sergeants who are the typical senior master chief diode types. Good guys, actually. They stay for a couple of days and come into isolation with us and show us how the things work. It is pretty much ape-proof.

A beacon is about five inches by three inches by three inches, about the size of a brick. It has two controls and some sort of hooterfritz that adjusts its bias or something, and has a little round thing that screws on top that is the antenna.

The two techies are absolutely awed at being this close to "The Front." I am perplexed because I never knew that the war had a front. Like all things, I guess this is relative. The week before, they were at Eglin Air Force Base in Florida. It shouldn't have been too big of a culture shock for them. Those crackers in North Florida fit the parameters for VC. They are farmers and traders and common folk by day, and by night they prey on GIs. And they both have a scary cellular infrastructure. Ever look at the genealogy of a redneck from North Florida? There are more kissing cousins than at a Norwegian bam dance. Maybe we should open a southern front. Now there's an idea that might catch on; we could go home on the weekends, but we probably couldn't whip that crowd, either.

The senior of the two techies is explaining the intricacies of the lithium candied, bromide, Alka-seltzer battery-powered hooterfritz, and how it develops memory so you have to discharge it completely, or it thinks it's dead when it's not. I'm wondering which "biggie" in the manufacturing superstar network came up with this baby. I bet this thing cost the military more than they paid all of us last year. The answer to that one comes up real quick, because the senior space cadet says that it is vital that the device not fall into enemy hands. Dickweed, it's essential that *Nick* doesn't fall into enemy hands, either. I am already formulating a plan where if they trap us on top of the hills over this bridge, I am going to stand up and put a gun to this little diode crapper and threaten to shoot it if they don't let us go. Yeah, maybe demand a plane to Cuba, a couple hundred thousand for pin money and the letter "m" removed from the English alphabet. That way I can plead insanity if I ever tire of Castro's paradise.

Airman the second, or whatever he is, is eyeballing the Cookie cleaning the silencer on his .22 High Standard. I can see that when he gets back to Florida being this close to a real "killer" is probably a guarantee to some prime shorts. If he could, he'd ask the Cookie to take a picture of the two of them together. Hey, wait a minute, what a great idea. We can probably get a hundred bucks out of the kid to have his picture taken with the Cookie. Throw in a couple of the Yards for another fifty, and if we let him hold the .22 we could make it an even two hundred. I'm going to tell the AST we need a Polaroid for taking pictures of the device. To get the film and the camera shouldn't be too hard, we just need plausibility. Yeah, we need to take pictures of the device so all three of us can study it. Brilliant! I get up and saunter over to the AST and tell him, in my best professional tone, that we are going to need a Polaroid and two packets of film. He looks at me and I whisper, "It's for the device." The AST suspects that we are up to something, but saunters off in curiosity.

I walk back over to where the Cookie is and start to explain the plan. He starts to crunch up that solid line of hair he calls eyebrows. It's like a film running across his face: Good idea, bad idea, maybe … and finally I see the larceny cells kick in. He finishes cleaning the gun, looks over at the kid and tells him to watch his weapon because he's going for a piss. "Don't touch anything."

I pull out a couple of mini grenades and clean them off with the oil rag Cookie has been using so they have a nice deadly sheen about them. Shit, I wish I had that Gerber mini-magnum commando knife Jimmy Reeves uses to clean his toenails. That's the only thing that so-called "fighting knife" is good for, but it looks neat. The Cookie comes back just as the senior Air Force guy finishes up. The brass files out, leaving us with the two techies in case we have any questions. I don't have any questions. We will take it in and probably get shot at by everyone who owns a gun. We will risk our hides and the thing won't work because somebody in Wichita forgot that green went to red in the tropics, not blue to white.

But the Cookie and I are ready to pounce. Best not to get the Mini-Mac involved at this point, he has important shit to do, like planning, and ordering up air packages, that sort of thing. More than likely, he will be grateful as hell if we don't involve him in anything this sordid. The AST shows up with the camera and the film packets. I take them from him and push him back out the door. I walk over and take the film out and load the camera. I take a few pictures of the device as the head space guy watches me. I can see he is already worried that I am going to have these in my pocket and leap into the arms of the North Vietnamese. After they capture us, they will find out that we have the super secret effervescent bromide battery-powered beacon wingding and western civilization will come crashing down because he didn't stop it. I smile at him and tell him that they will need these because the pictures will go in the file in the vault. The mere mention of the word "vault" conjures up images in his mind of NORAD, buried deep in the Colorado Mountains. In reality, the AST will probably put them in the target folder or sell them to the mail clerk.

Now if you have a Polaroid, and there are Yards around, it is instant "take my picture" time. They don't ask, but they start hamming it up to catch your attention. If you point it at them, whoever owns the aviator sunshades lets all the others wear them so they can look cool in the pics. I see the shades come out and the boys start primping.

I slide the two shots of the device in the target folder, taking care to paperclip them in the upper left hand corner like it was an official requirement. It puts them at ease. This is very important when shaking the Air Force loose from their money. You have to do things that are in their everyday environment. These guys are used to seeing request forms in triplicate for toilet paper. Cookie, God bless his little Ranger heart, says to remember that we have to secure all pictures that have team members in them because of MACV-SOG regulation title 18, paragraph 5, executive order number 1231.

"Oh come on, Cook. I know that. Besides, we will destroy all these, so we might as well use up the film." I take a couple of the Yards in posed shots and then Cook with a few more. Then I "discover" that they gave us two packets of film and I only signed for one. Heavens to Mergatroid!

Zoom Two says, "Uh, Sir, we are going back to the States as soon as you come back. Would it be alright if…"

Airman senior gives junior a look and waits to see what happens.

Zoomies are in the shallows. I can gaff the younger one now, but I have to have both in the reeds, first. Cook pipes up that it is totally out of the question, whatever Zoom Two is thinking. I become the bad kid, fuck authority, let's make some cash here, and after about ten minutes Cook "gives in." C'mon, before somebody comes back in, for Christ's sake.

We get down to the spit and crackle and soon we are taking pictures of them with Cook, them with me, them with the Yards, them with guns, them looking over a map, the whole shooting match. I make them promise to take the slime cards with them and bum them when they get to Da Nang Airbase. We are a hundred dollars richer by the time Mac gets back. The best thing is that the zoomies are so fresh from the States that they have real greenbacks, not Military Payment Certificates, the monopoly money that the Army uses in the war zone. That means we can trade them and maybe get more MPC for them. Perfect.

The two zoomies are in a hurry to get out of there because the "major," which is how we described Mac, is very touchy about these sorts of things. These two would never make it as kleptomaniacs. They don't even clear the door before Mac turns to us and says, "What did they steal?"

You get your entertainment where you can. We will put half in the special One-Zero fund that we have for keeping the kids in trinkets, and the other half we will splurge on ourselves. What good are secret things if you can't get some bennies out of them? They are happy; we are happy; no pictures of the secret hooterfritz, just two rear echelon guys who got to spend a couple of days with some real people. I hope they do get laid with those snapshots. It's a long career, and you never know when you might run into them again. Besides, they might be in supply or something lucrative by then.

Early the next morning we load on the truck and go out to the airfield that will take us up to Quang Tri. It's the usual jocular ride through Da Nang, then onto the sprawling airbase. By the time we get there, the C-123 that is our ride has arrived. Manes and a couple of others have come along to bid us "bon voyage."

Most people think that the Air Force is anal in its stringent rules about its toys. The crew chief is outside; the loadmaster is outside; they both have fire extinguishers and there is even a fire truck nearby. The normal answer from the Air Force is that after many years they have learned to be prepared for all contingencies, but there isn't anything to be worried about. These aircraft are built to military specifications. Bah! They were built by the lowest bidder, probably some Congressman's idiot cousin named Jasper. You can't fool enlisted people. That's why all the enlisted are out here with fire extinguishers and the fuzz-faced officers are applying combustion around all that fuel. Ever notice that the enlisted stand next to the plane while the officers run up the volume? Ever wonder why the enlisted guy gives the pilot the thumbs up signal, and then waits until the pilot gives him the thumbs up in return? That's to make sure that the officer doesn't have both thumbs up his ass during take-off.

As soon as the bird is safe for boarding, we traipse on. The Yards go onboard first, along with a couple of radio operators that are going to be put on Hickory. We wait until everyone else is on, and get ready to board ourselves. There is some hesitation; after all, Manes never comes out here to see us off. It must be something special, some word of encouragement he wants to share.

"What the fuck are you degenerates looking at? If you got any questions, I ain't got any answers. Now get on the airplane and go up there with your Daddy, Budrow, and if you fuck up and lose that gizmo, you better reenlist with General Giap, because my ass is going to be in a sling and you know where that will put you on the slope when the tidal wave of shit is rolling downhill." Maybe we should wound him before we get on the plane.

As the plane flies north, the three of us plan how the mission will go down. We have to get these babies onto a gradient that will allow them to offset each other.

One beacon is sufficient, but two is better, according to our instructions. So the plan is to drop down and place one at a higher elevation than the other, and separate them by a few hundred meters. That should give the Air Force all the parameters they need to hit this bloody bridge. Of course, none of us know that they have been trying to destroy this bridge for over a year. They have Arc Lighted the thing, low-level bombed it, high-level bombed it, even got their other manicured buddies in the Navy to bring the New Jersey up and shell it. But there the bridge stands like a hemorrhoid on the Air Services record. I remember the ANGLICO Team's comments on the target: It is masked by severe terrain on two sides and the gorge snakes so sharply that it is difficult to get a side angle and be able to direct fire off the gun target line. You definitely want to be *offiho,* gun target line when they are firing those big 16-inchers. They're more accurate, but if the Chief Gunner has had a bad day and he makes what the Navy calls "a slight elevation error," the Volkswagen-weight shell is going to land on you. And a 16-inch shell has a bursting radius of a kilometer.

The Air Force has never been able to call accurate fire because the place is crawling with troops. I wonder how many actual tons of goods are coming down that rail line. It isn't like the NVA to let themselves get bottlenecked like that. It sounds more like they are defending it, because every time we fail to blow it up, it's a propaganda victory for them. But on our side there is a totally different view, I am sure. Let's bomb it into toothpicks and scrap, and test our ability to hit a power plant at some other critical juncture. Either way we are going to see if we can pull it off. The mechanics of staying alive are our concern. What they do with the experience really is up to that crowd at the cocktail hour.

We land in Quang Tri and truck over to the launch site. The deuce we are riding in had been in fairly good shape just a couple of months ago. Now there is a gaping hole in the bed that has a piece of PSP covering it, and it looks like the rest of the truck has been used for a target down range. On closer examination, I can see that it's not the same truck; come to find out they traded the other truck to the Fifth Mech for a reefer full of meat and this vehicle. No sweat. We will steal the other one back while we are here. Nah, this one runs. It is not like we are going to have to cross the Serengeti with it.

We pull up and get the team settled. It will be a day or two before we get weather and assets in the same window. Until then, we will be the fill-in for Bright Light, so one of the returning teams can go back to Da Nang. That is what we think, anyway. When we get up to the TOC, we find that we are first in the slot. Surprise, surprise, they really want this beacon gizmo tested, probably because those Air Force guys are pulling maximum per diem and it's costing the Air Force an extra couple hundred a day. Budrow shows up with his usual charm to tell us he had to sacrifice a perfectly good truck in order to have enough food to feed us and the other teams and that we are going in as fast as they can give him the assets. He hopes we will be gone in four days and he will have enough steaks left to trade for something useful, like a recon team from the Rangers that at least act like soldiers. Home, sweet home.

We go over the plan, the SOI (Signal Operating Instructions), and everything for the nth time, and then break for chow and some judicious spirits, without getting stumbling drunk. There is nothing worse than being shaky going in; besides, war is noisy enough without the hangover. The other two teams will act as our Bright Light just in case we get into a real hornet's nest. We tell the guys on the other teams what's at the target, the types and placement of the enemy units. As we conduct the briefing, a team gets pulled out, thankfully, with no incident. They are lucky; they have been in for three days with no push. It was a dry hole and that is a rarity, especially up here.

Mission Control will start to stack up assets and the day after tomorrow, according to the weather guys, we should have a shot at a clear window. The F-111s can fly in soup. They will be the ones doing the "bombing by beacon," but we need clean air for all the air assets we use for insertion, extraction, survival, etc. The delay will give the team that was pulled out a chance to catch their breath before we launch. They are going to love this one; they will be our Bright Light. God gives you a break and then, as you are counting your blessings, the devil pulls up and offers you a ride.

The other team comes in about twenty minutes later. They offload and do their debrief. By the time the two Americans wander in, we are pretty much done with how we will use the Bright Light. We will brief the other team tomorrow. Tonight we will kick back, have a few beers and hear all about their nice little vacation. Then we will spring the good news on them. They walk in and look at us as if we are lepers. Somebody must've spilled the beans already.

It is much later and we have been talking about bridges. Through the fog that shrouds "Port Nick's Consciousness," I am trying to remember something about bridges. Ah well, it can wait. I can wait. The four beers that I have had make me sleepy. I go over to the team huts, take my boots off and strip down. I will get a good night's sleep, because tomorrow we will be fine-tuning everything with the launch site crew and talking with Covey.

We draw Chaney for Covey. Dave is a tall American Indian who is a very competent One-Zero, but has really found his calling in being a Covey rider. His calmness and ability to work the air assets is almost magical. Some guys are like that: they have a knack for putting all the pieces together. These guys are our mama hens; they are our link to the outside, to help line up everything that will save our asses.

There is nothing that gives you as much comfort after spending a terror-filled night in RON than hearing Covey gun his engines upstairs to let you know mama has come back to look over her chicks. These guys spend long hours in that bird, cramped in a tiny cockpit, with the tremendous responsibility of putting the right assets in the right place at the right time. Theirs is not a safe job, either. They are right down on the deck. When there aren't any air assets on scene, Coveys have been known to come in and fire their marker rockets at the bad guys to try and keep them off your ass. We have lost a good many who were shot down by ground fire, or ran into a mountainside because they cut it too close, or the normal accidental things that happen when you push men and machines to their limits.

Dawn comes when Pappy Budrow tells it to. By 0500 we are up and eating breakfast. We will do a mission brief and start sorting out with the launch site how we want to run this goat fuck. Budrow will call the ball after we outline what we want to do. Pappy is the consummate professional when it comes to the choreographing of all the extras.

We will launch after Covey has worked both sides of the gorge with sets of fast movers and Spads out of NKP, and from in-country, as well. The air support will make the two hilltops we want to use a dead zone before we get there. The air packages are hard bombs and napalm. Even if the NVA go underground, the nape will suck all the air out and suffocate anything not buried deep. We have even laid on a relatively new piece of ordnance. It is a propane bomb. When you pickle it, or release it, a chain reaction takes place. When the bomb hits, it breaks open and the gas spreads out and hundreds of little, time-release igniters spread out across the ground. Propane, or whatever the stuff is, is heavier than air, so it seeps into the low spots and down into bunkers and tunnels. Then the igniters go off. Pharoomph, followed by a ball of flame; it collapses bunkers and people's lungs. It is terribly effective, but the slopes are kind of steep so it may not work. Therefore, we are using a mixed bag of point detonating and delayed fuses on the hard bombs. Some will detonate in the trees and others will bury themselves before detonating. These will be important in and around the bridge approaches, where the AA is hiding. Then good old napalm turns everything into crispy critters. The shock and force of the preparatory should give us time to get in. It will give us time to dial in the transponders and get them up and talking to the flight of F-111s that will be in orbit waiting to hear from the boxes. After that they will come in fast and low, lock onto the signal, let the computers do all the fancy math work, and release the bombs on signal. Goodbye, bridge.

We aren't heavy enough to play Horatio at the bridge, so the flyboys are going to get one shot and then Pappy is going to pull the plug on the show. All things considered, we should be on the ground for about an hour, if we don't have suppressive fire layered up to the ceiling, if they haven't honeycombed the hills with elaborate tunnel systems with water traps to keep gas and exotics from getting to the upper chambers, if they haven't got eight million little rice eaters over the next hill, if we don't get shot down, and about a hundred more "ifs."

We argue about whether to use CBU-39 or whatever the number is, which is gas bomblets with CN gas. This stuff makes you throw up and basically incapacitates you. We have the little gas masks but no one can tell if the filters have been changed, and we don't know if we have enough filters to get everyone including the Bright

Light up. Besides, we have found out that if you use the stuff with WP it creates a primitive phosgene. Can't have that. Let us not use anything against The Hague and Geneva Conventions. If I could steal a tactical nuke, I would gladly strap it on an F-l 11 and buy the pilot champagne when he came back. In addition, I would, without a qualm, sign a statement swearing up and down that the conflagration was a result of children playing with kitchen matches. Well, that's out. There is not enough bamboo for a cover story on that end.

Bamboo! That's what I was trying to think of last night. Someone else had a bridge mission, and he blew it up. Castillo! That's right, the little Cuban weasel. I bet he knew this was coming up and took a Bright Light mission in NKP so he would be unavailable. We ought to fix his taco cart and tell Saigon that we need him here. As much interest as there is on this target, I am sure we can dig him out of whatever cushy deal he has buried himself in. I try to remember the details; unsuccessful, I grab Cook and Mac and we put all the pieces together.

Actually, it had been a really good mission. If you want sneaky and original thought, throw a Cuban or two in harm's way. The whole mission centered on blowing up this bamboo, timber, and rock bridge structure at a bottleneck in the trail system, across the fence in that country we are never in. Anyway, they had a Pink Team covering them and together they went in and moved parallel to the road, the Loach sitting right over his head. Knowing the Beaner, he was hanging onto the skids or he tied himself off to the pilot's family jewels to keep him close. But I digress. They ran up onto the bridge, cratering charges with the standoff already assembled in their rucksacks. All they had to do was place them on the right spot.

The Pink Team suppressed the curious while they dropped the rucksacks and fired up the non-electrics, giving themselves enough time to get to the extraction point before they blew the thing into matchsticks. He had even left some Black Psy-Ops in one of the bunkers. This was stuff they printed up in Saigon. It was written in dialect, on the right paper, right victory stamps, even scented with cheap perfume you could only buy in Hanoi. The usual content was some Nguyen's girl writing him that he has been gone so long she has struck up a romance with Ho down at The People's Collective No. 45, the place that makes Bata boots, and he is long stroking her every night because he has a deferment. His dad is a party official, got him out of being drafted, and because he is home every night, he is slapping the meat to all the girls whose boys are off fighting the imperialist running dog lackeys of the military industrial complex.

It's designed to break the morale of the troops. We get information from the Psy-Ops nerds that ASA intercepted radio traffic from some trying to find out if their girlfriends were screwing around, and that troops in such and such battalion mutinied and killed their political officer over the propaganda. Personally, I think the ASA types make the stuff up just in case someone needs bodies to fill a levy for the infantry.

Castro had left it as a cap on a very successful mission. But the idea of using the Pink Teams might work. We talk to Covey working out fuel loads. It's marginal, but might give us the edge. I still want to reach out there like the long arm of doom and pluck Castro from wherever he's hiding. He's our buddy, after all. What are friends for?

The day goes swiftly, the night even more so, and then it's dawn of the big day. One team is going to Bright Light us and another will go after any downed aircraft. We hope the punch we are going to put on them will be so bad there won't be any organized resistance. We get everyone geared and loaded as the air assets crank up. It is a beautiful day, with dawn starting to cast its rosy patterns in the east. The timing is such that Covey is already airborne and stacking up sets of bombers and fighters over the orbit point. There will be 30 minutes of pure hell for anyone on the ground around that bridge. By the time we are at the orbit point it should be but a few minutes until we start going in.

We fly up and over the flagpole. It is a tall flagpole inside the DMZ, with an NVA flag flapping on it. It is another propaganda coup from the other side's bag of defiant gestures. Everyone in the world has flown over and shot it up, blown it up, and generally tried to knock it down. It's gone down a couple of times and been back up in a matter of days. Someday we are going to come back here and that will be the target. If I could blow it down, take pictures of the wreckage, and recover remnants of the flag, I could make millions selling that flag over and over to every bomber/fighter jock in a three-nation area. I could probably get those Filipinos back at Da Nang to design a really neat plaque, with a remnant of the flag in the center and a reproduction of the flag destruction done on velvet. Sell the originals for five hundred apiece, easy. It's a big flag, I could probably make five or six thousand plaques. Let's see, that's two and a half million for five thousand ....

"Hey, we are getting ready to go in," the gunner shouts over the headset. The criminal mind that never sleeps comes back to the present. We are descending and can see that both sides of the gorge are a smoking ruin. But the bridge still stands.

I know Covey is having the devil's own time keeping the bombers from having a go at it. We are getting light AA fire but it's desultory. A couple of F-4 Phantoms streak past over the right side of the bridge. You can see the silver napalm canisters drop and tumble, and then it's like looking into the mouth of hell. The left side reverberates and the shock wave flashes out. Either that was a big rack of 250 and 500-pounders, or they dropped the gas bomb on the bunkers. We are coming to the smoking top of the first peak. Half our intrepid band, including me, will get off here and set the first beacon in place. The second drop is about two hundred meters higher up a ridgeline. If we get hit, or pressed, we will fight our way up to Mac. He has two extra little people and they are dragging a couple of M-60 machine guns along to give us supporting fires.

We have enough air up here to hold off the Golden Horde. I bet every pilot in Vietnam is up with ordnance this morning; hell, there is probably an Air Nuoc Mam flight full of picture-taking tourists somewhere in the traffic pattern, as well.

A couple of Navy birds go jinking down the gorge, and shortly afterwards some sort of twin-barrel 37mm opens up on them. We can see puffs of smoke above the jets because the boys on the opposing team have the fuse setting too long, and explosions on the rock wall explain why—Nguyen changed to a point detonating fuse and missed the aircraft. The jets pickle their loads, but they overshoot.

I get the magic box out as soon as we are on the ground and place it where it's got a clear radiating arc and turn it on. I tell Mac we are set and a few minutes later I hear him tell Covey that the door is open and unlocked. We will simply wait. All we have to do is hold until the boys come with the thinking bombs.

We are getting a little suppressive fire, but it's all coming from across the gorge. It is starting to range us, though, and soon it will be more than annoying. A 12.5mm starts its guttural pompom-ing and soon we are looking for dips in the ground as the rounds start chewing up the real estate. Whoever is on those guns has balls the size of buses. The whole side of the river they are on has to have been hit with everything they can load on a fast mover, and they naped it, as well. Everything is black and charred and smoking. Whoever these guys are on the gun, they have my vote for a six-week stand down in Hanoi. After all we've poured on them, they still have fight left. Hell, I would even buy the beer and the broads.

We talk to Covey, locating the guns for him. He rolls in and drops a Willie Pete in as a marker and then a set of fast movers come in to drop ordnance on the location. They streak off. A moment later it's "chugga, chugga, chugga," and the gun opens up again. A couple of Al-Es are next, big prop fighters, and they come in with their guns smoking as they descend. Shit, they are tearing up the hillside all around where the marker was. They drop ordnance and peel off and up. This gun is in a real good position, because the gorge is too twisty and the gunner is far enough down that everything goes off either to one side or above him.

Wait. There are two of them. I can hear the difference in the echoes coming from the canyon. If they had a quad set up, they would be knocking down aircraft. A couple of the birds have taken a hit trying to get at them. I can hear Covey talking to Mac; one of the sets of fast movers is going home, but the one that wasn't hit wants to invert and drop his remaining ordnance. They are setting up. He is going to do some sort of fancy birdman act to get rid of it. If it works, great; if it doesn't, he can escort his wingman back to the base. I see him loop in for the run, but I am also busy checking to see if anyone notices anything that is an immediate danger to us. I hear the "chugga, chugga, chugga" of the .51 caliber. The dirt and scrabble along the slope starts to kick up, with the last spurt zinging off the rocks just behind me. That was too bloody close. They must have a spotter up-slope directing them.

This guy is getting to be a real pain in the ass and when the ride home comes he will be able to cause us some real problems. I hear Covey say that the package is inbound and we should observe. Observe? Observe what? I can see about a third of the bridge. I wish Castro were here, he being the bridge-meister and all. He could give me observation tips.

They are still trying to slip some ordnance on the gun crews when I hear Covey tell me that I have movement coming up the ridge to the south. Coming up here? What the fuck did I do to them? No, no, no, go over there and shoot at those fancy airplanes.

Just like the Air Force to be late, probably had a pedicure and another cappuccino before they left to screw up everybody's day. I may take a few shots at them myself when they finally get here. And as if on cue, here they come, all flattened out, looking deadly, flying like someone had them on strings. Covey gives a "Hot Pickle" or some other bird signal and I see a little black object detach and fall away in a graceful arc, and then out of sight. There is a tremendous explosion; a huge spout of water rises from the gorge and pours down on us. There is a rain of falling rocks and debris. I hear a meaty thump and look over to see if one of the big chunks hit someone. Not five feet from me is a huge frog, deader than my chances for a date with anyone from a good family. It's not some teensy weensy little tree dwelling bit of bird bait, either. This thing looks like it is one of those Mississippi River bullfrogs that eat catfish for an appetizer.

My ears ring from the blast. I barely hear Covey ask what we see. Mac's slow drawl comes back to report that he sees a lot of churned up water, but unless the rascals have some real slick engineers and rebuilt real fast, the bridge wasn't hit. It's still there. No illusion. With all the iron they have dropped in this gorge they could build a dam from the debris.

We need to flee, boys. It is more than apparent that the super secret little beacon needs tweaking in order to hit the bridge. This is not the place for that. We need to get out of here now. Covey says he is going to have the Spads work the slope over below me, and a set of fast movers makes another pass on the guns. There is a big kaboom and the guns stop. Two Spads come in and CBU the slope below me. That's the spirit, boys, use all that stuff so I don't have to do anything but get on a helicopter and go home.

Should have sent a bridge expert like that malingering little Cuban. He would have gone down there with his little rucksack full of explosives, blown the thing into next month, and spread some "Dear John" letters and smut magazines around just for presentation. It would've saved money. I am going to recommend that when I get back.

The birds come in and flare, and I am on with the team as fast as we can board. We are away, with the pilots flying the envelope and then back across the DMZ. There's that flag again. I bet that Mac and I can hang underneath a Huey on strings and get that sucker with a pair of bolt cutters. We get back in and stand the package down. They tell us that we will be going back to Da Nang with the boxes. You bet we are. I am sure they are going to want to put the blame on someone. We are perfect chumps for that rap. I am going to memorize that little sequence chart so that by the time I get back I will know what I can't remember at this point. Like, what did I do?

That is another reason for an odd Cuban or two. They're expendable. His old man is in the Air Force, so he can probably get transferred. They will just send Mac and me out some day and never bother to come back for us.

All in all, this has been a good mission, no one dead, no one hurt other than a few shrapnel wounds from bomb trash. I should have brought that damn frog; it was the size of a dog. Wouldn't have done any good though, the Yards would have eaten it on the way home. In fact, Cuman is pissed at me because I didn't pick it up. He admonishes me by telling me that even the stupidest Sedang would have retrieved a morsel like that. We weren't fighting for our lives. I'll remember that next time, because I don't want the boys to think I'm slow or anything.

I wonder what kind of mischief we can get into tonight? Maybe we can sell the Cookie to the nurses as a sex toy. There ought to be some money in that.

CHAPTER 20

The Cuckoo's Nest

The air packages shuttle out while we sprawl under the shade and in the hut that doubles as the bullpen and drinking area in Quang Tri. No one pays much attention to the helicopters, you've seen one, you've seen them all, but now a Loach comes in, getting closer and closer. It overshoots the landing area and settles down right in front of us, blowing dust everywhere. It has everyone's attention now.

Before the engines finish shutting down, the door opens and Sneaky jumps out. Sneaky is an ex-Special Forces medic who decided he wanted to be a flying officer. As he describes it, the flying program is where they separate the men from the boys, then the men from the morons, and the morons fly Loaches.

He comes in, wiping the sweat from his brow. "I need a cold one." Someone tosses him a Black Label, which he deftly chucks out the window, unopened. "Not that crap. That's what you guys give the fucking tourists. I want a real beer." Someone grudgingly hands him a Budweiser. He is, after all, family, at least in the bastard stepchild category. Now he is back to plague us, bringing his infernal little noisemaker inside the camp to upset Pappy, who likes things ordered in his little world. Sneaky knows this and sticks out his jaw. "I was thirsty, okay? Besides, the bird is hot."

This particular bird is brand spanking new and has a crest on it that looks like crossed sabers over a verdant field. We steal jeeps; Sneaky has raised the bar. I see Budrow stomping across the open area between the TOC and where we are sitting. Every time his feet hit the dirt they kick up little puffs of dust. Good, I think. He will have someone else to chew on besides us. A forlorn hope, however, because Pappy always has enough left over to spread around.

Now that his throat has been lubricated Sneaky is telling us how those ingrates over in aviation have grounded him. It seems that the colonel is a bit peeved at him because he didn't fit the mold of the air cavalry.

Sneaky is a superb pilot. In fact, you could say that Sneaky takes flying a Loach to the level of religion. But despite the Army's efforts, Warrant Academy couldn't transform him into one of those almost gentlemen who know their salad fork from a back scratcher. He refused to conform to the Cav's proclivity of wearing the Civil

War style forage cap when drinking with his fellow officer types. Additionally, he is still prone to punctuate arguments with a left hook. What has kept him out of Leavenworth is that he has the best combat record with the Pink Teams.

We are about to get the rest of the story about why he has some General's personal bird when Budrow shoves his way into the hut. He stands there for a moment with that narrow-eyed, pit bull look. I'm sure Sneaky knows he's there, but he never turns around, he just keeps talking in a slow drawl. Budrow, never one to be bothered by either conscience or manners, starts right in with an insinuating growl.

"Who does that pile of junk belong to that is sitting in the middle of MY camp?" He gives the evil eye to everyone in the room, but he knows perfectly well to whom it belongs. Sneaky turns and lazily looks Budrow over, as if he were some interesting fauna specimen.

"Why Top, is that you? I believe that you are even balder and uglier than I remember," Sneaky smiles. Budrow and Sneaky were on the same team as NCOs back when Christ was a corporal.

"Is that your machine, Mister?" Budrow hisses. Budrow can make a particular form of respectful address like "Sir" or "Mister" sound like a suppurating wound, and that's how it comes out.

"Why no, Top," Sneaky drawls. "Technically that particular aircraft does not belong to me, just as this particular camp does not belong to you." We shoot a glance at Budrow, but Sneaky continues. "On the log books that particular aircraft is assigned to the commander of the Fifth Mechanized Division's air support," Sneaky pauses for effect. "I am sure that by some miracle of simian development, you have learned how to read since we last met. You can find it on the logbooks. Those would be the green vinyl-looking objects with the scratch markings inside."

The gloves are off and we are fortunate enough to be witnesses to this verbal ballet. Budrow hunches down his neck. "You know what I mean, you dick brain. Did you fly that bird in here and land it here instead of on the designated chopper pad?" But Sneaky and he have been at this for years, so Sneaky looks at him and deftly blows that inquiry aside.

"Why yes, Master Sergeant Budrow, I, as a commissioned *Warrant Officer*, noticed that I was having emergency technical failure in my hydraulics and tried to set down at the nearest emergency strip, which would be here, but alas I was unable to keep the aircraft aloft safely and actually make the PSP, so I, as a commissioned *Warrant Officer*, at great risk to myself, put down here. These gentlemen pulled me from the stricken craft, and thankfully have been re-hydrating me after my exhausting struggle at the controls." He's got you there, Budrow, I think, but I am wrong.

Budrow smiles that predatory smile that only loan sharks and rich ugly debutantes have perfected and says, "Well, why didn't you say so, *Mister* White? I have a suggestion."

"Why don't you come with me back over to the TOC and we will radio the unit that the bird belongs to, just to let them know that their star pilot has survived what appears to be shoddy mechanical maintenance. I am sure that they will be beside themselves with concern, and I am just as sure, and am willing to bet good hard dollars, that they will probably ask us to detain you. All the result of some paperwork glitch, I am sure. But I, being a *lowly Master Sergeant*, will be forced to follow a lawful order given by any officer appointed above me and restrain you from leaping into that pile of junk out there and breaking the bonds of the surly earth. I have just the Conex container that will serve as temporary Warrant Officers Quarters until your escorts arrive."

After that, it got ugly for a few minutes with deadly secrets about some whore with the clap in Okie and some colonel's wife in Hawaii and apparently some stolen or misappropriated funds, which is very interesting for we are, if nothing, the masters of blackmail. Us poor children of the night are sopping up the dirt and actually taking notes when they both stop and stare at us. Uh oh, they were uniting in their criminality.

"You got ears and a memory?" Budrow barks. "You will be digging piss tubes every time you come up here, understand?" He snags a beer and says to Sneaky, "They are looking for that pretty little bird you are flying. It is all over the radio. I would suggest that you get it out of here so I don't have a bunch of limp dick, leg officers trying to get in here." The verbal punctuation was followed by a long pull on the Budweiser. Of course, this has no effect on Sneaky, since he is a study in ignoring anything other than his own re-hydration.

Between sips of beer Sneaky tells us why he is flying stolen iron. It seems that the day before he had been flying the usual Pink Team formation, which consists of his flying low and being a tempting target while a Cobra gunship lies in wait above. Some NVA crew thought that they would do their bit for Communism by opening up on him with a 57mm. They were a little slower on the draw than he was. He hosed them down when he saw the foliage in a tree line move in a most unnatural way. He didn't even have to call his big brother down from above; he let loose with a long rip and no more gun crew. He drifted over and took a look, and sure enough, there was the side pan radar and all. The gun and crew were a little worse for the wear, though.

The team had come back in and given their daily shooting account to the intel folks and the colonel himself had guffawed and pooh-poohed his story as a bald-faced lie. "Why everyone knows they aren't using those types of guns this close in. Nope, guns like that are way too valuable." Ergo, Sneaky must be exaggerating. Of course, the gunship can't verify because they never saw anything except Sneaky doing some trim work on a hillside.

Sneaky was so mad he'd gone back out, grabbed his mechanic, who was about five bricks shy of a load because he actually liked Sneaky, and they flew back out to the AO alone, no guns. It took them about 20 minutes to find the site. They bobbed and weaved to see if anyone was around, but got no ground fire so they flew over the site. There it was. He hovered and the mechanic hopped out, took the sights, one of the pans, and loaded two of the bodies on the bird. Just as they were backing away from the slope, very smug in their accomplishment, an NVA officer popped up out of a spider hole not 20 feet from the bubble. He stood as if he was at the National Match and pulled a Tokarov 9mm out and shot at Sneaky.

Sneaky, though, has the honed reflexes of a pit viper, so he jerked the bird aloft, and the round missed him by a couple of feet, but got his mechanic in the shoulder. They flew back to camp and landed, but because he had called in wounded the brass was there to greet them. They shuffled the kid off to the hospital and Sneaky dropped the sights, pan, and bodies out and asked the brass if that was enough verification. That was too much for the staff. They grounded him and suggested, no, make that *ordered* him, to see the shrink.

To make a long story short, Sneaky did go to the funny doctor and while waiting there, his mechanic called to say they were sending him home. "Please come get me Mr. Sneaky. I don't want to go home." Well, Sneak grabbed the first thing he saw unattended and flew off on a mission of mercy. He grabbed the kid out of the field hospital and they made their getaway. He had stopped in here to see if he could leave the kid for a few days until he could get his paperwork straightened out.

He and Budrow are still arguing when I wander down to the Yard mess and sit down with the kids for some refried dog or something. I hear the little Loach fire up and leave, and see Budrow stomp back to the TOC. What happened to the kid is a mystery because an emergency news flash comes in from our fellow felons in Da Nang.

There is some new Provost Marshal in Da Nang and the MPs have set up roadblocks to check vehicles. So far they have nailed five of our jeeps. They can't hold our guys because of priority, arf, arf, but they have confiscated the jeeps. That is just like that bunch of self-righteous little pimps. I am sure that the MPs are going to get them back to their rightful owners, but they will keep the good ones. They and their other little buddies will justify it under some sort of seizure program. "Crooked cop" is a redundancy. Thank God the police in civilian life can't get away with crap like that. The country would be in a sad state of affairs. At least outside the UCMJ you have the Constitution. So tonight's mission, gentlemen, should you decide to accept …

We are gone by dark. They have two birds laid on to take us back, so we are going to purloin a few vehicles up here. Because we are outside the Da Nang Provost's jurisdiction, if we steal new vehicles there is no way to trace the numbers. They won't even show up on the master list as stolen for another two months. This is how the Army really works. Scrounging is a refined method of theft and barter. It's been that way since Caesar.

By dawn's early light we are all back. We have five jeeps and a pickup from the PA&E (We will give that one back; they are barter customers) and a Land Rover with USAID emblems on it. Screw that bunch of commies. We leave two of the jeeps, take the Land Rover and three jeeps, plus our own little bodies, and load on the birds. These are both dedicated air assets who are all over one of the jeeps because of its uniqueness. It is a Vietnamese copy of the original Willys jeep from WWII. We almost trade the Vietnamese jeep for a load of booze, but the deal falls through because the guy who stole it wants to keep it. It's actually a Philippine copy of the old Willys, not an M-151. We can't blame him there; besides, we can probably trade them one of the hot numbers in Da Nang so we get the ball back in court.

After a couple of hours we wind down through the air traffic pattern and land at Da Nang. A deuce and a jeep are there to deliver another team that will head back up to Quang Tri. We learn they are stopping all black vehicles and checking them at the I Corps Bridge. Are they? Well, these are all painted US army, OD green, so all the Americans grab a jeep and I grab the Land Rover and we convoy out of the airbase. We leave the jeep that came with the deuce with the aircrew. They are going on to Clarke, where they will offload it. The next bird north will be bringing our payment in the form of cognac, whiskey and other assorted liquor, plus a pallet of good German lager and a couple of cases of Mateus.

As soon as we clear the airbase we split and take different routes to the bridge. All the Yards are on the deuce. They are going to make a fuss at the checkpoint, get off, wander around with all those guns and such. That will keep the MPs busy and we will slide right through. By the time I get to the bridge, sure enough, they have stopped the deuce and are going over the logbooks. The little people are taunting the QCs and flipping them off, and about six of them have gotten off and are standing next to Fish as if they are his backup. There is some red-faced staff sergeant yelling at them and they ignore him. He starts to grab one of them and about 20 safeties go off. Fish says something to him that I can't hear, but the Spec-4 that's directing traffic waves us through. We make it back to the camp and pull all the vehicles up to the motor pool. Fish and his crew will have them painted in a day or so. The only concern is the Land Rover. It seems that some church group appropriated this particular vehicle on a loan basis and they are screaming bloody murder about its disappearance. Well, pray for a new one, brother, because this one is gone. Now if it had been the Catholic Church we might have sneaked it back; they are not a particularly forgiving crowd, but it's some evangelist crowd of Baptist tight skirts, so it is fortunes of war for the holy rollers.

The return to Da Nang means a first day of debriefs. I am right; the Zoomy Command is sure we screwed up the beacons. They have some sort of bubble theory that the sequence wasn't separated by enough lateral displacement or some kind of technical crap. I go through the rote of the turn on and aim sequence as best as I can remember it. They aren't all that displeased, although one of the light colonels, shit, there must have been eight of them there, starts to make some snide remark about we might have at least stayed there and had another flight laid on so they could recalibrate and try again. Both Mac and I are about to lean over and rip this pink-faced prick a new asshole when Manes, Colonel Donnie, and the grand Poobah himself, who had come up from Saigon, tell him it's the One-Zero's call when to come out. Evidently, this isn't good enough; he starts to say something else because he figures we don't look like we are lieutenant colonels. The dirty fingernails and two day growth of beard must give us away. Nah, it's probably because Mac looks like he is twelve; Cookie looks like those pictures in the Post Office; and, well, I just look. The grand Poobah shuts the impertinent prick up by asking Mac and Larry if we would be willing to go back on the target with the good colonel as escort so that the Air Force can be sure a technical expert is on-site properly handling their new toy. He turns white as a sheet. I'm trying to figure out if it's because someone might like the idea, or because he has overstepped his superiors.

After they file out, Chief SOG, Colonel Donnie, and our own little mini-planet tell us that everything actually exceeded their expectations. What we had done was to enable the military to develop a whole new generation of weapon platforms. Geez, and I thought they had expended that entire ordnance to get the killer frog.

No one wants to hear about the frog. I bet if they send some of those spandex heroes from the Navy up there, they could dog paddle up in the middle of the night, have a snarling hissy fit about their tan lines and maybe capture one. It won't work, though. That frog would whip the shit out of a SEAL team. Send some Marines because one of them would marry it and take it home. That's much more cost effective.

In the meantime, because I was foolish enough to mention the frog I take all the heat, Nick's killer frog, ha-ha-ha. If they had seen this thing they wouldn't go in the shower, much less some godforsaken stream out there in the bush.

We leave the briefing area and go outside. Now that the embarrassing little episode is over, we are off for three days. Whoopee. I have all kinds of shenanigans bottled up inside. We need to do something that will reestablish the pecking order down in Da Nang, with those heathen MPs first on the list. I'm all for just offing a few of them. If they think the VC are targeting them they won't go anywhere unless it is with 50 or more of the little plastic heroes, and that's if they are in V-60 Cadillac Gauge Armored cars with air support. Keep them locked up in their little guard posts and frightened for their little pantywaist lives. That's the way to keep them from bothering good honest soldiery. For Christ's sake, there are a couple hundred deserters involved in the black market running around Da Nang. Do you think those pretty boys are checking IDs and rounding up those junkies? Nope, a deserter has already slipped the surly bonds of discipline and regulations, so offing some little prick with an MP armband would not even work up a tickle of conscience. The Provost crew tried that a couple of years ago and about ten of them ended up with gunshot wounds. That was the end of that. But, I guess I am extreme; every time I bring up good solid suggestions like this, I get, "Shush, we can't do that."

In all my years of being shot at, fragged, mortared, bombed, stabbed, and generally mauled by the enemy, I have never looked up and seen an MP standing there, or even near there. All they have ever done is harass and interdict good honest, hardworking soldiers from letting off a little steam. Okay, we don't have to cap them; we just kidnap a few and take them with us on a mission. If they survive we can let them go and when they get back they can tell all their buddies not to screw with us. I like that idea. Better yet, let's grab this new Provost Marshal and take him out there. If he gets uppity we will leave him say, in Hotel-6. That's a nasty place. It is a brilliant idea, but I am sure that I can't talk Manes into this, not because he likes MPs, but because he would want something in return, like the Land Rover, or a case of Chivas. No, it's better to try the evil captain twins, Keith and Jimbo. They are psycho enough to see the simple justice in it. But that is impractical, as well, since they are both too psycho to see any profit motive. Captains are like Spec-4s with manners. Captain Robb would be a better bet since he was in the Phoenix program, and offing a few annoying functionaries wouldn't even prick his conscience. Best not to involve the captains at all; life is complicated enough without them running amok.

I get down to Recon, drop the equipment, clean the tools of the trade, oil everything, and do all the little housewife stuff. I strip down and head for the shower. Ah, the water is hot and relaxing. Cook and Mac are sitting in lawn chairs, fully clothed, and fully rigged up. The taps are directing a hot stream of water down on them, washing everything at once, clothes, harnesses, guns, grenades, ammo, and their nasty little asses. I am evolved, however pedestrian they are. In fact, I have brought my face mask and snorkel so I can use my spare toothbrush to clean out the small places in the equipment. Cook and Mac have already drunk a half a case of beer during their Recon bath.

Southerners. You should have to take a course in the care and maintenance of the grit-burning model before they make you have close daily contact with them. They are, I suspect, Kurt Von Daniken's theory aside, castaways from another star system.

Eons ago, the aliens came down here; taught the primitives how to farm and worship the gods, and provided them with a few simple math tools so they could build in a straight line. Then it was time to fire up the plasma engines and shag a star leg back home. But, somewhere deep down in the bilge area of that distant starship was the vacant duty station of the direct descendants of these two cretins lounging here in their own muddy water. I bet they were out fucking off somewhere when the mother ship blasted away from the planet, leaving them stranded here.

It's a safe bet that all those UFOs are full of alien anthropologists studying the human race, trying to decipher what happened when their gene pool experiment went off track. That's why they don't make contact. They know there is some ruthless lawyer that will try and pin the rap on them for the bloodline that led to these two genetic throwbacks.

You have to be amused by southerners as a genetic swipe. They have their own way about everything, from cuisine to the proper way to pleasure a sheep. God bless southerners, though, because if we didn't have any, the Germans and the Japs would have won the war and there wouldn't be the word "irony" in the *New Abridged*

Webster's. I have seen just about every place that you can find combat troops in the army, and if you have a bunch of good old boys it is usually a pretty good combat unit. Forget all that mean, inner city, black warrior and Chicano, knife fighting, swordsman bullshit. As a class of people that make a hard-edged weapon, give me southerners every time. They are the quintessential warrior types. And the skinnier and ganglier and more ignorant they are, the less you want to be on the opposing team if you back them into a comer.

All those good qualities aside, though, they do have their shortcomings. Don't argue semantics with one unless you know the finer points of picking a good orthodontist. Don't ever try to understand their cuisine or disparage it. Never ask them if being from California qualifies as being a Yankee as they suspect that Texas is leaning too far out of the saddle. Football is a religion and should never be taken in vain. They are sardonic, laconic, and a dozen other "ics."

My two comrades are just getting warmed up now as they finish the cleaning exercise in a sing-song litany of cute little country homilies. As they shuffle out I am finishing the last of a great hot shower. Nothing, not even sex, feels as good as a hot shower. Makes you feel like a new person. I dry off, wrap the towel around me, and head out the door. I am zoning as I shuffle up the sidewalk carrying my newly washed kit in one hand and hanging onto the towel with the other. I am mentally laying out the festivities for the evening. I notice the sand about two feet in front of me spurt up in a shower of dust, then another, then another. It dawns on me that I am being shot at. I move like a lizard. Zip, and I am crouched, and then I roll behind one of the grenade walls. Where is it coming from? I don't hear the report of a weapon. Maybe it is a sniper up on Marble Mountain? Then I hear a distinct "pffft" and turn towards the sound. I am all dirty and full of sand from my scramble for safety. There is only one place this could have come from and that is Wesley's hut. The noise registers in my mind, and I realize that the Weasel has been shooting at me with a silenced .22.

Okay Weasel, two can play that game. I walk calmly back to the hut. Mac and the Cookie are stripped down and reassembling their gear. They still have to go back to take their shower when this job is completed. I search their faces. Southerners are masters of the practical joke and born with poker faces. I give them a few moments for the hook to be cast. When it isn't, I am reasonably sure that Oog and Og here are not in on it. They are smoking cigarettes and drinking beer. I get out a set of NVA khakis and put them on, Bata boots, an AK vest with six mags, get an AK out of one of our team boxes and put on a pith helmet. They look at me quizzically, but protocol in our lunatic asylum prevents any serious questions, so they go back to nonchalantly reassembling their weapons. I do notice, though, that there is a serious hurry to get their little cannon collection back together.

"You might not want to go out for a little bit," I inform them. Then I lean out the door and dump about half a magazine into the roof of Wes's hut and yell,

"Come on out Yankee. You numbah ten; you die!" There is a moment of silence after the last round, and then he breaks out the back door of the hut, heading for the Yard huts. As he is sprinting for cover I yell after him, "You want to shoot at hardworking honest folk? Let's just see how you deal with VC on steroids, fucker!" For good measure, I put a burst behind him in the sand. He makes it around the corner of the Yard barracks. There is no sense chasing him in the hot sun. I come back inside and strip down. I need another shower. I tell Mac and the Cookie what happened on my way back from the shower. They think it is funny, but then Cookie reminds us how pissed Billy is getting about people shooting guns off inside the camp. Since retribution is a fine art, we all take a pistol along in case Wesley wants to stir up some more fun. Cookie has a silenced .22, but Mac and I have opted for big magnums: I have a .41 and he has a Dan Wesson .44, enough to discourage any further disquiet. We hang them around our necks on lanyards.

There is a hubbub of people stirring outside. Because it is best to blend in with the crowd to avoid any semblance of guilt, we want to appear to be three hardworking stiffs on their way to the shower. We head out the door holding our shaving kits, guns suspended around our necks, extra speed loaders, etc., all the stuff you need to take a shower at Insanity Central. We step outside and immediately run into the SMAJ and Frenchy standing on the walkway. Billy is rubbernecking the growing crowd and livid that his directive about shooting up the home court has been broken less than two hours after he issued it.

"I told you pencil-dicks to quit shooting up the company," he screams. We assume the blank "I don't know what you're talking about" look. I am not as good at it as the other two. Being southerners, they probably have been accused of cross-species dating and a whole series of other heinous acts, all before they were 14. This would give them a distinct advantage in assuming innocence.

"We heard an AK, SMAJ. We thought there might be trouble, so we are just taking some firepower with us while we shower." The second prime directive in any unit is "Thou shalt not rat," so we walk past him while he mumbles that he is going to kill the next son of a bitch that shoots in the company area.

Just as Billy says that, the Weasel comes sauntering around the corner, like he is James Bond. Billy spots him, sees the .22 with the silencer, and yells that if we suspect there is an attack on the camp, why in blue blazes is everyone running around with pistols? Get some rifles so you have some range. Unless, of course, you think this is the OK Corral. This is mixed with a vitriolic stream of invectives about being morons of questionable parentage, the usual stuff.

Wes stands there with that stupid look on his face, and as we walk past Mac whispers, "I got grenades in this shaving kit, and we are going back to the shower. A long hot shower, relaxing, with no interruptions, understand?" Wes stands there with that thought meandering through the bayou he calls a brain as we walk down to the latrine. We get inside the shower and are hosing down under the showerheads.

Billy pops in, looks at us, starts to say something, and then huffs back outside. It's a normal day in Recon. We finish, towel off, and head back to the hootch. All is calm. We dress in clean starchies, complete with team patch. There will be howling tonight. We take some Green Hornets with us for later; this could be a long night.

We head over to the club and there is the usual crowd around the bar and drifting out onto the floor. I suppose most people would call it dingy and dark, but it is our kind of chic. We have a TV room off to the side, and the TV is even operational. It is, except when some drunk has gotten pissed at Walter Cronkite and shot the TV. AFVN is the only channel, but I guess it's a form of entertainment. I usually go in there when I need a nap during a night of revelry.

The pistol incident has sparked my creative juices. We will all take the High Standards with us tonight and shoot the tires on any MP jeeps we see. We will start with low- level harassment and sabotage and see if that sends them a message. By 2100, we have been going at it enough with the other teams that we are ready for the half hour journey to the safe house downtown. Mac comes back with a jeep, and four of us pile in, all of us from Habu with Jimmy Johnson driving. A turn past the Yard huts and we are headed up to the main gate. We get up to the Officers Club and a truck is illuminated in the headlights. It sits squarely across the road effectively blocking traffic. There are figures around it carrying flashlights. It's Billy and Manes and "others." We have to stop. A dark figure, with the square mass of a bam, shines a light in our faces, blinding us.

"You morons are staying here tonight," Manes says.

"Why?"

"Somebody is firing up the population downtown," he says, and then searches each of our faces with the light as if we know something.

"Do tell. Why?" We try to hide the snickers. Manes is done with the subtleties of polite conversation, however.

"Yes, do tell, you morons. And The Old Man wants everyone to stay buttoned down tonight." He looks us over, under the glare of the flashlight. "Why?" he mimics us. "Are you three year olds? Do you need to know everything? They think it's a major VC infiltration. That's why."

"Are any MPs dead?" I ask, but quickly realize it is a blunder to have mentioned the MPs. Both of our adrenalin- fueled leaders whip in my direction and the flashlights pin me like an escapee from Stalag 13. Shouldn't have said that. I am sure that a hint of glee slipped through my voice, because both Manes and Billy tune their "I suspect he is involved" look at me. We have drawn way too much attention to ourselves. They are all now surveying us with that practiced look nuns have.

"What do you know about this?" Oops, time to go. Obviously the boys who left before us have been terrorizing the MPs. Best thing to do at this point is shut up lest we be blamed for it. I am pinned in the twin beams of light, but Mac comes to the rescue.

"Nothin', *Dai Uy*, we don't know nothin'," Mac says, and shoots me a warning glance.

Jimmy jumps in, too. "If we knew something, it still wouldn't amount to nothing." He squints at them blearily. Billy and Manes hover over us for a few minutes until they figure out that asking us questions about what they suspect, would be like getting a straight answer out of a preacher in a watermelon patch. We turn around and head back for the club. No use trying to leave because the Manes and Billy roadblock will be hovering in the shadows, staking out the gate, like lookouts on a bank heist. It's better that someone carried out the retribution plan early. Since we were here when all this shit happened we can't be blamed. We go back and tell the staggering survivors at the club we must seeketh fun in local quarters.

The night is spent at the club interviewing the returnees as they drift in. The lads shot out quite a number of tires, and not just the ones on MP vehicles. And as in all things, you must "up" the ante. They started shooting out their pretty little blue light bars and a few windscreens, etc. Then the boys started using the rooftops to move around and snipe. No one had been injured, but the MPs were convinced that VC hit squads were after them. They will probably write themselves up for valorous action. Every plastic one of them would get in on that frenzy. They would hand out a few Bronze Stars and think they survived a major offensive.

"Should have capped a few as long as the VC were taking the blame," I say, caught up in the enthusiasm. Of course everyone turns and stares at me as if my fly were open at a funeral. I get those looks again. Mac and Cookie are instructed to take me back to the hootch before I inflame the crowd.

The colonel takes it for granted that we are somehow responsible for last night's shenanigans, so we will have to settle for hanging around here for a day or so. No one is going to tell the MPs, but the more astute among their ranks will connect the dots. Really, they are more in the line of an annoyance than any hindrance. Besides, scaring the little pricks is well worth the cost of having to stay in camp for our stand down. I only wish I could have been in on it.

CHAPTER 21

Little Island in the Sun

The unit has been tasked for a raid, which is supposed to bring the combatants comfort because it conjures up images of Roger's Rangers and commando type operations, Indians in the bush, all that stuff you cut your teeth on when you were a kid. The only comfort that we can draw from it, however, is the fact that we will have two weeks to train, and that means two weeks that we won't be on the target lists. Two weeks away from getting our asses shot off while our hearts are in our mouths.

Training has started. Recently, we got some of the newer RPG-7s and we're going to practice with them. The Marines have agreed to let us use their ranges to the northwest of the city and the facilities around them. By using the range facilities they share with the ARVN Marines, we will have plenty of room to shoot all the guns.

There are a couple of gunnies here with a bevy of privates, and an equal number of their Vietnamese counterparts. The Marines are the only ones that seem to be able to impart their lore, pride, and craft to their Vietnamese counterparts. In fact, Vietnamese Marines and US Marines have interchangeable parts. This isn't, in truth, the only success story, because we have our carbon copies in the Yards. While the Marines are "The Few, the Proud, the Marines," our demented sideshow is more like "The Bizarre, the Insane, the Heavily Armed."

As we offload the assorted equipment and ammunition, the gunnies look us over as if we were low life scum. They probably have seen a bunch of ARVN with US advisors out here before, so I understand their contempt. But as we offload, I watch the two gunnies as they measure the types of weapons, the fact that they are well-maintained, the modifications and the sheer multitude of what we have brought to the range to fire that day.

There are three teams of us, about 30 people, and we have enough ammo and weaponry for three companies. The enlisted Marines are there as a detail to assist in running the ranges. We tell the two gunny sergeants we will set up our own targets and they give us the layout of the various ranges. God bless their little green hearts. Because the Marines still believe in marksmanship, they have a standard set of rifle ranges and a set of M-79 and anti-tank ranges with junk vehicles and bunkers as targets. They also have a 106 and mortar range. We need all of them.

You can see that the Marine NCOs don't like it, but they figure what the hell, HQ said we get the use of the ranges, so if we want to run things our way, why not, as long as we don't shoot up anything that isn't down range. We start out with fairly simple stuff, setting up some silhouette targets. As teams work out the kinks, we begin doing Immediate Action drills: action front, action rear, action either side, all done from our normal line formation.

The Marines know the drills on a smaller scale because in the Marine Corps the Navy makes them sign for every round. That way the Navy can afford all that white linen and the Filipino mess stewards for that class of patrician bigots who make up the upper strata of the white shoe Navy. This does not include naval pilots who, but for questionable parentage and being able to use a slide rule, should be Special Forces, or at least honest Marines at heart. But when we cut loose with a normal team drill it sounds like two companies in contact. We have no restrictions, whatsoever, on expending ammo. In fact, we have brought so much ammo that it took an extra truck, plus we have more in the trucks we were riding in.

Our next cardinal sin is that we are on a rifle range and we are firing rifles, sawed off M-60 machine guns, Russian RPDs, M-79s, shotguns, pistols, and at the same time, throwing grenades. This is how we break contact with the enemy, chew his little rice-eating ass up, and then move out. I have to hand it to the two Marine NCOs; they soon acquire the look of respectful tolerance and genuine interest.

The other ranks stand there in "Gaaahhhhlleee Sarge" silence. We do about four or five IA drills for each team then come back to the trucks and start reloading. I don't care how long you make your living with a gun, letting it rip on full automatic, feeling the thing alive in your hands, and hearing the roar stirs something exhilarating that pleases your inner child.

We dig open more cases and pull out grenades and all manner of exotica, and are going to give it another go before we get down to specific drills. The two NCOs saunter over and are nonchalantly eyeing the stash of ammo and weapons, asking a few polite questions here and there. I've been a sergeant long enough and a scrounger longer still, not to realize this is the recon for the filching they will extract as a courtesy. We have plenty of everything, so it won't even bother us, but I motion the two off to the side and tell them that the little people are real sensitive about "missing" their equipment, which in polite terms means that if knives, guns or trinkets disappear they will figure it is the ARVNs and will probably kill them. The Yards do not steal. In fact there is a story floating around that if you leave a hundred dollar bill lying in a Yard village, they will send out runners trying to find you and return it. Failing that, they will find another American to give it back to. They figure we are all one tribe or federation of tribes, just like themselves. The two gunnies get the message. I didn't call them thieves, just a polite warning that no theft would be tolerated. I use the ARVNs as the litmus test. Sergeant to sergeant protocol is much too complex for officers; they would do it in writing.

The exotic weapons fascinate the Marines. We are going to take a break, so I tell them that, if they want, they can fire everything they'd like. I give them my CAR-15, get an RPD, a sawed off M-60 and a sawed off M-79. I go over and pull a whole shit-load of ammo out for each weapon, and tell them to let it rip.

Now polite protocol would be to give them a couple of bursts worth of ammo and maybe a couple of grenades for the launchers to let them get the feel for it. Instead, I motion to the pile I pulled over and say, "Have fun." The two NCOs get to rip it up, and they also get to be elevated higher in the eyes of their charges. Very important sergeant political stuff happening here, so pay attention. To add to the cream, we give them a few more of the CAR-15s and tell them if they have any of their people or the ARVN Marines that would like to have a shot at it, go ahead. We are going to kick back for about 30 minutes. It's hot.

For the slow on the uptake, this puts them in the driver's seat. They are equal; we let them use our stuff, ergo, we are kindred. They then can bestow the privilege to those they deem worthy. It's a bad dog, guy thing. It involves some very heavy testosterone, and primitive rock language. It's sort of like territorial sniffing. Don't ever try and explain "alpha male stuff with stripes" to women or *officers*.

I go back with the team as Mac wanders up with Lieutenant Hagen. They give a few tips to the two regarding the sawed off M-79, and then they, too, wander off. We are sitting in the shade the trucks provide, cooling off, drinking water, just planning out the next stage. We will work the regular M-60s, the RPGs, and the minimortar in a support setting using the bunkers and the junked vehicles as targets. Then we will do it with the teams, fire and maneuver with support, and assault with support, so we can practice lifting and shifting fires. We get ready to start these drills as the Marines have almost finished. Selections of Vietnamese and American enlisted have also tried their hand at the weapons. We will oil them and switch to the other stuff, since we won't be using these for a while. The Marines offer to clean them, but that's a no-no; we clean our own stuff. These weapons are our lives. I don't mind letting them run ten or fifteen magazines through the CAR-15, but I'm the one who is going to disassemble, clean, and then reassemble the beastie.

We get up on the line and have five or six RPG-2s and an equal number of the bigger RPG-7s. The RPG is classified as a rocket-propelled grenade. It is an excellent tank killer, bunker buster and is used in assault or even in defense because it stuns, shocks, and kills. When that big 88mm warhead goes off, you want to find a hole to hide in. The old ones come in four parts. The front is a warhead the size of a football and then a silver detonator, which looks like a thick gas cap, fits in the base of the warhead next to the top of the rocket motor. Next comes the rocket motor and a booster that screws onto the base of the motor. The rocket is fin-stabilized. There are four to six fins at the base of the motor. If they are extended, you just twist them in the loading palm and screw the rocket into the tube. Most come with a retainer ring that comes off when the rocket is fired. The launcher is a tube with a pistol grip trigger assembly about 20 inches from the snout. It is set up for a right-handed firer, because there is a gas ejection port on the right hand side of the tube. If a lefty fires it from his left shoulder, his face is going to look like melted wax when he's done.

The newer model is essentially the same, a recoilless weapon. But it has an optical site with leads and all the fancy stuff instead of an iron site. There are hard plastic louvers over the tube, and the butt is a flared horn-type affair to help dissipate the gases. The rocket is also fin- stabilized but the fins are flat metal slats that fold forward against the rocket body and when it is fired they lock back from the force of the momentum.

This one has a different warhead, and as we are about to find out, it doesn't arm like the old ones, but does so as it picks up "g" forces. We get on line and everyone fires four or five rockets with the RPG-2 at bunkers and vehicles. Then we all get a quick rundown on the RPG-7 and the first order moves up to the line. There is no jolt, just a huge roar when they go off, with a bright flame as the rocket zips out at what seems to be the speed of light.

Everyone has a natural tendency to flinch; that's why we are here. We want to familiarize everyone with the weapon and work through the paces. The first four guys load their launchers and they go off, one after the other. One of the new guys on RT Kansas flinches, anticipating recoil, and the muzzle dips just enough that it strikes the dirt about 30 meters out. The booster kicks in and it cartwheels directly back at us. Everyone dives for the nearest cover: holes, dips in the ground, vehicles, you name it. I dive for a trench to my right and before I hit the ground, three Yards and two Marines run over my back and get there first. The round hits about 20 meters to my rear, the rocket motor kicks in and it sails another 70 yards or so before it hits the target shack. There is a tremendous explosion and the shack virtually disintegrates, with paper and boards raining down in all directions. Oh my, wasn't that lovely. I start to get up as one of the gunnies brushes the dirt off as well.

He looks at me and grins. "Secret weapon?"

"Yeah," I nod. "I think the Navy designed it. The Marines wouldn't accept it, so now we have convinced the NVA they are special." Needless to say, it scared the bejesus out of everyone. We get someone on the horn and find out it has a spin arm system in the detonator and has some peculiar quirks. Quirks? We spend another two hours practicing with the bloody thing. It's a good weapon, but I like the old one, the B-40. We will carry both on the raid. We are finding out which men on our team have the magic to operate the weapon, and they will end up being the designated hitters.

Now comes practice at providing cover fire with the mini-sixties. We have sawed off the normal 60mm mortar tube so we can carry just the tube and the jungle plate. If you want more base plate, fill a helmet with sand or clay and set it in there. Our Yards, and most of us, can put three in the air before the first one drops on the target. Most of the time we just use the base charge, that's all we need. But here we are shooting out around 300 meters, so we adjust by stripping "cheese" charges. We work all three systems together, mortars firing white phosphorous and then HE, machine guns, and RPGs, until we vaporize a couple of the bunkers. Then we get the teams out and do some "fire and maneuver" with the support sections, firing on the bunkers. Finally, we do fire and maneuver and then assault, with the support sections shifting fire as we hit the bunkers. A couple of guys get shrapnel, but it's minor.

This is how we train. The Marines love it. We let them watch, then let them try all the heavy stuff, and finally we do a full-on assault and let them fire the 60s for us, so the gun crews can get on focal in case we need more in the assault phase. It works well. By about 1500 we are finishing up. Cookie and I go back to the truck and we drag out some ice chests. The Marines are aghast that we have had the foresight to bring ice-cold beer along. Well, they act aghast, but I am pretty sure the two gunnies found it earlier during the theft recon. Everyone takes a break, sitting in the shade, while we begin to detail out the clean up and repacking. We give the gyrenes a case of beer; they will drink it after duty hours, which I believe will start as soon as we clear the range. As we are getting packed up, the two gunnies stand there by the truck as it is being loaded. They eyeball the little mini grenades and the mini CS grenades hungrily. Mac and I give them a case of each, some smoke, white phosphorous, and we manage to "lose a B-40" and 20 rockets. Now comrades in arms, we are assured that if we ever need anything, the Marine Corps will provide anything our little heinous hearts desire.

The one gunny tells us how the SEALs come out to use the range occasionally. They act as if everything is a secret. We all agree that everything about SEALs should be a secret, and furthermore, sailors with guns is basically a flawed concept. Sailors are lug wrench types. They were designed to travel around in the big blue bathtub, in behemoth iron ships that shoot big Volkswagen-sized shells at a similar tub full of enemy squids, blowing each other into scrap and little itty-bitty pieces of squid bait. They don't understand the finesse of the mud, never will; they are creatures of the sea. This is why the SEALs keep everything secret; they are busy figuring all this out. Give me a good old Marine any day. At the very least he is a rifleman. We load up and head back to the camp.

The plan for the raid is to use four teams like a platoon, but since we will be modified with straphangers, and since all of us are running heavy teams, it will work out to about a 50 man party. That will give us enough punch to do the job. We will have additional numbers in the snatch teams, which will be responsible for the actual securing and holding of any prisoners. We all hope that it will be a prisoner snatch involving getting Americans away from the enemy, but we are not being told anything at this time. They tell us to configure within our elements for at least two men who will secure any prisoners, plus a second special team that will be specific to that job. Fine.

Back at camp the teams break down to do weapons and equipment maintenance. We take some of the ammo and ordnance back to the supply point and the rest goes with us to the team area. This would horrify a conventional unit, because we have enough ammo and explosives in our team huts to make a sizeable crater if one of them ever accidentally torches off. In all the time CCN has been here, no such incident has occurred although, some of the collateral damage in 1968 was caused by the satchel charges thrown into some of the team houses.

Captain Larry is waiting for us. He will be the overall commander and has been "hush-hushing" with Saigon for over a week. We still don't know the target or what type of prisoners, but are speculating it's either an HQ unit and we are going straight for a grab of some high ranking officers, or it's POWs from our side. Everyone is hoping for the latter. It would really be something to free some poor son- of-a-bitch that has been living on rice chaff and cockroaches, dreaming of big tits and hamburgers, and hoping someday his comrades will come get him.

There is another alternative. This involves an imaginary set of circumstances where Billy has found out where there is a cache of freshly printed greenbacks (The NVA are reported to pay some of their agents in the south in dollars), and we are going in to seize these "documents." To add to the fun, Lamar suggests that Larry is in debt to some Chinese loan shark by the name of "Low Fat," and we are going in to cancel his contract for him. Personally, I like this last one. Billy is already making enough money and I like the Midget having a nemesis named Low Fat.

Manes comes down and we have a meeting with all the Americans targeted for the raid. We are to be prepared at oh-dark-thirty to move to the Da Nang Airbase, where we will transport south to Nha Trang. We will stay there overnight and transfer by LST (Landing Ship, Tank) to the island of Hon Tre. On the island, the Army has established their Combat Orientation Course and some other weenie stuff so that the incoming troops will get the idea that they are in a combat zone. It is all very functional from the standpoint of teaching the troops the basics, but because we will be using it as a training area, everything will be shut down. A romantic couple of days with the nuclear dwarf on a deserted isle. It's like winning one of those overnighters and finding out your cabin mate is a serial killer.

Now I've been to the COC course, back when I was a sober lad trying to earn an honest living, and the things I remember about the island are not likely to make a brochure that will attract the jet set. As I remember, everything on the island has a bite on one end and a stinger on the other. The plant life seems to be nature's experiments in poison, thorns, and sharp edges. The plants have stuff that makes you swell up; stuff that makes you itch, and one interesting variety of insect that actually lunges at body heat. This ought to be fun. I am telling the other guys about this when I notice that the Manes monster eyeballing me with that look that he reserves for his next victim. Time to sink down into the mass of huddled bodies; Larry has no patience when he is on the speaker's platform, which is whenever his lips are moving. We also get the EMMTW, the "Early Manes Murder Threat Warning." It's the usual diatribe about the first person that fucks up and gets drunk, abuses some REMF, gooses some round-eyed slut that hangs around headquarters, etc., will have to answer to him personally and he is going to twist the culprits head off like a ripe August tomato. We have nothing to worry about because the odds are in our favor that the very first person who will violate the above rules will be Little Squatty himself.

Nha Trang, I love the place. I have a semi-steady at the streamer bar. That is to say, she moves her client list aside when I roll into town, and since she usually only screws officers she is relatively unused. She is a big-titted, Cambodian-French mix. She is about five foot ten with long jet-black hair and green eyes. My heart is already getting knotted up in anticipation of some extreme physical exercise. She speaks almost flawless English and is funny. We like to hang together, go to some of the better dining spots, do a little shopping, and screw like we were the stars in a Masters and Johnson study. After three or four days I have to go back and get shot at; it's easier on the nervous system.

In Nha Trang there are all the tourist spots like "Sally Suck 'em Silly's," the huge Buddha monument, Francois by the Sea, the R and R center, as well as all the other sites. It's an interesting mix of locales that one gets in the urbane, manic mix of multi-culturals and homy GIs. On top of that, there is a complete mob of us to hang out with. I am sure that bunch of pansies at Nha Trang is trying to figure out how to make our stay in their fantasy war zone be measured in minutes, not days. I have never been overly fond of passing through the SFOB at Nha Trang. Oh don't get me wrong, there are always good friends passing through, but SFOB is the flagpole of Special Forces Command. Not our command because SOG is handled out of Saigon and reports directly to some other false idol, but all the other SF stuff is at Nha Trang.

You have to understand the mindset of the class of REMFs that are in charge of us, the "Great Unwashed." We would be the guys in Special Forces who are assigned to A Camps, the Mobile Guerilla Forces or Mike Forces, and Special Projects like MACV-SOG; the blue-collar workers of the war. Nha Trang and Saigon are the places that handle all the paperwork, logistics, and planning of strategic operations.

Consequently, we are the ones with the leaking holes and deranged ideas that we are doing the actual work, while the others try to look important lest they get transferred to where we are. There are people in Nha Trang who are on their third tour and have never fired their weapon in anger, much less in fear and terror. It is heavily populated with pencil-necked geeks, shirkers, and senior officers with commiserating staffs. All seem to think they are still at Ft. Bragg.

Among this crowd of half-steppers is a particularly disgusting group we call the Alpine Malingerers. They are a senior NCO clique of Bad Toelz, 10th Special Forces hemorrhoids, that finally has been driven out of Bavaria and actually made it to the war zone. They have made cushy little jobs for themselves, and when one rotates out, another one is prearranged to rotate in for that slot. I have met some real hard chargers who were in the 10th, but the group here is an anomaly. There is a particular E-8 that will eventually become the youngest SMAJ in the army. He runs the ice cream parlor. That wouldn't be so bad, but he actually thinks he is a combat soldier. Someone occasionally throws a rocket or mortar round in their direction and the next morning the Awards and Decorations clerks are working overtime filling out Combat Infantryman Badge requests. When Delta project was going full swing, they were a major embarrassment to that bunch of heroes, because Delta used to give them their rightful ration of bloody noses and bruises just for being the sorry malingering bunch of assholes they are. Since Delta is closed out, we will gladly fill that spot.

My guess is that Manes wants to make sure we are warned. We, on the other hand, bet he'll make it one night, max, before he punches out some pencil-dick, himself. Usually we get there, grab a bunk in the transient barracks, and then shag out the gate and stay downtown until we have to go back, give or take a few days. The weenies know we are coming, so that has sweetened the anticipation of the havoc we expect to wreak.

We get to the airport early and load all the stuff we are going to need for a projected six-day training period and a couple of day's stay in Nha Trang. REMFs don't normally let the Yards into their little pristine world of painted rock walkways and spit-shined jungle boots, but Saigon has told them that all of us will stay in the one compound. I bet that has their tits in a wringer.

We arrive in Nha Trang later that day; the trucks to transport us have been waiting with drivers. Real pretty trucks too, I think they wax them. We make the short haul over to the compound and unload everything, putting the Yards in a back barracks beyond the swimming pool and we billet right next to the pool. As soon as everyone has a bed, we assign guards for the equipment, because we are planning the night run to downtown. Unfortunately, we haven't even put our gear down before some E-8 ass-wipe comes in and tells us to hold here since the SMAJ himself wants to have a meeting with us. Manes has gone off with a couple of the other captains, but the rest of us are kicking back including Lieutenant Hagen and a couple of the other officers. Since no one is wearing rank, its just one big gaggle of NCOs to the casual observer. Some wit yells out, "If the SMAJ wants to talk to us, fine and dandy, but get his ass over here, because we are going to town tonight."

The E-8 about craps himself. I guess no one talks to these jerks like that here. The best part is that it is Hagen and one of our guys, who is also an E-8, giving him the "go get his Lordship" speech. He huffs out, and about 15 minutes later comes back with the SMAJ, who is a tall, skinny, acerbic looking individual. All of us peg him right off the bat as another one of the "cushy assignment crowd." He's either a homesteader from Bragg or Toelz, the kind of model that comes with pressed starched fatigues, shined jungle boots, and a whitewall haircut. He starts in about our appearance, our lack of military bearing, our everything that doesn't fit their little mold of the perfect public image of Special Forces. Barry Sadler did a little song called "Garret Trooper" that describes this type of insect.

I have just walked in wearing my toothbrush and toothpaste. Tony, Jesse and I have been getting cleaned up for the town run. The SMAJ turns and stares, aghast that we are naked during his briefing. Tony finally breaks the silence. "Sergeant Major! I think you're staring at my pee- pee!" We all think this is funny, but it only elicits a terse order of "At ease!" from the E-8 with him. Loosen up asshole. Unfortunately, our apparent disregard of the Sergeant Major's exalted rank drives the man into some sort of frenzy. He is hopping up and down, going on about how we are confined to the compound from this moment on. He wants a guard roster delivered to him, and as punishment we will take over guarding a section of the wall for the night.

"By God," the SMAJ says, "you are going to act like soldiers while you are here." Right, scumbag, so you and the rest of this pond scum can fuck-off and don't have to worry about us stealing your girlfriends, or maybe beating the shit out of the lot of you if we catch you downtown. I look at my comrades and can see that we are all thinking the same thing. We stare at the Sergeant Major in dead silence, until Hagen, who is standing there half-dressed like the rest of us, breaks the ice.

"No," Hagen says. The SMAJ goes ballistic and starts screaming about court martial and "who do you think you are" and then he makes the mistake of grabbing the Lieutenant's shoulder as he turns away. Hagen is a big boy, six foot, blond hair, and blue eyes, probably 195. We call him "Gringo." He has this flowing Zapata-style mustache that makes him look even more sinister. He spins, grabs the SMAJ in a wrist take-down, and drops him. "For your information, I am an officer, and I believe that you just assaulted me. I am sure that if I kicked your worthless, loud-mouthed ass right now, I have twenty witnesses that say you attacked me and I defended myself. We are not going to be pulling guard duty. We are not going to be confined to the barracks. We are not here to play games with the rest of you."

The SMAJ's flunky makes a break for the door. I think Thompson dropped him; can't be sure because he got hit several times before he hit the floor. Hagen continues. "We are not going to do anything but rest up and go do our assigned tasks in the morning. We get any crap out of you in-between and we will file charges, and you can be sure they will lead to a very nasty career end." He lets go and the SMAJ gets up; he hasn't got much to say. Can't argue with a stacked deck, besides he screwed his own pooch assuming everyone here was enlisted. He and his minion head out the door. Everyone continues getting ready.

Castro comes wandering out of the shower, looks around and asks, "What'd I miss?"

"The group Sergeant Major was looking for you," Tony says. "You have a promotion board tomorrow. He wants to see you before you go downtown."

Manes comes back, telling us to make sure that the Yards have what they need and to get them some beer, but not enough to get in trouble. We have to be ready to go at 0530 in the morning. He grimaces when we tell him the incident with the Sergeant Major. Someone asks him if we have to stay here tonight. He says, "You want to stay here? Well, I'm going downtown where the women are. If you all want to hang out here with these queers, just don't let anyone know you work for me." It's official, Squatty himself is telling us to go downtown.

We have a great steak dinner at the NCO mess. Before we left Da Nang everyone had been told to bring a pair of fatigues with all the proper unit patches sewn on. Those that didn't have at least some sort of uniform with, at minimum, their nametag and US Army sewn on in the proper place. I see a lot of Smith and Jones nametags.

After hanging around the club for about an hour having a few drinks, we decide to go to the city. We go out the front gate, grab a Cyclo-cab or three, and head downtown for some festivities. The night passes in an orgy of sights, smells, and tastes of the orient. I love Nha Trang.

It is about 2300 when I decide I have had enough fun and games. Some of us are going back to grab a few hours of sleep before we have to head to the island. There are six of us sharing a cab on the way back. As we near the main gate we see Charley Jay. He is riding a water buffalo. That isn't really odd; he probably couldn't find a ride, so he just borrowed the buff so he didn't have to walk. Charlie's old man had been a diplomat and Charlie has spoken Vietnamese since he was a kid. The buffalo, in the meantime, smells the swimming pool.

"Le buff" gives a shake, ejecting Jay onto the roadway, and takes off at a lumbering gait toward the water. He downshifts at the fence and sniffs around it, until he finally decides the fence is nothing in the way of an impediment. He puts his head down and uses his horns to deftly reduce the fence to twisted wreckage. Then he lumbers over to the edge of the pool and unceremoniously heaves himself into the shallow end. That's right, Old Paint; get in there where the bugs won't bother you. We watch the whole scene and then wander up to collapse on the bunks. Tomorrow will be another fun-filled adventure in the Land of Oz.

Oh-five-thirty rolls around much too quickly. I have a hangover from too much Ba Mi Ba and cognac. The headache is compounded with a horrible twisted knot in the front of my head. I get up, shower, go over and get the little people moving, and then cut over to the mess for breakfast. I need something to replace all the swirling indigestion in my stomach, plus a pot or two of coffee. To my amazement, I discover they have pastry, yes, delicate little pastry and all the trimmings. These goons really have it rough here. We eat well at Da Nang, but at the launch sites you might eat canned sauerkraut with beef for a month. This is delicious. Everyone is grabbing six or more of the little delicacies to stuff in their rucksack for later. It's going to be PIRs for the next six days.

As the sun starts to boil our brains, we load up the trucks to leave. The SMAJ comes out of his quarters, which are right next to the well-maintained swimming pool. He has on a store-bought, velour bathrobe, and is wearing a turquoise shower cap. He walks through the gate around the fenced pool and fails to notice the twisted wreckage at the back of the fence line. We can't see anything but a dark shadow, indicating that the buffalo is still in residence. Everyone nudges his neighbor as the SMAJ saunters to his reserved chair at poolside. He takes his little robe off, folds it neatly over a lawn chair, and walks over to the deep end, poised on the edge on his tippy-toes. The trucks pull out with us on them, but we are witness to the events as they unfold.

The SMAJ springs knifelike into the air just as the buff surfaces in the shallow end. I have never seen a man so desperately try to defy the laws of physics; he almost made it back. He hits the water in a tangle of legs and arms trying to go the other way, and surfaces right in front of the water buffalo. There are about two feet separating them and he is staring eye-to-bloodshot eye with "Monsieur Bison de tropics." Le buff snorts, sending a huge gob of green and yellow snot cannon-balling onto the SMAJ. It is a good thing he is wearing that cap. It looks like nearly two quarts of the slimy stuff is running all over one side of his head. The scene's unfortunate end is obscured as we round the comer are gone.

We are laughing our asses off when Manes says through his tears, "I never did like that prick. We were E-6s together. Which one of you degenerates did that?" Thou shalt not rat on thy fellow rodent is a rule. In fact, it is a prime directive. We are silent for a moment, before simultaneously saying, "Charlie Jay!" Jay tries to make himself smaller, but there is no pity in combat city.

The Yards thought it was funny even though they are not sure about the concept of swimming pools. To them any appreciable water supply is for drinking, bathing, and usually housing something that they can eat. Seeing the pool incident didn't generate any sort of response from them other than it was a natural place to find a water buffalo, which any fool should know.

Our four trucks wind down through the city of Nha Trang to reach the docks. The Navy has provided one of their LSTs and we herd aboard to find a comfortable perch for the ride to the island. The Navy finally gets the anchors and doors and ramps, whatever, up and locked. All this is accompanied by some sort of alien commands about port and starboard. Then with a gush of diesel exhaust the LST backs down the ramp and turns toward the open sea.

An hour later we are on the South China Sea. It is a beautiful day with the sun shining and the seas calm. We have a couple of trucks on the LST that we will use as a base camp. They hold our extra ammunition, rations, and creature comforts that we have brought along in order to make *pac* time a little more bearable. We have a couple of cases of beer stashed which we won't crack until the last day when we get ready to make the two hour ride back to the mainland. Right now, though, everyone is sprawled about, naked or near naked, sunbathing all over the ship. Even the Yards have gotten into the spirit of it and a few have stripped down to their loincloths or GI issue underwear. I haven't worn underwear since my first tour. It's the quickest way I know to develop some very painful ailments. No one in his right mind wears it. It's just one of those things you learn about living in the bush. I think the only time I have worn underwear was when I was down with dysentery, and that was so I could cut it off and wash myself. I can sympathize with King Hank's foot soldiers, especially the Irish who fought with him through France. Dysentery is a bane to all and sundry. Most people in a combat situation just cut their trousers away. It is a debilitating thing that I never want to go through again. The strain they have over here is amoebic, also, but it makes the Mexican version look like lactose intolerance by comparison.

I am up on the bow where the ramp is and I have a cravat tied over my hair with the loose ends flapping out behind me. In a Long John Silver voice, I provide my interpretation of the lyrics to *Sixteen Men on a Dead Man's Chest*. I am down to my cravat and a loincloth, but still wearing jungle boots. The Yards find it hilarious as Mac and I do a handy rendition of a hornpipe dance.

The Navy crew retreats to the confines of the bridge and the engine room. They had been nervous when we came onboard, giving us uneasy glances as we settled in, and now are alarmed as someone starts using an M-79 for target practice on a couple of 55 gallon drums and some plastic containers floating 200 meters in front of us. The commotion increases when someone else joins in with an M-60. Soon the crowd is blasting away, blowing drums, containers, and driftwood into so much scrap and seaweed that the "captain" of our good vessel, who is some kind of lieutenant, sends someone forward to demand to see our commander. He is extremely distressed when he finds out that the one blasting away with the M-79 is, in fact, our esteemed commander. He is even more distressed when informed by the Midget to "just drive the fucking tub, and I will worry about what I shoots at." I think the captain was more upset that Larry used the word "drive" than anything else.

The Navy has all kinds of Navy-speak for everything. You don't go to the latrine, it's "the head." You don't chow down, you "mess"; left is port, right is starboard … lee, aft, astern, here come the bloody torpedoes. Only the Marines can understand them.

The LST slows as it approaches the island, where there is a ramp and pier for unloading. By this time we are all pretty much dressed. True to naval tradition, they run the thing up on the beach and the ramp goes down. We rush up the beach about 50 yards, screaming "Banzai! Banzai!" It is great fun for us. The Navy looks relieved that we have gotten off their floating bathtub. The trucks trundle down and we march a few hundred meters up a dirt road to a clearing that we will use as a base camp. Each team sets out to build huts and lean-tos for sleeping, and soon the place looks like a movie set for South Pacific. We have a fresh water point that is not far from the COC School, but we stay out of that area, although we will use their Vietnamese village as a mock up. We have the run of the island for the next six days.

By nightfall we have organized the place and gone out on a couple of walk-around tours to look at the various ranges and get a feel for the terrain. This place has been here for so long they actually have a garden and some banana trees. With the abundance of fruits, herbs, and tubers, the Yards are in seventh heaven. We have the sea nearby to catch fresh fish, at least for the next two nights, then we will work our way inland and do some platoon tactics and movements so we can attune ourselves to moving and fighting as a large unit.

It is an idyllic place; I can't imagine anyone considering being here a hardship tour. I wander down to the COC course. It is canned plastic, right out of Fort Benning, with neat little trails and round robin type teaching stations covering things like Malayan swinging gate booby traps. Shit, I have never seen one of those out in our AO. It's the classic booby trap with sharpened stakes that comes swinging out of the foliage and impales Aldo Ray or some other supporting actor in all the Hollywood versions of the war. These are remnants of the old war.

In the new war, they booby-trap the area with big, bloody, Chinese-type claymores, made from a 55-gallon drum. When that particular baby goes off, there isn't enough left of you to wet a hanky, much less impale. They have *punji* pits and *punji* fields at the next two stations. Now that's real. We even use them on static positions, a sharp stake cut from bamboo or anything, with a little human excrement to dip the end in. You set them in little depressions around your perimeter. I've seen plenty of these, and I have seen the wounds they produce. If the injured man doesn't get somewhere with real medicine, real fast, he'll go poisonously septic, get gangrene, and then a host of other nasty things set in. At that point, he'll be lucky if they only amputate.

On the island there is a complete mock up of a Vietnamese village. There are actually two of them, one is "all pretty" and has chickens and hogs running around. The other one is used for firing exercises. They are at different ends of the area. I wander around the neat, pretty one, wondering why there is such an abundance of domestic potluck running around. As soon as the Yards discover them, the chickens and pigs will be on the menu, as well as a few of the quackers. I wonder how they have escaped the notice of the Yards, when I get that feeling, the sixth sense. I crouch and start looking for whatever or whoever is watching me. I scan the undergrowth and see two of our Yards and two more from Castillo's team, grinning at me from the brush not 20 meters away. I stand back up and they come out. They already have a chicken and three ducks trussed up for the pot. Bop and Xaung grin at me. They pat me on the arm.

"Ummm *Trung Si*, numbah one," they say, while rubbing their bellies and gesturing at the chickens and trussed up members of duckdom.

Bop can't resist adding an admonition, "You same same shleep, *Trung Si*. No see *Tahan*." He looks at me as if I have committed some sort of heinous lack of protocol by daydreaming. Yeah, my fine little forest denizen, you got me there. I was daydreaming. You have to watch the rear; you think it is safe and someone blows you out of your knickers. VC still wander around here. We have gotten so used to fighting the NVA that we forget the VC are still active all over the rest of the country. That's all I need, to get smoked by some part-time asshole who is probably a hair dresser by day. I watch them as they bag a couple more chickens and a fat little squealer. They look at me as if to ask if it's all right. I just shrug. What the hell, if the COC weenies want their livestock safe, they should take it with them. They were probably so excited about five days with their girlfriends that there was a rush to the boat. Screw the livestock.

We meander up to the camp, gathering stuff as we go. More forage parties are coming in. There is the start of a huge bonfire going and the remaining coals from an earlier one are being shoveled into a nearby pit. An assortment of cleaned, gutted wildlife and the domestic victims are being rolled up in banana leaves to be placed amongst the coals. A bigger pig has been spitted and placed over the coals. The smell is delicious. It looks like a luau. The only thing missing is Wheeler, and it is too bad he isn't here. He could strip down, paint himself up, and parade around making Hawaiian noises and maybe brain a pig or two. It might be entertaining if we could dress Manes up as Captain Cook and let him and the Big Kahuna have a go at a reenactment. Nah, Larry would cheat and then both of them would be pissed off. In that case, there are not enough places to hide out here.

We are almost to the camp when I see Mac and Cook over by the beach so I split off from the boys and wander over to them. When I get there they are talking to Tony, Hagen, and Berg. Berg is very laid back. I went to One-Zero school with him. Hagen, nicknamed "Festus," is steady as well. Tony, well, Tony and I go back to weapons training together. I wonder how we survived. His nickname has always been "Fast Eddie." We were broke and had been in weapons training when Nail, Sergeant First Class Nail, told us that you could get high eating a tiny bit of the cheese-like charges that are on the 4.2 inch mortar. He said they had done that at some A Camp he had been in when they couldn't get booze.

At that point we could have been convicted of being morons on two major counts, the first being in believing anything that comes out of Arkansas, the home swamp for Nail. Jesus, the state was settled by a family of six that survived some Cherokee attack in Georgia and moved west, deeper into them thar hills. That would be a family of one brother and his five sisters. They started the white population there. I guess on the frontier, little things like kids with one eye and grotesque physical attributes didn't matter in those days, as long as you could shoot. That's why today it's the safest place in America to commit a crime; they all have the same DNA. The second count was compounding the original stupidity by trying Tony's "cheese."

Tony and I had gotten a Charge 52 or something, and nibbled a few little bites. Sure enough, we were soon zipping along at 30,000 feet, washing it down with root beer. There was only one small detail that the "Swamp Thing" left out. The special effects come from the nitroglycerine, and as it wears off the capillaries snap down from being inflated and give you a migraine that feels like the Jolly Green Giant is stepping on your nuts. We had to be taken to Womack Army Hospital because they thought we were infected with spinal meningitis. Ah yes, Fast Eddie, my friend and fellow test pilot in discovering better living through chemistry.

We lay out tomorrow's festivities, because the next day their team and Habu will be working together as an integrated raiding element. The other two teams will split off and do the same. Manes has a meeting planned for the morning, but tonight it's just kick back and relax.

An hour later our stomachs are distended from gorging. There is a constant stream of Yards coming over to drop off some delicacy from the fire. The Yards are perfect for living off the land and preparing terrific feasts. If you leave them alone, within 30 minutes of being in an area they have collected anything of nutritional value and will, subsequently, eat at any hour that affords them the opportunity. They are perfect hunter-gatherers.

Dawn breaks and I awaken in the hootch that the little people have made for us. It is a pole affair, with a palm thatch roof and a sleeping platform made from split bamboo. This keeps you about 24 inches off the ground and prevents some of the more unpleasant critters from crawling in and sleeping with you. Sleeping on the bamboo has been softened somewhat by a grass mat that they've made. It's warm and dry and cozy.

In fact, I had slept like a baby. I spent the night wrapped in an indig sleeping bag. Guards rotated throughout the night, with two Americans staying awake for each shift. I'd pulled my shift around 2400. I had gotten up and walked around the camp on our side to ensure that everyone who was supposed to be awake was awake. There were even a few of the Yards worrying the leftovers of the pig. Ah, nothing like the midnight munchies from the Stone Age. Scratch the guns and the modem equipment and this looks like a hunting party from a thousand years ago.

What wakes me up is the smell of frying pork. I sit up and stretch, working the kinks out. The Yards are all up and around the fire. Cook is up and so is Mac. I wander over and am immediately offered a banana leaf with some rice and some fruits, and what looks like fried pork skin with a chunk of golden brown meat attached. Can life get much better than this? I think not. I squat down with them and Mac starts going over the drills that we are going to do. In about an hour the whole camp is bustling and everyone is getting ready to move out and begin our daylong training formats. The plan is to break at noon, wherever we stop, and meet back here for the final night before we move out to the far side of the island for the practice raid. Manes is stomping around making official noises. Thank God he will be going with the other group and their designated snatch team. Tomorrow he will join us. That will be soon enough.

The raid elements are mirror images of each other, and each is capable of performing the mission should the other one get wiped out on insertion. That's war, mate. We finish up and move out in separate formations, each team moving towards a rally point about a klick and a half away. We will join up and conduct platoon operations as combined teams and do our fire and assault patterns all day. The forest closes around us and we practice transitioning and trying to coordinate our movements so that we arrive at the arranged checkpoints at staggered times, but on schedule. We want one team to get there and set up security shortly before the other team, so that we don't run into each other. This is so one team is ready to receive when the other team gives a vector that is coded red, blue, green, or yellow. The points of true direction are given on numerical increments by ten- degree jumps. Say North is blue and East is yellow and your team is moving at 60 degrees, the direction given is "Blue 60." The other team knows you are coming in to its southwest. Any noise or movement coming from anywhere else has to be the bad guy.

It is a pretty simple code system, and every once in a while you rotate the colors clockwise. This prevents the enemy from picking up on the system and either laying in ambush or waiting for your next move to figure out where the group is going. We alternate the terrain, so on one leg you have it relatively easy and on the next you get terrain found only in goat country. It's sweaty work. Just because it's double or triple canopy doesn't mean there is cool shade. It is darker under all that foliage, but it's like a steam bath. When we come across streams, it's a welcome relief to break, go admin, and use your cravat to wash off a bit. The relief from the sticky, sweaty feeling only lasts for a few minutes, but it feels so good. We test the ability of the radio to communicate between teams. We have opposing ridgelines between us and we want to see how well we can get a signal on the little blade antennas. In the actual mission we will have Covey as a relay station, but it doesn't hurt to see what kind of ranging problems we are going to have.

We do this until about 1400 and then join forces. We come across a small waterfall in an area that is relatively clear of the thick undergrowth and the other team comes to us. Our afternoon exercise will be in some open savanna about 250 meters farther out. This is a nice spot so we stay here for now. I can't believe it, there is actually a breeze coming up from the stream, which drops off to the north. We must be near the ocean in that direction, or the terrain drops off and a natural flow of air is forced up the tunnel created by the stream and its overhanging vegetation. The other team comes in and we extend the perimeters and send a few spider probes out to see what is beyond our eyesight on all sides. Visibility is about 75 meters, which is fairly open compared to what we have been traveling through. We eat chow and get ready for the next two hours of work. We will do a platoon assault on a little clump of trees that are at the north end of a fairly large clear area, about 250 meters by 150 meters. We will take the trees under fire with the M-60s, and the mortars and rockets, while the teams get on line and assault. This way we can look at our alignment and adjust. We will start from the wood line, and will have only about 80 meters of open ground top cover. The support element will be to our right rear on the long axis of the clearing. This will allow us to be offset from the gun target line. Since we don't have a fire direction control, this is going to have to be done all in the head.

This works fine, but it takes a couple of tries. Our mortars are hand-held, or rather, hand-directed so it is all done by what we call "Kentucky windage," but it works all right. We calculate that we want to be no more than ninety degrees, or near perpendicular, to make it simple. Think about throwing a rock in a pond. Your brother is standing on the east side of the pond, and you are throwing rocks at a tin can floating in the middle, from the south end. You throw a rock and it lands over the can by three feet. Your brother sees it hit to the right of the can, so he would say "Left three feet" so you can adjust for the rock falling on the can. But, in reality to you, the person throwing the rock, you would need to drop, or subtract, three feet. It's fairly simple stuff. The Army complicates it by giving new names to everything from the can to the arc the rock makes in flight.

The exercise works well. We manage to scare the hell out of everything with fur and feather and blow the hell out of the silhouettes we put in the clump of trees. We identify a couple of problem areas and correct them. Basically, this has been a rehearsal for the real thing and a fun day, with lots of loud noises and the smell of cordite, more fun than a rock fight when you were twelve. We move back as one group trying out what they now call a "bounding over watch." It is a formation that is pretty hard to do in thick vegetation, but workable as the terrain opens. The first thing you learn in combat movement is to use flankers and a point element in front of the main body. If you have these out effectively you can scare up the other side and give yourself some fighting time. We don't have that problem because we are so compact, but in large units the tendency is for troops to bunch up. There is something comforting about being close to the next guy. More than likely he will get it, not you, right? The reality is that there is more chance "they" will get all of you. I've heard it before in training, "One grenade will get you all! Spread out." A more dispersed target is harder to hit.

We work our way around in a loop and arrive back at the beach around 1700. This will be the last day here. Tomorrow we will move out into the interior and do drills and rehearsals for the next three days. Tonight is the same as last night. Kick back, talk tactics and methods, everyone putting in his observations and going over the rough spots to figure ways to smooth them out.

After dark, Castillo comes walking into the firelight. He is dressed in palm fronds with a string of seashells around his neck. He is carrying a homemade spear and starts dancing around the fire waving the thing around. He looks like Che Guevera, made up for a bad night at the Tiki Lounge. Someone finally gets tired of his antics and shoves him in the direction of the fire. His hula outfit catches fire and he heads for the breakers, flaming like a shot down aircraft.

The next three days are the same, except we are tactical the entire time. We move, call in a couple of air strikes, and then move again. We will repeat the process until Uncle Larry is satisfied that we are operating like a well-oiled machine. The last time we do a practice assault we use the Viet Village and bomb, shoot, mortar and rocket the place into rubble and burning wreckage. This part is the most enjoyable since it is like being a Vandal. We do the searches and find all the hidden bunkers, then rally at a point on the other side.

Larry gives us the order to split into teams and move to the north end of the island to await pickup on the beach. It is tough moving. We have to make the pickup point by a prescribed time, so we are moving a lot faster than we would on a normal operation. We have been tactical for three days and, with the exception of talking the air strikes in and the assault, haven't spoken above a whisper in all that time. As we near the beach, we suddenly hear the angry snapping sound made by bullets. That snap is caused by the bullet breaking the sound barrier. The louder the snap, the closer to your sacred vessel it is.

Mac, Cook and I work our way up to the berm created by the tidal surges and look out on a little bay. Sitting in the bay is a white and aqua-colored Chris-Craft with outboard motors. It is about 100 meters offshore and there are four Caucasians in it: two guys, and two women. The guys are obviously officers with their nurse dates and have come out here from God knows where, probably one of the R and R centers, for a little afternoon of fun with the boat, deserted isle, white sand beaches, a little wine, and a little poontang. One of the girls has an M-16. The two studs are evidently showing their manliness by letting the girls take turns getting a feel for chopping away on full auto at the beach and foliage. Had the berm not been there, they would have probably hit someone. While we are lying there, the Midget comes up on the horn demanding to know who is popping caps. Mac tells him what we see and so does Castillo, who is just down the beach from us. Larry radios back to hold in place; he is coming up Red 20, which is to our direct rear. He arrives in about five minutes with one of the other teams. He looks the situation over with his usual assessments like "stupid shits," and "dumb son of a bitches," interlaced with the admonition to all present to "keep yer heads down." Then, he gets the last team on the radio to tells them to be careful coming in. They are about 20 minutes out, and our ride, which will be the LST, is about an hour out.

By now Larry has become annoyed by the zip, zip, crack, crack, followed by feminine giggles and lusty stud shouts coming from the pinheads in the boat. It's bad enough that he is stuck on a beach with us, but he is more frustrated that he can't figure out a way to get out to the boat and the women. Now if the Midget were one of the guys out in the boat doing the, "me Tarzan, you Jane act," he wouldn't be annoyed at all. In fact, he would probably insist that one of us stand up, so the fluff would have something to shoot at, and then justify the sacrifice by claiming that it was good training. But this is not the case. I can see the ideas going through his square

Slavic head, which in Larry's case is a short trip. He grins and tells Mac, "Give me that radio." He fiddles around and goes up on the frequency with the LST and tells them where we are, and that we are going to have a mad minute in just a little bit. Then he gets all the Americans together and tells us to get M-79s, machine guns, anything we want, and to tell the Yards they can watch, but not shoot. After that, we get directly in front of the boat and strung out about 25 meters just off to the right of where these "num-yums" have been cracking away. He tells us that when he says "go" we'll shoot all around the little boat. Don't hit it, and don't get closer than say, 75 meters, with the big stuff, but tear the shit out of the ocean. This is going to be good.

Three of the miscreants are sitting down in the boat swilling beer. The two girls have taken their tops off and are sunning their respective racks when one of the guys stands up, slaps a twenty-round magazine in, and strikes a John Wayne pose like he is Sgt. Rock, then rips up the beach on full auto.

Manes waits until he dumps the last round. "GO!" We open up with CAR-15s, two M-60s, and two M-79's. It sounds like a battalion. The water on both front and rear of the boat erupts in white geysers. The M-79s make impressive whomping explosions, ringing the boat. No worry about shrapnel. The effect on the tourists is predictably chaotic. When we open up, the one that is standing literally drops the M-16 overboard and dives for the bottom of the boat. They are all screaming. The women are hysterical and one is screaming to start the motor.

The other guy says, "Fuck you, I ain't standing up!" We see a hand reach up and turn the motor over; it won't start. Then there is a frantic search for the gun, punctuated by "Where the fuck is the gun?" We can barely hear because the women are screaming and crying. The motor catches and the little boat almost swamps itself, making a hard right as it zings out to sea. With the motor at full throttle, it is bouncing on the swells, and every time it slaps back down we see bodies bounce up for an instant then fall back out of sight. They are about a quarter of a mile out when someone stands up and actually starts driving the thing. It is one of the nurses. She is wearing no top, her hair blowing in the wind, glancing over her shoulder every once in a while, and heading for the safety of the sea.

She looks magnificent, that's one thing we all agree on. The boat was a good mile out before we even saw the guys reappear. I watch through the glasses, giving the others a play by play. She is yelling at the guys. One reaches over like he is going to emphasize something and she slaps him so hard he falls back out of sight.

We are laughing so hard that we are getting hiccups and it is hard to see. Castillo looks at Manes and says, "See, typical officer shit. If an NCO would have been in charge, he'd have been quick enough that when he saw the dummy drop the gun overboard he would have backed out of the jungle and shot up the area and yelled out to them to save themselves; he would hold them off." Castillo pauses for a reaction and then leers at him and adds, "He would probably get a medal AND some drawers."

Larry looks at him as if he were something on the bottom of his boot. You can see the wheels turning, though. He will be looking for the two nurses tonight, I bet with some story that will insert the Midget as holding off an entire sapper regiment to save some unknown American women in a pleasure boat that cruised into a cove at a secret VC frogman island. I can imagine the dialogue. With all that gratitude, he will naturally be overwhelmed and do the "Aw shucks ma'am, I'm just grateful you got away" bit. "I lost half my guys, had to kill the biggest one who followed me right into the water, must have been a Chinese, almost seven feet tall. I had to bite his throat out, he was so maddened by the prospect of raping a white woman."

One thing is certain. The two heroes in the boat are not going to be enjoying anything other than that special kind of scorn only the female of the species is capable of delivering. Those boys are permanently off the dating list. With the grapevine that the sisterhood has, they'd better change their names; or, if they have any sense at all, throw their dates overboard in the shipping channel and hope the sharks get them.

Castro moves off before Captain Chunk decides he might need the dropped M-16 for props tonight. Bob is, after all, SCUBA qualified. The idea pops into my head to bring this up to our beloved leader, but the Cuban is quick and can obviously read minds, because he is looking at me while he explains the possibility that the reef is spotted with deep tidal pools and this is where, in all probability, the M-16 now rests. You can see deep blue spots out where the boat was; these are obviously those deep holes that go to the bowels of the earth, according to him. He goes on to tell Larry how these holes are typically hundreds of feet deep, swarming with sharks and all manner of things.

The way he describes it, one would expect Captain Nemo and the boys to surface at any moment. But you only have to look at Manes to understand why *Sea Hunt*, with the Cuban, seems appropriate. Manes is too chunky, too dense, to be involved in water operations; there is no positive buoyancy in the Midget. It is most unlikely he went to SCUBA school. And if he did, he didn't like it. It's hard to intimidate anyone with your lungs full of water.

The LST comes chugging around the island, backwaters about a 150 meters out, and drops its ramp. We start wading out to it. The reef is anywhere from boot deep to waist deep. All the Yards on the team are sticking close to me, until they realize that the Cookie is a much better height to climb if it gets too deep. He is slogging along, making little Ranger wakes behind him, followed by the Bru who will swarm up on him like fire ants. There are tidal pools out here, vindicating Castillo's sea rant. I walk past one and notice that there is a grouper down about 20 feet. I stand there in knee-deep water looking down. It is probably 35 feet to the bottom. I can see spiny little sea critters on the bottom, and a long, silver fish about six feet long with rows of teeth. It is slow going carrying all the equipment.

As I get nearer, I can see that the LST crowd have stopped on the other side of the island and retrieved our two deuce and a halfs. We help each other transition up out of the water from the lip, to the ramp of the LST, and soon all are onboard. It looks like one of those movies from the South Pacific campaigns. I would hate to do this under fire. The Marines who did the landings out there had to have some gigantic *cajones* back then. Gives you just a small measure of the guts it took to do that in The Big One.

We get loaded. The LST raises its ramp, backs out, and swings around, heading back for Nha Trang. The rest of the trip is like going out, although the swells are a little larger. One of the crew comes by and says, "Didja hear?" He is almost aglow with excitement.

"Hear what?"

"Some guys and a couple of nurses were out here and got attacked by hundreds of VC," he informs us breathlessly, as if sharing the war story made him part of the experience.

"No shit? Right here?" Castillo asks.

"Yeah. They barely made it out alive," the swab answers.

"You sure it was this island?" someone else queries, but he has no answer to that. What does come out in a few minutes is that our little attack was probably why we had to wade. Good move, Midget. The squid relates that they had been the first ship that the idiots had come across after escaping. They stopped the LST and babbled their tale of terror. They left as soon as the crew relayed the information to Swabbie HQ. Evidently, when our Sea Scouts were told that they were picking up troops who had been on that very same island, they elected to park just out of rifle range. As nervous as sailors are around small arms fire, I am surprised that they hadn't parked farther out. They probably didn't have a manual on the VC and figured that 150 meters is all a bullet goes. We're lucky we didn't have to swim back to Nha Trang. I hope those guys with the nurses were MPs.

The weather turns nasty about halfway back and by the time we get to Nha Trang all of the little people are seasick and a few of us as well. This tub we're on rolls like a round-bottomed garbage scow. The crew hates us, mostly because the little people have thrown up everywhere. There are some spectacular projectile vomiting cases. They throw up on the vehicles, in the vehicles, on the deck, even down something called a scupper, whatever that is. The only place they haven't thrown up is over the side. I'm starting to get a little green myself when we finally pull up to the dock. We get a hose from the boat and power wash off the worst of it. We have a moment to readjust to our land legs while organizing the offloading. Larry gets in a jeep and makes some sort of "forward, ho" signal and we motor off in the direction of the SFOB.

We get to the base and everyone goes back to his assigned billets. Only one small problem this time, they have billeted the Yards away from everyone else, in what had been the Vietnamese laundry workers' billets. Not that it's bad accommodations, but it is right next to the chicken and duck pen. We get them settled in, look at each other and smile. The fowl kingdom is about to have night visitors. Whoever the genius is that decided to billet the little people in the VN barracks rather than have those savages close to their lily-white American quarters is going to pay for that one dearly.

We saunter back to the barracks to find out that we aren't going to be able to get out until late tomorrow afternoon, maybe even the next day. We are, as you can imagine, just crushed by this news; but not as crushed as the staff. I bet they wish they had something they could divert to pick us up, something flying a mission that is not as critical as getting us out of their safe little world, such as, say, a B-52 assigned to striking SAM sites in and around Hanoi. But they are stuck with us. Chin up lads and make the best of it.

We strip off and get our weapons clean. The first phase is, of course, the showers. Once we have washed and rinsed our weapons and ourselves, it is towel and loincloth time and the second phase begins. Take all the equipment out of the pouches. Get a *Stars and Stripes* newspaper. Dump all the ammo out of your magazines and disassemble the guns. Get a t-shirt, if you don't have one at hand look for someone else's. Get out the handy can of WD-40 and spray everything down. The areas that may have carbon build-up, such as the gun chambers and bullet ramps, magazine wells, barrel gas ports, gas plugs, whatever, work over with a tooth brush. If you lost the one that you use on your weapon, then the choice is between a flashing smile and the carbon deposit. Go for the carbon. A lot of us carry a small tube of diesel fuel for this purpose. The Army strictly forbids the use of diesel fuel to clean weapons, but it is the best thing for cutting carbon deposits. Split the T-shirt into swatches; some are used for cleaning and some for oiling afterwards. Once all the metal is clean, spray it down again with WD-40, and wipe it down with the oil rags. Most people don't know this, but weapons sweat the oil into themselves. A green trooper will oil his weapon once and happily assume that it is a bright, oiled, killing instrument, and will stay that way. It will be covered with what we call GI gold, that's rust to the layman, before 24 hours are up.

As we are cleaning, some staff twinkie comes flying up with the distressing news that our savages are despoiling the swimming pool by doing their laundry in it. We go over to the window and, sure enough, there are the lads happily squatting next to the pool. Actually, they are scrubbing their laundry in the little wading pool. A couple of stalwart types from the HQ are physically trying to keep them from the main pool. They have a Vietnamese interpreter who is talking to the Yards, and they eye him like a pack of wharf rats looking over a nice ripe corpse. We go down and get the lads out of the line of fire before the situation gets too intense. We find a laundry spot for them. When we come back our piles of sodden uniforms have been whisked away, and we are told that our laundry will be returned by this evening. We still have clothes we'd left to be laundered before we went to the island. Sure enough, as only a well-oiled, military, rear unit can operate, there are the clean, starched, and pressed duds we'd left behind.

We go to the shower after retrieving our STABO rigs and harnesses that have been drying in the sun for the last two hours. We reload everything, and tape what needs taping, then stack our combat equipment at the head of our beds with the weapons. This is giving the REMFs the queezies; they normally have ammo, but it is locked down in the barracks, with the key in the possession of the one guy who won't be there when they need it. On top of that we have grenades and all that other horrid stuff. They are going to have a guard on the barracks anytime we are not there. Not a bad idea, since there is probably one or two VC working here at any given time. A couple of fresh-faced, Spec-4s show up to watch the door for us.

We go to the shower for the final scrub and a shave. I've said it before: there is nothing that feels as good as being clean. Sex is great but it doesn't come close to being clean after living in your own juices for a while. Ask any combat troop, shower or sex? Ten to one he heads for the shower. That is, unless of course he likes the gamey feeling, or he's French.

We decide that since there's a pool, we might as well take a dip. We grab beers and bottles and head out towards the pool, intent on doing a little skinny-dipping.

"Hold it right there fellows. The sign says you must have proper swimming attire on."

"No problem, we will just cut the legs off these jungle fatigues and go that way."

"No way, you have to have a store-bought suit on, no cutoffs."

"Well, we forgot to pack a store-bought swimsuit as part of our combat load." This little exchange is going on between us and an E-7, whose job it is to be the lifeguard at the pool. No shit, that's his only function, and he has three guys, all NCOs who are his first, second, and third assistant lifeguards, plus two Spec-4s as well. I'll let you guess who gets to clean the place up. We are tired of listening to him. He is trying to get a message to the Head Office that the barbarians are at the gates, when our patience wears out and we chuck two of them into the pool, followed by us in a mad rush. Charlie Jay strips down to his birthday suit and steps in. He has secured an inner tube and he plops down in it, shades on, cool beer in hand, snub-nosed revolver around his neck. He floats over to the far end where there are four or five Vietnamese girls sunning themselves on lawn chairs. These are obviously the girlfriends of the staff weenies.

We get a visit shortly after that from some major who barks at the side of the pool for a while, and then Hagen and one of the captains go over and have a little conversation with him. The boyfriends of the little bevy of voluptuous, bikini-wrapped womanhood come out and try to pry their girls away from the pool to no avail.

Charlie has floated a Baby Ruth out near his inner tube, and yells out, "Some dirty bastard has shit in the pool!" The few twinks who had stayed in the pool abandon the water at this point. Charlie reaches over, takes a bite out of it and announces, "It's okay. It's a Yard turd." This can't go on long before we are declared *personas non gratis*. I bet that when the next poor sod comes strolling in here expecting to kick back for a few days after having been at some camp up-country for the last six months, these same assholes do their best to make his life miserable. Our arrival in their safe little world is almost too much for them to take. There are just too many of us. If it were up to me I would dynamite the fucking pool so they would have to go to the beach. Then I'd slip down to the beach and chum the current to draw the sharks. In fact, a couple of months later I hear some guy from One-Zero school does just that, only he uses detonation cord and some data sheet. Same reason, no trunks.

We get about an hour before the brass and other heavies show up with Manes in tow, and he tells us we have to abandon our boyish antics. In addition, Manes informs us that we are leaving first thing in the morning and everyone will stay here tonight. The mission has been moved up. No sweat, I can get drunk here as well as downtown. Besides, that Cambode will probably finish me off if I go another session with her.

That evening we go to the NCO club and sit around slowly getting sozzled until about twenty-late-thirty, or some military time. I am up in the transient barracks with Mac, the Cookie, and the Cuban. We are drinking cognac and mixing it with warm root beer. I don't think it will catch on; it's pretty horrid. We are sitting there just dreamily discussing things like food, women, and friends, and are starting to get maudlin when some kind of siren starts up. We hear bustling and much shouting. Castro walks over to the door and peers outside.

A couple of our guys are standing on the stairhead looking back in the compound when a mortar round lands in the next compound. Not a barrage, one round. It lands on a cement pad and sends a shower of hot shrapnel around. The tires of a nearby truck go flat. Then nothing. It's not a ranging round like someone registering a mortar on target. More likely it is some bozo out there in the paddies to the west, trotting out and firing his shot for communism, then packing the tube back down a *benjo* hole, all done and proper. Then he heads home to the wife and kiddies for a little fish and *nuoc mam*, and maybe later a beer with the other heroes of the revolution.

But the scene at the SFOB is different. People are running everywhere. We are in various stages of undress. I have on a loincloth and my Luger. We killed the lights when the round went off so now we are standing in the dark on the upper stairwell waiting for another round. You don't just fire one round and then lay the barrage in. Where it hit is nowhere. They will have to adjust, and that means firing at least two more rounds. The hubbub below is increasing in its frenzy. People are spilling out of the barracks, running amok in their efforts to stumble to their assigned sectors. A mortar crew heads over and gets in their nice, pretty mortar pit. Ah, cries of despair, where is so and so with the key to the ammo? Just as predicted, he isn't to be found. Someone takes a crowbar and beats the lock off. The place is still lit up like normal. If I were Sir Chuck out there in the paddies I could adjust my fire so quickly it would be "snuff city" after the first barrage. When is someone going to kill the master generator and darken this place? The mortar crew gets the four deuce out and set up.

Mac and I had wandered by the mortar position when we first arrived. It was ludicrous. They had, in their zeal to make everything look so rigidly military, cemented the base plate into the ground. Oh it looked neat, but I wouldn't want to be there when they drop the first round down the tube. That cement is going to shatter and fragment. It'll look like someone dropped a hand grenade amongst the crew. Someone is yelling, "One-twenty-twos! One-twenty-twos!" I guess he means the infamous 122mm rocket, which can be fired in volleys. This boy has never been around a 122mm when it goes off. By comparison, it makes that mortar round sound like someone popped a paper bag. Then the hue and cry resounds throughout.

"Rockets! My God, they're firing rockets!" Finally, the lights go out, and though that is a tactical improvement, it is a bad move with this hysterical crowd. "Oh God, sappers have knocked out the generators!"

We continue to see dark figures run for the trench line, some dropping gear on the way. It suddenly occurs to us that this is not a good place to be with all these nervous ninnies running about. Then someone on the line starts up with a 40mm Bofors. Shooting at what, I don't know, but it's certainly impressive. We are half-laughing at these poor idiots, and yelling down to them, "It was ONE round, guys!" At that moment a figure bounds up the stairs.

"What do you think you are, bulletproof?" he screams. "Get out on the bunker line!" It's the Sergeant Major, fully equipped, complete with helmet and parachute chinstrap, flak vest, armed with a CAR-15. What the holy hell is this rear muffin doing with a CAR-15? It's brand new, too. We apologize for not being scared shitless of one mortar round, but he isn't hearing rational observations and starts screaming that they need every man at the bunker line. Well, why didn't you say so? Obviously, we didn't realize the severity of the single round opening gambit.

If they are going to be hysterical about this we might as well add to the insanity. We grab our gear and rush out to meet the yellow horde that we know isn't there. Do they want a firepower demonstration? Hell, we specialize in that. Some of us are wearing nothing but web gear, guns, and boots. We hit the trench line and pile in doing our best John Wayne shit. Charlie Jay lands on two Donut Dollies that have run there for protection. It appears that attack hysteria has driven everyone in the camp to safety either in one of the command bunkers or in the trenches. These two delicate flowers opt for being with the relative safety of the fighting force, versus being part of the jittery crowd that is probably crammed in the command bunker. On the way, we mutually decide that the best way to get this battle over with is to open up as if hordes of Chinese, left over from the Chosin Reservoir, are piling up in the paddies. Christ, on a clear day you can see for almost six miles out to the base of the mountains in that direction.

We are just in position when the 40mm opens up again. As if on cue, we all stand up and start hosing down the rice paddies. I look over and Charlie is firing away and yelling dialogue right out of the comic books.

"Take that you murderous scum! Here they come black as hell and thick as grass! ARG! ARG! ARG!" We bum up probably three magazines a piece this way. Then we stop, but the twinks are shooting their hearts out.

A grenade goes off down the line and one of our wits yells out, "They're in the wire." The Bofors keeps pinging away at the same area, out about 2000 meters. I wish I had one. I wonder if we can steal it. Nah, it's too heavy to get on the plane tomorrow. It takes about 30 minutes to get all the nervous trigger fingers quieted down after that. As we sit with our backs to the front wall, just bullshitting, some idiot from the HQ slams into the trench in a modified Batman flying leap.

"Why aren't you firing?" he screams and Castro tells him we have already killed our quota and we are on break. He skitters off down the trench. The SMAJ and some light colonel come striding down the line with a bullhorn ordering everyone to stop.

"Cease fire! Cease fire!" The firing slowly peters out in their wake. I have to get one of those bullhorns. Maybe I'll lift that instead of the Bofors. I wonder where they keep this one? Probably, under some major's bunk. Or maybe one of those Bad Toelz fairies has a job as the official bullhorn custodian. Maybe if we steal it they will get so pissed off that they will transfer him to an A Camp that's actually in the war.

Looks like the war is over and soon the call is shouted out to check for casualties. This is all becoming boring, so we start to drift back over in ones and twos to the barracks. The rest of the poor snots are out there for another two hours before someone gives the all clear. The generators start up, and we stand on the stairhead again, drinking beer and watching the wind down. Out in the paddies, at the edge of where the lights from the perimeter end, is a wounded buffalo. We can see it clearly. It has wandered in after the mad minute of about thirty minutes ago. Obviously, the ninnies from Weenie HQ cannot make up their mind if it is a buffalo, or some cunning group of NVA that have rigged up a buffalo skin and are creeping up under it. They actually mount a combat patrol. About 20 guys leap and bound out there in the human excrement that is so vital to good rice production, and when they are about 50 meters from the bull, they open up on it. Eventually, in about an hour, they come back.

Yes sir, we have one dead VC transportation asset to report. I'd love to see the AAR (after action report) on this one, but I have participated in enough of this silly horseshit and I am going to sleep. I drift off, dreaming of the nurse with the magnificent rack. I want to marry her and have her children. She could probably whip all the plastic heroes in this Hollywood puzzle palace and still be able to soothe my fevered brow. It is a very nice dream.

CHAPTER 22

King of the Cannibals

We still don't know our exact mission, just that it is a prisoner snatch of some kind. We don't know what kind of prisoners. Are we taking prisoners or rescuing our own? After a while you get used to the secrecy, no sense stuffing our heads with the big picture.

I like sleeping on C-130s. They have a drone and rhythm to them that lends itself to rapid eye movement. The only thing to worry about is the temperature control. If you get an experienced loadmaster who has a few hours under his belt, he knows the proper temperature to keep everyone comfortable. If you get some green, right-out-of-Omaha type, you either burn up or freeze. In this case we have the latter. I sleep fitfully for about 45 minutes, when I begin to rouse with cold, aching discomfort. I sit up, stiff, cold, and cramped. Most everyone is conked out or in the stages of coming back to fully awake.

The inside of the aircraft is as familiar as my own home. These big lumbering birds are the backbone of the Air Force. I have ridden in them so many times that I can tell them apart by model and year of manufacture. I struggle up and stretch, trying to shake off that sweat-sock-in-the- mouth, grumpy feeling of napping. I start towards the back of the aircraft stepping gingerly over legs like a slow motion high jumper. Back here is where we stacked the rucksacks. They are covered with a cargo net and lashed down. Normally there would be two or three guys stretched out asleep on the top of this load, but not today.

My plan is to retrieve a poncho liner and go back to sleep. I should be able to reach my rucksack without having to unsnap the whole net. The poncho liner is in the top waterproof pocket. I see the loadmaster eyeballing the rucksacks with some apprehension. He is talking into the boom mike on his headset. The reason that he is puzzled or paranoid, whichever, is not because there are live grenades and such, visible in the outer pockets. No, the reason that he is apprehensive is because the rucksacks are occasionally moving on their own. In fact they are moving as if they were alive. This is also the reason that nobody is sleeping on top of the stack. Before we left Nha Trang the Yards had stuffed every fowl and piglet that came within their grasp into their rucks.

Whoever came up with the bright idea of billeting them in Nha Trang next to the livestock pens is doing a major explanation dance this morning. This would have commenced upon discovery of the pens now being empty of all but the slickest chicken and sneakiest duck. A Yard is so slick he can steal the duck and leave the quack. As the people in charge stand there in shock, listening to mother pigs wailing in grief over their stolen offspring, their paperwork reassigning them guard duty on the Ho Chi Minh trail is on the way.

I get up to where the loadmaster is and start pulling at the pile to get at my rucksack. It's a bit of a struggle since the load has settled and the net has been pulled tight. I am bending down working the net aside so I can get to the top pocket of the ruck when he leans down and puts one hand on a rucksack near the top. "There appears to be something in these things," more as an interrogative than a statement.

"Yeah, these are hill tribesmen, the staples of their diet are snakes, like pythons, and lizards. But their favorite cuisine is a smaller version of a Komodo dragon, vicious things with mouths big enough to take a bite the size of a softball out of you." He looks at me with that look people give you when they don't want to hear what you just said.

"Say again?"

"I said, they eat lizards and snakes, and it's part of our commitment to them to supply them. They have to have fresh game. They get sick if they eat processed food. About the only thing their metabolisms can handle is rice and very little of that, so we supply them with fresh game." I retrieve my poncho liner and start to shake it out so I can wrap myself in it. There are a couple of Sedang from one of the teams sitting at the base of the pile. They have primitive tattoos on their faces, which is weird enough, but as youths they file their teeth into points. One of them looks up at me and smiles. The loadmaster gets a look at those choppers, and now he is positive that he heard me right. His hand comes off the rucksacks like someone put a flame to it.

"These things are full of snakes and lizards?" his voice rising a bit at the end.

"Yeah, but you don't have to worry," I reassure him. "They shoot them up with curare or some kind of poison that knocks them out for about three hours. It doesn't taint the meat, just keeps them quiet. By the way, how long before we get to Da Nang?" I look at my watch as if measuring the time for the dosage to begin wearing off. It is wasted theatrics because he is talking into his little boom mike with little furtive glances at the pile. I wrap the poncho liner around me and lean back against the pile. See here, space cadet? I am not scared of any snakes and lizards.

He comes back over a little closer and tells me, "The pilot says we are about an hour and ten out. Will those things stay drugged that long?" I take his arm and look around until I spot Manes's square form wedged against the forward section of seats.

"You see that guy there that looks like a refrigerator with a head on it, the blonde one?" He nods and I continue. "He's been living with these people for five years.

They actually regard him as their war chief. He has gotten them to work for us and not eat their enemies anymore. He speaks the language fluently." I pause and the zoomy is nodding, and listening, nervously.

"Well, he knows all the stuff about the dosages. In fact, he was the one that put the really big lizard to sleep. He has some more of the stuff on him. I never mess with it because if you do it wrong it can paralyze your face for days. You got to chew this root then force them to eat the chaw. It is all really complicated. Anyway if you think that these here rucksacks get a little too active just go wake him up and he can come back here with those two medicine men there." I point at the two Sedang, who grin at me with a mouthful of filed teeth, adding to the effect. "Be careful though, he's been with them a long time, he's a little jumpy."

He goes over the whole scenario. "Which guy? That one? He's got the drug?" He asks to make sure I am pointing out the right one. I look at Larry peacefully snoozing away and make sure Zoomy understands that, oh yes, he is the one. He says something into the mike and heads for the front of the airplane, I guess to tell them that they are carrying cannibals, snakes and Komodo dragons, along with their deranged, blond-haired king. As soon as he gets about halfway there, I find a spot over on Captain Chunk's side of the aircraft, snuggle in and lose myself amongst the bodies.

I wait about 20 minutes. During that time zoomy number one comes back with one of the flight deck crew. He points at the stack, looks around for "Mr. Information," but I am well-hidden. There are several poncho liner-covered forms around the cabin. Not spotting me they look down at the Sedang, and get a fang smile for their troubles. I sink a little lower down so just my eyes are peeping over the next man's shoulders. They scratch their heads, then their asses, shuffle back and forth, talk a little, and then talk on the boom mike to the front. The loadmaster a couple of times points out Larry's sleeping carcass at the front on my side. They talk a little longer on the mike again. Then here they come, stepping carefully between the sleeping forms. I cover my head; they are past me. I look over and they are standing a safe distance from Larry's sleeping form, while the lieutenant firmly grips Larry's toe and shakes it gently. Larry moves in his sleep. The lieutenant waits, and then shakes it a little more vigorously. Manes comes awake with his usual, roused-the-sleeping-dragon, finesse. He sits up, wiping a slab-like hand across his face. They bend over, talking quietly to him. I can see the emotions flit across his face, his countenance going from confused to irritation. They are in a tight knot. I don't have long to wait.

"What fucking lizards? Cannibals? What did he look like?" I trade my poncho liner for the poncho covering the Yard next to me, tucking it in around him. Sure enough, here they come, shaking awake everyone covered in a poncho liner. Manes is shoving bodies aside, and people are sitting up. They shake the Yard awake next to me. Larry is standing on my calf but I don't move. The crew chief shakes his head, no, and they move on.

They get all the way to the rear of the aircraft and Manes stands there with his hands on his hips looking like a miniature behemoth. He reaches through the net, snags a rucksack and snakes a bound up duck out of it, amid a flurry of feathers and a stream of duck shit. He holds it up at shoulder height. The duck can't move. It is trussed, bill to webbed feet. He is holding it by its feet; the duck knows this is the end, and lets out another squirt of fear-induced bowel ammo, splattering the three of them. Everyone is awake now, and you can plainly hear Larry.

"Does this look like a fucking dragon?" followed by another stream of invectives. Larry looks at the Sedang. They both smile at him. He drops the duck down on the rucksacks and starts bulling his way to the front of the aircraft. God, I would love to hear that conversation. I can see the crew chief talking on the boom mike. I bet that he is warning the flight deck that the "King of the Cannibals" is heading their way.

Better exercise discretion. With the Midget on a rampage, too much visibility at this point could be fatal. Everyone is sitting up and looking around. A couple of the Yards, who own the released quacker, go back with the Sedang and capture it. It would seem that Larry's rough handling has loosened its bindings. That takes about ten minutes with everyone trying to grab the duck. This results in more duck shit all over the place. That duck shouldn't have anything in its bowels but acid by now. They get it under control but the place smells to high heaven. No one will sleep through that. Mac and the Cookie grab me and look me over.

"You're involved in this, aren't you?" Ah, the accusatory case, I know that case from grammar lessons.

After 20 minutes, Larry comes back from the front shaking his head and mumbling something under his breath. The loadmaster is very busy doing anything that will prevent the bull from coming back into his comer. Larry shoves someone aside and sits down with Castillo and starts talking at him. Good, go after the Cuban. If there is anyone likely to be involved in this sort of sordid joke, it is the Cuban. Good track *Dai Uy*, you might make major after all. When is this plane going to land? The first thing this planeload of snitches will do is sacrifice my little white ass to Manes, god of the volcano. My only hope is that we spiral into the sea and I swim free of the wreckage.

Fifteen minutes later we land and taxi up with all the doors open. The plane smells like a pig sty, and as I suspected, I am hauled out of the crowd for summary identification. The loadmaster readily identifies me with "Yeah that's him. I'm sure of it."

We spend the trip back to the main camp with me as the wicker man, and everyone gets to worry me over the details. They think it is hilarious. All I wanted to do was get even for the heat being too low. Ah well, like my granddaddy used to tell me if you're going to practice humor you have to pay the piper, or something like that. Mac and the Cookie are having a grand old time ribbing me. That is, until I point out I can probably get out of this by volunteering us all for a DMZ target. That ensues an argument about whether the One-One can volunteer the whole team or just himself. I don't care, we are going there eventually. The whole troop is having a good time watching the three of us sort it out.

We get back, expecting to go into isolation to prepare for the grand mission. Larry and a couple of the officers have gone ahead of us from the airport. When we pull up we are told to send the Yards back to the Company and to wait for Larry. He comes out and tells us the mission has been canceled and that we should plan on getting regular targets in the next few days. It is a let down. Personally, I am ready for something new. I have had all I care to experience in the way of being a pop-up, shoot-back, target. Manes tells us that he is just as disappointed as we are that it didn't go through. He is absolutely sure we could have pulled it off. Then he dismisses us, but not before he pointedly tells me that he is going to make an extra effort to see if they can find a target with cannibals in it, just for me. He, as supreme commander of the nut ward, will make that effort, just for me, even if they have to search the entire greater Asian war zone. They still have cannibals in Malaysia. He has connections with the Brits, or whoever is running the place this month, and will make sure I get a chance to run through the jungle. Not the whole team for this little get-even trip, just me.

We break down and wander down to the Company. I am currently in the barrel, but it doesn't bother me. I know in my heart of hearts it was funny, and before 24 hours are up someone will be in so much hot water that I will be completely out of the line of fire.

We go over and tell the Yards no big raid. We go back to missions. They take it with their usual aplomb; they are already plucking the purloined fowl for dinner. The story has filtered down to the Montagnard level because before we leave, Cuman drags me aside.

"*Trung Si* Nick, Bru no hab king." End of story for them, despite the fact that if they were cannibals, his bulk represents a year's supply of protein. In some odd way, they think it is funny that Mac and the rest of us are always getting caught doing something and irritating him. They are that way. They have the practical joke down to a fine art, so they like to see it in other people.

We get all the equipment stowed and head over to the club. It's easy to find today; the whole area reeks of CS gas. We have periodic outbreaks of gas in the compound. You never gas another guy's hut, that's a bad thing. But every once in a while, someone gets a wild hair up his ass and tosses a mini CS grenade in the club. Then for three or four days we have to leave the doors open and air the place out. It's annoying and sooner or later the fun wears off. The next one that tries it usually gets the snot pounded out of him. We walk in with the intent of grabbing a hamburger, but can't stand to be inside for more than a few moments. We hack our way outside and opt for going to the mess hall. Nobody ever gasses that place. The food is good. In fact, we have probably one of the best mess facilities around.

Better than the General's mess in I Corps. The mess sergeant is a bit of a twink, but he is a genius when it comes to food. You want steak, you get steak, as well as lobster, fresh seafood, you name it. In fact, I remember we had lamb chops, complete with a light rice pilaf and mint jelly, just before we left. The aroma tells my stomach to get it on.

We are in luck; they are having some sort of seafood buffet. They make good bisque. I forget where they got the mess steward; I think the colonel stole him from Saigon.

We fill our plates and look for an open spot. There are quite a few teams represented here, which is unusual. I see Bernie and Doug Laurent in a corner as we walk over, and yes, Doug has a bandage on him. This time it's on his head. He is like Davidson except every time he goes out he gets wounded or injured in some way. He is all of 20 and looks like the guy on the Zig Zag package, the spitting image of a real French Canadian. He is the perfect straight man for Bernie, who is old enough to be his father.

"Anybody else get hurt in the accident?" Mac asks.

Doug immediately comes back with, "Who says it was an accident?" We wait in silence. Doug starts again. "No, it was 20mm shells that did this." I know French Canucks have hard heads, but he must mean the casings. We love to pick on Doug. He's like everybody's kid brother. There are four or five of us from Minnesota; Doug is by far the cutest of the litter. He hangs around with Keith Larson. Larson is a sick, sick, puppy. Nice guy, good on the ground, but I think he may have been smoking those pinecones. And they are chums with Steve Dokken. Dokken is the mental picture that is conjured up for what a juvenile delinquent should look and act like. He has a constant little smart-ass smirk, like he just got done screwing some cheerleader in home economics class. He's another good one. There is something about Minnesota that breeds this intrepid little throwback crowd. Hell, I am from Minnesota. I must be an anomaly though; I am normal.

Bernie is ribbing Doug about the location of his wound. "Doug, how come it is that you always get hit in the back? Back of the head, back of the shoulder, in the butt, back of your legs with shrapnel, huh?" he categorizes Doug's last four injuries. "Doug, the enemy is that way." He says pointing to the front. Doug immediately goes into this litany of how it isn't his fault. We know Doug isn't running away, but he falls for Bernie's ribbing.

When he sees that we are all laughing, he says, "Aw, you guys," and gets up and leaves the table. Like I said, he is like your little brother. That is, if your little brother is built like a tank and has to shave three times a day. Of course, Bernie gives him hell about that, too. He tells him that clinical tests have proven if you masturbate too much your hair grows faster.

We get the full skinny out of Bernie. They had been using Spectre, trying to extricate them from some hilltop. The One-Zero of the team is a guy named Sparling. Sparling has maybe three tours in projects. Cool, collected, he is a quiet customer.

Anyway Sparling, had been calling in Spectre and they had been working it in real close. So close in fact that they had been driving it right in on the team, another prime example of shoot or die. One of their last passes broke the pressure on the team, but the gun casings being ejected out of the aircraft had fallen on them as well. One of the Yards was burned badly on his neck, and of course, one hit Doug square in the back of his head. That shell casing, falling from that height and speed, should have cracked his skull open like a ripe tomato. He was lucky he survived. Of course, everyone was giving Doug a hard time about having a moose skull.

Bernie is also messed up and will not be going out in the bush anymore. They were going to put him in the club, but Jimmy Reeves is running it. He got shot and got his leg messed up, so now he is the club manager.

That explains why the club smells like CS. Reeves likes gas and uses it for punctuation. I guess he wanted to close up at 0200, or so, and had gone to the back to rack out. At 0500, they were still making loud noises, so he put on his mask and threw a full size CS grenade in amongst the crowd, and then went back to sleep. That took care of the noise.

They're lucky. Jimmy has been known to pop a cap on people that cross his tolerance line. He normally doesn't kill them, but there have been some fools that have gone off leaking. So far, it hasn't been anyone in the unit. Yet. Great, we have a crazed coonass running the club. Better take a gun along. Bring your mask for the drink run.

We ask Bernie if he knows what they are going to do with him. He says he doesn't know, but Manes suggested that he become the safe house manager downtown. Good idea, none of us want Bernie to go to the Security Company, or worse yet, get sent back to the States. He is 41, for Christ's sake. He has broken every regulation there is to get over here and into this war; besides, I have almost forgiven him for his buddy, Kevin. After all, I don't want to be anywhere else now. If they send him back to the States they will take him out of SF and probably board him out of the army. Screw them; we will hide him out over here. Wait for the war to end in ten or twenty years. By that time we might own half of Da Nang, and we will all retire here and raise kids and hell.

We are about to get up when Dokken comes sauntering in. He tells Mac and me that Butler is looking for us. Captain Psycho, I wonder what he wants. Les has gone off to fly Covey and there is talk of sending Butler over to Thailand in a couple of months to take over NKP. Meanwhile, he is running loose. He has become sort of a one-man think tank for special projects. Between him and Sergeant Major Billy dreaming up crazy shit, we are liable to end up jumping into Hanoi with a nuke device strapped to our asses. There is no place to run; the pricks know all our hiding places. The only chance we have is to make it downtown. There we have some running room. Then Dokken drops the hammer. The Sergeant Major is with him. Ah shit, double trouble.

I am sure that we will know how suicidal whatever it is they have dreamed up, if they insist on buying the drinks. It is too late to borrow a whole bunch of money from them. We should have done that before we went to Hon Tre. We are dead meat. The Cookie is still not dialed in. He wants to do it the Ranger way.

"Well, let's just go see them," he starts out. He hasn't learned the subtle danger signals of a mission impossible yet. If Waugh wants to go along, or Butler, I am personally going to shoot myself or pay the Yards to wound me real messy like, so it takes ten years of therapy just to be able to hold my own John Henry. There isn't a chance I would let myself be in the bush with those two wackos. Being in the same war zone is hazardous enough. I must find Manes. Maybe if I piss him off enough he will send us into the DMZ targets, armed with only BB guns. At least we will have a chance.

CHAPTER 23

Rubik's Cube

The problem with being on top of your profession is that, eventually, someone is going to give you a task that is teetering on the edge of disaster. Of course, we have no concerns about this since we consider our current task in CCN as near suicidal.

Judging by that criteria, the idea of raids into the enemy's hinterland sounds relatively safe. The idea itself has Cookie almost inebriated in some sort of Ranger bliss. Mac and I are looking for a Boson's mortar so Cookie can lug it along. Somewhere out there is a super cliff that he can run up to and fire the little sucker off to send a grappling hook and line aloft to lodge itself against some bunker-lined bluff. Cook can then scramble up, throw a few grenades, shout a few Ranger slogans, spread a bit of murder and mayhem about, and then come back down. Short of that, there is little chance we can dampen his enthusiasm unless we plan on wounding him and shipping him off to some leg unit as the mail clerk.

We are preparing ourselves for the inevitable, since all this training will not be allowed to go to waste. The question for us is: who will initiate the plan? Will it be Saigon and the war whores in the planning center? Or, will it be our own esteemed, band of insidious miscreants. Personally, we are hoping that Saigon is the initiator, since we can probably adapt a plan that includes our survival. If the unholy troika of Manes, Billy, and whoever is the designated cerebral floater for the week, gets involved, we are most certainly going to be homogenized, parkerized, and sodomized by events out of our control.

Mac and I run interference, keeping the Cookie from making us too visible to the Sergeant Major. We have been sending him to the S-4 with a host of menial tasks, lest he get drawn into a conversation with the powers that be and impart his overwhelming desire for some killer raid operation. I am for sedating him, but Mac reminds me that would result in our having to find a tranquilizer that will work. Somewhere in the S-4 is the answer to our dilemma. Way in the back is probably some dusty crate full of Mark 20 blowguns with curare tipped darts. Why not? They seem to have everything else.

Mac looks out the door of our hut, a Quonset that is divided in half to house two teams, just in time to see Billy wandering around the company area. We have prepared for this sort of situation by installing a crawl hole above my bunk that leads to the top bunk of the team next door. It is covered by a German naval ensign that I liberated somewhere.

Mac hisses a warning that Billy is not only loose, but is coming our way. He and I slither up into the next room, waking Fred Adams in the process. We are all three huddled on his bunk and staring through the slight crack between the wall and the flag. Billy comes into the hooch after calling out from the sidewalk. The door is open because we had been cleaning our guns with diesel and needed ventilation. His hailing before entering might be good etiquette, but here it's a survivalist tradition since most of us are nervous sleepers and it's not a good idea to jolt us awake. He "transitions" into the room. I put it that way because the Sergeant Major has a way of just materializing next to you. It's spooky.

He stands in the door for a moment looking over the abandoned evidence of our recent departure. There is a cigarette in the ashtray with a little ash on it. Billy looks at it for a moment then reaches over and examines it. He sniffs the end of it while his eyes dart around the room as if he suspects that we have discovered the ultimate recon tool: invisibility. But the Sergeant Major is the eternal pragmatist if nothing else; he keeps looking for physical clues as to why his trap is empty. I am sure he has been stalking us all morning. Everywhere we have been I have been catching glimpses of him out of the corner of my eye. For sure he is stalking us, and only our finely tuned ability at squeezing out every day of stand down we can has saved us so far. That is why we were discussing what to do with the Cookie. With him *trying* to run into Count Dracula here, it's like going to the ball with a sign that says, "I like queers."

Billy gives the hut a complete scan. He's been on the ground. His bush wire tells him something is not right, so he's tracking us like we were Nguyen. We try not to peek at him directly, just like in the bush. With Dracula's sense of "bush ESP," we need to stay on our toes. Billy shifts his eyes over to the fridge. We hear somebody call out from the sidewalk and the Sergeant Major turns towards the door. A figure steps into the doorway. It's the Weasel, Wesley, who stands there diddy-bopping from one foot to the other. The Sergeant Major looks at him and strikes the Heinz Guderian pose that gives me the spooks.

"You know where these pencil-dicks are making themselves scarce?" he growls at Wesley.

"I ain't seen 'em, Sergeant Major," Wes snickers. "They probably are hiding from you."

"When you see either of these two lads," Billy pauses and looks around the room as if not quite sure that we aren't really there somehow, "tell them that I am looking for them." He shifts past Wesley and disappears out the door. Wesley looks at his back for a moment then turns and looks around the room before he, too, leaves. We heave a collective sigh of relief.

"Git!" Fred shoves me with his foot. "You guys are dead meat, hexed, bad ju-ju, unclean. That pretty much describes the two of you. Git and keep on going. We just got back yesterday. Being around the two of you is like being covered with honey in grizzly land." He rolls over and pulls his poncho liner around him as Mac and I crawl back into our hut. "And plug up that hole!"

Friggin' ingrate. If we get sucked into some death defying horrible Billy trap, I'm going to insist that he and Reeves, his illustrious Cajun cohort, are the only two guys that we feel comfortable working with. And we'll include Wesley in that invitation, to pay him back for running around acting as the Sergeant Major's radar. We are cooked. The more the merrier. Ho-ho-ho.

Mac scans the area around the hut to make sure Billy isn't hanging upside down in the eaves with the rest of the bats, before pulling the door closed. He walks over to the fridge and fishes out two beers. We pop the tops and sit down to finish cleaning our weapons. We have cleaned virtually everything in our team box in addition to our own personal weapons. The table and the floor, as well as the bunks, have weapons and other paraphernalia stacked all over them. The sawed-off M-60s, the equally shortened RPD, as well as all its drums and belts, glisten deadly from the top of Cook's bunk. All the silenced weapons and our own belly ordnance are on top of the table. I have my sawed-off, double-barreled shotgun and am giving it a final loving finish, as Mac reassembles both of the big Magnum revolvers that we keep for traveling companions when we are back in camp. Cook's stuff has been clean for two days now, since he stripped everything down the night we got back. He stayed up all bloody night with his little Ranger illuminator, cleaning his guns until the place smelled of WD-40.

The door swings open and Cookie comes in dragging a box full of goodies for the kids and a few items that we needed personally from S-4. With the Yards, every scrap of clothing, extra blankets and other geegaws we give them is like the gift bag at Christmas. Cookie has gotten his hands on poncho liners and indig sleeping bags, as well as some jungle sweaters. He piles his loot on the floor and looks at the two of us. His face is aglow and it isn't from the exertion. Usually he would be bitching about something, but from under the single eyebrow that extends from side to side, he fixes us with a glare.

"Did you know the Sergeant Major is looking for us, Stretch?" he directs the question at me. I look up at him and then over at Mac. Mac looks at the Cookie and smiles blandly.

"We know. Who did you hear it from?" We both know who that would be, but no fun in not asking.

"Wesley. He caught me over by the truck when I came back. He said the Sergeant Major was looking for you two, specifically. Are we going into isolation?" he sits down on my bunk since his is covered with the tools.

"Nope, not yet, at least. We haven't talked to Billy yet. Don't be so anxious, Cookie. We will get our chance at the title soon enough. The Sergeant Major might find a different set of victims if we can avoid him for another twenty-four hours." Mac says and we start to put the gear away. Cookie looks at us as if we were a couple of draft dodgers.

"We can't hide from him forever," Cook says as if it were a capital crime and stares at us glumly. I almost feel sorry for him. Almost. He is right, of course. We are going to have to gird our loins and surface sometime. But avoidance is an art form, and it's good training for staying out of harm's way in the bush. We will let it run its own course. There is a knock on the door and a voice mumbles something from the other side. Mac and I are positive it isn't Billy; he would just emerge from a green gaseous cloud in the middle of the room. Cookie, on the other hand, is so sure that the moment, *his* moment, in history has arrived that he shoots past us so fast he creates a breeze and pulls the door open, His hope that a messenger from War Central has arrived with the news that we have been selected for "Bloody Dawn," or some other operation, is dashed.

Something even more disastrous than that shuffles into the hut. It's Les Chapman. Since they have broken up him and Butler, they have become the separate poles on the magnet of sanity. Butler has been running around like some sort of roving ambassador of mayhem, and Chapman got sent up to Phu Bai to be a Covey rider. Everyone knows most Covey riders are held together with rubber laces.

The man now standing in front of us, Chapman, is no exception. He has taken to emulating Dave Chaney and Dallas Longsteath, both primary riders. Dallas is some sort of fashion slave. He wears these weird flight suits with garish patches, the ones all the flying crowd get a woody over, with dragons eating MIGs or some killer insects with machine guns. Chapman is walking the same runway; he is dressed in some sort of coal black flight suit with maps and papers coming out of some side pocket, and he is wearing his survival vest over one shoulder. Les has some serious self-destruct issues, coupled with combat narcissism. Any one of a host of other cranial twists he possesses should have kept him not only out of some small aerial cockpit, but completely away from anything that goes boom.

Chapman saunters in the room and, almost on his heels, Dave Chaney steps into the room behind him. He looks at Mac and shrugs. Chapman snickers at us.

"We're going to be down here for the night before we head north. Rumor has it that you and *wienerschnitzel* there," he motions at me, "are going to be sacrificed on the big altar. We might as well go downtown; because wherever they send you, we'll be flying Covey for you. I guess that means you buy."

Mac looks at him and makes a face, then studiously ignores him as he exchanges greetings with Dave. I mumble a weak hello to Dave, and try not to make eye contact with Chapman in the hope that he will disappear. This is bad. With these two adrenalin ghouls and the Cookie trying to get our heads in the noose, we are more than cooked, we are doomed. As we finish organizing the hut the two of them rifle through the fridge. Cook keeps suggesting that we find the SMAJ. We tell him that if he doesn't shut up we are going to tie garlic around his neck so the SMAJ can't find him. We get a Ranger scowl for that one. Sure as shit Billy will find us before the night is out. Going downtown actually is a good plan. After shooing junior birdman and Chaney out, we head for the showers. It is late in the afternoon by now and others are headed for the same. We pass Case and McDowell and they make the sign of the cross and hiss at us. Everyone knows.

Well, we will just gut it through. Let them work at finding us. In the meantime, we might as well have as much fun as we can. It will take at least three days from entering isolation to whenever they can possibly shove us up the dragon's ass, so there is plenty of time to sober up. Dulling the fear with alcohol doesn't work. It just pushes the thought of what might happen to the back of your peanut. Be audacious; act like you don't give a damn; stay the course. I keep running these brave thoughts through my head, but the dialogue sucks. Sniveling and whining won't work either, since we are expected to hold up our end. Besides, we don't even know what it is that Billy Incorporated has dreamt up. How bad could it be?

I look up from under the hot stream of water and realize I have been thinking out loud. Mac is standing at the next nozzle shaking his head at my musings. Cookie, however, sees a ray of hope and says that nothing is ever as bad as it seems. Humph! He doesn't know. Whatever it is, we will just go do it. The shower helps; I am already thinking about rewards for survival and success, versus the thought of dying.

Maybe the mission will be a wire tap. OOOOOHH wouldn't that be nice: sneak and peek, sit off a trail somewhere for three days changing the tapes every 24 hours. Nah, too simple and, besides, you can't sneak and peek anywhere west of Hawaii by now. Maybe they want us to do something like a prisoner snatch. Now that makes sense. Land somewhere in the DMZ and grab a hilltop. Pretty soon plenty of prisoner candidates will show up. All we have to do is time it close enough that we grab one rushing the chopper as we try and extricate our shot-up asses. I might even suggest it, by God. If they think we can grab one they might just give us a couple of extra sets of gunships. As far as volunteering for the DMZ, it doesn't much matter. Wherever they are going to send us will be at least that hot.

Clean and full of fresh ideas about how to spend the evening, we walk up the middle of the company as if daring the powers to be to grab us, like a Shanghai crew of victims from the Barbary Coast. Once we are back at the hut we dress in our go-to-meeting clothes, and slide over to the mess hall. We stand in the door for a moment surveying the crowd. Butler and his former One-One, Chapman, are sitting with Dave Chaney, watching Manes shovel fried chicken and mashed potatoes as well as cold slaw into his maw, like some excavator at a Minnesota pit mine. Chapman spies us and waves us over, but we ignore that. It is best to get in with the rest of the unwashed, and not get directly in Manes's sights. Butler just smiles at us benignly, like some mutant bam owl and Homo sapiens hybrid. That is definitely a table to avoid. He and Chapman were bad enough when they were running recon together. Here in the company of Manes, the two of them would gut you, just for entertainment purposes.

We go through the line and, taking our trays, head for a table with Laurent and Larson sitting at it. They take one look at us as we are sitting down, and move to another table. Laurent looks apologetic. Larson looks at us as if we were the doorway to an open abyss. They scuttle off and we start eating. Cookie keeps glaring at the rest of the crowd as if they had betrayed some sacred trust. He will learn. When Billy and the Manes brain trust have something in mind for you, your friends are already dividing up your stuff.

I keep scanning the crowd looking for Billy, but he is conspicuously absent. Not that it will matter, because Captain Manes will tire of reenacting the shovel brigade as soon as his tummy hits the full meter. At that point, he will lean back to start the digestive process and survey the crowd for victims. Chapman and Butler will point us out, directly. Chaney won't; he is probably communing with the Great Spirit or something. RT Habu isn't even on his radar screen until we get the actual word, then we will be fair game. The rest of our peer group avoids us like lepers. I go to get a cup of coffee and run into Castillo. He just looks at me sadly and holds his hand out as if to ward me away.

"Don't even try," he says. "We are already in this. We are supposed to be Bright Light for another team. And I am willing to pay good money and give away all my toys to make sure it isn't you guys. We have our pride, you know." He pauses and dips his finger in his gravy, then licks it before continuing. "More importantly, we still have our skins and intend to keep 'em. Rumor has it that being around you and Gator Breath, is a surefire way to lose that. So no, *nein, nichts*, is the answer to whatever you are going to suggest. Take it like a man and stay away from me." He starts to slither away, but I grab his arm.

"Not so fast you refugee from Castro's paradise." He reacts like I was a plague victim. "Just to show you how badly you miscalculated, for your information we already got our mission. Yep, and you could have been part of it. RT Habu is going to Okinawa for some sort of classified mission. We are supposed to be there for six months. I just came over to say goodbye and to tell you that I would try to get you on it. It's probably just as well that you have this attitude, since they specifically wanted people that spoke German and had the ability to blend in as a foreigner other than American. I was willing to lie for you, but it probably would have been discovered sooner or later. So all the best, okay?" I hold out my hand. The Cuban is made up of pure survival organisms, though. He stares at me for a moment and snickers like a three year old in day care.

"Mac doesn't speak German." He thinks he has me, but I just smile at him.

"He doesn't have to. Both he and Lamar speak Creole. Rumor has it, that we all will have to learn Navajo. Might take us six months before we are ready to be deployed." I walk away from him. He stands there for a minute after scanning the crowd for Lamar, and then shakes his head. He catches me looking at him and flips me the digit and cackles off into the crowd.

I come back to the table and haven't even settled into my seat when Billy materializes next to Mac's chair. There is no chance to slip away. I try to get my signal mirror out to see if it will actually catch his reflection or not, but he is too fast. He looks at all of us, placing one hand on Cookie's shoulder and the other on the back of Mac's chair, and leans over our table.

"You men are going into isolation tomorrow. Captain Manes will brief you on the details." He looks at us for a moment then pats Cook on the shoulder. "Good men," he mumbles and then slides off towards the door. Cook looks like the Big Ranger slipped him a blessing. I look at Mac for a moment. He sighs and casts a look at the Cookie as if he were a child that just couldn't understand that the stove was hot to the touch. He chuckles after scanning our contemporaries, who studiously avoid us.

"You know, don't you, that we can drink for free tonight," he smiles at the crowd.

"Yep," I agree, "and the rest of this family of girls know that we are going to need backup. They will pay almost anything not to be on the list." I take a sip from the coffee that has grown cold. "Let's go make our friends nervous, shall we?" Mac laughs and we get up and head for the club. Mac sends the Cookie off to get our jeep. We have taken to hiding it near the Yard latrine, since it is relatively new and still has the canvas intact. The interval will give us a chance to figure out how to dampen his enthusiasm some so we can let it all hang out tonight.

We walk into the club, get a drink and settle ourselves into chairs. Now that we have been sentenced, so to speak, we are at least touchable. The rest of our peers are traipsing through and giving us either the finger, or the high five, depending on what they consider is the likelihood of their being picked as our back up. Castillo walks in and saunters up to the table, looks us over and snorts before heading for the bar. Mac looks at me and smirks.

"I betcha that we can probably get laid downtown and someone will pay for it." He surveys the room, his gaze landing on Pulley, who snorts and gives us both the finger and turns his back on us. No hope there. Tarheel is so tight he would rather die than part with a nickel. Besides, taking Pulley along is like dragging along bad luck in a big keg full of black cats. Pulley has a way of attracting trouble; best to leave him alone. He knows it, too. He smirks at us like some weird Tobacco Road denizen.

In the middle of this sits Cookie, almost aglow with the mere thought of the whole affair. I want to shoot him, but we might need him to fight our way out. Chapman saunters in from outside and heads our way. He pulls up a chair and slides his flight-suited persona into our midst. He looks at Mac.

"We are flying whatever package you guys have," he says. "If I were you I would be ecstatic since we can almost guarantee that you will come back, for a fee, of course." He chortles at his last bit of birdman witticism. Cook looks at him distastefully as if the thought of bribing Covey for extra assets somehow violated the UCMJ. If I thought it would help, I would go get the magnums, and start mugging some of the camp pedestrians for their pocket change. Besides, I know that historically, Covey will always do whatever is humanly possible to maintain our lifeline.

Mac is busy draining a Jack Daniels. He finishes up and looks at the rest of us. "I am for going downtown and doing some serious hell-raising. Let's go." He looks at Chapman and adds, "You can come along, but only if you are going to be of some help with either the money or the entertainment of ourselves."

Chapman just looks at him and stands up with the rest of us, his only comment being, "Why not? You are going to be entertainment enough to an entire Corps area when they hear you sniveling and whining on the radio in about three days."

"No go there, gallant bird rider," I say as we go out the door of the club. "We will be on secure voice, so only a select few will be able to hear us."

"I am going to transfer you over to the guard freq," he smirks. "That way everyone who has an airplane west of Honolulu can hear." We pile into the jeep with Mac driving and turn out towards the main gate. Fred "Injun" Adams is walking towards the club. As we slowly pass him we all give him the eyeball. He looks at us and does some sort of movement from the chest-hand-extended-toward-the- horizon, Sioux thing.

"White man screwed," he says as we pass him. Chaney flags us down as we pass Headquarters and squeezes into the back. Then we pass the front gate and turn north towards Da Nang. There is a thunderous clap behind us from the top of Marble Mountain, and we watch a 106 round go streaking out to splash with a distant boom somewhere in the river delta.

"What the hell are they shooting at?" I ask.

"They are probably bored," Chapman says, just as they let loose with another one. "They aren't just bored; they must be drunk." This little nighttime display of firepower is somewhat uncommon. Ever since the camp was overrun in 1968 they have kept a fighting/observation post on top of the mountain. During the past years, and right after the battle, they sealed up most of the cave entrances and buried a lot of Uncle Ho's children in the caverns that honeycombed the massif.

Usually it is someone on the perimeter that fires up imagined, and sometimes real, antagonists in and around the wire. Other times, Manes and the Head Shed send a Recon team to perdition duty on the wall for some misdeed, and this usually results in a mad minute of firepower demonstration at night. But to be firing the big gun, they must be eating mushrooms or they have gone completely insane. Whatever they are shooting at has to be two klicks from us and obviously out on the river. They better have a good excuse or a fabulous lie to cover their asses on this one.

By now we are at the I Corps bridge and the MP checkpoint is holding up traffic. The bridge spans the river and leads into the center of the city. The machine gun posts that are spaced on the bridge open up on something in the river in the same direction as our gun crew had been firing. I see a line of green tracers come up from the ground to the south, near the far bank of the river. We get out and, like everyone else, stare off in the direction where the firefight is taking place. A gunship, that is making runs over that area, opens up with his chin turret and a stream of red tracers punctuate the "brrrrrrrrp" of the Mini-gun.

The MPs are running back and forth all crouched and yelling at each other about some perceived threat. Jesus, the fight has to be at least two klicks away. You would think by the way they are acting, that General Giap and some of his boys were sawing away at the bridge abutments. We watch as the 106 fires again at some target up river.

The MPs see the muzzle flash and start screaming, "One twenty-twos! One twenty-twos!" The round splashes in the river and skips into the brush on the far side, to detonate with a sharp crump. These ninnies are starting to make me nervous. We climb back into the jeep.

Chapman, still in his birdman costume, could be mistaken for some black-clad VC infiltrator. I look at Mac and we both look at Chapman. I contemplate the entertainment value of kicking him out of the jeep and yelling "VC!" He must be reading our minds, because he pulls out a pistol, eases off the safety, and grins at us from the back seat.

I quiz Chaney about any rumors he might have heard about what we might be force-fed on the morrow, but he goes into his Plains Indian bullshit and stares off into the distance as if I didn't exist.

Mac slaps me on the arm and says, "Don't bother him. He has gone into the spirit world to think us through the mission." Chaney frowns at him and belches.

"If he starts screaming," I say to Mac, "shoot me in the foot and I will do the same for you, okay?" Chapman is busy telling Cook why it won't be a Bomb Damage Assessment.

Normally, when the mighty Air Force does a "Rolling Thunder" Arc Light, they trundle out six to fifteen odd B-52s, load them with a week's production of bombs and fly out to the designated area. They put down their martinis and one of them walks back to the john, pressing the "bomb" button on the way. All that ordnance falls down and turns several square kilometers of the ground into mulch and bone fragments. Then they send a group of stalwart lads out to see what got destroyed. This is a job for the Hatchet Force. There are enough blown down trees to get choppers in to land a platoon or a company. Since it is usually a police call (pick up the scraps and see what they were), the Hatchet Force has the bodies for that, unless of course it was somewhere like 0-8 (Oscar-Eight) or DM-10. Then they send a Recon team. The team goes in when there is just enough oxygen to revive any survivors. In that situation, they are still a bit sluggish when they crawl out of their holes, pissed off, concussed, and looking to hurt somebody, just about the time you arrive. That is a perfect situation for a Recon team. And if you run fast enough, you might make it back onto the same chopper that brought you in. In that case, the team provides intel with how many they missed with the bombs.

Chapman looks at Cook and tells him cruelly, "They will probably use an Arc Light just to soften up the target you guys are going to get." His subtle attempt at sarcasm is lost on the Cookie, though. You can see that Cookie wants more than that. Cookie wants them to drop the Arc Light while he is on the ground. The louder, more violent the *Gotterdammerung*, the happier he will be. He has been positively buoyant since Billy put the curse on us.

The roadblock clears as the weenies decide they have gotten whatever it is up river. We get back in the jeep and wind our way with the hundreds of other vehicles getting across the bridge. It takes us about 20 minutes to get to the China Night, where good food and cheer can be had by all. There are already several jeeps from the project in the lot as we pull in. Mac pulls our chariot into a back recess and we untangle ourselves from the jeep, walk up to the front and into the garishly lit interior.

The place is its usual rowdy bedlam. We find a table and Chaney wanders off to do some forgotten task. Chapman sticks to us like gum on the bottom of your shoe in August. We sit down and order some food and drinks. This is Da Nang, considered an in-country R and R center. When it isn't off limits because of some bombing or other minor detail, that is. It is always on-limits to us, but tonight they apparently have eased the restriction because there is a fair mix of the regular soldiery in the crowd. The Pink House, or steam bath for Korean officers, is next door. We will get to that later. Mudhole comes in and stops at our table. It seems that the battle at the river was the result of the MPs seeing sampams upriver after curfew, and had taken the precaution of lighting up their asses. Lo and behold, their suspicions were confirmed when Nguyen fired back from shore and from the sampams. Their hysterical calls for help had, evidently, been heard by the TOC and the lads on top of the hill. Not to miss any opportunity to break the boredom, they had lobbed a 106 shell at the barely discernable boats.

Apparently they had found that by adjusting their aim a bit they could skip a round off the water and hit near and beyond the far shoreline. That's pretty good shooting in anybody's book. The air cavalry finally arrived shortly after they sank one boat, and finished the job with a couple of gun runs. The secondary explosion, that turned the sampan into kindling, means they found explosives on the remaining boat. Everyone is surmising that it was for the bridge or one of the ships in the harbor. Heathens! They might have hit the Helgoland, the German Hospital ship, and the only source for good white wines in the country.

The night becomes a blur as we wind our way through the spots offering even a modicum of entertainment. We are finished and broke by 2300. We have run into just about everyone who is at the camp. When we are ready to head back we are a convoy of three jeeps. The alcohol consumption has taken control of driving technique and we breeze past the MP checkpoint on the bridge with a bleary wave to their attempt to stop us and check our IDs. By the time they call the other end of the bridge it is too late, and we blaze by their belated reaction.

Jimmy Johnson is driving and I am opposite him in the front. Cookie is sitting on the right side in the back, propping Mac's head up. As we turn at the crossroads, I notice a three-quarter ton pulling up behind the jeeps. I think it's the MPs so I suggest to Johnson that he pour on the coal. We accelerate and soon leave a wide gap between us and the other two jeeps behind us. The three-quarter ton pulls out to pass them.

Just as they are abreast of the second jeep, I see two muzzle flashes from the back of the truck. The other jeeps slam on the brakes and the truck shoots past them, gaining on us.

I yell out to Jimmy that it looks like they are shooting. Mac is awake now. We are scrambling to pull our weapons free from wherever we stashed them. The truck closes and I see someone fire what appears to be an M-79 grenade launcher. The round slams into the back of our jeep with a sickening, meaty thump. Jimmy slams on the brakes. As they careen past us, I see two black GIs in the front and four black GIs in the back, holding on for dear life as the driver struggles to control the vehicle. One of the ones in the back is still holding onto the M-79. Mac and I let loose with some 30 rounds. I see one of the assholes grab his side and fall back into the mass of bodies in the back, and they are gone. The driver turns out their lights in an attempt to disappear into the night. A few moments later the brake lights flash just long enough for us to see them turn into one of the support camps on the right.

We stop and the other two jeeps pull up. Cookie is in a bad way; so is Mac. The M-79 round is imbedded in the rear seat, unexploded. It caught Cook in the back and broke some of his ribs. Either part of the seat or the round itself has screwed up Mac's elbow, which is swollen as hell. The other two jeeps have no casualties, but there is a shot out windscreen. Both have the same story.

The occupants had screamed out something like, "Die, whitey motherfucker!" and opened up on them with no warning. They couldn't shoot back, for fear of hitting us.

There is a lot of racial tension in Da Nang. The trash from the "MacNamara 100,000 Program" makes up the majority of the support troops in and around the 80th Group. They are also most of the junkies that inhabit the warrens of Gonorrhea Gulch. We are all checking our ammo supplies and redistributing to make sure everyone has enough. We send one jeep back to the camp to get reinforcements and prepare to go after those who tried to kill us. The mood is universal: I didn't survive the A Shau and all the Laotian targets to be blown away by some hopped up "don't wannabe" shipped over here from the States.

We go around the back of the jeep to examine the damage. The grenade is lodged in the seat back. After examining the round we discover it is one of the old ones that are spin activated. It has to go 30 meters out of the barrel before it arms itself. They had been too close when they fired it. Instead of a grenade, it turned out to be a very large bullet. Cook is in real pain, but won't go back because he is in a murderous rage. All of us are.

Three more jeeps of our guys arrive and we roll up on the compound. Jimmy slides our jeep into the gate and we all pile out. We snatch the weapons out of the hands of the guards and those in the two nearest bunkers. We have to punch a few down to the ground and Jimmy paces back and forth, asking them who was in the truck that pulled in the gate. The guards are pissing themselves as we have smacked a couple of them around pretty bad. One of them says that he doesn't know who they are, but they headed for what they call "the junkie hootch." I guess this is one of the barracks where all the dopers hang out. We are jabbing him to get the location when our other jeep pulls up with a deuce and a half filled with two teams of Yards. One of the teams is Jimmy's hoodlums.

About this time, the first sergeant of the unit shows up. It is a bad moment to play first weenie. On top of that, he is carrying a brand new CAR-15. Jimmy snatches it out of his hand and jacks him in the forehead with the butt. He falls down on the ground with Jimmy yelling at him, demanding to know what a rear echelon pig like him is doing with a CAR-15. Mac is leaning against the truck and so is the Cookie; both are hurting. I lose it. I take my gun and shove it up under the first sergeant's nose and tell him what happened and why we are there. I tell him that we are going to get the rest of our Yards and turn this place upside down until we find the fucking trash that shot at us. I pull the hammer back and am ready to kill the worthless toad. He is scared shitless. Hell, they all are.

We are used to staying alive in worse conditions than these bunnies could even imagine in their worst nightmares. Our survival is keyed on pure aggression, and we *are* pure aggression at this point. I want to kill all of them. None of them are innocent. Whoever these shits are that tried to kill us, these assholes know them. They are either too scared of them to confront them or they are part of the same crowd. Their NCOs don't deserve to wear the stripes. If they had done their job they wouldn't have a unit full of hopheads.

Another truck rolls up and more Yards join us. By now, we have blocked the highway and seized about half of their perimeter. Behind them come Captain Manes and the Executive Officer. They quickly slow things down and start to ease us out of "cocked and ready to shoot first" mode. The MPs show up and Manes goes out to talk to them. He comes back and tells us that we are going to stand down. There is some grousing, but eventually we back off. We get Cookie and Mac in the jeep and Jimmy and I climb in. Both of them are in serious pain by the time we get back to the compound. We take them up to the infirmary, and Doc Wang clucks his way through the triage and starts to bind up their injuries. Cook has three broken ribs and a severely wrenched back; Mac's elbow is cracked. Both of them are swollen and succumb to the Demerol. Jimmy and I head down to the club as the last of the raiding party comes straggling in.

When we get to the club, Manes collars us and tells us to just cool it. He asks how Cook and Mac are and we tell them they are peacefully under Doc's dream juice. He gets everyone in the club quieted down and explains the incident, and what is transpiring as a result. The MPs are shaking down the whole compound and so far have found the one that we capped, and one other with a leaking wound. Both are junkies. The MPs are in the process of sorting out the wicked. The one that didn't make it had bled out by the time they found him. He was so hopped up he probably didn't know he was checking out. Billy comes in and asks us what happened. He is solicitous about Mac and the Cookie. I wander over to our hut and lay down about an hour later, still trying to come down off the adrenalin.

The next morning I have to go with the SMAJ and Manes to give a statement to a couple of dicks from CID. Nothing is said about our terrorizing the whole camp. Evidently, this crew of hopheads has been a chancre for quite a while. The whole thing will get swept under the rug by the Army. With the war being so unpopular they won't risk making it into an incident that would draw the leftwing press in for a feed.

The maintenance outfits are where they dump all the undesirables from the line units. Da Nang is bulging at the seams with deserters and those wanting to desert, all fueled on cheap, and readily available, heroin. We should have capped the whole crew. The only reason they shot at us was because we were white. If it had been some poor mail clerk, they would have taken their time and killed him. Their NCOs and officers are scared shitless of them. As it was, *we* scared the shit out of *them*.

I go over to tell Cuman, but the Yard mojo wire has already informed him of the details. He and the team are up at the infirmary making a nuisance of themselves. With Mac and Cookie both incapacitated, we are unable to run. It looks like it will be two weeks before we are able to get back in the slot. We are off the target list, if only temporarily. I make plans to let the Yards go home as soon as Mac comes limping in from the infirmary and Manes tells him that he isn't going anywhere so get his ass back in bed or he will assign him to Security Company. The Yards have instructions to return in a week. I come back from giving them the news in time to find both of my stalwart companions back in the hut. Since we can't run, we are eligible for an in-country R and R. What a turn of events. Had the idiots been another ten meters away, they would have killed all of us.

Castro comes in and wants to rub our heads for luck. We have been saved from the jaws of fate by this accident. I tell him that for a small fee he can buy items of their clothing and trinkets for good luck. We are going to need cash to fuel the R and R. He just laughs and tells the other two that he suspects I paid off the hopheads to shoot them just to get out of the mission.

We are effectively out of action until Mac and the Cookie recover. No fault of our own, we were just at the wrong place at the wrong time. Jimmy comes by to commiserate with us and our anger, which is somewhat softened by the fact that we won't be first in the batter's box. It was idiocy and bad timing. After surviving all that we have, we came very close to becoming just another incident swept under the rug.

We sit, quietly going over the incident, when Billy materializes in the doorway. "You men all right?" he asks, but doesn't wait for and answer. "Too bad. We could have done some great things together." He shakes his head and actually seems to have some sort of compassion at our misfortune. I look over at Castro and he is trying to be invisible.

"Yeah, Sergeant Major, we really wanted the chance at this mission. It would have been a great opportunity to try out something new. Who knows? We might have caught them with their pants down." I sigh as if I carry some great regret. Mac looks at me as if I have a screw loose, and Cookie scowls at me before he looks at the Sergeant Major.

"We could still make it happen, Sergeant Major. I'm feeling better already." He winces as he tries to sit up. Castillo, his eyes darting in my direction, is looking for an opportunity to slip out of the room. I smile at him.

"Yeah it's too bad that we are all banged up, but there are plenty of others," I look at Castro again before turning back to the Sergeant Major, "that are up to snuff on the raid concept." Billy, though, is lost in some sort of thought process that doesn't involve victims, so he misses the murderous look the Cuban gives me. He mumbles something and then pats Mac on the shoulder.

"Good men," he says and leaves the hut. Castro lets out an audible sigh and turns back to me.

"You know if he picks us I am gonna demand that you straphang just to get even for that ambush." He glares at me.

"No can do Sarge," I reply. "I am eligible for an in-country R and R and the trauma of seeing my two brothers here shot before my very eyes has unhinged me. I am unfit for combat. Hell, I might have some sort of horrible flashback out there and just start shooting, because in my delirium I am reliving the awful event." Cookie scowls. He would go out there wrapped up in surgical tape and plaster of paris looking like a tamale if he could. Mac is much more pragmatic. Take the time to heal; we will get thrown back into the fray soon enough. We are called over to the orderly room and informed that we are to either assist around the camp or take an in-country R and R. That's a tough choice. We go back to the hut and give the news to the Cookie with glee. He is visibly despondent. I am starting to feel sorry for him, but then, even the Titans took a break from their labors.

We decide to go to Nha Trang, but that idea is nixed by the powers. It seems that in light of our recent rowdy behavior, the SFOB now has some sort of vendetta in mind against any of the Special Projects personnel. Manes and Colonel Donnie are loath to give them any sort of excuse. We are the least likely to keep a low profile so we will go to Saigon, and then to Vung Tau. Ah, lovely Vung Tau. The city is perched on the South China Sea like a jewel. It is almost like a dream. We spend the night with Castillo and Jimmy Johnson simultaneously castigating us for our seeming lassitude and choking on their obvious envy at our good fortune.

CHAPTER 24

Gin and Heartbreak

I am asleep on the plane carrying us to Saigon. I am having pleasant dreams of home and my childhood when I am jolted awake. Jolted is an understatement because it is searing pain that rockets me from unconsciousness. My two baboon companions leer at me and I smell something burning. This is always a bad sign on an aircraft.

The pain is emanating from my crotch. It feels as if someone has taken a branding iron to it. I sit up abruptly, almost bashing Cookie in the face with my head. I look at my fatigue trousers; there is a hole burned in them to the right of the fly. There is also a brown, wet stain around the hole and extending down the leg.

"You fell asleep with a cigarette and set yerself on far!" Mac drawls, and then he and Cook both break into giggles. "Cookie put you out with his coffee." With that, they laugh uncontrollably. Perfect.

Cookie manages to wheeze between giggles, "We were going to pat it out but we didn't want these zoomies to think we were queers!" More giggles. The hole is about two inches across. I wonder how long these two had watched the process before they decided that I might be needed later, like when we get back to running for our lives. I realize any sort of complaint would be wasted on these two. They would only use it as an excuse for more of their humor. Instead, I rise and try to keep from wincing.

"Oh? Are you sure you two weren't just careless and this is your crude and opaque way of covering up your own crimes?" The two of them just grin like a pair of weasels at the window of a chicken coop.

Looking around the cargo bay, the rest of the passengers are a mixed lot of soldiers from various units, all dressed in their khakis. This is the regulation uniform for Saigon. Most of these guys are going there for the same purpose as we are. Saigon is one of the main in-country R and R centers. It is the heart of the apparatus that runs the war and is full of staff officers and the usual crowd of rear echelon twinkies that surround them.

We have been spared the khaki travel attire by the fact that we are delivering some equipment to House 10. The two footlocker-sized crates are lashed down on the rear ramp of the aircraft. We are in our fatigues and armed as if, by all appearances, we are escorting classified material. The arrangement is a "don't ask, don't tell" type of mission. For all I know, the boxes are full of the colonel's laundry, or maybe full of outdated Military Payment Script that Billy had been unable to unload after the last currency change. We don't care because it's our ticket for priority on a direct flight to Saigon.

We are not wearing any rank insignia and the only ID we are to show is our "walk-on-water" pass. In addition, we are carrying our best sporting iron. Mac has a CAR-15, I have a Czech 63 Skorpian machine pistol, and the Cookie has an Ingram and a High Standard with a silencer. The weapons are enough to discourage any normal questions, because it is obvious they aren't normal issue. I have my Browning, and a .44-caliber derringer as well, because the little Czech machine pistol is great for show, but is basically a crowd clearer. When we get to House 10 we will lose most of the hardware so I will need to get something more concealable and, more importantly, disposable.

After we had gotten ourselves moving this morning, we were trucked over to the normal air terminal and deposited at the operations center to wait for the air truck to arrive. The two crates were secured behind the desk and one of us had kept an eye on them while the other two generally wandered around aimlessly. Cookie found some Air Force guy who showed him where the coffee was hidden, and we managed to secure three gigantic plastic cups and filled them from the reservoir. I had a bottle of cognac with me so we spiked the contents liberally. About half an hour later the plane pulled up to the ramp and the Air Force motioned for us to load our crates and get onboard first. We had already settled near the back when the rest of the troops filed on.

There are a couple of officers who mostly ignore us as well as the other troops, except for some snooty major who keeps eyeballing us with a mixture of disdain and a desire to challenge our behavior. The major has seated himself where he can keep an eye on us. He is wearing the crossed cannons of a cannon cocker. It doesn't matter because his whole demeanor spells p-r-i-c-k.

When Cookie opened the cognac to sweeten his coffee, the major had sniffled to himself and said something to the captain sitting next to him. The captain was from the 101st and more or less ignored whatever the major seemed to have on his mind. The captain was looking forward to the same pleasures that we were, and obviously had no interest in engaging in some chickenshit games.

Obviously the major's pique is heightened by the pyro demonstration of my two companions, and now he is steeled to straighten out the pecking order. As I clear my head, I see him rise and walk over to say something to the loadmaster, who shakes his head while making the universal "beats me" shoulder shrug. This only encourages the major and he starts making his way over to where the three of us are sitting. I nudge Mac and whisper a quick "prick warning" as the major covers the last few steps and draws up before us in an officious manner.

"Let's see some identification and your orders," he commands and looks down his nose. We ignore him and continue to chat amongst ourselves, which causes him to rise to an apoplectic rage. "Stand at attention when an officer is addressing you!" he storms. We laugh at him. I am growing annoyed, but the Cookie pulls himself erect and flashes his walk-on-water ID and shows it to the major. Cook is the epitome of the super soldier. Usually his answer to annoyances like this is to smash flat whatever, or whoever, it is. But today he is full of condescending protocol. He leans over and very calmly starts in.

"Major, you are obviously under the impression that we are in the Armed Forces. Let me dispel that illusion right now. Not only are we not, but in effect I am about three grades higher up the food chain from your rank and position, which would leave you in a very bad position. Now I suggest that you return to your seat and remain there for the duration of the flight, or I will have you restrained, and when we get on the ground, have you arrested. If you want to carry this further since you are an officious ass, go right ahead because I am bored, and you richly deserve the shit-storm that will envelope your ass." He looks the major over as if he just discovered something particularly odoriferous. He continues in an even tone, as the major stands there with his mouth partially open. "I already don't like you, but even a fool deserves a fair warning. Do you understand me, Major?" He punctuates his statement with a stare that would have intimidated a wolverine. The major is out of his league; he knows it, or at least suspects it. He stands there with his mind trying to wrap itself around the events as Cook sits down again. Cook looks up, and obviously disturbed that he is still standing there, scowls at him. This time when he speaks it is not softly. "I said 'git,' Major! What part of that don't you understand?" The major turns and hurries back to his seat, red with embarrassment. The rest of the passengers snicker.

"You know Cookie might just be officer material some day if he keeps retrogressing like that," Mac grins. "For a minute, I wanted to lock my heels and salute. We should use his talents more often."

I look at him and the Cookie, as I try to adjust my burned and scalded locale. "It's more likely that his talent, as you put it, will probably get us all thrown into L.B.J. (Long Binh Jail—the main stockade in Vietnam). The major, there, is going to be in officious shock just long enough after we get on the ground for us to possibly escape. That is, if our ride is waiting for us." I look at Cookie and shake my head. "See if you can plan phase two or a plan B, instead of setting fire to anything else."

The plane starts to descend as we enter the busy traffic pattern over Saigon. Within minutes we land. The big props reverse and the lumbering sky truck rolls and turns onto the taxiway. I look out the door window as we draw up to the terminal ramp; one of the SOG vehicles is parked there. Thank God for small favors. The plane comes to a halt and the ramp goes down. The loadmaster dismounts, pulls the chocks out behind him, and then disappears around the starboard side. He returns, points to us and the crates, and makes a motion to deplane.

As we are helping the assistant loadmaster undo the straps that hold the crates down, the truck from House 10 pulls up. We get off the plane and muscle the crates onto the back of the truck. After securing them, Mac goes around to the passenger side and gets in. Cook and I get on the back of the truck and the driver gets in. We pull away from the plane as the loadmaster gives us the thumbs up. He had seen the potential for being up all night giving depositions if the prick with the oak leaves got his steam up. He deftly averts catastrophe by unloading us first. We are gone and away before the rest of the passengers start coming out.

Saigon is the flower of the Orient. As we wind our way from the big air base to House 10, we lounge in the back of the truck taking it all in. We will stay here for a few days before we take off for Vung Tau.

When we get to the safe house there is the usual band of hangers-on as well as a few transient reprobates like ourselves. We get our sleeping arrangements worked out and take a shower. Before returning to the lounge area, we take the TWs we brought with us to get cleaned up for a night on the town. As I walk into the lounge, I am snatched from behind and someone gives me a wet tongue in the ear. I turn around in the midst of the struggle and see an old friend of mine from Bragg. It's Rocky.

Now Rocky is a legend among demolition men, and has a love for explosives that borders on the sexual. He is all done up in his class As and has his beret cocked back on his head like a Sicilian cheroot smuggler. The last I had heard was that Rocky was up-country with one of the Mike Forces, or safely sequestered in some remote A Camp. His being here at the same time we are has all the makings of a potential court martial. Rocky has been promoted and demoted so many times it is rumored he puts his stripes on with Velcro. He grins and punches me playfully in the solar plexus.

"Yah! Good thing you showed up. I was getting bored!" he grins from ear to ear. The one saving grace about Rocky is his infectious good humor. I introduce him to Mac and the Cookie. He grabs me around the shoulders and squeezes me in a cross between a hug and foreplay with grizzly bears. He inquires how long we are going to be there. Uh oh, I can see the wheels of mayhem spinning in his head and am attempting to stall off the inevitable. Before I can stop him, the Cookie gives him our entire itinerary.

It's not that I don't like Rocky; in fact, I love the little Sicilian chunk. But he is a magnet for craziness. I came here to relax and get away from the war for a few days. Hanging in there with Rocky for longer than 48 hours is hazardous to your life, limbs, and property. I can almost guarantee that going back to the war will seem like a relief. Right up front I try to explain this to my compadres, but they think that I am just building up Rocky's reputation like some flatboat legend so that he will feel like he is among friends. Rocky just grins. I finally give up, and decide to let them find out for themselves.

As Rocky bear hugs both, he realizes, through the winces and oinks from them, that the two of them are injured and he tones his act down a notch so that he doesn't produce any further pain. Injuries or not, after seeing the Ranger tab on Rocky's uniform Cookie latches onto him like a long lost relative. I want to tell Cook that Rocky was a distinguished graduate of his Ranger class by virtue of the fact that he had been sent there as punishment for some misdeed, and anything less would have not been sufficient to get him out of the trouble he was in at the time. But, why bother? They are soon bosom buddies and in a Ranger-induced bliss.

We are off to go bar-hopping our way through the many delights that Saigon has to offer. As the evening wears on I find out that Rocky is tucked away on some training project and is in town for a break from the dull routine. That is his story, anyway. I suspect that it is more likely that there is a demolition accident involved somewhere in the affair. I let him spend the night wiling away the hours with Cook, comparing notes and garnishing the truth. With Rocky it all sounds like some sort of wild bullshit story. For the uninitiated, the truth would be truly frightening. I have never met anyone with so little regard for any sense of propriety or, for that matter, the consequences of playing with things that vaporize solid objects. Mac catches my attention a few times as the night wears on, and rolls his eyes in exaggeration. It's possible he and I might survive.

Before the night is over we manage to get into two fights, and Rocky punches some leg sergeant so hard he pukes all over himself. We wander back and collapse in our temporary quarters around 0200. I consider it a quiet night since no one has been dismembered and none of us are in leg irons. Since Rocky is going to be here for a week, I go to bed plotting to escape before he gets up in the morning.

I get up before 0700 and go down to where Mac is to wake him up. I want to go to Vung Tau, but he and Cook want to stay in Saigon for a few days. They have to have their respective dressings and wraps examined, so I decide to go ahead and try to get a few days of rest. Mac grins lopsidedly.

"You mean that you don't want to hang around here with Rocky?" he laughs at his own remark, then groans in pain from the effort.

"Nope. I figure to leave the Cookie with him so that he gets the finish on his education. You keep an eye on them. I have other interests in mind, like staying in one piece. I know Rocky; he was just getting warmed up last night." I lean against the wall as he sits up in the bed.

"Maybe we can adopt him and take him back up north with us," Mac muses groggily. He shakes his head. "Nah, bad idea. That boy is a magnet for trouble, and if he and Wesley ever got together they would most likely blow up the camp. You go on ahead. We'll come down in a few days." He thinks to himself for a minute then laughs. "That is, if I can pry Cook away from him." I leave as he rolls over and lies back down. It will take them several hours to sleep off last night. By that time

I will be long gone. Mac knows I want some time alone and will cover my tracks with some plausible story. Rocky is a creature of the moment; if I am not there he will find someone else to include in his self-destruct plans.

It's easy to make arrangements for a lift into Vung Tau and soon I am sitting in the doorway of a chopper on its regular ash and trash flight into the coastal town. There are a couple of correspondents on the same flight, heading down there to cover whatever they had bullshitted their editor into thinking was newsworthy. It's a beautiful day and the flight is serene. After we land, I thank the crew for the lift and hail a tricycle cab to find a place near the ocean. I have been here before and it hasn't lost its charm. I get a bungalow at the old Michelin complex, unpack my stuff, and spend the next few hours traveling around the old town.

Passing up the usual GI haunts, I eat at a small provincial around 1400, enjoy an iced drink on the veranda, and watch the traffic and the steady flow of pedestrians that pass by. The girls in Vung Tau are truly the loveliest in Vietnam. Just when you think you have seen the love of your life, one comes along that makes her look like she ought to be on an Alpo diet. I am lost in my thoughts of their beauty and quietly grading them on a scale of one to ten behind my sunglasses. It is peaceful here and the war seems so very far away.

The soft tinkle of laughter behind me causes me to turn to see who it is. I am quite surprised to see two round eyes, that is, two white women, enter the veranda and take a table over by the wall looking down on the street. From their accents, they are Aussies. Both are quite lovely but the smaller of the two is stunning. She has long dark hair and elfin features. She sees that I am looking at them and flashes me a brief, yet shy, smile before they sit down.

The waiter comes back and I order an iced beer as well as an espresso. When he returns I pay my bill and relax back into the seat to enjoy the parade of sights below. I catch drifts and bits of their conversation as a backdrop to my daydreaming. They are nurses and are here for the same reason everyone else comes here, bit of rest and relaxation. The one who smiled at me is named Judith and her friend, who appears to be a few years older, is named Glenda. They will have no problem finding escorts in this town. The place is brimming with soldiers, correspondents, construction honchos, embassy types and the odd spook or two. In fact, I am surprised that they haven't got two or more lovesick lieutenants attached to them already. I finish my beer and the espresso and rise to leave. I give them a brief nod of hello and goodbye as I walk out through the interior and down the stairs.

I grab a pedicab and go back to the bungalow. It's still early afternoon and I want to swim for a while before taking a nap, so I strip down and, wearing a pair of faded scuba trunks, go for a dip in the ocean. The water is cool and the breezes are full of the salt air and the many flowers that proliferate here. The sea is crystal clear and I spend the next hour or so just enjoying the feel of it and the many brightly colored fish that abound in its shallows.

As I come out of the water and start to trudge up the sand, I run into two gents who are sunning themselves on a pair of lawn chairs they have dragged down from the short pad of a patio that faces the ocean from each bungalow. This place had originally been a rest center in the late fifties for the *pied noir* of the French Indochina social structure. It has the decaying ambience of age yet still retains some of its colonial charm. Some of the newer additions to the decor are garish; plastic patio furniture is gradually replacing the wicker, which hasn't handled the abuse of the many guests. My patio has a couple of wicker papa-san chairs with bright aqua cushions.

The two men are fit and muscular, and from the Ray Ban sunglasses apparently have some connection to aviation. They see me coming up from the sea and wave me over. Between them is a cooler and it is brimming with bottles of Ba Mi Ba beer. They stand up and introduce themselves as Patrick and Dave. I was right. They both are flight officers. Dave is a captain and Patrick is a Warrant Officer. They fly as part of a Mohawk squadron. This is a twin-engine, weird looking, fixed wing aircraft. Most of these birds are equipped with electronic countermeasures or surveillance equipment. I accept a beer and sit down in the sand to enjoy the warm breeze and the cold beer.

I respond to their questions of who and what I am by merely telling them my name and that I am in Special Forces. This satisfies their curiosity, more so when I add that I am in Special Projects. We interface with these guys as far as mission formats, and some of the side-looking airborne radar imagery we get is generated by their squadrons.

They, like me, are on an in-country R and R. I tell them what I know about the city and the nightspots, as well as the best places to eat. They are going up to the base at Long Than later in the day to pick up the makings of a barbeque. We agree to pool our resources and I go over to my bungalow and return with some money to split the costs. They are nice enough guys, like all aviators a bit on the dashingly disturbed side, but firmly rooted in the knowledge that what they do is fraught with mortality.

We are sunning ourselves when we hear women's voices from the bungalow next to mine. It had been vacant when I checked in, but apparently not now. This place is popular with the civilian side of the war effort and I pray that my new neighbors aren't a pair of Donut Dollies with an attitude. If I want to bring some company back at night I don't need a couple of estrogen kitties sitting in judgment next door. I am almost flabbergasted when the two Aussie nurses step out on the patio. They both survey the view and pick us up on the radar almost immediately. It isn't hard since the three of us are staring quite pointedly at them. The shy one recognizes me and gives a bit of a wave in my direction and I return it. The airborne libido twins wait until they step back inside before pouncing on me as a source of information about the other one, assuming that the delicate one and I know each other. I tell them that I don't know either of them, but relate where I had seen them and what

I had overheard. I also make it clear that the way is clear for their intended pairing, because I don't have any desire to be matched with some round-eyed skirt in this town.

It's not that the two are dogs, in fact, quite the opposite. The little delicate one is just my type, but I would spend all my time running interference to keep the rest of the wolf pack from attempted theft. I came here to relax and get away from pressure. Patrick is warming up with the intention of swooping down in true aviator fashion and sweeping the ladies off their proverbial feet. Why not? He is funny and charming; I am sure that unless the two nurses are Carmelite nuns he has a chance at the title. I say my excuses and thank them for the brews, agreeing to meet them later for dinner. I pick my way the short distance up to the bungalow and after brushing off the sand, go inside and strip down. I go into the small bathroom and take a luxurious shower. As I dry myself off, I hear Patrick on the patio next door giving the ladies of mercy the full dose of his charm. Soon I hear Dave's voice join the conversation.

I turn on the rotating fan and lie down on the bed. The beer and the swim have made me drowsy. The breeze coming off the ocean is cool and the soft hum of the fan lulls me to sleep. My dreams are disjointed and mixed with images of happier times and parts of the war that don't involve death. The peacefulness of being out of harm's way, if only for a few days, allows me to drift off into a deep sleep.

It's late in the afternoon when I wake up and the sea has taken on the mirror quality of a perfect setting. I catch the faint whiff of perfume as I lay there in half-wake fulness. I look at my watch. It is nearly five. I stretch and quietly will myself to sit up. My pistol and cigarettes are in the *idi-wa* stand next to the bed. I open the drawer, take a cigarette out of the pack and light it up, then stand and go in the bathroom. Putting the cigarette in an ashtray next to the toilet, I throw some cold water on my head and face and rinse the sleep from my eyes. I wrap the towel around me like a sarong, recover the cigarette and walk out on the patio to watch the sea.

I miss Mac and the Cookie, but they will be along soon enough. Hopefully they will have lost Rocky by then or peace as a concept will be long lost. The thought of Rocky here in this place makes me chuckle. I catch a movement out of the comer of my eye and turn to the left. Judith is standing on her patio doing much the same as I. She looks at the cigarette and smiles wryly.

"Those things will kill you, you know," she says, and laughs at the ludicrous statement. I bow slightly.

"In this place there are a great many things that are more sudden and direct, but yes, you are correct," I reply. She laughs again. Her laughter has a musical quality to it and her voice has a husky sensuality. She points in the direction of Dave and Pat's place.

"Your mates have offered to take us to eat tonight. They got back about an hour ago with enough food to feed a mob. They said it was for tomorrow, some sort of

Yank tradition, called a cowboy barbeque. We wanted to meet you, but they said that it was best not to wake you. They said you were a snake-eater. From the way they said it I assume it is a compliment." She pauses for a moment. "Oh, I am so sorry. My name is Judith, Judith Patterson." She held out her hand. I step over and grasp it gently, holding onto the towel, which is starting to obey gravity.

"My name is Nick. I am pleased to meet you, Judith. Are you any relation to Banjo Patterson?" I ask jokingly, for Banjo Patterson is the Kipling of Australia. I had stumbled across one of his books while working with the Aussies. She laughs, and tilts her head back when she does.

"Gor no, my family is in the cattle business, though," she says. "Imagine that, a Yank who reads Banjo Patterson. You musta been stuck someplace where there was a limited supply of books." She cocks her head slightly. "A bit more odd, a Yank that reads Patterson and eats snakes." She must have noticed the slight frown at the mention of snake-eaters and she blushes slightly, before following it up with, "I'm sorry, no offense meant."

"None taken," I reply. "Snake-eater is slang for Special Forces. I have been called worse. Your lot, the SAS, has some unique nicknames as well. It goes with the territory, I guess." There is a bit of an awkward silence and then she looks at me again.

"And, gracious too, my, my, Nick with no last name," she pauses for a moment. "I think I like you. We have been here for five minutes and you haven't made the usual Yank pass." I look at her and laugh. She is right of course, most GIs have an over-active libido and we, as a group, are extraordinarily aggressive in that respect.

"I'm not awake yet. Give me fifteen minutes and I'll be rutting with the rest of the pack." I smile at her. She is quite something. She is about my age but there is a tired quality around her eyes. We chat for a while. She gets my last name out of me, and I find out that she and Glenda work for one of the USAID programs. I mention that I once stole a Land Rover from some AID project and she laughs again, adding that they were given quite a briefing about the light-fingered qualities of "your lot," as she puts it. We both laugh at that one.

Our interlude is interrupted as Glenda walks out rubbing the sleep from her eyes and we are introduced. She has the same musical quality of laughter as her friend. I like Australians; they have a simple straight-forward quality about them.

It seems the two Mohawk pilots have made arrangements for dinner and have included me in the plans. Quite nice of them, considering I was the only one who knew where the French restaurant was that they had been bragging about. No matter, the girls seem to be fun and since they were paired up with the flying crowd I could slip off and satisfy my prurient urges later.

Patrick must have had his interference receptors on while he was napping for he appears as if by command from the recesses of his bungalow to make sure I am not poaching. He steps over the small wall that separates the patios and joins the conversation. Glenda looks at me and remarks that I should probably dress or find a pin to hold the towel up. I excuse myself and say that I want to have a shower. We agree to meet in about an hour. I leave the three of them chatting on the patio and go inside the bungalow.

After another heavenly shower, I towel off and dress in the civvies I bought yesterday in Saigon, nothing fancy, just a pair of khaki trousers and a pale blue silk shirt that resembles a short-sleeved safari jacket. We can wear civvies on R and R, so I don't have to bother with a uniform. The town is full of soldiers in uniform. I would just as soon be mistaken for some embassy twink, thank you. Besides the two aviation twins will be in their war suits. With the girls as their dates, they will have to wear them. That way, only brother officers and civilians will be trying to steal them away. That cuts the competition in half.

I ditched my Browning for a Walther PPK in Saigon. It is easier to hide under a shirt. I have two extra magazines for it, so I have almost the same firepower. I doubt that I will need it, but guns and staying alive had become synonymous. I hear voices outside in the twilight, so I step out on the patio and Dave as well as Pat are on the girls' patio. The first thing I notice is that Dave has become a major. These two are brighter than I thought. That will cut the competition down even more if the wolf pack thinks he is a field grade. I am starting to warm up to these two. They have potential. The girls are looking exactly as one would imagine, alluring and desirable. I step over the low wall to greetings from all four. Glenda disappears inside and comes back out with a glass of chilled white wine and hands it to me with the remark that at least with it I look civilized. I catch her glance and she is looking at the slight bulge on my belt line in the back. She winks and does the Mae West line about being glad to see her, smart and observant girl. She hovers over Judith like a protective veil. Patrick is going to have his work cut out for him.

We stand there in the twilight and toast our respective countries, and damn each other's bureaucrats. Everyone is in a festive mood. Patrick and Dave have a jeep, but I dissuade them from taking it, pointing out that the cabs are cheap and you don't have to worry about some thug stealing it. Judith remarks that I appear to be somewhat of an expert on grand theft auto, which makes everyone laugh. We go out and hail one of the taxis and wind our way along the seashore to the place that Robbie had told me about.

As we get out, there is a steady flow of people coming in and leaving the establishment. We make our way inside. The girls are head-turners in their own country, I am sure, but here their entrance is causing some serious cervical injuries. We are ushered to a prime table by the maitre d', an astute man who realized the drawing power of the aviators' dates.

Robbie, I think, deserves a major pat on the back for this place. White tablecloths, uniformed waiters, and a sumptuous menu, make the place a jewel on anyone's itinerary. The staff fusses over us and we enjoy a pleasurable meal over even more pleasant conversation. Pat and Dave are wowing the girls with daredevil tales of their exploits flying missions in the dark of night. The girls, in turn, are relating the sometimes humorous antics of the nursing profession. There is a dance floor on the veranda and a band is playing a mixture of rock and soft ballads.

By the time we are into the coffee and after dinner wines, Dave has primed himself for evening exercises. He and Pat invite the girls to the dance floor. I enjoy a cognac, while watching the lithe movements of Judith under her white knit dress as she slow dances with Pat. This starts the fires burning in me for the company of a woman. She is truly lovely. I am not the only one who notices. Hell, you would have to be three months dead not to be aroused by the sight of either one of them. I like Pat; in fact, he and Dave are good people. I envy them their luck, but at the same time am happy for them. Dave is married, I am sure. He has that guilt about him that shrouds the chained. But in reality, no one is married in a war zone. Life is too fragile for that.

As I am watching, a rather inebriated civilian walks, or rather weaves out onto the dance floor and attempts to cut in on Patrick. The warrant officer handles it in a firm but gracious manner, and he finishes the dance with Judith. They come back to the table and as they sit down Judith smiles at me and asks if I am not bored here all alone. I look at them both and say that I am having sport watching Pat defend his territory. A brief dark look passes Pat's face, followed by a glance in the direction of the inebriated civilian as he agrees that some of the crowd has bad manners. Judith touches his arm as if to reassure him and they both start chatting about something else.

My mojo wire starts to tingle and I look up at the crowd again. The asshole that had been bothering Pat is sitting with three others and they are talking loud enough to be heard above the murmur of the crowd. I can't catch what they are saying. The tables nearest them are glancing embarrassedly and apprehensively in their direction, with the exception of a table full of Australians who are eyeballing the three with the look of a feral dog pack.

I see Dave start to break away from Glenda after one particularly nasty remark, but she pulls him back as the dance ends, and they make their way back to our table. The band stops and declares they will take a break between sets. I can see that Dave is upset. He sits down and tries to put a good face on it, but Patrick sees it too and leans over and they whisper between themselves. They both glance in the direction of the table where the drunks are. The civilian gives the two of them the finger and says something to his companions. Pat starts to get up, but the girls switch the conversation, drawing them both in and averting a confrontation. I am watching the table of drunks. Assholes are the same, no matter what rank or circumstance.

I see the drunken civilian get up and head for the latrine. I give it a moment of thought before excusing myself, and I walk off in the direction of the entrance. I go outside and quickly come around the building and in the side entrance. The doors have been opened to let in the sound of the sea and the fresh breeze. As I come in, I look at the table the civilian had come from. His two companions are talking animatedly. One appears to be a Navy Petty Officer and the other is another civilian. They don't see me, as their attention is on the table with the girls.

I slip behind them and go into the latrine. There are three others besides the drunken asshole standing next to the urinal trough. Two of them have their wits about them as they turn and see me. They leave quickly. The drunken civilian doesn't sense me until I am right behind him and slightly to the left. He turns, putting himself back in his trousers. He looks up and recognizes me from the table.

"What the fuck are you looking at? Are you queer? Is that why you ain't got one of those snotty round-eyed cunts?" he slurs and grins crookedly. I guess he was used to verbal sparring, which was a mistake, because I kick him as hard as I can in the side of the kneecap and hear the gratifying snap as the knee dislocates. The pain is so intense and sudden you can't even scream. He does manage to vomit all over himself, though. He falls over sideways, and I kick him in his right kidney as he lies there choking. He flops over on his back gasping. I step up and bring my heel down as hard as I can on his genitals. The pain makes him pass out. The other guy in the john looks at me and then at the asshole and grins. By the uniform he is wearing and his accent, he is an Aussie.

He gives me the thumbs up and says, "Good on you, mate. If you need some help with his friends just call out." He steps over to the door and slips out.

I flip the drunk over and douse his face in the urinal drain and he sputters awake. I take out the Walther and stick the barrel up one nostril. He is semi-awake. "I'm not queer. And you can thank your lucky stars for that, you piece of shit, or I would use you like the bag of shit you are." His eyes are wide with shock and fear, so I slap him with the pistol on the side of his face, before I continue. "What I am, is the last thing you will ever see in this world, if I see you again. You drag yourself out of here or I am going to kill all three of you. I won't even bat an eye about it or hesitate one instant." I slap him again with the pistol, opening a cut above his eye. "Do you believe me?" He nods yes, his head making nervous twitches up and down. I drop him on his back and slide the Walther back into my pants. I step on his unbroken knee for good measure and he groans in pain and passes out again. I walk over and open the door to the latrine. There is a commotion coming from the direction of his friends' table. I slip outside and start back the way I had come.

The Aussies have decided to end their annoyance with the loudmouth crew in much the same manner. The Aussie I had seen in the latrine has one of the other two by the shirtfront and has slapped him. His friend is watching, open-mouthed and impotent, because there are two other burly members of the Australian Infantry standing next to him, making him promises of the same treatment. The Aussie with the handful of shirt spies me, grins, and winks as I turn and slip out the door. I walk slowly around the side, letting the adrenalin drain out of my system. I light a cigarette and my hand shakes. I hate assholes. I hate drunken assholes even more.

The civilian was a big, beefy, red-faced, mean drunk. Obviously, he had been getting away with being a bully for a long time. He picked on Pat first because he was a lowly Warrant Officer and smaller. Whatever he said to Dave about Glenda, he said just loud enough to be heard and yet, not directly at him. He and his friends would have been trouble before the night was over.

Some would say it was excessive, but that is the only way I have been trained to act toward threats. Quick, violent action has saved Mac and my cookies in the bush so many times that it now comes naturally.

I am coming around to the front door just as the other two assholes are being escorted out the main gate by the staff. They have their broken friend suspended between them, and their departure is being ensured by the watchful Aussie and six of his mates.

Pat, Dave, and the two girls are at the top of the stairs. I walk up to them, look at the scene below and ask what happened. Pat looks at me and at the asshole escort before answering. "Those guys that were giving us a hard time must have said something to the Australians, because they beat the shit out of one, and slapped the other two around. They are getting thrown out now." He has his arm around Judith protectively.

"We are going to go somewhere a little more quiet," he says, looking at me. "Do you want to come along?" Translation: I'm being polite, not sincere. I look at them and decline, asking how much I owe them for the meal. They wave off the offer and suggest we meet up tomorrow. I nod and say goodnight to them as the Australians start coming back up the stairs. They all nod at the girls and make their excuses for their rude behavior, grinning like baboons. The two couples thank them and Dave offers to buy them a round. The one who had been in the john thanks them, but says no. He turns to me.

"Looks as if you are stag, my friend. I always wanted to have a drink with a dervish. How about it? Can Her Majesty's Forces offer you a drink?" He grins again. He is wearing the uniform of a leftenant in the light infantry. With him are four warrants, or sergeant majors. They are all grinning. I return their grin and tell him I would be honored. The girls look at me, perplexed, and ask if I am sure. I assure them that I have other plans for the evening. Dave is his usual quiet self, and I am sure that he suspects I was involved. He nods a goodbye as they go out and board one of the taxis. The Aussie lieutenant comes up and holds out his hand.

"I am pleased to make your acquaintance, mate." We turn and go back inside to the bar area. The evening is one that I shall not soon forget. There is only one group that relishes mayhem and alcohol more than the Australians, and they were the Visigoths. We manage to put a serious dent in the local alcohol supply and end up touring the various houses of ill repute as a nightcap.

The dawn is starting to peek over the land when the whole rousing crew deposits me at the compound. I am sure we woke everyone within a one-mile radius, and blearily remember seeing Pat and one of the girls at the door of his bungalow for an instant before I stumble into my room and go to sleep.

I have a jarring headache when I am awakened by the heat. I forgot to turn on the fan in the room, so I am drenched in sweat. I slowly force myself up and manage to retrieve a bottle of mineral water from the small refrigerator in the corner. That helps some. I pop two Darvons to dull the headache. I navigate to the bathroom without any major injuries and take a long shower, the last part as cold as I can get it. When I finally come out I feel almost human. I get dressed and make my way to the little cafe where I had first met the girls and slosh enough strong coffee to wake the dead. After about an hour, I am fit enough to substitute food for the cigarettes, and by the time I have finished the meal I am almost perky. Thank God for sunglasses, though.

A weapons carrier pulls up and two of the Aussies from the night before get down and look up at the veranda. Spying me, they wave and come up the stairs. They come over to the table and pull up like relatives who heard you just won the lottery. The short burly one is called "Bluey" because of his red hair and his mate is a tall lanky raw- boned type named John.

"You look terrible," Bluey starts in as the waiter arrives. They both order a beer. I can't think about beer much less drink it at this hour.

"You two don't look so chipper, either. Where is the rest of your mob? Intimidating some poor staff officer or beating up some poor sod because he looks odd?" They both grin and shake their heads as if shocked at my accusation.

"No, they are all down at the beach with your two mates, the aviators. The sheilas are due back in half an hour and we are going to barby. The leftenant says that we should come up here and fetch you, you know," John adds, as an explanation as to why they have hunted me down. They wave the waiter over for a re-supply of beer, and I order one, too, since the day apparently has started to get into swing.

Bluey is about thirty-something, so is his companion. They both take a long pull on their beer as soon as it arrives and lean back a bit, looking over the crowded street. Bush sense tells you to always keep your senses about you. They are watching the background like we all do. Bluey turns from his scanning and grins at me as I gag on the beer.

"'Ere you might want to take it slowly on the first one," he cautions. "By the way, one of your lot showed up this morning about the time we came by to see if you were still alive." He pauses for a moment then adds, "Speaks sort of odd he does, like he was talking through syrup. Said 'e was your mate. Came down looking for you. He's a tough looking little wart." It can only be Mac. I am wondering where the Cookie is.

"Does he have another one with him that looks like a shaved bear?" I ask, thinking of Rocky. Bluey laughs and puts down his bottle.

"No, just the one. He said he had to leave your other two mates in Saigon, and came down 'ere to make sure you weren't in trouble. Leftenant Macguire was telling him about your bad manners in the loo last night. They were 'aving a good laugh when we left." He takes out a cigarette and offers me one. I take it and light up. The smoke feels good.

"He said you were often prone to violence, so he came looking for you to keep you out of bad habits. It appears the two pilots are now informed that you were up to mischief, so now all and sundry want you to come back for the barby." I motion the waiter over and pay the bill. It would appear that we are going back to the compound. I see the weapons carrier pulling up down below.

"Our chariot has arrived. Shall we?" John asks. We get up and walk down the stairs. One of the other warrants from the previous evening, Taffy, is driving. He grins and motions to the back. We get in and he turns out into traffic. We haven't gone a block when there is a tremendous explosion about 100 meters in front of us. The unmistakable clap of high explosives followed by dust and debris fills the narrow street to our front. We are all up and out before the vehicle rolls to a stop. Everyone has a weapon out and is scanning the street.

People are screaming and fleeing in our direction. We start walking towards where the blast has gone off. As we get closer we start to come across people who are wounded, staggering out of the blast area. Then we start coming across bodies. The center of the explosion is in front of a row of shops and small outdoor cafes. There are more bodies now and pieces of bodies. The bodies are mostly soldiers, with a sprinkling of civilians. Bluey swears softly and a woman is screaming across the street. I bend down to check on a young sergeant from the infantry, who is lying on his side. As I roll him over I see that a jagged piece of metal has cut him almost in half. He is very dead. There is a woman's leg still in its nylon, lying severed and surreal, near his head.

I straighten up and look over to Bluey. He and John are trying to help someone on the ground. It is a woman and she is screaming and sobbing at the same time. I walk over to where they are and am shocked when I see that it is Glenda. She is missing her left foot and part of her lower leg. They have rigged a tourniquet by the time I get there and Bluey is holding her and murmuring words of comfort to keep her from blacking out. He waves John off, telling him to go get the vehicle. John takes off up the street. I turn around to follow his movements and that's when I see Judith.

She is across the street and she is dead. She looks so small and frail lying there in the dust and debris. The blast has blown off all her clothes except her bra, and one leg is missing. I walk over and look down at her. For some reason it seems obscene for her to be lying there exposed like that.

I get what looks like a bolt of cloth that has been blown out of a tailor shop, and cover her with it. John comes back with the vehicle and we load Glenda and a wounded soldier from the 9th Division on it. John helps me gather up Judith's remains, now wrapped in the cloth, and we load our package into the truck as well.

We turn the vehicle around and, once clear, race through the streets to the medical center at the R and R headquarters. They are just starting to get the few survivors into receiving when we finally get done. They have taken Glenda and are going to medevac her to Saigon; Judith's body will be shipped in the following days.

By the time we get to the bungalows most everyone has heard about the bomb. Bluey goes over and tells Patrick and Dave about the girls. Mac comes over and we lean on the fender of the truck. He looks at me, and then over at Patrick who has taken the death of Judith very hard. Dave wants to go down to the hospital to see Glenda, but Bluey tells him it will do no good, since she will most likely not be there by the time he arrives.

The bomb was concealed in a motorcycle driven up in front of one of the cafes and parked. After the driver walked away, it detonated. The final count was eight dead and some 40 wounded. The Viet Cong managed to sneak their bomb into the rear area, because it was the perfect place to terrorize an occupying force.

The Army reacts in the usual knee-jerk fashion of the static defender. The word passes quickly that Vung Tau is considered a closed and controlled zone with a curfew. What help that will be I have no idea. By all accounts this was a daylight operation, and the chances of closing a ring around the city and enforcing a curfew is not going to do anything but slow down commerce. The VC cell that planned and executed the operation is, by now, deeply hidden or long gone.

I only knew the girls for a few days and regret the terrible loss their families will experience. Judith had been a bright and delicate light in this world. She came over here because she truly believed in her profession; now she was just a memory. All that was left was a cold mangled shell that would be taken back so that her family could grieve and try to make sense of her sacrifice.

Mac and I watch Patrick. He is shocky and wandering about in a daze. Who knows? Perhaps he and Judith found something in their few hours together. It does happen, I suppose. Poor bastard.

The Aussies are a good lot. They go through the girls' room and gather up their things, and contact the organization they worked for. From this point on the whole affair will be handled by the organizations connected with their embassy. These are set up to deal with notification and the return of remains. Dave and Patrick decide to catch a lift up to Saigon to see if they can get in to see Glenda, whenever she comes out of surgery. They say their goodbyes and leave in the jeep they used from the airfield.

Bluey comes over and asks us if we need a lift. I look at Mac and decide we might as well pack up and leave since the MPs will close the city down for at least 72 hours. The Aussies have a chopper coming to pick them up in the afternoon, and offer to drop us on the way, if we like. We decide to go to Long Than, which is just a hop away by chopper. The One-Zero school is there and we can hang out with our peers for a day or so, and then catch one of the trash flights back to Saigon. We call Cookie and tell him we will meet up with him in Saigon. No sense in his coming down here. Mac wants to cut the cast off his arm, saying it itches more than it hurts.

It's been a nice couple of days, before the war came back to remind me of where we are and how fragile life is. That's the trouble with this place, it doesn't do you any good to try and forget it, because it's almost always an illusion. Even if your bush sense is dialed in, you can still be in the wrong place at the wrong time.

We will go back to that war, the one where the fighting and dying is up close and reasonably predictable. It doesn't make sense, the bomb and the girls, but I have seen a lot of dead people over the years, and very few of them make sense. Only the times when it was their survival or mine make sense to me. The resulting bodies are incidental in that case.

We will go back to that war, where the circumstances are constant and the danger has a naked face. Maybe we can survive. At least one can prepare for the inevitable. As we wait for the chopper, I idly watch the clouds in the distance and marvel at the contrast of the beauty in this world with the ugly uncertainties of life. I am not at all surprised at the cruel twists of fate. Most people, if they are lucky, never have to face their fears of mortality. We live with them every day. To me it is just another day; I will wrap myself in the comfort of my friends and get on with it. Regret and compassion have little to do with the course of events here. Survival depends on your inner strength.

We are but warriors for the working-day;
Our gayness and our gilt are all besmircht
With rainy marching in the painful field;
Henry V

William Shakespeare

10/18